Interactive Data Visualization

Interactive Data Visualization

Foundations, Techniques, and Applications

Second Edition

Matthew Ward
Georges Grinstein
Daniel Keim

CRC Press
Taylor & Francis Group
Boca Raton London New York

CRC Press is an imprint of the
Taylor & Francis Group, an **informa** business

AN A K PETERS BOOK

CRC Press
Taylor & Francis Group
6000 Broken Sound Parkway NW, Suite 300
Boca Raton, FL 33487-2742

First issued in paperback 2021

© 2015 by Taylor & Francis Group, LLC
CRC Press is an imprint of Taylor & Francis Group, an Informa business

No claim to original U.S. Government works

Version Date: 20141027

ISBN-13: 978-0-367-78348-8 (pbk)
ISBN-13: 978-1-4822-5737-3 (hbk)

Library of Congress Cataloging-in-Publication Data

Ward, Matthew, 1955-
    Interactive data visualization : foundations, techniques, and applications / Matthew Ward, Georges Grinstein, Daniel Keim. -- Second edition.
      pages cm
    Includes bibliographical references and index.
    ISBN 978-1-4822-5737-3 (alk. paper)
      1. Information visualization. 2. Computer graphics. 3. Image processing. I. Grinstein, Georges G. II. Keim, Daniel. III. Title.

    TK7882.I6W37 2015
    001.4′226028566--dc23
                                                                                              2014039562

Visit the Taylor & Francis Web site at
http://www.taylorandfrancis.com

*To our spouses
Meredyth,
Janet,
and Ilse*

Contents

Preface to the First Edition

Our goal in writing this book is to provide readers and students with the theory, details, and tools necessary to be able to build visualizations and systems involving the visualization of data. There are a number of books that provide visualization taxonomies with numerous examples, but none that look at the algorithmic and software engineering issues in building such visualizations and systems, and none that discuss visualization theory. Furthermore, this book covers the spectrum of data visualizations, including mathematical and statistical graphs, cartography for displaying geographic information, two- and three-dimensional scientific displays, and general information visualization techniques.

We believe that it is not enough to provide detailed descriptions of each visualization or of the key techniques. We discuss implementation and language issues, performance demands and limitations, and application requirements and results. We also describe how visualizations are used in knowledge discovery and problem solving, as well as how to evaluate different visualizations. We also discuss the various roles visualization plays in larger application frameworks, such as those in knowledge discovery and visual analytics. This will provide a view into the various visualization interfaces that can be delivered and will help explain the design process.

Goals of This Book

The main goal of this book is to enable readers and students to expand their understanding of the field of interactive data visualization. To achieve this, we explore the fundamental components of the visualization process, from the data to the human viewer. At each stage, we present the basic terminology and concepts, along with techniques and algorithms in common use today.

The book is geared towards practitioners and developers, as well as those just wishing to gain some exposure to the field, for which we present topics at multiple levels of detail. Those wanting an in-depth understanding of techniques are provided with sufficient information, often with full source code, to complete an implementation, while those with more modest aspirations can focus on the concepts and high-level algorithm details.

For developers, we provide guidance in the design of effective visualizations, using methods derived from the study of human perception, graphical design, art, and usability analysis. While we cannot guarantee the effectiveness of a visualization designed using these guidelines (in fact, some guidelines may be contradictory), it is a good idea to examine the resulting visualization using different evaluation criteria.

For practitioners, we describe a wide range of existing visualization systems, both public and commercial, and show how these are used to solve specific problems in a wide range of domains. This will enable users of visualization systems to select appropriate tools for their tasks.

Finally, for researchers in visualization, we describe directions for current and future research, identifying some of the emerging technology and hot topics being developed at academic and industrial centers today. We hope that the information contained in this textbook is sufficient to enable researchers new to the field to acquire the background necessary to understand the details and significance of current research being presented in conferences and journals in this field.

Assumptions about the Reader

We assume readers are conversant with some programming language and have some understanding of algorithms. The more knowledgeable readers are, the more they will get out of the book, as the topics are covered in great detail. Each chapter contains programming activities that will help readers better understand the process of developing and testing a visualization. Some of these can be performed using Excel and its built-in plotting techniques. Others assume the use of regular programming languages such as Java or C++, as long as they have graphics libraries available. Readers should feel free to develop their code in other languages as well.

Outline of This Book

The book consists of 15 chapters:

Chapter 1 presents an overview and history of visualization and its connection with computer graphics.

Chapter 2 provides the foundations and characteristics of data, which forms the beginning of the visualization pipeline.

Chapter 3 explores the human component of the visualization pipeline, with descriptions of the perceptual system and the roles it plays in understanding and interpreting visualizations.

Chapter 4 deals with the foundations of the visualization processes, from basic building blocks to taxonomies and frameworks.

Chapters 5 through 10 cover a wide gamut of visualization techniques, loosely grouped by data characteristics, describing the methods and algorithms used to map data to graphical depictions.

Chapters 11 and 12 describe the role of user interaction within visualizations, and presents a wide range of interaction techniques and styles.

Chapters 13 and 14 discuss the visualization design process, presenting principles and guidelines to improve the effectiveness of specific visualizations, as well as techniques for evaluating the resulting visualizations.

Chapter 15 reviews a variety of available visualization systems, identifying key features and observed limitations.

Chapter 16 touches on directions for future work for those wishing to advance their knowledge of the field beyond what is covered in this book.

Discussion of Exercises

Several types of exercises are provided at the end of each chapter. Some are review questions that are geared towards reminding readers of the significant concepts covered by the chapter. Others are expansion questions designed to encourage students to think beyond the material covered, to build on the concepts to design alternate approaches to solving a problem. Both types of questions would be appropriate for use in examinations.

We also provide programming projects. Some require very little in the way of graphics support, and thus can be implemented readily on any platform, including those discussed. This minimal configuration would simply require the ability to set a pixel and a line on the screen and control its color. On the web site we provide demonstration programs for a number of languages and operating systems that could be used for this. Other projects require a more extensive graphics package, such as OpenGL, to support 3D viewing, lighting control, and so on. Students who have completed a course in computer graphics should have already obtained the background necessary to use these packages. Programming projects range from the simple implementation of algorithms provided in pseudocode in the text, to extending various algorithms or techniques or even to programming techniques significantly different from those presented in the text. We expect that this last type of project will take more time to complete than the others, and may be the basis for term projects and/or advanced studies.

Web Site for This Book

The web site associated with this textbook (http://www.idvbook.com/) contains a wealth of valuable information for both instructors and students. This web site includes downloadable software tools (described in Appendix C) along with example data sets (Appendix B), providing hands-on experience for understanding the various techniques described in this book. Additional links to useful data repositories, as well as sites describing data file formats, are also provided. As new visualization tools are always becoming available, and companies active in the visualization field come and go, we maintain an up-to-date listing of software packages and vendors, with an occasional review written by one of the authors or contributed by others in the field.

Instructional tools, such as reading lists, slides for lectures, and demonstration programs, are also available. It is hoped that as more faculty use this text in their courses, additional material will be contributed, including additional exercises, supplementary web pages that expand on particular topics, and software to provide students good starting points for their own implementations.

The web site contains updates and corrections to the printed text, along with a mechanism for readers to electronically submit identified bugs, and suggestions for improvements to both the text (for future editions) and the web site.

Reliability of Programs: Disclaimer

The programs in this book and on the web site have been written carefully. Use of these programs is, however, at your own risk. The authors and publisher disclaim all liability for direct or consequential damages resulting from use of the programs.

Acknowledgments

The authors wish to thank all the students in their visualization courses and research labs who have, over the last ten years, supported the evolution of the book materials through reviews, edits, figures, code, and comments. Special thanks go to Dr. Alex Gee and Curran Kelleher for their strong editorial participation, and to Loura Costello, Dr. John Sharko, Dr. Jianping Zhou, and Heather Byrne for their meticulous editorial support. Thanks to Dr. Jing Yang, Zaixian Xie, Zhenyu Guo, Wei Peng, Qingguang Cui, and Anil Petro for their work in developing software to generate many figures in this book. Michael Regenscheit, Fabian Fischer, Florian Stoffel, and Dr. Peter Bak provided essential SVN support, helped with LaTeX problems, and provided figures. Dr. Haim Levkowitz provided reviews and edits on the early versions. Christopher Healey contributed wonderful material for the chapter on perception.

The authors also wish to thank Alice Peters, Charlotte Henderson, Camber Agrelius, and all the other people at A K Peters who helped make this book a reality. Their tireless efforts at finding and fixing the many bugs with this manuscript are greatly appreciated. We would also thank all of the many people who gave us permission to use their images for this book.

Finally, the authors wish to thank their spouses and children for their countless hours of support and sacrifice that were required to complete this project. We couldn't have done it without you!

Preface to the Second Edition

Several corrections, enhancements, and additions are included in this second edition of *Interactive Data Visualization*. Grammar and technical bugs were discovered and fixed in every chapter. Material was updated and new related readings, exercises, and programming projects were added. Several figures were replaced with better-quality ones, and a number of new figures were added. A new chapter, entitled "Visualization Techniques for Time-Oriented Data" and written by Wolfgang Aigner, Silvia Miksch, Heidrun Schumann, and Christian Tominski, was added. We feel that all of these changes have greatly enhanced the value and usefulness of this book.

The authors had a great deal of assistance in the creation of this new edition. Matthew Ward would like to thank the students of his data visualization course, especially Michael Barry, for help finding related readings and new content. Georges Grinstein would like to thank Ekaterina Galkina and John Fallon for their help in collecting new figures and content.

CHAPTER 1

Introduction

This chapter provides a high-level introduction to data and information visualization, what visualizations are, and why imagery is so important. It presents reasons for using visualization, shows how visualizations are applied to problem solving, and discusses the process of visualization. The visualization pipeline is presented with its relationship to other data analysis pipelines. Finally, the importance of human perception in connection with visualization is introduced. We assume that the reader already has a basic understanding of computer graphics.

1.1 What Is Visualization?

We define *visualization* as the communication of information using graphical representations. Pictures have been used as a mechanism for communication since before the formalization of written language. A single picture can contain a wealth of information, and can be processed much more quickly than a comparable page of words. This is because image interpretation is performed in parallel within the human perceptual system, while the speed of text analysis is limited by the sequential process of reading. Pictures can also be independent of local language, as a graph or a map may be understood by a group of people with no common tongue.

1.1.1 Visualization in Everyday Life

It is an interesting exercise to consider the number and types of data and information visualization that we encounter in our normal activities. Some of these might include

- a simple formatted number representing a single item of interest, such as the gross national product (GNP) of the U.S.;

- a table in a newspaper, representing data being discussed in an article;

- a train and subway map with times used for determining train arrivals and departures;

- a map of the region, to help select a route to a new destination;

- a weather chart showing the movement of a storm front that might influence your weekend activities;

- a graph of stock market activities that might indicate an upswing (or downturn) in the economy;

- a plot comparing the effectiveness of your pain killer to that of the leading brand;

- a 3D reconstruction of your injured knee, as generated from a CT scan;

- an instruction manual for putting together a bicycle, with views specific to each part as it is added;

- a highway sign indicating a curve, merging of lanes, or an intersection.

Visualization is used on a daily basis in many areas of employment as well, such as

- the result of a financial and stock market analysis;

- a mechanical and civil engineering rotary bridge design and systems analysis;

- a breast cancer MRI for diagnosis and therapy;

- a comet path data and trend analysis;

- the analysis of human population smoking behaviors;

- the study of actuarial data for confirming and guiding quantitative analysis;

- the simulation of a complex process;

- the analysis of a simulation of a physical system;

- a visual representation of Facebook friends and their connections;

- marketing posters and advertising.

In each case, the visualization provides an alternative to, or a supplement for, textual or verbal information. It is clear that visualization provides a far richer description of the information than the word-based counterpart. But why is this so? In what kinds of situations are visualizations effective? What types of information can and cannot be visualized? How many different ways are there to show the same data, and which ones are best for particular circumstances? In this book, we will explore these and other questions. Perhaps the most important question is this: why should we study visualization?

1.1.2   Why Is Visualization Important?

There are many reasons why visualization is important. Perhaps the most obvious reason is that we are visual beings who use sight as one of our key senses for information understanding. The two examples below highlight why visualization is so important in decision making, and the role of human preferences and training. One example focuses on data distortion, and the other on human interpretation.

What is the effect of the presentation of data on the decision-making process? Can the presentation of data impact the decision, and can we say which presentations are better or more influential than others? In Figures 1.1(a) through 1.1(d), we show several views of the same data set. In Figure 1.1(a), data are shown at a large uniform scale (equally) in both x and y; the scale is so large that the values of the data are all close to each other, resulting in a blob that does not allow the differentiation of individual data points and gives the appearance that the data is tightly clustered. In Figures 1.1(b) and 1.1(c) we alter the scales. In (b) the y-axis is scaled larger, thereby clustering the data in the vertical direction, resulting in a linear horizontal pattern. In (c) the scaling is in the x-direction, producing a strong linear pattern in the vertical direction. Finally, in Figure 1.1(d), we do not scale at all, but use the range of the data to determine the scaling (from min x to max x and min y to max y of all the values). By changing the origin of the graph with alternative scalings, we can produce graphs that look startlingly different (even turning linear data into quadratic data). Looking at any of

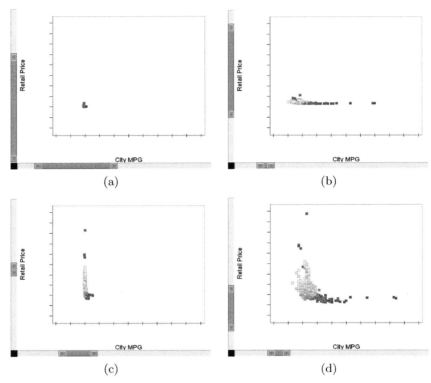

Figure 1.1.   The same data plotted with different scales is perceived dramatically differently:
                  (a) Equally (uniformly) large scale in both x and y. (b) Large scale in y. (c) Large
                  scale in x. (d) Scale determined by range of x- and y-values.

these figures, we would be tempted to categorize the data's "natural" structure (we discuss this data in greater detail at the end of this chapter). We
might be inclined to say the plot is very linear (a–c), while it is actually
inversely proportional (d). Thus scaling as well as outliers can distort the
"truthful" representation of data and in fact can be used to do so.

    A second example is very real and highlights the need for testing user
interpretation of visualizations in specific decision-making processes. In 1999
Linda Elting and colleagues [113] presented to 34 clinicians the preliminary
results from hypothetical clinical trials of a generic conventional treatment
compared with a generic investigational treatment, both treating the same
condition, using four different visualization techniques. The two treatments
differed from one another, with one of the treatments made to appear much
better than the other. Clinicians seeing that difference should then decide
to stop the trial.

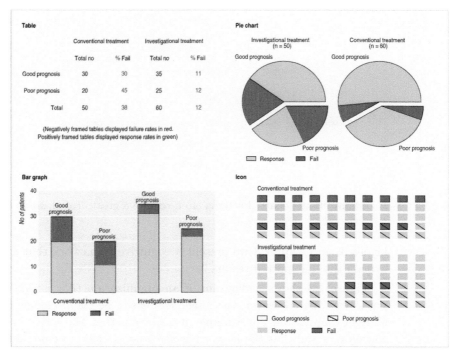

Figure 1.2.   Various visual representations of a hypothetical clinical trial. The icon display (lower right) was the most effective for the decision to stop the clinical trial. The bar and pie charts were the least effective. (Image courtesy [113], © 1999 BMJ.)

Figure 1.2 shows the four presentations of the same data. In the upper left we have a simple table, in the upper right pie charts, in the lower left stacked bar charts, and in the lower right a sequence of rectangles, each representing a patient. In all representations, both the conventional and the investigational treatments are presented. The green color shows that the drug induced a response and the red that none occurred.

The decision to stop varied significantly, depending on the presentation of the data. Correct decisions were 82% with icon displays (lower right), 68% with tables, and 56% with pie charts or bar graphs. In actual clinical practice, up to 25% of the patients treated according to the data displayed as bar or pie charts would have received inappropriate treatment. Clearly, the choice of visualization impacted the decision process. Elting noted that most (21) clinicians preferred the table, and that several were contemptuous of the icon display. This emphasizes that it is not only the visualization that is key in presenting data well, but that user preferences are heavily

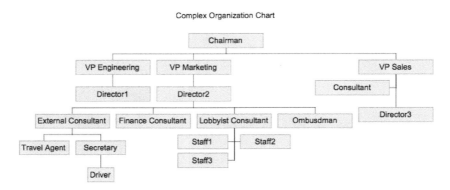

Figure 1.3.   An organizational chart. Patterns often require a great deal of words to describe.

involved. In Chapter 3 we present a cognitive framework that attempts to explain the unexpected results.

Figure 1.3 shows a diagram of an organization that is difficult to describe verbally. However, the image can easily be comprehended with only a brief examination. For example, it is obvious that Marketing has the most consultants and that the Driver has the longest chain of command.

The flood of data, its democratization, and the web have brought about an increasing use of both static and interactive visualizations that are much more aesthetic and understandable to the user. The exploration and analysis of large marketing, financial, security, medical, and biological data sets has led to results needing to be explained. Visualization is a cornerstone of these new knowledge discovery tools. Applications often use visualizations within larger applications to provide alternative views of the data and to help describe some structure, pattern or anomaly in the data. One thing is certain: given the increasing levels of information available to people to run their businesses, solve their problems, and assist in decision making, there is a growing need for tools and techniques to help make effective use of this information overflow. Likewise, there is a growing need to find mechanisms for communicating information to people in an efficient and effective manner, and to help educate them about processes and concepts that affect everyday life, from global warming to economic trends to genetic engineering. In virtually any domain, visualization can be, and is becoming, an effective tool to assist in analysis and communication.

1.2   History of Visualization

As we embark on the study of visualization, we start with a quick look at the history of the field. This is by no means a thorough review, but a cursory one aimed at piquing your curiosity. See Michael Friendly's web site [136] for a wonderful collection and more details.

1.2.1   Early Visualizations

Perhaps the first technique for graphically recording and presenting information was that used by early man. An example is the early Chauvet-Pont-d'Arc Cave, located near Vallon-Pont-d'Arc in southern France [491]. The Chauvet Cave contains over 250 paintings, created approximately 30,000 years ago. These were likely meant to pass on information to future generations. See Figure 1.4 for an example of a cave painting.

The oldest writing systems used pictures to encode symbols and whole words. Such systems are called *logograms* [88]. The Kish limestone tablet (see Figure 1.5) is considered the earliest written document. It is from Mesopotamia and is mostly pictographic, but it has the beginning of syllabic writing found in cuneiform scripts. It is located in the Ashmolean Museum, Oxford [395].

Figure 1.4.   One of the Lascaux cave paintings on the northern slopes of the French Pyrenees on the banks of the Vézère River [386].

Figure 1.5.   Early graphical writing. The Kish limestone tablet from Mesopotamia [395].

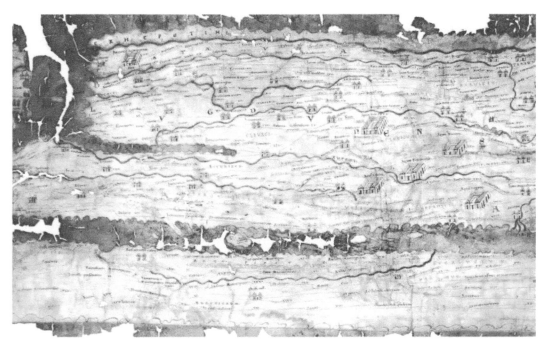

Figure 1.6.   A copy of one of the 12 pages of the Peutinger Map set, showing the roads of the
Roman Empire. (Image courtesy http://www.livius.org/pen-pg/peutinger/map
.html.)

Another early writing system, which came from the ancient Egyptians, is called *hieroglyphics* [9]. Hieroglyphs are divided into three major categories: logograms, phonograms, and determinatives. Hieroglyphic logograms are signs that represent morphemes, "the smallest language unit that carries a semantic interpretation" [193]. Phonograms are signs that represent one or more sounds. Determinatives are signs that help to join logograms and photograms together to disambiguate the meaning of a sequence of glyphs.

Early visualizations came about out of necessity: for travel, commerce, religion, and communication. Maps provided support for travelers where planning or survival was the key. The Peutinger Map or cartogram, one page of which is shown in Figure 1.6, was an early road map of the 70,000 miles of imperial highways of a section of the Roman world, with roads (in red) and their approximate mileage. It adds key landmarks such as staging posts and distances between large rivers and forests. One interesting aspect of the map is that distances are distorted. East-west distances are scaled up more than north-south ones. Thus, Rome appears nearer to Carthage than Naples is to Pompeii. Such distorted maps arose for many reasons. Relative positions were more important than actual accuracy, and in some cases the distortions were due to the medium being used (the map itself is 22 feet 1.75 inches by 13.25 inches): "The archetype may well have been on a papyrus roll, designed for carrying around in a capsa [tool box]. As such, its width would be severely limited, whereas its length would not" [169]. The original map is now in the Österreichische Nationalbibliothek in Vienna, Austria.

There were qualitative maps of land that highlighted the number of rivers to cross, mountain passes, and in some cases, the location of known brigands. There were maps showing the trade winds for sea travelers and maps used for battle planning. The European medieval world depended on sea trade for wealth. Thus, maps drawn by explorers and voyagers provided a great deal of information and were kept secret. However, as is usual, the information leaked, and a number of maps and books became available.

The Hereford map (see Figure 1.7) is an approximately four and a half feet by five feet calf skin map of the world that can be seen in the cathedral at Hereford, Wales. It depicts the land masses of Asia, Africa, and Europe, with Jerusalem at the center and the Holy City at the exact center (where, in fact, an image of the crucified Jesus appears). Some real and some religious information is available on the map. On the external boundaries of the map, where little was known at the time but where there was much superstition, one can find numerous mythical figures. See [458] for a very detailed analysis of the map. Note that there were earlier maps.

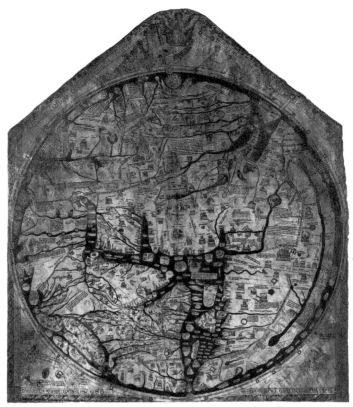

Figure 1.7.   The famous Hereford map, the largest surviving map of the Middle Ages (1280s).
                   (Image courtesy Wikimedia Commons.)

Figure 1.8 shows a portion of John Snow's map of the deaths resulting
from cholera in London in 1854. Each stacked bar within the houses represents one deceased individual. There's much that can be done with such a
map. For example, the overview map in Figure 1.9 highlights a concentration
around the central water pump. What caused this concentration? Why were
there individuals who died far from that center? Tufte [424] stated, "Snow
observed that cholera occurred almost entirely among those who lived near
(and drank from) the Broad Street water pump. He had the handle of the
contaminated pump removed, ending the neighborhood epidemic which had
taken more than 500 lives." It is maps such as these that allowed one to
explore and communicate geographical links to disease and other time-based
events.

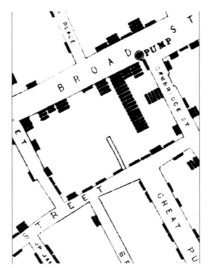

Figure 1.8.   A section of John Snow's map of the deaths from cholera in London in 1854.
Each bar within the houses represents one deceased individual. (Image courtesy
Wikimedia Commons.)

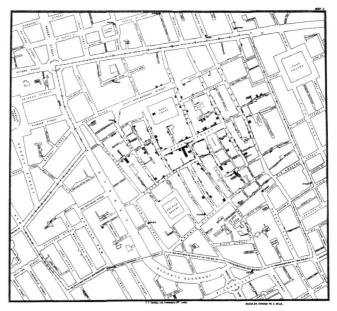

Figure 1.9.   Overview map of the deaths from Cholera in London in 1854. Note the concentration around the Broad Street Water Pump. Note as well the outliers. (Image
courtesy Wikimedia Commons.)

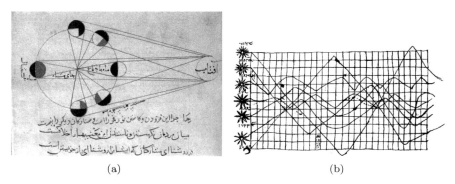

(a)   (b)

Figure 1.10.   Two early time series visualizations: (a) produced by Biruni circa 1030, shows the phases of the moon in orbit; (b) drawn around the same time, shows planetary motion. (Image courtesy Wikimedia Commons.)

Time series visualizations had been around even prior to Descartes in the 1600s. One of the earliest was a circular representation of the phases of the moon by Abu Rayhan Muhammad ibn Ahmad al-Biruni, born in Kath, Khwarezm. Biruni was well known in the Muslim world and one of the most encyclopedic and broadest scientists of his time. Biruni completed his extensive astronomical encyclopedia Kitab al-Qanun al-Mas'udi in which Figure 1.10(a) appears. Figure 1.10(b) appeared about the same time, but in the Western world. It displays the movement of the planets.

Minard's Napoleonic march representation was a brilliant tour-de-force, presenting linked geographic and time-series data on a static representation. This is one of his last maps, perhaps to appeal the destruction of France through war. The map strongly emphasizes the loss of troops during the Napoleonic Russian expedition. There were actually two maps, one of Hannibal's campaigns and the one shown in Figure 1.11. The armies are represented as flows whose width corresponds to the size of the army, and time is annotated. The size of French army went from over 400,000 to 10,000. The image is one of the most reproduced and has often been used as a test of the capabilities of visualization systems.

A clear breakthrough for information visualization was the abstract representation for axes, allowing other parameters to be used as the coordinates. Without the abstract (mathematical) interpretation, we would stay with strictly planar geospatial interpretations. Thus one could have density as one axis and temperature as the other. For example, Figure 1.12(a) shows

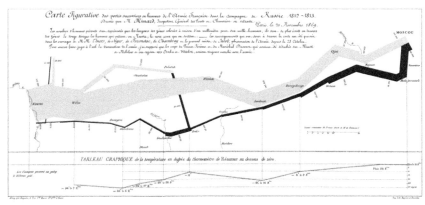

Figure 1.11.   Minard's map, showing Napoleon's march on Moscow. The width of the line
                conveys the size of the army at that location. Color indicates the direction of
                movement. The temperature is plotted at different points along the retreat at the
                bottom. (Image courtesy Wikimedia Commons.)

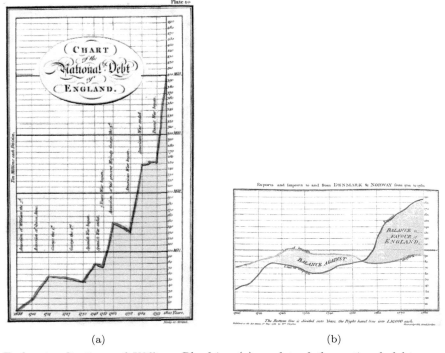

(a)   (b)

Figure 1.12.   Early visualizations of William Playfair: (a) a plot of the national debt over
                time; (b) a display of the balance of trade between England and Norway/Den-
                mark (1786). (Image courtesy Wikimedia Commons.)

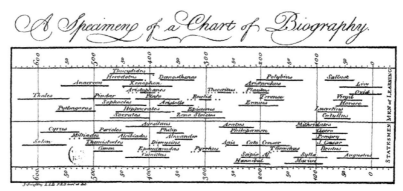

Figure 1.13.   Joseph Priestley's display of the longevity of famous people (1765). (Image courtesy Wikimedia Commons.)

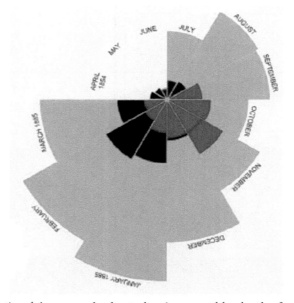

Figure 1.14.   Florence Nightingale's coxcomb chart showing monthly deaths from battle and
other causes. Blue represents the deaths from disease, red represents deaths from
wounds, and black represents all other deaths. (From an interactive on-line tool
at http://understandinguncertainty.org/node/213.)

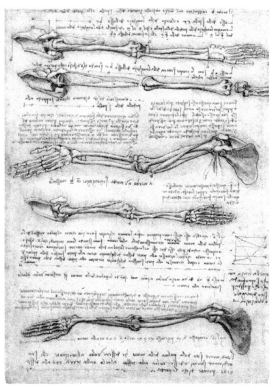

Figure 1.15.   Leonardo Da Vinci's study of the motion of the human arm (1510). (Image courtesy Wikimedia Commons.)

the national debt over time, as developed by William Playfair [322], one of the pioneers of information visualization. Other examples of early information visualization include Playfair's plot of the balance of trade between England and Norway/Denmark over a number of years (Figure 1.12(b)), Joseph Priestley's display of the life spans of famous people (Figure 1.13), and Florence Nightingale's presentation of monthly deaths within the army, comparing those who died in battle with those dying from other causes (Figure 1.14). Medical visualizations were also quite popular, particularly for the training of new doctors. Many examples exist, though few are more famous than Leonardo Da Vinci's amazing drawings of human anatomy (Figure 1.15).

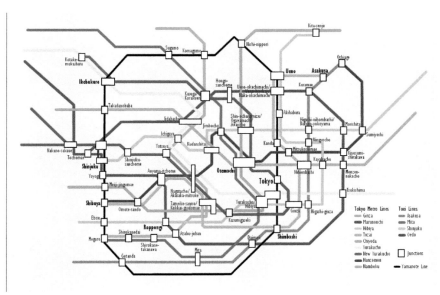

Figure 1.16.   The Tokyo Underground map. A logical representation of the metro highlighting
                 qualitative relationships between the stops. (Image courtesy Wikimedia Com-
                 mons.)

1.2.2   Visualization Today

Visualization most often provides different levels of both qualitative and
quantitative views of the information being communicated. For example,
Figure 1.16 shows a map of the Tokyo underground. It provides an easy-to-
read yet logically distorted view of the criss-crossing network of the subway
system to facilitate interpretation; similar techniques have been used for a
number of subway and other transportation systems as well as for processes
and their flows.

Distorted views are often interpreted imprecisely and depend on the
viewer. Most representations of two-dimensional maps exhibit some degree
of distortion due to the 3D-to-2D projection (globe to plane). However,
since a small area on the globe is well approximated by a plane, local street
maps have minimal distortions and thus can provide strong relative detail
and especially link information, including connectedness, closeness, above, or
below. Figure 1.17 displays Google map directions between two local street
addresses, indicating the roads, intersections, and turns to make throughout
the trip.

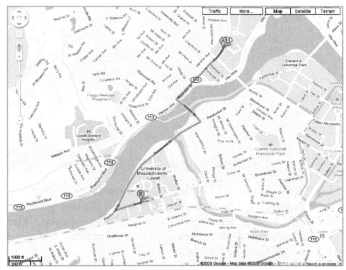

Figure 1.17.   The google.com map directions from 198 Riverside St., Lowell, MA (UMass Lowell, North Campus) to 883 Broadway St., Lowell, MA (UMass Lowell, South Campus). Google.com maps provide graphical cues drawn on top of road maps to indicate driving directions from point A to point B. (Image © 2009 Google.)

The difference between a statement such as "the Dow Jones average rose by 125 points today" and a plot of the Dow Jones average (Figure 1.18) is that the sentence provides a single, exact piece of information, while the plot provides several pieces of imprecise information; a viewer can gauge the degree and direction of the change, along with trend information, but may only have an approximation for the numeric values involved. This becomes even more pronounced over larger plots, where more patterns may be discerned.

It is possible for visualizations to provide very precise views of the data. Figure 1.19 provides such precision. Numbers and text definitely are visual representations and are considered visualizations, as is a table or a document. They are representations of data. The figure is the running U.S. National Debt Clock. With a population of about 300 million, the average debt share was around $27,000 in January of 2006. As of May 2008, the average debt share had risen to over $30,000. As of July 2009 it was $37,826 and in 2014 it reached over $38,000!

Modern visualizations harness digital media. For example, Figure 1.20(a) shows a normal ECG (electrocardiogram) while that of Figure 1.20(b) shows

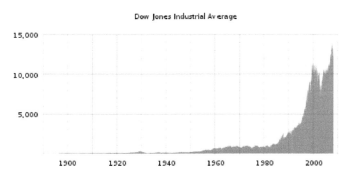

Figure 1.18.   Dow Jones Industrial Average (DJIA) from 1900 to 2000. The Dow Jones Indus-
                  trial Average is a U.S. stock index based on the weighted average of the stock
                  prices of 30 large and actively traded U.S. companies. The divisor changes over
                  time as stock splits, so as not to alter that average in those cases. (Image courtesy
                  Wikimedia Commons.)

$11,956,584,748,608.58

Figure 1.19.   The outstanding United States public debt as of January 22, 2006.

an 83-year-old man with left ventricular and arterial hypertrophy. An ECG
is an electrical recording of the heart in action (beating) and is used to
identify heart ailments or problems [205]. The diagnosis is based on differences from the normal or base ECG. Many such differences can be seen in
Figure 1.20(b).

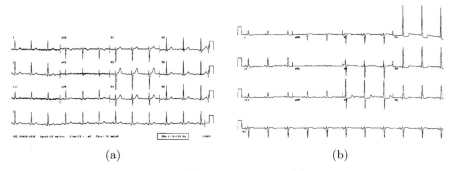

                              (a)   (b)

Figure 1.20.   Two examples of 12-lead ECGs: (a) a normal adult; (b) an 83-year-old adult with
                  heart problems. (Image courtesy http://www.ecglibrary.com/ecghome.html.)

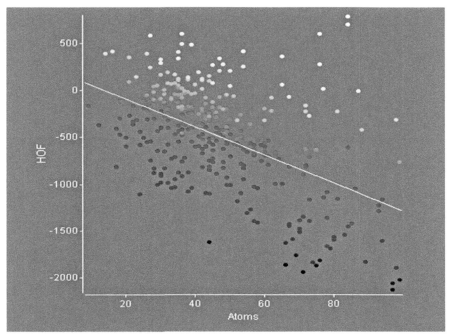

Figure 1.21. Yeast mechanism of action data with regression line. (Image Generated by UMass Lowell UVP Software.)

Figure 1.21 displays a scatterplot for analyzing the mechanism of action for yeast. The x-coordinate represents the number of atoms and the y-coordinate, heat of formation. We do not need to understand the parameters nor the domain to see the scatterplot representation of the data and to recognize the line of regression. Clearly that regression line can be computed from the data without using the image. The result is an equation of the form $y = mx + b$, where m represents the slope of the line and b the y-intercept (here $m = -12.5$ and $b = 50$). The analyst would then have the regression. However the figure allows the user to explore more detail, such as the spread, what outliers are present, and other patterns. For example, the user might notice the color trend (which conveys the Gibbs energy at each point) from bottom left to top right, which might not have been identified in a statistical analysis. This ability to provide rich descriptions of the data is one of the key strengths of visualizations.

Anscombe [20] provided an example of 4 totally different data sets consisting of 11 points each, and having identical (to 2 decimal places) mean

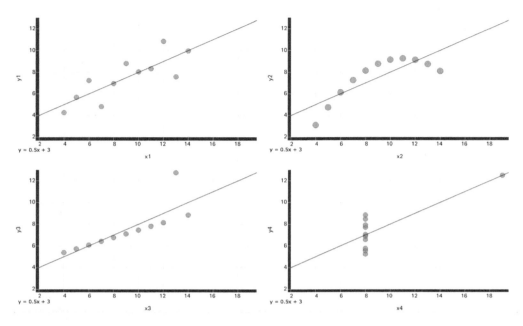

Figure I.22.   Plots of four data sets with identical statistics.

in x and y, sample variance in x and y, correlation between x and y, and a linear regression line.

Figure 1.22 shows the 4 data sets, and Figure 1.23 shows their shared statistics. The upper left of Figure 1.22 is typically the one that would be thought of when looking at the statistical values. However the three other versions display some possible alternatives. This highlights that the

Property	Value
Mean of X	9
Variance of X	11
Mean of Y	7.5
Variance of Y	4.1
Correlation	0.816
Linear Regression	y = 3.0 + 0.5x

Figure I.23.   Statistics of four distinct data sets.

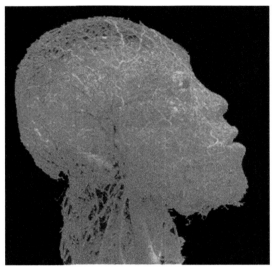

Figure 1.24.   Blood vessel configuration of the head and brain. (Image © Gunther von Hagens, Institute for Plastination, Heidelberg, Germany, www.bodyworlds.com.)

dependency only on statistics can be problematic and that a visualization could help eliminate misconceptions.

We now deal with data every day and are quite familiar with maps, simple graphs and charts. These more abstract representations of data (graphs and charts) have gone beyond their first applications (trading, economic analysis) and are much more widely used. Visualization provides a visual representation of objects that may include data, algorithms, results of computations, processes, user controls, and numerous other components of an application. These visual representations provide information through the use of computer-generated graphics. In an interactive visualization the user can query the display and thus interact with the application display directly rather than using menus. It is even possible for an application to be totally driven through its visualizations.

The following are a collection of modern visualizations from a variety of applications, including medical reconstruction, aerospace simulation, and bioinformatics. Figure 1.24 shows the blood vessels in red overlaid on a skull. Figure 1.25 shows the airflow generated by a jet during take-off.

The background image in Figure 1.26 comes from the Kyoto Encyclopedia of Genes and Genomes web site (KEGG), which provides XML files containing the coordinates of the genes in the image. Expression data from

Figure I.25.   Simulation visualization of the air flow generated by a Harrier jet when taking off. Here, color depicts the amount of force exerted by the underlying representation, red being the highest and blue the lowest. (Image courtesy http://quest.nasa.gov/aero/background/tools.)

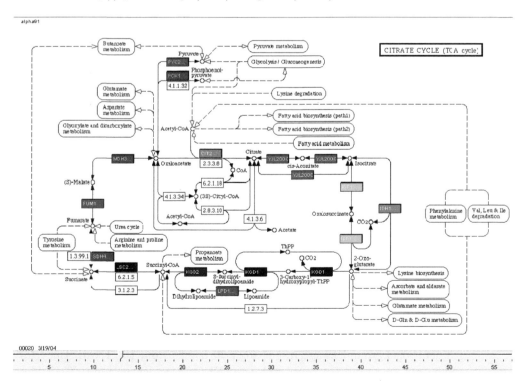

Figure I.26.   A pathway represented by a network with nodes representing genes and color the level of expression. (Image generated using UMass Lowell UVP software.)

the Stanford web site for yeast expression data has been overlaid. The slider along the bottom indicates a specific microarray experiment. The colors indicate the expression level for the gene. Green is low and red is high.

Network representations are now increasingly in use. They can represent traffic patterns, communications between computers, e-mail exchanges, Facebook friend relationships, and numerous other relationships.

Figures 1.27 and 1.28 show a social network where a point represents a person and an edge a relationship. Figure 1.27 is a simple one with Figure 1.28 a much more complex social network (VAST Challenge submission by Penn State University). Finally, Figure 1.29 shows the interconnections between genes in human DNA (See Circos.ca). Chapter 9 discusses these in more detail.

1.3   Relationship between Visualization and Other Fields

1.3.1   What Is the Difference between Visualization and Computer Graphics?

Originally, visualization was considered a subfield of computer graphics, primarily because visualization uses graphics to display information via images. As illustrated by any of the computer-generated images shown earlier, visualization applies graphical techniques to generate visual displays of data. Here, graphics is used as the communication medium.

In all visualizations, one can clearly see the use of the graphics primitives (points, lines, areas, and volumes). Beyond the use of graphics, the most important aspect of all visualizations is their connection to data. Computer graphics focuses primarily on graphical objects and the organization of graphic primitives; visualizations go one step further and are based on the underlying data, and may include spatial positions, populations, or physical measures. Consequently, visualization is the application of graphics to display data by mapping data to graphical primitives and rendering the display.

However, visualization is more than simply computer graphics. The field of visualization encompasses aspects from numerous other disciplines, including human-computer interaction, perceptual psychology, databases, statistics, and data mining, to name a few. While computer graphics can be used to define and generate the displays that are used to communicate the information, the sources of data and the way users interact and perceive the data are all important components to understand when presenting information.

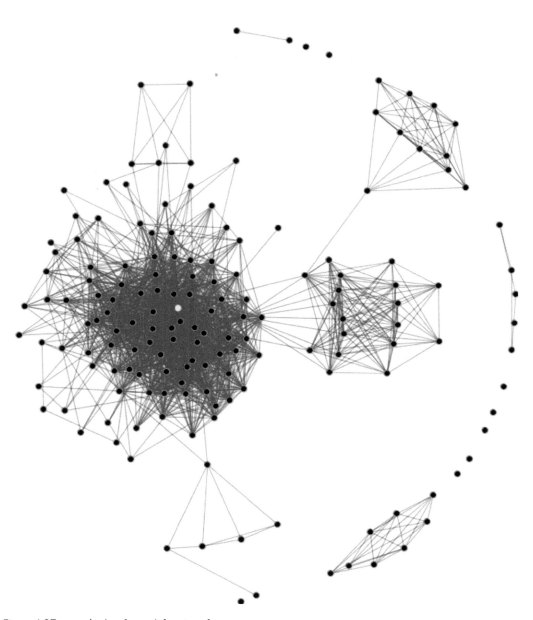

Figure 1.27.   A simple social network.

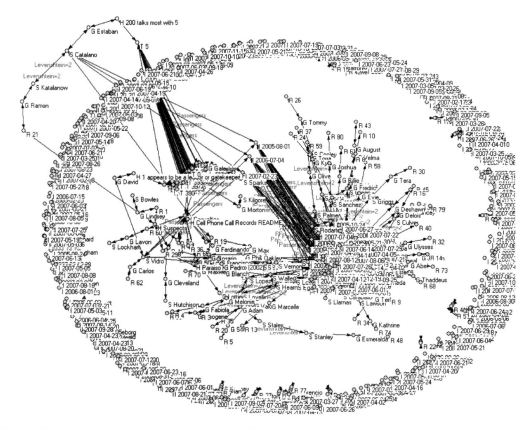

Figure 1.28.   A more elaborate social network.

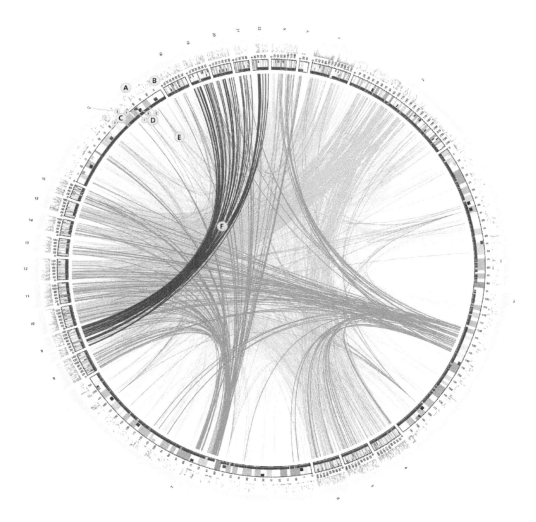

Figure 1.29.   A network showing the relationships between genes in human DNA, generated
                with the Circos package.

The sources and types of data will be described in Chapter 2, perception in Chapter 3, and interactions in Chapters 11 and 12.

Our view is that computer graphics is predominantly focused on the creation of interactive synthetic images and animations of three-dimensional objects, most often where visual realism is one of the primary goals. A secondary application of computer graphics is in art and entertainment, with video games, cartoons, advertisements, and movie special effects as typical examples. Visualization, on the other hand, does not emphasize visual realism as much as the effective communication of information. Many types of visualizations do not deal with physical objects, and those that do are often communicating attributes of the objects that would normally not be visible, such as material stress or fluid flow patterns. Thus, while computer graphics and visualization share many concepts, tools, and techniques, the underlying models (the information to be visualized) and goals (what the viewer hopes to extract) are fundamentally different.

Thus, computer graphics consists of the tools that display the visualizations seen in this book. This includes the graphics-programming language (OpenGL, DirectX, Processing, Java3D), the underlying graphics hardware (NVidia or ATI/AMD graphics cards), the rendering process (flat, Gouraud, Phong, ray tracing, or radiosity), the output format (JPEG, TIFF, AVI, MPEG), and more. We consider computer graphics to be the underpinning of visualization and thus need to keep abreast of it. In Appendix A we provide a brief history of computer graphics.

The visualization in Figure 1.30 shows the dependency of interactive visualization on computer graphics. The visualization displays a patient's heart (scientific/medical visualization) in the upper left window with two other frames showing additional parameters not easily displayable on the heart. These last two are the ones that are often considered information visualizations, but clearly all three are! Computer graphics is the rendering engine for this integrated visualization.

1.3.2 Scientific Data Visualization vs. Information Visualization

Although during the 1990s and early 2000s the visualization community differentiated between scientific visualization and information visualization, we do not. Both provide representations of data. However the data sets are most often different. Figure 1.30 highlights the importance and value of having both. Biomolecular chemistry, which once only considered the visual representation of molecules as stick and balls, has migrated over time

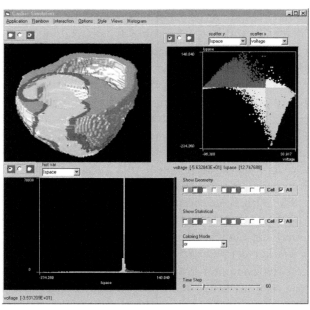

Figure 1.30.   A visualization of a patient's heart, along with visualizations representing additional parameters not easily representable on that 3D model. (Image from [159], © 2000 IEEE.)

to representations as spheres with rods, to more realistic ones, as shown in Figures 1.31 and 1.32, to now include information visualizations (scatterplots and other visualizations). This book takes the view that both scientific visualization and information visualization are allied fields. In some cases, the data being visualized begs for different handling: a large volume (1K × 1K × 1K = 1 billion points) requires dealing with large numbers of memory accesses and large-scale computations, whereas displaying a scatterplot of a million patients from a file is more concerned with reading the data from the database or file; the computations are much simpler.

1.4   The Visualization Process

What is involved in the visualization process? The designer of a new visualization most often begins with an analysis of the type of data available for display and of the type of information the viewer hopes to extract from or convey with the display. The data can come from a wide variety of sources

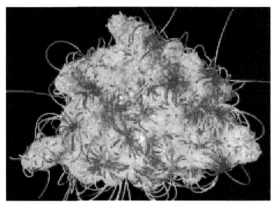

Figure 1.31.   An example of a drug that targets HIV-I reverse transcriptase. (Image courtesy IBM OpenDX Highlights.)

and may be simple or complex in structure. The viewer may wish to use the visualization for exploration (looking for "interesting" things), to confirm a hypothesis (either conjectured or the result of quantitative analysis), or to present the results of one's analysis to an audience. Examples of interesting results are *anomalies* (data that does not behave consistent with expectations), *clusters* (data that has sufficiently similar behavior that may indicate the presence of a particular phenomenon), or *trends* (data that is changing in a manner that can be characterized, and thus used for predictive models).

Figure 1.32.   Electron microscopic image of filaments of DNA, generated with Alias/Wavefront Visualizer. (Image courtesy Ed Egelman.)

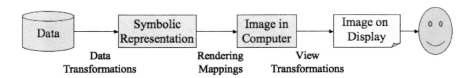

Figure 1.33.   The visualization process at a very high or primitive level view.

To visualize data, one needs to define a mapping from the data to the display (see Figure 1.33). There are many ways to achieve this mapping. The user interface consists of components, some of which deal with data needing to be entered, presented, monitored, analyzed, and computed. These user interface components are often input via dialog boxes, but they could be visual representations of the data to facilitate the selections required by the user. Visualizations can provide mechanisms for translating data and tasks into more visual and intuitive formats for users to perform their tasks.

This means that the data values themselves, or perhaps the attributes of the data, are used to define graphical objects, such as points, lines, and shapes; and their attributes, such as size, position, orientation, and color. Thus, for example, a list of numbers can be plotted by mapping each number to the y-coordinate of a point and the number's index in the list to the x-coordinate. Alternatively, we could map the number to the height of a bar or the color of a square to get a different way to view the data. In this book we present dozens of possible mappings (see Chapters 5–10), along with strategies for selecting effective mappings (see Chapter 13).

Another significant, yet often overlooked, component of the visualization process is the provision of interactive controls for the viewing and mapping of variables (attributes or parameters). While early visualizations were static objects, printed on paper or other fixed media, modern visualization is a very dynamic process, with the user controlling virtually all stages of the procedure, from data selection and mapping control to color manipulation and view refinement. There is no formula for guaranteeing the effectiveness of a given visualization. Different users, with different backgrounds, perceptual abilities, and preferences, will have differing opinions on each visualization. The user's task will also affect the usefulness of the visualization. Even a change in the data being visualized can have implications on the resulting visualization. Thus it is critical to enable users to customize, modify, and interactively refine visualizations until they feel they have achieved their goal, such as extracting a complete and accurate description of the data contents or presenting a clear depiction of patterns that they want to convey.

Visualization is often part of a larger process, which may be exploratory data analysis, knowledge discovery, or visual analytics. In this discovery process, the preparation of data depends upon the task and often requires massaging erroneous or noisy data. Visualization and analysis go hand in hand with the goal of building a model that represents or approximates the data. Visualization in data exploration is used to convey information, discover new knowledge, and identify structures, patterns, anomalies, trends, and relationships.

The process of starting with data and generating an image, a visualization, or a model via the computer is traditionally described as a *pipeline*—a sequence of stages that can be studied independently in terms of algorithms, data structures, and coordinate systems. These processes or pipelines are different for graphics, visualization, and knowledge discovery, but overlap a great deal. All start with data and end with the user. These pipelines are presented in the next three sections.

1.4.1 The Computer Graphics Pipeline

For computer graphics the stages are as follows (see Figure 1.34):

Modeling. A three-dimensional model, consisting of planar polygons defined by vertices and surface properties, is generated using a world coordinate system.

Viewing. A virtual camera is defined at a location in world coordinates, along with a direction and orientation (generally given as vectors). All vertices are transformed into a viewing coordinate system based on the camera parameters.

Clipping. By specifying the bounds of the desired image (usually given by corner positions on a plane of projection placed in front of the camera), objects out of view can be removed, and those that are partially visible can be clipped. Objects may be transformed into normalized viewing coordinates to simplify the clipping process. Clipping can actually be performed at many different stages of the pipeline.

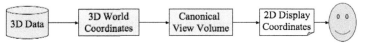

Figure 1.34.   The graphics pipeline.

Hidden surface removal. Polygons facing away from the camera, or those obscured by others, are removed or clipped. This process may be integrated into the projection process.

Projection. Three-dimensional polygons are projected onto the two-dimensional plane of projection, usually using a perspective transformation. The results may be in a normalized 2D coordinate system or device/screen coordinates.

Rendering. The actual color of the pixels associated with a visible polygon depends on a number of factors, including the material properties being synthesized (base color, texture, surface roughness, shininess), the type(s), location(s), color, and intensity of the light source(s), the degree of occlusion from direct light exposure, and the amount and color of light being reflected off of other objects onto the polygon. This process may also be applied at different stages of the pipeline (e.g., vertex colors can be assigned during the modeling process); however, due to its computational complexity, it is usually performed in conjunction with projection.

Ray tracing, a variant on this pipeline, involves casting rays from the camera through the plane of projection to ascertain what polygon(s) are hit. For reflective or translucent surfaces, secondary rays can be generated upon intersection with the surface, and the results accumulated (we shall see examples of this sort of accumulation when we discuss certain methods of volume rendering). The key algorithms involved include determining where rays intersect surfaces, the orientation of the surface at the intersection point, and the mechanism for combining the effects of secondary rays. Since each ray needs to be intersected against many, if not all, polygons, significant effort is often involved in pruning objects that will be unlikely to intersect a given ray prior to performing the intersection formulae.

1.4.2 The Visualization Pipeline

The data/information visualization pipeline has some similarities to the graphics pipeline, at least on an abstract level. The stages of this pipeline (see Figure 1.35) are as follows:

Data modeling. The data to be visualized, whether from a file or a database, has to be structured to facilitate its visualization. The name, type, range, and semantics of each attribute or field of a data record must be available in a format that ensures rapid access and easy modification.

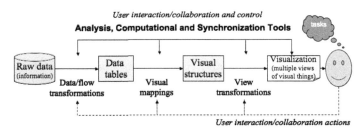

Figure 1.35. One example of the visualization pipeline. There are many variants, but all transform data into some internal representation within the computer and then use some visual paradigm to display the data on the screen.

Data selection. Similar to clipping, *data selection* involves identifying the subset of the data that will be potentially visualized. This can occur totally under user control or via algorithmic methods, such as cycling through time slices or automatically detecting features of potential interest to the user.

Data to visual mappings. The heart of the visualization pipeline is performing the mapping of data values to graphical entities or their attributes. Thus, one component of a data record may map to the size of an object, while others might control the position or color of the object. This mapping often involves processing the data prior to mapping, such as scaling, shifting, filtering, interpolating, or subsampling.

Scene parameter setting (view transformations). As in traditional graphics, the user must specify several attributes of the visualization that are relatively independent of the data. These include color map selection (for different domains, certain colors have clearly defined meaning), sound map selection (in case the auditory channels will be conveying information as well), and lighting specifications (for 3D visualizations).

Rendering or generation of the visualization. The specific projection or rendering of the visualization objects varies according to the mapping being used; techniques such as shading or texture mapping might be involved, although many visualization techniques only require drawing lines and uniformly shaded polygons. Besides showing the data itself, most visualizations also include supplementary information to facilitate interpretation, such as axes, keys, and annotations.

1.4.3   The Knowledge Discovery Pipeline

The knowledge discovery (also called data mining) field has its own pipeline. As with the graphics and visualization pipelines, we start with data; in this case we process it with the goal of generating a model, rather than some graphics display. Figure 1.36 presents one view of that pipeline.

Note that the visualization pipeline can be overlaid on this knowledge discovery (KD) pipeline. If we were to look at a pipeline for typical statistical analysis procedures, we would find the same process structure:

Data. In the KD pipeline there is more focus on data, as the graphics and visualization processes often assume that the data is already structured to facilitate its display.

Data integration, cleaning, warehousing and selection. These involve identifying the various data sets that will be potentially analyzed. Again, the user may participate in this step. This can involve filtering, sampling, subsetting, aggregating, and other techniques that help curate and manage the data for the data mining step.

Data mining. The heart of the KD pipeline is algorithmically analyzing the data to produce a model.

Pattern evaluation. The resulting model or models must be evaluated to determine their robustness, stability, precision, and accuracy.

Rendering or visualization. The specific results must be presented to the user. It does not matter whether we think of this as part of the graphics or visualization pipelines; the fact is that a user will eventually need to see the results of the process. Model visualization is an exciting research area that will be discussed later.

Interactive visualization can be used at every step of the KD pipeline. One can think of this as *computational steering*.

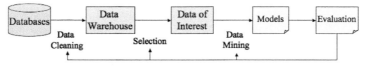

Figure 1.36.   One view of the knowledge discovery pipeline or process.

Figure 1.37.   How many legs does this elephant have? (Image from http://www.ilusa.com/gallery/elephant-illusion.jpg.)

1.4.4   The Role of Perception

In all visualizations, a critical aspect related to the user is the abilities and limitations of the human visual system. If the goal of visualization is to accurately convey information with pictures, it is essential that perceptual abilities be considered. A well-drawn picture can be stimulating, but if we are presenting a conclusion, we do not want ambiguities such as Shepard's many-legged elephant in Figure 1.37. The following illusions, and many more very interesting ones, are from http://www.ritsumei.ac.jp/~akitaoka/index-e.html.

Consider a collection of black squares spaced slightly apart (Figure 1.38). Note the effect these squares have as you stare at them. There are, of course, no moving black dots at the intersections of the white lines, but clearly such a presentation of data would create instabilities. It thus makes little sense to map a variable to a graphical attribute that humans have limited ability to control or quantify, if the goal is to communicate a numeric value with accuracy. For example, most people cannot gauge textures accurately

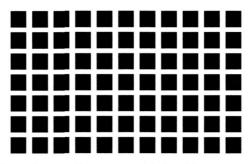

Figure 1.38.   The strength of the eye's saccadic movement is hard to overcome.

("Is texture A twice the value of texture B?"), though our abilities to perform relative comparisons are much stronger than absolute judgment (see Chapter 3).

Users interact with visualizations based upon what they see and interpret. Understanding how we see should help us produce better displays, or at least avoid producing very poor ones. About half of the human brain deals with visual input, and much of the processing is parallel and effectively continuous. Texture, color, and motion are examples of primitive attributes that we perceive. What are good colors for data? How does motion perception work? We discuss these in Chapter 3, but here we quickly review some of the key issues. For example, eight percent of males are color deficient. This implies that good visualization software should provide the ability to change the color of objects on the screen. What colors to use will depend on the user's deficiency and what the visualization is trying to convey. In the rest of this section, we present some key perceptual processes, so that we can use these in discussions on visualizations.

As in the pipelines briefly discussed earlier, the human perceptual system receives input data and processes it in various ways. The first process is *preattentive processing*, a fast, high-performance system that quickly identifies differences in, for example, color or texture. There are other features that the visual system deals with, such as line orientation, length, width, size of an object, curvature, grouping, and motion.

Figure 1.39 shows a set of colored points with a distractor that can be easily distinguished from the others. Figure 1.40 also shows a distractor with targets. In this case, line orientation is the perceptual element explored. Note that it, too, is processed in parallel (preattentively). Figure 1.41 shows an example of a display in which identifying the distractor is done attentively, with focused attention. The identification of preattentive primitives has helped in the development of modern display techniques for harnessing human perceptual capabilities.

Understanding visual perception leads to certain guidelines. For example, the Gestalt School of Psychology, started in 1912, attempted to define a set of laws by which we perceive patterns. These laws included rules about proximity, similarity, continuity, closure, symmetry, foreground and background, and size. We discuss these laws in detail in Chapter 3 and how they can be used in the visualization design process in Chapter 12.

Several steps are involved after the pre- and post-attentive processes. Cognition forces some visual interpretations, and thus understanding its role clearly helps in the development of task-oriented visualizations solutions.

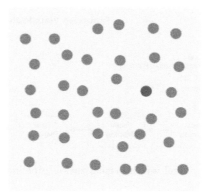

Figure 1.39.   A display showing one distractor (red) in a sea of blue-colored points. It is preattentively distinguished.

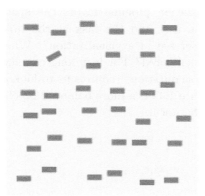

Figure 1.40.   A display where orientation is the key perceptual factor explored.

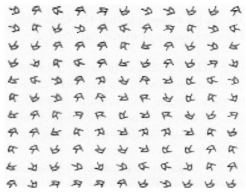

Figure 1.41.   It is difficult in this display to identify the inner square consisting of right-handed Rs.

Proposed Visualization Model

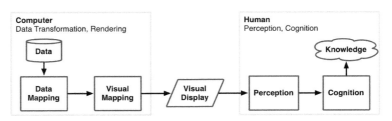

Figure 1.42.   A proposed model for the visualization pipeline.

1.5   The Role of Cognition

The visualization pipeline favors the synthesis of the visualizations and presents the user and the task as the target of the visualization. What does the user see in a visualization? What information gets understood, missed, remembered? For how long can such information be remembered? Each of these questions requires us to look beyond perception and into cognition. Figure 1.42 is a more balanced pipeline, which is discussed in greater detail in Chapter 3.

1.6   Pseudocode Conventions

Throughout the text we include pseudocode wherever possible. In our pseudocode, we aim to convey the essence of the algorithms at hand, while leaving out details required for user interaction, graphics nuances, and data management. We therefore assume that the following global variables and functions exist in the environment of the pseudocode:

- *data*—The working data table. This data table is assumed to contain only numeric values. In practice, dimensions of the original data table that contain non-numeric values must be somehow converted to numeric values. When visualizing a subset of the entire original data table, the working data table is assumed to be the subset.

- m—The number of dimensions (columns) in the working data table. Dimensions are typically iterated over using j as the running dimension index.

- n—The number of records (rows) in the working data table. Records are typically iterated over using i as the running record index.

- NORMALIZE(record, dimension), NORMALIZE(record, dimension, min, max)—A function that maps the value for the given record and dimension in the working data table to a value between min and max, or between zero and one if min and max are not specified. The normalization is typically linear and local to a single dimension. However, in practice, code must be structured such that various kinds of normalization could be used (logarithmic or square root, for example) either locally (using the bounds of the current dimension), globally (using the bounds of all dimensions), or local to the active dimensions (using the bounds of the dimensions being displayed). Also, in practice, one must accommodate multiple kinds of normalization within a single visualization. For example, a scatterplot may require a linear normalization for the x-axis and a logarithmic normalization for the y-axis.

- COLOR(color)—A function that sets the color state of the graphics environment to the specified color (whose type is assumed to be an integer containing RGB values).

- MAPCOLOR(record, dimension)—A function that sets the color state of the graphics environment to be the color derived from applying the global color map to the normalized value of the given record and dimension in the working data table.

- CIRCLE(x, y, radius)—A function that fills a circle centered at the given (x, y)-location, with the given radius, with the color of the graphics environment. The plotting space for all visualizations is the unit square. In practice, this function must map the unit square to a square in pixel coordinates.

- POLYLINE(xs, ys)—A function that draws a *polyline* (many connected line segments) from the given arrays of x- and y-coordinates.

- POLYGON(xs, ys)—A function that fills the polygon defined by the given arrays of x- and y-coordinates with the color of the current color state.

For geographic visualizations, the following functions are assumed to exist in the environment:

- GETLATITUDES(record), GETLONGITUDES(record)—Functions that retrieve the arrays of latitude and longitude coordinates, respectively, of the geographic polygon associated with the given record. For example, these polygons could be outlines of the countries of the world.

- PROJECTLATITUDES(*lats, scale*), PROJECTLONGITUDES(*longs, scale*) —Functions that project arrays of latitude values to arrays of y values, and arrays of longitude values to arrays of x values, respectively.

For graph and 3D surface data sets, the following is provided:

- GETCONNECTIONS(record)—A function that retrieves an array of record indices to which the given record is connected.

Arrays are indexed starting at zero.

1.7   The Scatterplot

We conclude our introductory chapter with a detailed discussion of one of the most basic visualization techniques, one we have already used in previous illustrations: the *scatterplot*. We include it early in the book to provide a basis with which to discuss visualization in general, and to provide exercises for both coding and theory/applications. This will give us some experience with transforming data into a visual representation that is understood by most readers. The scatterplot is one of the earliest and most widely used visualizations developed. It is based on the Cartesian coordinate system.

The following pseudocode renders a scatterplot of circles. Records are represented in the scatterplot as circles of varying location, color, and size. The x- and y-axes represent data from dimension numbers $xDim$ and $yDim$, respectively. The color of the circles is derived from dimension number $cDim$. The radius of the circles is derived from dimension number $rDim$, as well as from the upper and lower bounds for the radius, $rMin$ and $rMax$.

SCATTERPLOT($xDim, yDim, cDim, rDim, rMin, rMax$)

```
1   for each record i ▷ For each record,
2       do x ← NORMALIZE(i, xDim) ▷ derive the location,
3          y ← NORMALIZE(i, yDim)
4          r ← NORMALIZE(i, rDim, rMin, rMax) ▷ radius,
5          MAPCOLOR(i, cDim) ▷ and color, then
6          CIRCLE(x, y, r) ▷ draw the record as a circle.
```

Vehicle Name	Sedan	Sports	SUV	Wagon	Minivan	Pickup	AWD	RWD	Price
Acura 3.5 RL 4dr	1	0	0	0	0	0	0	0	43755
Acura MDX	0	0	1	0	0	0	1	0	36945
Suzuki XL-7 EX	0	0	1	0	0	0	0	0	23699

Table 1.1.   A simple partial table of the car and truck data. Note that you can think of this as a row-based table (cars and trucks) or a column-based table (car attributes).

We consider the 2004 new car and truck data set, which consists of detailed specifications for 428 vehicles. The variables included are dealer and retail price, weight, size, horsepower, fuel efficiency for city and highway, and more (see the book's web site). Although it looks like there are 19 variables for each vehicle, columns 2–7 effectively identify the type of car, and columns 8 and 9 the wheel-drive type. Table 1.1 shows three records of the data; the table in Figure 1.43 shows a subset of the complete data focused on Toyota vehicles. Some records have missing entries. The column variables are as follows:

1. vehicle name (text 1–45 characters);

2. small, sporty, compact or large sedan (1=yes, 0=no);

3. sports car? (1=yes, 0=no);

4. sport utility vehicle? (1=yes, 0=no);

5. wagon? (1=yes, 0=no);

6. minivan? (1=yes, 0=no);

7. pickup? (1=yes, 0=no);

8. all-wheel drive? (1=yes, 0=no);

9. rear-wheel drive? (1=yes, 0=no);

10. suggested retail price, what the manufacturer thinks the vehicle is worth, including adequate profit for the automaker and the dealer (U.S. dollars);

11. dealer cost (or "invoice price"), what the dealership pays the manufacturer (U.S. dollars);

12. engine size (liters);

13. number of cylinders (=-1 if rotary engine);

Vehicle Name	Small/Sporty/Compact/Large Sedan	Sports Car	SUV	Wagon	Minivan	Pickup	AWD	RWD	Retail Price	Dealer Cost	Engine Size (l)	Cyl	HP	City MPG	Hwy MPG	Weight	Wheel Base	Len	Width
Toyota 4Runner SR5 V6	0	0	1	0	0	0	0	0	27710	24801	4	6	245	18	21	4035	110	189	74
Toyota Avalon XL 4dr	1	0	0	0	0	0	0	0	26560	23693	3	6	210	21	29	3417	107	192	72
Toyota Avalon XLS 4dr	1	0	0	0	0	0	0	0	30920	27271	3	6	210	21	29	3439	107	192	72
Toyota Camry LE 4dr	1	0	0	0	0	0	0	0	19560	17558	2.4	4	157	24	33	3086	107	189	71
Toyota Camry LE V6 4dr	1	0	0	0	0	0	0	0	22775	20325	3	6	210	21	29	3296	107	189	71
Toyota Camry Solara SE 2dr	1	0	0	0	0	0	0	0	19635	17722	2.4	4	157	24	33	3175	107	193	72
Toyota Camry Solara SE V6 2dr	1	0	0	0	0	0	0	0	21965	19819	3.3	6	225	20	29	3417	107	193	72
Toyota Camry Solara SLE V6 2dr	1	0	0	0	0	0	0	0	26510	23908	3.3	6	225	20	29	3439	107	193	72
Toyota Camry XLE V6 4dr	1	0	0	0	0	0	0	0	25920	23125	3	6	210	21	29	3362	107	189	71
Toyota Celica GT-S 2dr	0	1	0	0	0	0	0	0	22570	20363	1.8	4	180	24	33	2500	102	171	68
Toyota Corolla CE 4dr	1	0	0	0	0	0	0	0	14085	13065	1.8	4	130	32	40	2502	102	178	67
Toyota Corolla LE 4dr	1	0	0	0	0	0	0	0	15295	13889	1.8	4	130	32	40	2524	102	178	67
Toyota Corolla S 4dr	1	0	0	0	0	0	0	0	15030	13650	1.8	4	130	32	40	2524	102	178	67
Toyota Echo 2dr auto	1	0	0	0	0	0	0	0	11560	10896	1.5	4	108	33	39	2085	93	163	65
Toyota Echo 2dr manual	1	0	0	0	0	0	0	0	10760	10144	1.5	4	108	35	43	2035	93	163	65
Toyota Echo 4dr	1	0	0	0	0	0	0	0	11290	10642	1.5	4	108	35	43	2055	93	163	65
Toyota Highlander V6	0	0	1	0	0	0	1	0	27930	24915	3.3	6	230	18	24	3935	107	185	72
Toyota Land Cruiser	0	0	1	0	0	0	1	0	54765	47986	4.7	8	325	13	17	5390	112	193	76
Toyota Matrix XR	0	0	0	1	0	0	0	0	16695	15156	1.8	4	130	29	36	2679	102	171	70
Toyota MR2 Spyder convertible 2dr	0	1	0	0	0	0	0	1	25130	22787	1.8	4	138	26	32	2195	97	153	67
Toyota Prius 4dr (gas/electric)	1	0	0	0	0	0	0	0	20510	18926	1.5	4	110	59	51	2890	106	175	68
Toyota RAV4	0	0	1	0	0	0	1	0	20290	18553	2.4	4	161	22	27	3119	98	167	68
Toyota Sequoia SR5	0	0	1	0	0	0	1	0	35695	31827	4.7	8	240	14	17	5270	118	204	78
Toyota Sienna CE	0	0	0	0	1	0	0	0	23495	21198	3.3	6	230	19	27	4120	119	200	77
Toyota Sienna XLE Limited	0	0	0	0	1	0	0	0	28800	25690	3.3	6	230	19	27	4165	119	200	77
Toyota Tacoma	0	0	0	0	0	1	0	1	12800	11879	2.4	4	142	22	27	2750	103	*	*
Toyota Tundra Access Cab V6 SR5	0	0	0	0	0	1	1	0	25935	23520	3.4	6	190	14	17	4435	128	*	*
Toyota Tundra Regular Cab V6	0	0	0	0	0	1	0	1	16495	14978	3.4	6	190	16	20	3925	128	*	*

Figure 1.43.   Toyota vehicle table. All variables are shown. Notice that there are a few missing values.

14. horsepower;

15. city miles per gallon;

16. highway miles per gallon;

17. weight (pounds);

18. wheel base (inches);

19. length (inches);

20. width (inches).

We can look at the table of data for some of the variables. What patterns can be seen in the table? Now let's try using graphical methods. Let's begin to explore the data. Suppose we select all Toyota vehicles (see Figure 1.43). It is difficult to get a sense of the data just by looking at even this small subset of 28 records. Specific questions about the data can be asked. For example, what are the relationships between weight and length? Is there a correlation between vehicle model and MPG (specific models have specific ranges of MPGs)? Does the dealer price mean we have a better performing vehicle (higher price implies better MPGs)? Do foreign vehicles perform better than domestic ones?

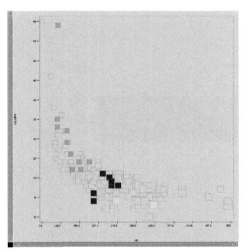

Figure 1.44.   A scatterplot of horsepower versus city MPG for Toyota vehicles. The vehicle class
                   is mapped to color.

In fact, even when looking at just three of these records the task is not simple. Imagine looking at tables with hundreds of records—how would one answer these questions? Figure 1.44 represents two selected variables for those 28 records.

Much can be quickly and easily discerned from the visualization. For example all Toyota vehicles are broken down into three categories and there is clearly a close to linear relationship between horsepower and city miles per gallon. Is this a general rule? If we select another model, say Kia vehicles, we find a very similar relationship (see Figure 1.45).

So we have a hypothesis! In fact, there may be several. Increasing horsepower in 2004 vehicles yields a decrease in MPG. Perhaps that is too broad and we should restrict it to foreign vehicles. Let's test that hypothesis. We want to confirm that increasing horsepower in foreign vehicles yields a decrease in city MPG. There are many ways to do this. We'll jump right to another foreign car to check it out. Consider the Lexus data in Figure 1.46. It's clear that there are relationships, but they are not necessarily as simple as we stated earlier. Consider the whole data set plotted (see Figure 1.47). This is where we can start to explore the data further.

There are a number of questions we can ask:

   1. Do the trends defined for 28 records apply to the whole data set, or if not, what specific subsets do they apply to? In other words, can we generalize the model we've discovered or identified?

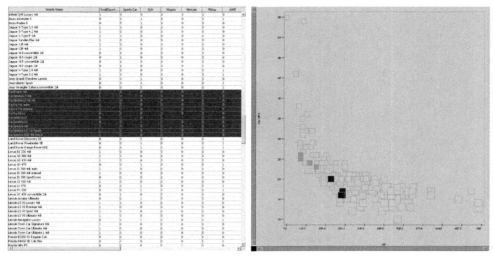

Figure 1.45.   Table and scatterplot of the Kia vehicles. Note that here, too, a linear relationship
                holds.

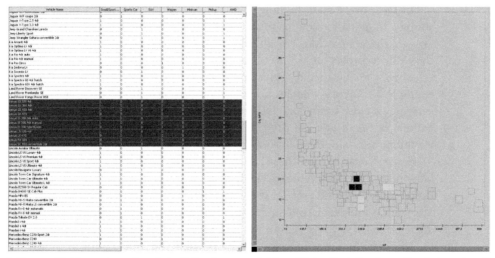

Figure 1.46.   Table and scatterplot of the Lexus vehicles. Note that the hypothesis is not vali-
                dated.

2. How many records have missing values, and for what fields (attributes)?

3. What can we say about the missing data?

4. What can we say about the data overall?

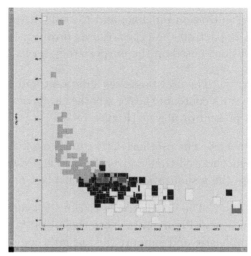

Figure I.47.   Scatterplot of all vehicles. There is lots to explore here.

(a) What is the distribution of MPG?

(b) Are there trends?

(c) Are there groups?

There are many more questions that could be asked and discoveries that could be made. We will discuss further analyses of this data set in the exercises. Before leaving this example, we note that one can criticize the visualization. There is no legend. Some rectangles are bigger than others. What happens if points overlap? Why does it use squares?

I.8   The Role of the User

In computer graphics, the role of the user is predominantly at either of the two ends of the pipeline, either in creating the model of the scene to be rendered or observing the end results, perhaps with some interactive control of camera or animation parameters. As what is being rendered is often a simulation of a three-dimensional "world," it is assumed that our innate perceptual abilities are sufficient and well trained for the task. In addition, the role of the resulting image is generally straightforward, that is, to convey to the user the scene contents and the actions and interactions of the objects within the scene.

On the other hand, the user can be involved in most, if not all stages of the visualization pipeline, and the role of the visualization can have significant impact on the types of user involvement. It is useful to categorize visualizations based on the purpose they serve. These include the following:

Exploration. The user possesses a data set and wants to examine it to ascertain its contents and/or whether a particular feature or set of features is present or absent (Figure 1.47).

Confirmation. The user has determined (e.g., via computational analysis) or hypothesized that a given feature is present in the data and wants to use the visualization to verify this fact or hypothesis (Figure 1.45).

Presentation. The user is trying to convey some concept or set of facts to an audience (Figure 1.2). Note the added labeling and stronger colors to emphasize and support the author's conclusion.

Interactive Presentation. The user is providing a presentation as above but one that is interactive typically for an individual to explore. Interactive presentations such as those available nowadays on the web take much more time to prepare. There are numerous constraints that have to be present so as not to allow the user to get lost, such as zooming out to a point where nothing is visible. Such interactive presentations are engaging when well done and are becoming more common as users are becoming more facile on the web.

The major experience most people have had with visualization is in presentations, where a speaker or author uses a bar chart or line graph to indicate a set of values and their relationships. Other common visualizations, such as maps and organizational charts, also primarily serve this purpose. The creator of the visualization is fully aware of the information that he/she wishes to convey and usually has a reasonable idea of the types of visualizations with which the intended audience is familiar. The reason that presentation visualizations are the primary visualization experiences for most people is that, until recently, visualizations have been mostly static images requiring significant efforts to generate. The advent of more powerful computers and easier mechanisms for creating visualizations has made possible the other types of visualization. Presentation visualizations take a great deal of time to produce and are used in a wide variety of areas, such as training and education. Figure 1.48 presents screen shots from animations used for explaining a complex model over time, showing the evolution of a storm.

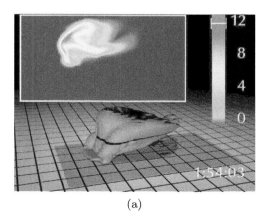 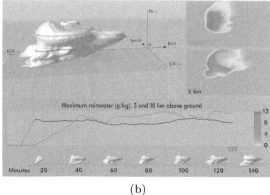

(a)   (b)

Figure 1.48.   (a) A storm over time with a horizontal cross section in the small window. (b) The
same storm with different views [24]. (Images © 1995 IEEE.)

In exploratory visualization we look for patterns in the data to explain
its structure. Figure 1.49 displays the gene expression patterns of selected
genes measured from a number of patients' tissue samples and controls. The
higher-expressed genes are portrayed in red; the lower-expressed genes are
in green. Along the two dimensions, the tissue samples are organized by
disease type, and genes are organized by their discriminative disease type in
terms of analytic. This visualization allows one to see quickly which genes
are related to which diseases.

Each of these categories of visualization has its own special tools. For example, presentation visualizations more commonly use presentation graphics
as their layout and visual control tools. Many products, such as Photoshop,
provide rich controls for fine tuning the visualization.

1.9   Related Readings

There are several web sites and articles written on the history of visualization
and related topics. Here is a brief list:

History. The National Science Foundation (NSF) has a brief document on
the history of its funded pioneering visualization activities, mostly
centered on scientific visualization. See http://www.nsf.gov/about/
history/nsf0050/pdf/visualization.pdf. See also Michael Friendly's paper on the history and evolution of data visualization from the 17th
century to modern times [135].

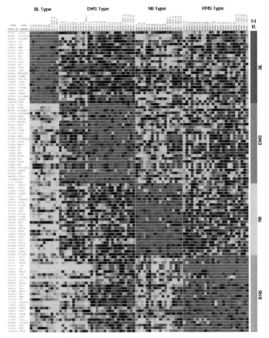

Figure 1.49.   Exploratory visualization used in microarray gene expression experiment analysis.
                    (Image courtesy [489].)

Siggraph. The Association for Computing Machinery (ACM) Special Inter-
    est Group in Computer Graphics has a great deal of information and
    education materials. See http://education .siggraph.org/.

Cartography. Michael Friendly and Daniel J. Denis maintain a web page
    with numerous beautiful images on Milestones in the History of The-
    matic Cartography, Statistical Graphics, and Data Visualization, an
    illustrated chronology of innovations. See http://www.math.yorku.ca/
    SCS/Gallery/milestone/.

Visual analytics. The   National   Visualization   and   Analytics   Center
    (NVAC) has a wonderful book available online entitled *Illuminating
    the Path: The Research and Development Agenda for Visual Analyt-
    ics.* See http://nvac.pnl.gov/agenda.stm.

John Snow. A great deal of history is associated with Dr. John Snow's map
    of the deaths from cholera in London. Snow used bars and an in-
    terpretation by Gilbert replaced the bars with dots [146]. Sedwick,

Tufte, and others credited the dots map to Snow. A nice description of the evolution of Snow's maps and different usages was done by Tom Koch [147].

1.10 Exercises

1. Choose a topic from computer graphics or visualization and research its origins. Feel free to skim ahead in this book to find a topic, such as volume rendering or parallel coordinates. Send your contributions to the authors via the book's web site. If we can verify it, your findings may be placed in our online history page.

2. Describe the linkages between the stages of the graphics pipeline and those of the visualization pipeline. Are there any stages in one pipeline that do not have a clear linkage in the other pipeline?

3. Describe the linkages between the stages of the visualization pipeline and those of the knowledge discovery pipeline. Are there any stages in one pipeline that do not have a clear linkage in the other pipeline?

4. Give an example of each of the four categories of visualization: interactive presentation, presentation, confirmation, and exploration.

5. Give an example of existing websites relevant to data visualization that show data visualization can be both interesting, useful, and revealing. What type of visualizations do they provide? Do they engage you? What ideas do they evoke?

6. Explore some visualizations and think about how to distort them to "hide" the truth.

7. Familiarize yourself with scatterplots: write up a summary of what they are, how they are created, and how they are used. There are hundreds of different variations on scatterplots, so select one or two as examples in your summary.

8. Describe the similarities and differences between clipping in the computer graphics pipeline and data selection in the visualization pipeline. What would happen to each if this step were removed?

1.11   Projects

1. Using the vehicle data set and an existing visualization tool (e.g., Excel, Weka, Weave, or XmdvTool), or an analytic tool such as R, perform the following tasks.

   (a) Read the full data set into the program.

   (b) Select a subset of the data that contains an obvious correlation (exploratory visualization).

   (c) State a hypothesis and confirm it using the full data set (confirmatory visualization).

   (d) Present your results in a PowerPoint slide (presentation visualization).

2. Write a scatterplot program from scratch, using the following steps.

   (a) Write a program that reads the data, stores that data internally, and identifies which records have missing values. Keep track of the minimum and maximum of each variable.

   (b) Select two of the variables as your axes. Draw coordinate axes and label them with the names of the variables.

   (c) Loop through all nonmissing data records and plot a circle or square at location (x, y) based on your selected variables. Skip any record that has missing values.

   (d) Additions to consider: color the square or circle by some other value; use size to represent yet another value of the record; have the user select which variables to use as the axes; handle missing values by replacing the missing data with some very large number, some very small number, or the average value for that variable.

CHAPTER 2

Data Foundations

Since every visualization starts with the data that is to be displayed, a first step in addressing the design of visualizations is to examine the characteristics of the data. Data comes from many sources; it can be gathered from sensors or surveys, or it can be generated by simulations and computations. Data can be *raw* (untreated), or it can be derived from raw data via some process, such as smoothing, noise removal, scaling, or interpolation. It also can have a wide range of characteristics and structures.

A typical data set used in visualization consists of a list of n records, $(r_1, r_2, \ldots, r_n)$. Each record r_i consists of m (one or more) *observations* or *variables*, $(v_1, v_2, \ldots v_m)$. An observation may be a single number/symbol/string or a more complex structure (discussed in more detail later in this chapter). A variable may be classified as either *independent* or *dependent*. An independent variable iv_i is one whose value is not controlled or affected by another variable, such as the *time* variable in a time-series data set. A dependent variable dv_j is one whose value is affected by a variation in one or more associated independent variables. *Temperature* for a region would be considered a dependent variable, as its value is affected by variables such as *date*, *time*, or *location*. Thus we can formally represent a record as

$$r_i = (iv_1, iv_2, \ldots iv_{m_i}, dv_1, dv_2, \ldots dv_{m_d}),$$

where m_i is the number of independent variables and m_d is the number of dependent variables. With this notation we have, $m = m_i + m_d$.

In many cases, we may not know which variables are dependent or independent.

We can also think of data as being generated by some process or *function*. In this case, the independent variables would be considered the *domain* of the function, and the dependent variables would be the *range* of the function, as for each entry in the domain there is a single unique entry in the range. Note that, in general, a data set will not contain an exhaustive list of all possible combinations of values for the variables in its domain.

2.1 Types of Data

In its simplest form, each observation or variable of a data record represents a single piece of information. We can categorize this information as being *ordinal* (numeric) or *nominal* (nonnumeric). Subcategories of each can be readily defined.

Ordinal. The data take on numeric values:

- binary—assuming only values of 0 and 1;
- discrete—taking on only integer values or from a specific subset (e.g., (2, 4, 6));
- continuous—representing real values (e.g., in the interval [0, 5]).

Nominal. The data take on nonnumeric values:

- categorical—a value selected from a finite (often short) list of possibilities (e.g., red, blue, green);
- ranked—a categorical variable that has an implied ordering (e.g., small, medium, large);
- arbitrary—a variable with a potentially infinite range of values with no implied ordering (e.g., addresses).

Another method of categorizing variables is by using the mathematical concept of *scale*.

Scale. Three attributes that define a variable's measure are as follows:

- Ordering relation, with which the data can be ordered in some fashion. By definition, ranked nominal variables and all ordinal variables exhibit this relation.
- Distance metric, with which the distances can be computed between different records. This measure is clearly present in all ordinal variables, but is generally not found in nominal variables.

- Existence of absolute zero, in which variables may have a fixed lowest value. This is useful for differentiating types of ordinal variables. A variable such as *weight* possesses an absolute zero, while *bank balance* does not.

Scale is an important attribute to examine when designing appropriate visualizations because each graphical attribute that we can control has a scale associated with it. Ideally, the scale of a data variable should be compatible with the scale of the graphical entity or attribute to which it is mapped, though it is somewhat dependent on the task to be performed with the visualization.

The type of data also determines the operations that can be applied to the data. While the equality and inequality operators $(=, <>)$ can be applied to any type of data, comparison operators $(<, >, <=, >=)$ can only be applied to ranked nominal and ordinal data types, and mathematical operators and distance computations $(+, -, *, /)$ can only be applied to ordinal data types.

2.2 Structure within and between Records

Data sets have structure, both in terms of the means of representation (*syntax*), and the types of interrelationships within a given record and between records (*semantics*).

2.2.1 Scalars, Vectors, and Tensors

An individual number in a data record is often referred to as a *scalar*. Scalar values, such as the cost of an item or the age of an individual, are often the focus for analysis and visualization. Multiple variables within a single record can represent a composite data item. For example, a point in a two-dimensional flow field might be represented by a pair of values, such as a displacement in x and y. This pair, and any such composition, is referred to as a *vector*. Other examples of vectors found in typical data sets include position (2 or 3 spatial values), color (a triplet of red, green, and blue components), and phone number (country code, area code, and local number). While each component of a vector might be examined individually, it is most common to treat the vector as a whole.

Scalars and vectors are simple variants on a more general structure known as a *tensor*. A tensor is defined by its *rank* and by the dimensionality of the space within which it is defined. It is generally represented as an array or matrix. A scalar is a tensor of rank 0, while a vector is a tensor of rank 1. One could use a 3×3 matrix to represent a tensor of rank 2 in 3D space, and in general, a tensor of rank M in D-dimensional space requires D^M data values. An example of a tensor that might be found in a data record would be a transformation matrix to specify a local coordinate system.

2.2.2   Geometry and Grids

Geometric structure can commonly be found in data sets, especially those from scientific and engineering domains. The simplest method of incorporating geometric structure in a data set is to have explicit coordinates for each data record. Thus, a data set of temperature readings from across the country might include the longitude and latitude associated with the sensors, as well as the sensor values. In modeling of 3D objects, the geometry constitutes the majority of the data, with coordinates given for each vertex.

Sometimes the geometric structure is implied. When this is the case, it is assumed that some form of grid exists, and the data set is structured such that successive data records are located at successive locations on the grid. For example, if one had a data set giving elevation at uniform spacing across a surface, it would be unnecessary to include the coordinates for each record; it would be sufficient to indicate a starting location, orientation, and the step size horizontally and vertically.

There are many different coordinate systems that are used for grid-structured data, including *Cartesian*, *spherical*, and *hyperbolic* coordinates. Often, the choice of coordinate system is domain-specific, and is partially dependent on how the data is acquired/computed, and on the structure of the space in which the data resides. Generally, a straightforward transformation matrix can be used to convert positions in the data space coordinate system into positions on the display space coordinate system.

Nonuniform, or *irregular*, geometry is also common. For example, in simulating the flow of wind around an airplane wing, it is important to have data computed densely at locations close to the surface, while data for locations far from the surface can be computed much more sparsely. For irregular geometry it is, of course, essential that the coordinates are explicitly specified in the data file. As the geometry changes from a uniform to a nonuniform or irregular grid, the computations for display increase in complexity.

2.2.3   Other Forms of Structure

A timestamp is an important attribute that can be associated with a data record. Time perhaps has the widest range of possible values of all aspects of a data set, since we can refer to time with units from picoseconds to millennia. It can also be relative or absolute in terms of its base value. Data sets with temporal attributes can be uniformly spaced, such as in the sampling of a continuous phenomenon, or nonuniformly spaced, as in a business transaction database.

Another important form of structure found within many data sets is that of *topology*, or how the data records are connected. Connectivity indicates that data records have some relationship to each other. Thus, vertices on a surface (geometry) are connected to their neighbors via edges (topology), and relationships between nodes in a hierarchy or graph can be specified by links. Connectivity information is essential to support the processes of *resampling* and *interpolation*. This form of structure can either be included explicitly in the data record (e.g., with a fixed or variable length vector identifying the records to which the current record is linked) or as an auxiliary data structure.

The following are examples of various structured data:

MRI (magnetic resonance imagery). Density (scalar), with three spatial attributes, 3D grid connectivity;

CFD (computational fluid dynamics). Three dimensions for displacement, with one temporal and three spatial attributes, 3D grid connectivity (uniform or nonuniform);

Financial. No geometric structure, n possibly independent components, nominal and ordinal, with a temporal attribute;

CAD (computer-aided design). Three spatial attributes with edge and polygon connections, and surface properties;

Remote sensing. Multiple channels, with two or three spatial attributes, one temporal attribute, and grid connectivity;

Census. Multiple fields of all types, spatial attributes (e.g., addresses), temporal attribute, and connectivity implied by similarities in fields;

Social Network. Nodes consisting of multiple fields of all types, with various connectivity attributes that could be spatial, temporal, or dependent on other attributes, such as belonging to the same group or having some common computed values.

2.3   Data Preprocessing

In most circumstances, it is preferable to view the original raw data. In many domains, such as medical imaging, the data analyst is often opposed to any sort of data modifications, such as filtering or smoothing, for fear that important information will be lost or deceptive artifacts will be added. Viewing raw data also often identifies problems in the data set, such as missing data, or outliers that may be the result of errors in computation or input. Depending on the type of data and the visualization techniques to be applied, however, some forms of preprocessing might be necessary. Some common methods for preprocessing data are briefly discussed later in this chapter. The interested reader is directed to the many fine textbooks dedicated to these topics for more in-depth coverage.

2.3.1   Metadata and Statistics

Information regarding a data set of interest (its *metadata*) and statistical analysis can provide invaluable guidance in preprocessing the data. Metadata may provide information that can help in its interpretation, such as the format of individual fields within the data records. It may also contain the base reference point from which some of the data fields are measured, the units used in the measurements, the symbol or number used to indicate a missing value (see below), and the resolution at which measurements were acquired. This information may be important in selecting the appropriate preprocessing operations, and in setting their parameters.

Various methods of statistical analysis can provide us with useful insights. *Outlier detection* can indicate records with erroneous data fields. *Cluster analysis* can help segment the data into groups exhibiting strong similarities. *Correlation analysis* can help users eliminate redundant fields or highlight associations between dimensions that might not have been apparent otherwise.

The most common statistics about data include the mean

$$\mu = \frac{1}{n} \sum_{i=0}^{n} (x_i)$$

and the standard deviation

$$\sigma = \sqrt{\left(\sum (x_i - \mu)^2\right)}.$$

The most common statistical plot is the distribution of data, in the form of a histogram.

2.3.2 Missing Values and Data Cleansing

One of the realities of analyzing and visualizing "real" data sets is that they often are missing some data entries or have erroneous entries. Missing data may be caused by several reasons, including, for example, a malfunctioning sensor, a blank entry on a survey, or an omission on the part of the person entering the data. Erroneous data is most often caused by human error and can be difficult to detect. In either case, the data analyst must choose a strategy for dealing with these common events. Some of these strategies, specifically those that are commonly used in data visualization, are outlined below.

Discard the bad record. This seemingly drastic measure, namely to throw away any data record containing a missing or erroneous field, is actually one of the most commonly applied, since the quality of the remaining data entries in that record may be in question. However, this can potentially lead to a significant loss of information, especially in data sets containing large numbers of records. In some domains, as much as 90% of records have at least one missing or erroneous field. In addition, those records with missing data may be the most interesting (e.g., such as due to a malfunctioning sensor or an overly high response to a drug).

Assign a sentinel value. Another popular strategy is to have a designated *sentinel* value for each variable in the data set that can be assigned when the real value in a record is in question. For example, in a variable that has a range of 0 to 100, one might use a value such as -5 to designate an erroneous or missing entry. Then, when the data is visualized, the records with problematic data entries will be clearly visible. Of course, if this strategy is chosen, care must be taken not to perform statistical analysis on these sentinel values.

Assign the average value. A simple strategy for dealing with bad or missing data is to replace it with the average value for that variable or dimension. An advantage to using this strategy is that it minimally affects the overall statistics for that variable. The average, however, may not be a good "guess" for this particular record. Another drawback of using this method is that it may mask or obscure outliers, which can be of particular interest.

Assign value based on nearest neighbor. A better approximation for a substitute value is to find the record that has the highest similarity with the record in question, based on analyzing the differences in all other variables. The basic idea here is that if record A is missing an entry for variable i, and record B is closer than any other record to A without considering variable i, then using the value of variable i from record B as a substitute in A is a reasonable assumption. The problem with this approach, however, is that variable i may be most dependent on only a subset of the other dimensions, rather than on all dimensions, and so the best nearest neighbor based on all dimensions may not be the best substitute for this particular dimension.

Compute a substitute value. Researchers in multivariate statistics have dedicated a significant amount of energy to developing methods for generating values to replace missing or erroneous data. The process, known as *imputation*, seeks to find values that have high statistical confidence. Schafer [362] has developed a model-based imputation technique (see the projects at the end of the chapter).

In all cases where a value is substituted for the missing or erroneous value, it is critically important that the fact that this value is "suspect" be preserved, and that any visualization of this data must convey this information.

2.3.3   Normalization

Normalization is the process of transforming a data set so that the results satisfy a particular statistical property. A simple example of this is to transform the range of values a particular variable assumes so that all numbers fall within the range of 0.0 to 1.0. Other forms of normalization convert the data such that each dimension has a common mean and standard deviation. Normalization is a useful operation since it allows us to compare seemingly unrelated variables. It is important in visualization as well, since graphical attributes have a range of values that are possible, and thus to map data to those attributes, we need to convert the data range to be compatible with the graphical attribute range.

For example, if $d_{\min}$ and $d_{\max}$ are the minimum and maximum values for a particular data variable, we can normalize the values to the range of 0.0 to 1.0 using the formula

$$d_{\mathrm{normalized}} = (d_{\mathrm{original}} - d_{\min})/(d_{\max} - d_{\min}).$$

To ease interpretation, we sometimes choose the scaling and offset factors to coincide with intuitive maximum and minimum values, rather than the ones the data possess. For example, if the data corresponds to percentages that fall between 40 and 90, we might use the full range of 0 to 100 instead.

If the data has a highly non-linear distribution, a linear normalization will map most values to the same or close-by values. In this case, it may be more appropriate to perform a non-linear normalization such as a square root mapping

$$d_{\mathrm{sqrt-normalized}} = (\sqrt{d_{\mathrm{original}}} - \sqrt{d_{\min}})/(\sqrt{d_{\max}} - \sqrt{d_{\min}})$$

or even a logarithmic mapping

$$d_{\mathrm{log-normalized}} = (\log d_{\mathrm{original}} - \log d_{\min})/(\log d_{\max} - \log d_{\min}).$$

Note that such a mapping changes the data values and distribution, and it is essential that it is communicated to the user in the visual mapping.

Normalization may also involve *bounding values*, so that, for example, values exceeding a particular threshold are capped at that threshold. In this way the details falling within the specified range can be more effectively interpreted when mapped to a specific graphical attribute. For example, density values in a tomographic data set may have a substantial range, yet the range of interest for someone interpreting the data may be a very small portion of that range. By truncating the range and normalizing, the variation across the shortened range will be more easily perceived. This is especially important when extreme outliers exist.

One method of automatically obtaining appropriate bounding values is to compute $\alpha - Quantiles$ with appropriate α-values. If we expect, for example, no more than 1% outliers at the top and bottom spectrum of our data distribution, we can use $\alpha = 1\%$ and $\alpha = 99\%$ as lower and upper bounding values.

2.3.4 Segmentation

In many situations, the data can be separated into contiguous regions, where each region corresponds to a particular classification of the data. For example, an MRI data set might originally have 256 possible values for each data point, and then be segmented into specific categories, such as bone, muscle, fat, and skin. Simple segmentation can be performed by just mapping disjoint ranges of the data values to specific categories. However, in most situations, the assignment of values to a category is ambiguous. In these cases, it is important to look at the classification of neighboring points to improve the confidence of classification, or even to do a probabilistic segmentation, where each data point is assigned a probability for belonging to each of the available classifications. Figure 2.1 shows an image with 256 levels of grey segmented into four classes, based on the analysis of subranges of data.

A typical problem with segmentation is that the results may not coincide with regions that are semantically homogeneous (*undersegmented*), or may consist of large numbers of tiny regions (*oversegmented*). One solution to this problem is to follow the initial segmentation process with an iterative *split-and-merge* refinement stage. The structure of such an algorithm is as follows:

```
similarThresh = similarity measure indicating two regions have
                similar characteristics
homogeneousThresh = uniformity measure indicating a region is
                    too nonhomogeneous
do {
    changeCount = 0
    for each region
        compare region with neighboring regions to find most
        similar
```

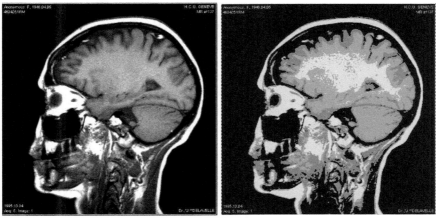

Figure 2.1.   Slice from skull data set, with original values and after segmenting into four subranges.

```
      if most similar neighbor is within similarThresh of
      current region
          merge two regions
          changeCount++
      evaluate homogeneity of region
      if region homogeneity is less than homogeneousThresh
          split region into two
          changeCount++
} until changeCount == 0
```

The complex tasks of the above algorithm consist of:

- determining if two regions are similar—a simple procedure is to compare the average values within each region;

- evaluating the homogeneity of a region—one possible algorithm is to evaluate the histogram of the values within the region to determine if it is unimodal or multimodal;

- splitting a region—a typical algorithm creates two (or more) subregions at the points where the values are most different and *grows* regions around these seed points until all data points within the region have been reassigned.

Care must be taken to avoid an infinite loop caused by repeated splitting and merging of the same region. A solution to this problem is to tighten the similarity threshold or loosen the homogeneity threshold as the algorithm progresses. More sophisticated algorithms can incorporate other features of the regions, such as smoothness of boundaries or the size and shape of regions, to obtain desirable characteristics in the resulting segments.

2.3.5 Sampling and Subsetting

Often it is necessary to transform a data set with one spatial resolution into another data set with a different spatial resolution. For example, we might have an image we would like to shrink or expand, or we might have only a small sampling of data points and wish to fill in values for locations between our samples. In each case, we assume that the data we possess is a discrete sampling of a continuous phenomenon, and therefore we can predict the values at another location by examining the actual data nearest to it. The process of *interpolation* is a commonly used resampling method in many fields, including visualization. Some common techniques include the following:

Linear interpolation. Given the value of a variable d at two locations A and B, we can estimate the value of that variable at a location C that is between A and B by first calculating the percentage of the distance between A and B where C lies. This percentage can then be used in conjunction with the amount the variable changes in value between the two points to determine the amount the value should have changed by the time point C is reached. If we assume the points lie on the x-axis, then we know the following equation is true:

$$(x_C - x_A)/(x_B - x_A) = (d_C - d_A)/(d_B - d_A)$$

or

$$d_C = d_A + (d_B - d_A) * (x_C - x_A)/(x_B - x_A).$$

This is similar to the normalization transformation we encountered in Section 2.3.3. To remove the restriction of the line being on the x-axis, we can use parametric equations to define both the change in position and change in value between points A and B, compute the value of the parameter in the line equation that defines point C, and use this number in the value equation to generate the value at location C. The parametric form of a line is $P(t) = P_A + Vt$, where $V = P_B - P_A$. Note that this will work for arbitrary spaces, as we haven't specified the number of dimensions used to define P. By setting the left-hand side to P_C, we can then compute the value of t and use it in the associated equation for the value change, $d(t) = d_A + Ut$, where $U = d_B - d_A$.

Bilinear interpolation. We can extend this concept to two dimensions (or to an arbitrary number of dimensions) by repeating the procedure for each dimension. For example, a common task in two dimensions is to compute the value of d at location (x, y) given a uniform grid of data values (i.e., the space between points is uniform in both directions, as in an image). If the location coincides with a grid point, the answer is simply the value stored at that location. But what happens if (x, y) lies between grid points? To solve this, we first find the four grid locations that surround (x, y). If we assume the grid positions are all whole numbers with a spacing of 1.0 and that (x, y) both have fractional components, the bounding box of grid elements containing the point will be (i, j), $(i+1, j)$, $(i, j+1)$, and $(i+1, j+1)$, where i is the largest whole number less than x and j is the largest whole number less than y.

We will first interpolate horizontally, and then vertically. Reusing the one-dimensional interpolation above, we compute the percentage of the way that x is between i and $i+1$. Let us call this value s. We can now compute the value of d at positions (x, j) and $(x, j+1)$ using the values at the four grid points. Next, we compute the percentage of the way that y is between j and $j+1$. Call this percentage t. We finally compute the value at position (x, y) by interpolating using the above calculated values from our horizontal interpolation and the percentage t, namely,

$$d_{x,y} = d_{x,j} + t * (d_{x,j+1} - d_{x,j}).$$

In the end, $d_{x,y}$ is simply a weighted average of the four grid values nearest to it. Calculating the closed form solution for this weighted average is left as an exercise.

Nonlinear interpolation. One of the deficiencies of linear interpolation techniques is that, while the local change in values is smooth, the changes on opposite sides of a grid point can be noticeably different. In fact, the continuity at a grid point is only order 0, as the first derivative on either side will, in general, be different. We can improve on this by using a different formulation for interpolation, namely a higher-order polynomial equation, as a means of estimating the intermediate values. Several quadratic and cubic curves known as *splines*, and commonly found in graphics, have been employed. Indeed, the primary purpose of those curves has been to interpolate surface positions, given a set of control points and blending functions. For our purposes, it is important that the data values at the grid points be preserved, i.e., the curve defining the changing values must go through the control points. A popular curve satisfying this condition is the *Catmull-Rom* curve, which we describe below.

Given control points (p_0, p_1, p_2, p_3), the cubic curve that goes through these points is defined as

$$q(t) = 0.5 * (1.0 \; t \; t^2 \; t^3) * \begin{pmatrix} 0 & 2 & 0 & 0 \\ -1 & 0 & 1 & 0 \\ 2 & -5 & 4 & -1 \\ -1 & 3 & -3 & 1 \end{pmatrix} * \begin{pmatrix} p_0 \\ p_1 \\ p_2 \\ p_3 \end{pmatrix}$$

or

$$q(t) = 0.5 * ((2 * p_1) + (-p_0 + p_2) * t + (2 * p_0 - 5 * p_1 \\ + 4 * p_2 - p_3) * t^2 + (-p_0 + 3 * p_1 - 3 * p_2 + p_3) * t^3).$$

Figure 2.2 shows a sparse grid of random values with the intermediate values computed using Catmull-Rom interpolation. Data values are mapped to grayscale.

Depending on the density or sparsity of the data, it might be possible to either selectively sample the data to reduce its size, or use data replication

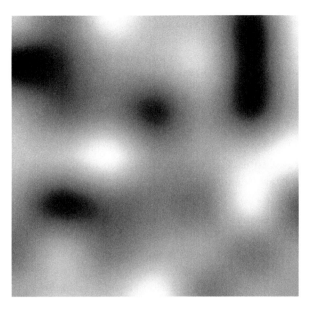

Figure 2.2.   Nonlinear interpolation of a 5 × 5 grid of random values provides smooth transi-
                   tions between adjacent points.

to expand the size. Subsampling can be fairly simplistic, such as choosing regularly spaced data from the original set. However, this can easily
lead to lost data features. For example, selecting every fourth point on a
map could easily miss important objects such as roads and streams. Other
approaches involve averaging neighborhoods, selecting median or random
points in the subregion of the original data that will map to a single point,
or domain-specific feature preservation. Figure 2.3 shows a low-resolution
medical image using two methods for resampling: *pixel replication* and *averaging neighborhoods.*

Data subsetting is also a frequently used operation both prior to and
during visualization. This is especially helpful for very large data sets, as
the visualization of the entire data set may lead to substantial visual clutter.
A user may specify a set of constraints (a query) to retrieve for visualization
only the data that meet the desired conditions, such as all the data for a
specific time period, or all data for which the change in stock value exceeds
a particular threshold. Subsetting may also be performed on the visualization itself, with the user highlighting, painting, or otherwise selecting the
data subset of interest (see the discussion about interactive techniques in
Chapter 11). The results of this selection can either be deleted (as currently

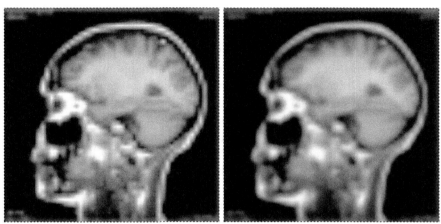

Figure 2.3.   Low-resolution version of skull data shown above, using pixel replication and averaging to interpolate additional data points.

uninteresting), masked (i.e., remove all data other than the selected subset), or simply highlighted. Interactive subsetting is generally easier to control than query-based subsetting, as the user can see the characteristics of the overall data set and make an informed decision as to which portion of the data he or she wishes to explore in more detail. Query-based subsetting has the advantage of not requiring the loading of the entire data set into the program, and allows users to specify precise boundaries for their region of interest.

2.3.6   Dimension Reduction

In situations where the dimensionality of the data exceeds the capabilities of the visualization technique, it is necessary to investigate ways to reduce the data dimensionality, while at the same time preserving, as much as possible, the information contained within. This can be done manually by allowing the user to select the dimensions deemed most important, or via computational techniques, such as *principal component analysis* (PCA) [385], *multidimensional scaling* (MDS) [259], *Kohonen self-organizing maps* (SOMs) [248], and *Local Linear Embedding* (LLE) [350]. Each of these can be used to convey, within the dimensionality of the display, a description of the data set that covers the majority of significant features, such as clusters, patterns, and outliers. However, it is important to note that most of these techniques do not produce unique results. Starting configurations, parameters of the calculations, and variations in the computations can lead to quite different results, as we will encounter in the aggregation techniques. In Figure 2.4 we can see the results of reducing a four-dimensional data set to two dimensions using PCA and plotting the resulting points. In fact, we use a form of glyph, called a *star glyph*, to convey the original data points. Clearly, the PCA algorithm does a good job of separating data into clusters.

Principal component analysis (PCA) is a popular method for dimension reduction [385]. PCA is a data-space transformation technique that computes new dimensions/attributes which are linear combinations of the original data attributes. The advantage of the new dimensions is that they can be sorted according to their contribution in explaining the variance of the data. By selecting the most relevant new dimensions, a subspace of variables is obtained that minimizes the average error of lost information. An intuitive description of PCA is as follows:

1. Select a line in space that spreads the projected n-dimensional data the most. This line represents the first principal component.

2. Select a line perpendicular to the first that now spreads the data the most. That line is the second PCA.

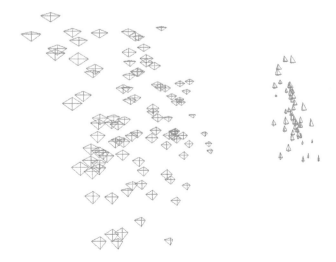

Figure 2.4.   The Iris data set in star glyphs, with the position of each point based on the first two principal components. The star glyph represents four variables as the lengths of the each of the lines emanating from the center of a four-pointed star. Reasonable clustering can be seen.

3. Repeat until all PC dimensions are computed, or until the desired number of PCs have been obtained.

More formally, the steps in computing the PCA are as follows (from [385]):

1. Assume the data has m dimensions/attributes. For each member of a record, subtract the mean value for that dimension, resulting in a data set with mean=0.

2. Compute the covariance matrix (see any statistics book).

3. Compute the eigenvectors and eigenvalues of the covariance matrix.

4. Sort the eigenvectors based on their eigenvalues, from largest to smallest.

5. Select the first m_r eigenvectors, where m_r is the number of dimensions you want to reduce your data set to.

6. Create a matrix of these eigenvectors as the rows, with the first one being the top row of the matrix.

7. For each data record, create a vector of its values, transpose it, and pre-multiply it with the matrix above. This completes the transformation; each data record is now represented in the reduced dimension space.

As another example of a dimension reduction process, we present below the steps for computing a form of multidimensional scaling known as a *gradient descent approach*. Briefly, MDS tries to find a lower dimensional representation for a data set that best preserves the inter-point distances from the original data set. In other words, we wish to minimize, for every pair of points (i, j), the difference between d_{ij} (the distance between the points in N dimensions) and δ_{ij} (the distance between the points in the reduced space). This discrepancy is usually referred to as the *stress* of the configuration. The procedure is as follows:

1. Compute the pairwise distances in n-dimensional space. If there are n data points, this requires the calculation of $n(n-1)/2$ distances.

2. Assign all data point locations (often random) in the lower dimensional space.

3. Calculate the stress of the configuration (a normalized, signed value or a mean-squared error are just two of the possibilities).

4. If the average or accumulated stress is less than a user-prescribed threshold, terminate the process and output the results.

5. If not, for each data point, compute a vector indicating the direction in which it should move to reduce the stress between it and all other data points. This would be a weighted sum of vectors between this point and all its neighbors, pointing either toward or away from the neighbors and weighted proportional to the pairwise stress. Thus, positive stresses would move the points away from each other, and negative stresses would bring them together, and the greater the absolute value of the stress, the larger the motion.

6. Move each data point in the lower dimensional space, according to the vector computed, and return to step 3.

Care must be taken to avoid infinite loops caused by points overshooting their "best" configuration. Likewise, as in all optimization processes, the algorithm can become stuck in a local optimum. This can be caused by *blockages*, where some points that should be close together are caught on opposite sides of a repulsive force (points that are trying to maintain a long distance from the points in question). In this case, repeating the algorithm with different starting conditions, or allowing, as in simulated annealing [261], an occasional *jump* with a magnitude and/or direction different from the vector calculated, to enable a point to clear such blockages if they exist, may improve the solution. There are also a number of non-linear dimension reduction techniques which use a non-linear mapping from high- to low-dimensional space. Two widely used methods are emphSelf-organizing maps (SOMs) [248] and *Local Linear Embeddings* (LLEs) [350].

Many visualization and statistical graphics packages include both MDS and PCA implementations. In fact, some will even use PCA to compute initial positions to be used in the MDS process, which can greatly reduce the number of iterations required to converge on a low-stress configuration. It is worthwhile to note that there are examples of higher-dimensional data where the first few principal components do not separate the data well, but the later principal components with small eigenvalues do.

2.3.7 Mapping Nominal Dimensions to Numbers

In many domains, one or more of the data dimensions consist of nominal values. We may have several alternative strategies for handling these dimensions within our visualizations, depending on how many nominal dimensions there are, how many distinct values each variable can take on, and whether an ordering or distance relation is available or can be derived. The key is to find a mapping of the data to a graphical entity or attribute that doesn't introduce artificial relationships that don't exist in the data. For example, when looking at a data set consisting of information about cars, the manufacturer and model name would both be nominal fields. If we were mapping one or both of these to positions on a plot, how would we do the assignment of positions to names? One might simply assign integers to different names, perhaps using an alphabetic ordering. However, this might imply some false relationships, such as Hondas being closer to Fords than Toyotas. Clearly, we need a better approach. While ranked nominal values can be readily mapped to any of the graphical attributes at our disposal, nonranked values pose a more significant problem.

For variables with only a modest number of different values, there are several options for graphical attributes that have less of an ordering relation than position or size. These include color and shapes. Indeed, most plotting programs support a number of different plotting symbols to enable easy separation of modest numbers of distinct values or classes of data, and significant research has gone into identifying colors that are readily separated, and in general, do not imply an ordering relationship (see the discussion of color perception in Chapter 3).

If there is a single nominal variable, there are a few possible techniques we can use. The simplest is to just use this variable as the label for the graphical elements being displayed. This works fine for data sets with modest numbers of records, but it quickly overwhelms the screen for large data sets. Innovative strategies include showing random subsets of labels and changing the points with labels being shown on a regular basis, and showing only the labels on objects near the cursor [121]. For mapping this single variable to numbers, we could look at similarities between the numeric variables associated with a pair of nominal values. If the statistical properties of the records associated with one nominal value are sufficiently similar to the properties of a different value, then that implies that these two values should likely be mapped to similar numeric values. Conversely, if there are sufficient differences in properties, then likely they should be mapped to quite distinct values. Given all the pairwise similarities, we could then use a technique such as MDS to map the different nominal values to positions in one dimension. This is a simplified variant of a technique called *correspondence analysis* in statistics [158]. It can even be applied if all dimensions of the data set are nominal, which is termed *multiple correspondence analysis*.

2.3.8   Aggregation and Summarization

In the event that too much data is present, it is often useful to group data points based on their similarity in value and/or position and represent the group by some smaller amount of data. This can be as simple as averaging the values, or there might be more descriptive information, such as the number of members in the group and the extents of their positions or values. Thus, there are two components to aggregation: the method of grouping the points and the method of displaying the resulting groups. Grouping can be done in a number of ways; the literature on data clustering is quite rich [204]. Methods include bottom-up merging of adjacent points, top-down partitioning of the data space, and iterative split-and-merge methods. In all cases, the important computations are the distance between data points, the *goodness* of the resulting clusters, and the quality of separation between adjacent clusters. Variations in these computations can lead to quite different results. Indeed, there is often distrust of cluster results by people knowledgeable about their data. Again, it is important to convey to users when and how aggregation has been done.

The key to visually depicting aggregated data is to provide sufficient information for the user to decide whether he or she wishes to perform a *drill-down* on the data, i.e., to explore the contents of one or more clusters. Simply displaying a single representative data point per cluster may not help in the understanding of the variability within the cluster, or in detecting outliers in the data set. Thus, other cluster measures, such as those listed above, are useful in exploring this sort of preprocessed data. Figure 2.5 shows the Iris data set using parallel coordinates, with one side showing the original data and the other showing aggregations resulting from a bottom-up clustering algorithm. The dominant clusters are clearly distinguishable.

2.3.9   Smoothing and Filtering

A common process in signal processing is to smooth the data values, to reduce noise and to blur sharp discontinuities. A typical way to perform this task is through a process known as *convolution*, which for our purposes can be viewed as a weighted averaging of neighbors surrounding a data point. In a one-dimensional case, this might be implemented via a formula as follows:

$$p_i^1 = \frac{p_{i-1}}{4} + \frac{p_i}{2} + \frac{p_{i+1}}{4},$$

where each p_i is a data point.

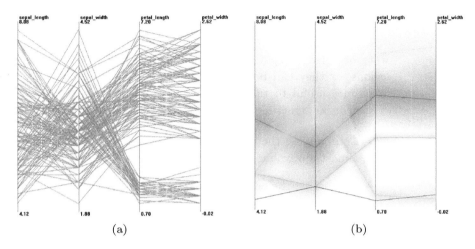

Figure 2.5. The Iris data set in parallel coordinates: (a) the original data; (b) the centers and extents of clusters after aggregation. Each axis in parallel coordinates represents a dimension, with each record being drawn as a polyline through each of the coordinate values on the axes.

The result of applying this operation is that values that are significantly different from their neighbors (e.g., noise) will be modified to be more similar to the neighbors, while values corresponding to dramatic changes will be "softened" to smooth out the transition. Many types of operations can be accomplished via this *filtering* operation, by simply varying the weights or changing the size or shape of the neighborhood considered.

For time series, it may be desired to weight older values less than more recent values. A popular method for obtaining this behavior is *exponential smoothing* [141]. The idea is to weight older data exponentially less than the more recent data. For a data series $x_0, x_1, ..., x_n$, the exponential smoothing is calculated recursively as

$$s_0 = x_0,$$
$$s_t = \alpha * x_{t-1} + (1 - \alpha) * s_{t-1},$$

with α being the decay factor.

2.3.10 Raster-to-Vector Conversion

In computer graphics, objects are typically represented by sets of connected, planar polygons (vertices, edges, and triangular or quadrilateral patches), and the task is to create a *raster* (pixel-level) image representing these objects, their surface properties, and their interactions with light sources and other objects. In spatial data visualization, our objects can be points or regions, or they can be linear structures, such as a road on a map. It is sometimes useful to take a raster-based data set, such as an image, and extract linear structures from it. Reasons for doing this might include:

- Compressing the contents for transmission. A vertex and edge list is almost always more compact than a raster image.

- Comparing the contents of two or more images. It is generally easier and more reliable to compare higher-level features of images, rather than their pixels.

- Transforming the data. Affine transformations such as rotation and scaling are easier to apply to vector representations than to raster.

- Segmenting the data. Isolating regions by drawing boundaries around them is an effective method for interactive exploration and model building.

The image processing and computer vision fields have developed a wide assortment of techniques for converting raster images into vertex and edge-based models [153, 371]. A partial list of these include the following:

Thresholding. Identify one or more values with which to break the data into regions, after which the boundaries can be traced to generate the edges and vertices. The values may be user-defined, or computed based on histogram analysis, and may be adjusted for different regions of the image (termed *adaptive thresholding*).

Region-growing. Starting with seed locations, either selected by a human observer or computed via scanning of the data, merge pixels into clusters if they are sufficiently similar to any neighboring point that has been assigned to a cluster associated with one of the seed pixels. A major problem is defining a suitable measure of similarity.

Boundary-detection. Compute a new image from the existing image by *convolving* the image with a particular pattern matrix. Convolution is a straightforward process. Each pixel and its immediate neighbors are multiplied by a value corresponding to their position in a pattern matrix (with the selected pixel mapped to the center of the pattern).

These products are then summed, and the corresponding pixel in the result image is set to this value. A vast assortment of image transformations are possible, based on the contents of the pattern matrix. For boundary detection, we use patterns that will emphasize (set to high values) either horizontal, vertical, or diagonal boundaries, while deemphasizing (setting to low values) pixels that are very similar to all their neighbors.

Thinning. The convolution process mentioned above can also be used to perform a process called *thinning*, where the goal is to reduce wide linear features, such as arteries, to a single pixel in width. These resulting connected pixels form the center or *medial axis* of the regions that were thinned.

A wide range of such operators have been developed. A good text on the subject is [389].

2.3.11   Summary of Data Preprocessing

While these and other processes can improve the effectiveness of the visualization and lead to new visual discoveries, it is important to convey to the user that these processes have been applied to the data. An understanding of the types of transformation the data has undergone can help in properly interpreting it. Likewise, misinterpretation or erroneous conclusions can be drawn from data that has been preprocessed without the user's knowledge (see Chapter 13).

2.4   Data Sets Used in This Book

Throughout this book, we will give numerous examples of data visualizations. While each may be appreciated without understanding the data being displayed, in general, the effectiveness of a visualization is enhanced by the user having some context for interpreting what is being shown. Thus, we will draw most examples from the following data sets, each of which may be downloaded from the book's web site. A wealth of additional data sets can be found on the U.S. government's open data portal *www.data.gov* and the European Union's open data portal *open-data.europa.eu*.

djia-100.xls. A univariate, nonspatial data set consisting of 100+ years of daily Dow Jones Industrial Averages.

Source—http://www.analyzeindices.com/dow-jones-history.shtml

Format—Excel spreadsheet. After the header, each entry is of the form YYMMDD followed by the closing value.

Code—file can be viewed with Excel.

colorado_elev.vit. A two-dimensional, uniform grid, scalar field representing the elevation of a square region of Colorado.

Source—included with the distribution of OpenDX (http://www.opendx .org/).

Format—binary file with a 268-byte header followed by a 400×400 array of 1-byte elevations.

Code—file can be rendered with TopoSurface, a Processing program included in Appendix C and on the book's web site.

uvw.dat. A three-dimensional uniform grid vector field representing a simulated flow field. The data shows one frame of the unsteady velocity field in a turbulent channel flow, computed by a finite volume method. The streamwise velocity (u) is much larger than the secondary velocities in the transverse direction (v and w).

Source—Data courtesy of Drs. Jiacai Lu and Gretar Tryggvason, ME Department, Worcester Polytechnic Institute (http://www.me.wpi .edu/Tryggvason).

Format—plain text. After the header, each entry is a set of 6 float values, 3 for position, 3 for displacement. There is roughly a 20:1:1 ratio between the 3 displacements.

Code—file can be rendered with FlowSlicer, a Processing program, and FlowView, a Java program (also need Voxel.java) included in Appendix C and on the book's web site.

city_temp.xls. A two-dimensional, nonuniform, geo-spatial, scalar data set containing the average January temperature for 56 U.S. cities.

Source—Peixoto, J.L. (1990), "A Property of Well-Formulated Polynomial Regression Models." *American Statistician*, 44, 26–30. Also found in: Hand, D.J., et al. (1994) *A Handbook of Small Data Sets*, London: Chapman & Hall, 208–210. Downloaded from http://lib.stat .cmu.edu.

Format—Excel spreadsheet. After a header, each entry is a city name and state, followed by three numbers: average January temperature, latitude, and longitude.

Code—file can be viewed with Excel.

CThead.zip. A three-dimensional uniform grid, scalar field consisting of a 113-slice MRI data set from a CT scan of a human head.

Source—Data taken on the General Electric CT Scanner and provided courtesy of North Carolina Memorial Hospital. From http://graphics .stanford.edu/data/voldata/.

Format—Each slice is stored in a separate binary file (no header). Slices are stored as a 256×256 array with dimensions of $z = 113$, $y = 256$, $x = 256$ in z, y, x order. Format is 16-bit integers—two consecutive bytes make up one binary integer (Mac byte ordering). $x : y : z$ shape of each voxel is 1:1:2.

Code—file can be rendered with VolumeSlicer, a Java program included in Appendix C and on the book's web site.

cars.xls, detroit.xls, cereal.xls. Several multivariate, nonspatial data sets commonly used in multivariate data analysis.

Source—http://lib.stat.cmu.edu

Format—Excel spreadsheets, mostly with no headers.

Code—files can be viewed with Excel.

Health-related multivariate data sets. Subsets from UNICEF's basic indicators by country and the CDC's obesity by state; several multivariate, spatial data sets used with Geospatial Information Systems.

Source—http://OpenIndicators.org

Format—Excel spreadsheets.

Code—files can be viewed with Excel, with Weave, and with many other visualization systems.

VAST Contest and Challenge Data. Several heterogeneous data sets that represent realistic scenarios (though they are synthetic) and have embedded ground truth. These were used in the various IEEE VAST contests and challenges.

Source—http://hcil.cs.umd.edu/localphp/hcil/vast/archive/index.php

Format—tables, text files, spreadsheet, images, videos, and others.

Code—files will likely require work to be read into a typical visualization system. For example, the text files require some processing to be dealt with. Several tools are available that analyze the data and even provide various visualizations, including Weka, RapidMiner, and Jigsaw.

U.S. Counties Census Data. A subset of the U.S. census for the 3137 counties in the U.S. (including the District of Columbia) that includes county and state, total population broken down by age, race, family relationships (number children, age of children, ...) and household parameters (own, rent, ...).

Source—http://www.census.gov and cleaned subset is at http://www.openindicators.org/data

Format—comma-separated values.

Code—The file can be viewed in Excel and in Weave (http://www.openindicators.org/).

iris.csv. Size data for Iris plants classified by type.

Source—http://archive.ics.uci.edu/ml/datasets/Iris

Format—comma-separated values.

Code—The file can be viewed with Excel or as text.

2.5 Related Readings

In the chapter "Data Preprocessing" of [352], the author provides a mathematical overview of data preprocessing including error handling, data transformation, and data merging. Details on dimension reduction, including principal component analysis (PCA), dimension estimation, and manifold modeling, can be found in [53]

Collecting data sets for visualization and analysis quickly leads one to realize the incredible number of distinct file formats that need to be parsed in order to start analysis. For image data, one of the best sources for format information is the book by Brown et al. [49]. Another somewhat dated web site on data file formats is [402].

The web is overflowing with data sets available for analysis. A few of the ones that have been around for a while include StatLib [394], a library of statistical data sets and algorithms, the UC Irvine KDD Repository [430],

NOAA's collection of public climate data sets [306], and the Human Computer Interaction Lab's archive of VAST and other related data sets [431].

2.6 Exercises

1. Give examples, other than the ones listed in this chapter, of data sets with the following characteristics:

   (a) with and without an ordering relationship,

   (b) with and without a distance metric,

   (c) with and without an absolute zero.

2. Describe the difference between a data attribute and a value. Use examples to clarify your response.

3. There are numerous strategies for dealing with missing data in a data set. These include deleting the row containing the missing value, replacing the missing value with a special number, such as -999, replacing the value with the average value for that data dimension, and replacing the value with the corresponding entry from the nearest neighbor (using some distance calculation). Comment on the strengths and weaknesses of each of these strategies: what is gained or lost by following one approach over the others?

4. Perform a web search looking for repositories of publicly available data. Retrieve two or three, and analyze them in terms of their structure and meaning. Does the data have spatial or temporal attributes? Is it nominal or ordinal (or both)? Does it come in a standard or custom file format?

5. Repeat the above process, using a newspaper as your source. What sorts of data can you extract from the newspaper? What are the data types? What data sets could you derive by processing the information in the newspaper? Try to design at least one data set for each section of the newspaper.

6. List at least ten sources of data from your normal daily activities (you'll be surprised—data is all around us!). For example, nutrition labels from the food we consume have a wealth of information, some of which you probably don't want to know. Start gathering one or two types of data to be used for future projects in this course.

7. Find the data for temperature highs from the last two weeks in your region and apply the convolution smoothing technique to smooth the temperature curves.

2.7   Projects

1. Write a program that accepts as input a uniform, 3D scalar field (each record is an integer) whose dimensions are $(height_i, width_i, depth_i)$ and that computes and outputs a file with dimensions $(height_j, width_j, depth_j)$. Assume the program is invoked with the command:

```
resample file1 height1 width1 depth1 file2 height2 width2 depth2
```

2. A common task when dealing with data is dividing it into categories, such as *low*, *medium*, and *high*. There are numerous strategies for performing this task, each of which has strengths and weaknesses. Write a program that reads in a list of integers and divides them into a given set of bins (this number can be passed into the program), using one or more of the following strategies:

   - uniform bin width—the size of the range of values for each bin is the same;
   - uniform bin count—as best as possible (without dividing a single number between multiple bins), each bin has about the same number of elements in it;
   - best break points—start with everything in one bin. Search for the largest gaps, and divide at those locations. If no gaps exist, break at values with low number of occurrences.

3. *Normalization* is a process in which one or more dimensions are processed so that the resulting values have a particular range and/or mean. This allows two or more dimensions with very different characteristic ranges (such as temperature and elevation) to be combined into a distance calculation. Given a list of floating point values, write a program that normalizes these values into one or more of the following ranges (you will see why this is useful when we start mapping to graphical attributes):

   - all values fall between 0.0 and 1.0;

- the values are mapped such that the resulting set has a mean of 0.0 and standard deviation of 1.0;

- all values are integers between 0 and 255.

4. Imputation for a single variable or column is rather straightforward. However, in situations where numerous values are missing in many columns, Schafer [362] has developed a model-based technique. Test Schafer's technique on a data set having missing values, and then implement the technique yourself and compare your results. The R project [326] is an open-source and free software environment for statistical computing and graphics where you can find an implementation of Schafer's algorithm.

5. Implement the *Principal Component Analysis* technique and apply it to the Iris data set. Which linear combination of original dimensions defines the first principal components?

CHAPTER 3

Human Perception and Information Processing

This chapter deals with human perception and the different ways in which graphics and images are seen and interpreted. The early approach to the study of perception focused on the vision system and its capabilities. Later approaches looked at cognitive issues and recognition. We discuss each approach in turn and provide details. Significant parts of this chapter, including many of the figures, are based on the work of Christopher G. Healey (http://www.csc.ncsu.edu/faculty/healey/PP/index.html) [174], who has kindly granted permission for their reuse in this book.

3.1 What Is Perception?

We know that humans perceive data, but we are not as sure of how we perceive. We know that visualizations present data that is then perceived, but how are these visualizations perceived? How do we know that our visual representations are not interpreted differently by different viewers? How can we be sure that the data we present is understood? We study perception to better control the presentation of data, and eventually to harness human perception.

There are many definitions and theories of perception. Most define perception as the process of recognizing (being aware of), organizing (gathering and storing), and interpreting (binding to knowledge) sensory information. Perception deals with the human senses that generate signals from the environment through sight, hearing, touch, smell, and taste. Vision and audition

Figure 3.1.   Two seated figures, making sense at a higher, more abstract level, but still disturbing. On closer inspection, these seats are not realizable. (Image courtesy N. Yoshigahara.)

are the most well understood. Simply put, perception is the process by which we interpret the world around us, forming a mental representation of the environment. This representation is not isomorphic to the world, but it's subject to many correspondence differences and errors. The brain makes assumptions about the world to overcome the inherent ambiguity in all sensory data, and in response to the task at hand.

Visual representations of objects are often misinterpreted, either because they do not match our perceptual system, or they were intended to be misinterpreted. Illusions are a primary source of such misinterpretations. Figures 3.1 and 3.2 highlight our inability to notice visual problems except on more detailed perusal. The drawings are those of physically nonrealizable objects.

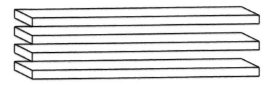

Figure 3.2.   Four ≠ three. As in Figure 3.1, this object would have a problem being built (there are four boards on the left and three on the right).

Figure 3.3.   A more complex illusion: there are two people drawn as part of the face.

Sometimes the ambiguity presented is easily seen, but more difficult to explain. Sometimes it is not even perceived.

Figure 3.3 highlights that on first glance an image may represent a primary object, one that is perceived more obviously than the secondary others that may require more effort or time. There are many such illusions, and these are easy to construct. In effect, the artist puts together a primary image out of secondary images. There may even be tertiary ones. Tools have been developed to support such imagery. For example, Rob Silvers uses a computational technique to form an image composed of a mosaic of smaller given images (see Figure 3.4 and Figure 3.5, which contains a detailed view).

Our visual machinery also performs similar computations, but perhaps not as we would expect. Figure 3.6 highlights that our vision system is, foremost, not static, and secondly, often not under our full control. It is clear that there appear to be black squares being generated between the white spaces in Figure 3.6(a) and black circles in Figure 3.6(b). Why? If we forcibly stare at an intersection of the spaces between the black squares, we can actually stop the "spots" from appearing. This is akin to our stopping breathing. When we visualize data, we need to make sure that no such interferences are present that would impede the understanding of what we are trying to convey in the visualizations.

Figure 3.4.   Photomosaic of Benjamin Franklin using images of international paper money or bank notes. (Photomosaic® by Robert Silvers, http://www.photomosaic.com.)

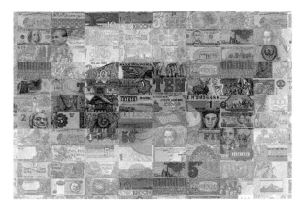

Figure 3.5.   Close-up view of the eye in Figure 3.4. (Photomosaic® by Robert Silvers, http://www.photomosaic.com.)

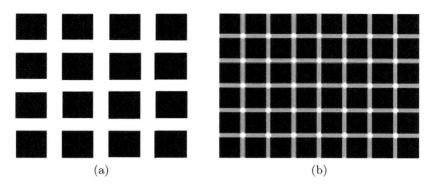

Figure 3.6.   The Hermann grid illusion: (a) illusionary black squares appear over the complete image as you gaze at it; (b) similar to (a) but even more dynamic and engaging.

Similarly, Figure 3.7(a) and (b) highlight that there is more to our visual system than meets the eye (pun intended). In both of these images, we seem to have machinery forcing the interpretation of the objects we see in a specific manner. The study of perception is to identify not just this machinery, but the whole process of perception, from sensation to knowledge. What is causing the lines not to appear perfectly straight, or the triangle to stand out? More generally can we explain the causes of these and other illusions we see? These are the important questions we need to answer in order to be able to generate synthetic images that will represent data unambiguously and not pop out an artifact.

Figure 3.7.   (a) The Hering illusion: red lines are straight. (Use a straight edge to verify.) (b) The Kanizsa illusion: a triangle seems to pop out of the image even though no such triangle is drawn.

These illusions are due to our perceptual system's structure, and the assumptions it makes about an image or scene. The interpretations are due to a variety of reasons and are the result of how the process works. To understand this process and identify its structure, we first need to measure what we see and then develop models explaining the measured results. These models should also help explain the illusions.

There are two main approaches to the study of perception. One deals with measures, and the other with models. Both are linked. Measurements can help in the development of a model, and in turn, a model should help predict future outcomes, which can then be measured to validate the model. We can measure low-level sensory perception (which line is longer) or higher-level perception (can you recognize the bird in this scene?). Each requires a different set of tools and approaches. This approach, however, still does not explain why we see these differences, or why we recognize objects. That requires a model of the process.

Not paying attention to perception will lead to problems in visualization. For example, Figure 3.6 clearly shows how visual patterns can impact a display. We need to understand, at least rudimentarily, what aspects of visualization cannot be violated. Some of these involve color (perceived differently by individuals) and three-dimensional perception (forced interpretations by inherent perceptual assumptions, such as where a light source is typically placed). We will see several more examples later in this chapter.

3.2   Physiology

The main sensory component of vision involves the gathering and recording of light scattered from objects in the surrounding *scene*, and the forming of a two-dimensional function on the photoreceptors [217, 353]. Photoreceptors are generally very small sensory devices that respond in the presence of photons that make up light waves.

3.2.1   Visible Spectrum

Visible light, the light waves that are capable of being perceived by human eyes, actually represents a very small section on the electromagnetic spectrum (see Figure 3.8). This sub-spectrum ranges from about 380 nm (nanometers) near ultraviolet, up through to about 700 nm toward the infrared. This range is very much dependent on the individual and generally

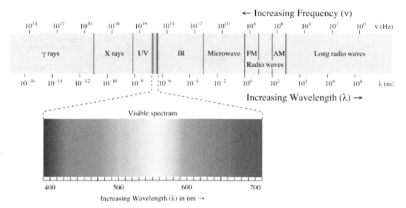

Figure 3.8.   The electromagnetic spectrum with an expanded visible light spectrum [269]. (Image courtesy Wikimedia Commons.)

shrinks in size after the age of twenty [269]. Color blindness and total blindness in humans are the result of an individual not responding to certain wavelengths.

Beyond just the consideration of light is the importance of physical object properties. It is through the visual system that information concerning the external objects in the surrounding environment is captured. This exchange of information between the environment and the observer is presented to the eyes as variations of wavelengths. These variations are a result of object properties that include object geometry, scene illumination, reflectance properties, and sensor photoreceptor characteristics.

3.2.2   Anatomy of the Visual System

The human eye is a marvelous organ, yet its construction is quite simple. Figure 3.9 shows a horizontal cross-section of the right eye, viewed from above. This diagram provides names for most of the fundamental macro-structures that provide humans with the ability to *see* their surrounding environment. The major parts that directly involve the path taken by light waves include the cornea, iris, pupil, lens, and retina. Overall, the eye is a fluid-filled sphere of light-sensitive cells with one section open to the outside via a basic lens system, and connected to the head and brain by six motion-control muscles and one optic nerve.

Lens System and Muscles. First, the six muscles are generally considered as motion controllers, providing the ability to *look* at objects in the scene. The

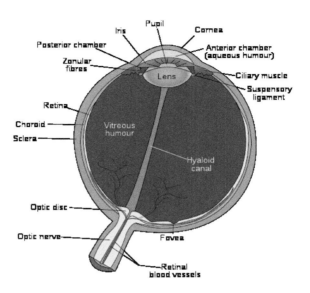

Figure 3.9.   Horizontal cross-section of the human eye, viewed from above. (Image courtesy Wikimedia Commons.)

action of looking at specific areas in the environment involves orienting the eye's optical system to the regions of interest through muscle contractions and relaxations. Also, the muscles tend to maintain the eye-level with the horizon when the head is not perfectly vertical. These muscles also play another important role in the stabilization of images. Continually making minor adjustments, eyes are never at rest, although we do not perceive these actions visually. In an engineered system, such motions are usually considered as imperfections, yet they have been found to improve the performance of the human visual system [310].

The optical system of the eye is similar in characteristic to a double-lens camera system. The first component is the *cornea*, the exterior cover of the front of the eye. Acting as a protective mechanism against physical damage to the internal structure, it also serves as one lens focusing the light from the surrounding scene onto the main lens [148]. From the cornea, light passes through the *pupil*, a circular hole in the *iris*, similar in function to an aperture stop on a photographic camera [269]. The iris is a colored annulus containing radial muscles for changing the size of the pupil opening. Thus, the pupil determines how much light will enter the rest of the internal chamber of the eye. The third major component is the *lens*, whose crystalline structure is similar to onion skin. Surrounded by the *ciliary body*, a set of muscles, the lens can be stretched and compressed, changing the thickness and curvature of the lens and consequently adjusting the focal length of the optical system. As a result, the lens can focus on near and relatively far objects. The elasticity of the lens determines the range of shape changes possible, which is lost as one ages, leaving the lens in a slightly stretched state [148]. Once the light has passed through this lens system, the final light rays are projected onto the photoreceptive layer, called the *retina*. The process is not as precise as camera optics, however. As Overington states:

> An important point to note about the lens system is that is has very little facility built-in for correction of many of the aberrations which are normally corrected in good quality instrumental optical systems. This inevitably means that the image produced is far from perfect. Yet the apparent image perceived appears very sharp, whilst quite phenomenally fine subtleties in the image can be observed. [310, p. 7]

The Retina. The *retina* of the human eye contains the photoreceptors responsible for the visual perception of our external world. It consists of two types of photosensitive cells: *rods* and *cones* (see Figure 3.10) [148, 269]. These two types of cells respond differently to light stimulation. Rods are primarily responsible for intensity perception, and cones for color perception. Rods are typically ten times more sensitive to light than cones. There is a small region at the center of the visual axis known as the *fovea* that subtends

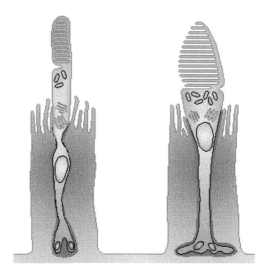

Figure 3.10.   Human rod (left) and cone (right). (Image © Colour4Free.)

1 to 2 degrees of visual angle. The structure of the retina is roughly radially symmetric around the fovea. The fovea contains only cones, and linearly, there are about 147,000 cones per millimeter [148]. The fovea is the region of sharpest vision. Because the human eye contains a limited number of rods and cones (about 120 million rods and 6 million cones), it can only manage a certain amount of visual information over a given time frame. Additionally, the information transferred from these two types of cells is not equivalent.

Another interesting fact is that the optic nerve only contains about one million fibers; thus the eye must perform a significant amount of visual processing before transmitting information to the brain. What makes the retina an unusual layer for light stimulation is the orientation of the photoreceptive cells. The whole layer of cells that makes up the retina is actually backwards; the light rays must pass through the output neurons and optic nerve fibers first, before reaching the photosensitive cells, which are also facing away from the light source. The reason suggested for this arrangement in all vertebrates is that "eyes are actually part of the brain and represent an outgrowth from it," and that "the cells of the retina are formed during development from the same cells that generate the central nervous system" ([148] p. 18).

The eye contains separate systems for encoding spatial properties (e.g., size, location, and orientation), and object properties (e.g., color, shape, and texture). These spatial and object properties are important features that have been successfully used by researchers in psychology for simple tasks such as target detection, boundary detection, and counting. These properties have also been used extensively by researchers in visualization to represent high-dimensional data collections [448].

Rods. Rods are the most sensitive type of photoreceptor cells available in the retina; consequently, they are associated with *scotopic vision*, night vision, operating in clusters for increased sensitivity in very low light conditions. As these cells are thought to be achromatic, we tend to see objects at night in shades of gray. Rods do operate, however, within the visible spectrum between approximately 400 and 700 nm [269]. It has been noted that during daylight levels of illumination, rods become *hyperpolarized*, or completely saturated, and thus do not contribute to vision [148].

Cones. On the other hand, cones provide *photopic vision*, i.e., are responsible for day vision. Also, they perform with a high degree of acuity, since they generally operate individually. There are three types of cones in the human eye: **S** (short), **M** (medium), and **L** (long) wavelengths [148]. These three types (see Figure 3.11) have been associated with color combinations using

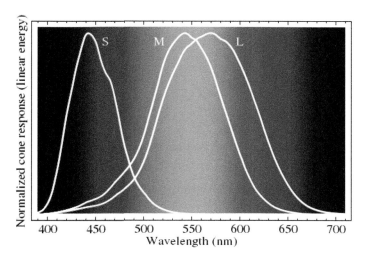

Figure 3.11.   The retina layer contains the three types of cones (short, medium, and long). (Image courtesy Wikimedia Commons.)

R (red), **G** (green), and **B** (blue). The long wavelength cones exhibit a spectrum peak at 560 nm, the medium wavelength cones peak at 530 nm, and the short wavelength cones peak at around 420 nm. However, it must be noted that there are considerably fewer short cones, compared to the number of medium and long wavelength cones [310]. In spite of this, humans can visually perceive all the colors within the standard visible spectrum. Unlike rods, cones are not sensitive over a large fixed wavelength range, but rather over a small moving-window-based range. Cones tend to adapt to the average wavelength where there is sensitivity above and below their peaks, and a shift in their response curve occurs when the average background wavelength changes [148].

Blind Spot. Given that humans have two types of photoreceptors with three types of cones, how are these cells distributed on the retina? First, there is an overall distribution of all cells across the retina, with the highest concentration occurring at the center of our visual field in the fovea and reducing in coverage toward the edges [148]. Where the optic nerve meets the retina, a *blind spot* occurs, due to the lack of photoreceptive cells. Second, there is a striking separation between the locations of rods and cones. The fovea consists of only cone receptors, and no rods, for highly detailed and exact vision [269]. Surrounding the fovea are three concentric bands: *parafovea*

Figure 3.12.   Blind spot discovery by identifying disappearance of target.

with an outer ring of 2.5-mm diameter, *perifovea* with an outer ring of 5.5-mm diameter, and the *peripheral retina*, covering approximately 97.25% of the total retinal surface and consisting largely of rods [269]. Each of these areas is marked by a dramatic reduction in cones, and it is significant to note here that within the parafovea there already are significantly more rods than cones.

The identification (more really verification) of one's blind spot can be done simply with this Optic Disk experiment (see Figure 3.12). Close your right eye and look directly at the number *3*. You should see the yellow spot in your peripheral vision. Now, slowly move toward, or away from the screen or paper image. At some point, the yellow spot will disappear, as its sensory reflection hits the blind spot.

There are some very interesting outcomes resulting from the physiology of human eyes. First, the photoreceptive cells are packed into the retina parallel to each other, and are not directed toward the pupil [148]. Thus, the eye obtains its best stimulation from light entering straight on through the pupil.

Next, the rods and cones are packed in a hexagonal structure for optimized coverage. Such a packing scheme, in conjunction with an initially blurred image, resulting from cell sampling, has been demonstrated to provide near-optimal information transfers [310]. Another fascinating fact about the retina concerns the sampling rate of the photoreceptive cells. Through the effects of *temporal smoothing*, where receptors only respond every few milliseconds, humans perceive flickering lights up to a certain frequency, beyond which the eye only registers a constant light source [148].

It has been said that the United States Air Force tested pilots' ability to respond to changes in light by flashing a picture of an aircraft on a screen in a dark room for 1/220th of a second. According to these anecdotal reports, pilots were consistently able to detect the afterimage of the flash, and were also able to identify the aircraft type.

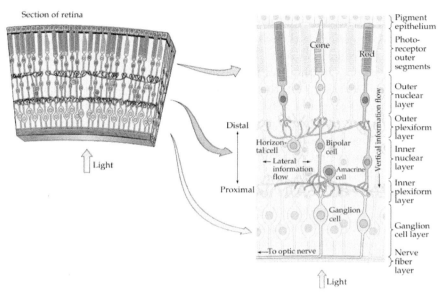

Figure 3.13.   A representation of a retinal cross-section. (Image © The Brain from Top to Bottom.)

Finally, it has been shown that the human eye responds to *ratios* of intensities and not absolute values [148]. These ratios play an important part in adaptation and contrast sensitivity and the eye will adapt to changes in wavelength ranges.

3.2.3   Visual Processing

Signal processing in humans is performed by *neurons*, the elementary biological components that make up the nervous system. This system operates on sequences of frequency-modulated pulses sent between two neurons in communication. Through chemical actions, each neuron stimulates other neurons—possibly hundreds to thousands of other nervous system cells—causing information to travel.

Retinal Processing. The retina of the eye is actually a complex layer of many neurons and photoreceptive cells, as depicted in Figure 3.13. This illustration has the photoreceptors pointing up; thus, the front of the eye is pointing down, so that light first hits the bottom layer and progresses through the various layers, until it stimulates the rods and cones. The relatively large black bulbs represent the nucleus of each neuron.

There are four neuron layers within the retina that perform initial image processing on the stimulations resulting from the individual photoreceptors, the cones and rods. Figure 3.13 is a highly stylized diagram of the human retina, showing the four layers plus the top layer of receptors; again, the light enters from the bottom. These four layers are composed of individual types of neuron cells, based on their connectivity properties: *horizontal cells* only connect sets of receptors, *bipolar cells* connect receptors to other layers, *amacrine cells* join numerous bipolar and ganglion cells, and *ganglion cells* transmit retinal stimulation from the eye to the brain via the *optic nerve* [269].

As mentioned previously, the retina develops directly from brain cells; thus the obvious ability for preprocessing of the stimulus image. Like the individual groups of photoreceptive cells, there are also various types of bipolar and ganglion cells that have very distinct properties dealing with the combinations of rods and cones [310]. Some cones within the fovea are connected to individual ganglia via a single bipolar link. Rods on the outer periphery of the retina are grouped together and joined with bipolar cells, where several bipolar groups output to a single ganglion. Hence, the retina is already performing some kinds of image compression, and possibly segmentation. This reduction of retinal stimulation is required, as there are only about a million optic nerve fibers relaying image information to the brain, which is

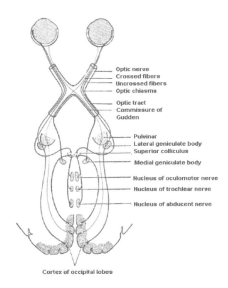

Figure 3.14.   The anatomy of the visual system. (Image courtesy Wikimedia Commons.)

a hundred times less than the total number of rods and cones [8]. There is also other valuable information formed during this compression. Individual rods and cones by themselves do not provide much information, due to the limitations of the optic nerve. Furthermore, individual cones only respond to fixed wavelength ranges; thus one cell cannot provide color information. Consequently, it is through the combinations of photoreceptor stimuli that intensity and color descriptions can be obtained, which is believed to happen at a very early stage in visual processing [148].

The Brain. The *brain* is the center of all bodily functions and is composed of the majority of neurons found in the human nervous system. The overall structure of the brain is divided into two hemispheres, left and right, with the addition of a few smaller structures located under these hemispheres. Of importance is the fact these hemispheres have relative functional regions, one of which is designed for processing visual stimulation [269]. Before the optic nerves from each eye reach the inner regions of the brain, they partially cross at the *optic chiasma*—half the fibers from each eye cross to the opposite side of the corresponding brain region (see Figure 3.14). Thus, each hemisphere receives visual information from both eyes, possibly to help with the perception of depth. As there is so much visual processing performed at both the eyes and within the brain, these linked organs form an integral visual system [8].

3.2.4 Eye Movement

Perhaps the most critical aspect of perception is the importance of eye movement in our understanding of scenes, and therefore images. It explains, for example, the illusionary black dots in the earlier figures [143,364,391]. There are a variety of eye movements performed for scene interpretation.

Smooth pursuit movements. These are just as their name implies. The eyes move smoothly instead of in jumps. They are called *pursuit* because this type of eye movement is made when the eyes follow an object. For example, to make a pursuit movement, look at your forefinger at arms' length and then move your arm left and right while fixating on your fingertip. Such movements are also called *conjugate eye movements* or *coordinated eye movements*. The angles from the normal to the face are equal (left and right as well as up and down).

Vergence eye movements. These result from nonconjugate movement and yield different angles to the face normal. Moving a finger closer to the face

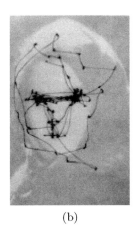

(a)   (b)

Figure 3.15.   (a) The face used to study eye tracking. (b) The results of the tracking of the gaze.

and staring at it will force the eyes inward, resulting in vergence movement. Defocusing to merge depths in illusions is another example.

Saccadic eye movements. These result from multiple targets of interest (not necessarily conscious). The eye moves as much as 1000 degrees per second, bringing the gaze on those targets within 25 msec. It holds its position once on target. Selected targets are determined in the frontal part of the cerebral cortex. The selection is discriminatory, dependent on a variety of parameters, and somewhat random.

Saccadic masking. Saccadic masking or suppression occurs during two states between saccadic views. The gap produced is ignored (some say blocked). A continuous flow of information is interpreted, one that makes sense. The higher-level visual system filters out the blurred images acquired by the low-level one, and only the two saccadic stop views are seen.

Marketing research has helped identify how to set up advertisements to force the visual focus on objects of interest. For example, when looking at the face in Figure 3.15(a), we find that the eye moves as in Figure 3.15(b). Note how the concentration of vertices highlights the targets to which the eye is attracted. The same tracking for the left image is shown on the right one in Figure 3.16. Note the role of the boundaries and the key focal points of faces.

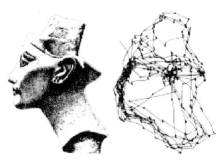

Figure 3.16. The right image shows the path followed by the eye in looking at the image on the left. Note the targets, which can easily be identified from the concentration of vertices of the path, and note the role of the boundary.

3.3 Perceptual Processing

We use the classic model of information processing [86] for understanding the flow of sensory information, from the low-level preattentive to the higher cognitive levels (Figure 3.17). This model highlights that memory is involved in post processing, but this is known to be only partially correct. Perception can be intrinsic and uncontrolled (preattentive) or controlled (attentive).

Automatic or preattentive perception is fast and is performed in parallel, often within 250 ms. Some effects pop out and are the result of preconscious visual processes. Attentive processes (or perception) transform these early vision effects into structured objects. Attentive perception is slower and uses short-term memory. It is selective and often represents aggregates of what is in the scene. Low-level attributes are rapidly perceived and then converted to higher-level structured ones for performing various tasks, such as finding a door in an emergency. We first focus on low-level attributes, then turn to higher-level ones, and finally put it all together with memory models.

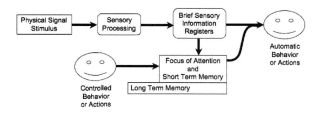

Figure 3.17. Classic model of the flow of sensory data for cognition (based on [86]).

3.3.1 Preattentive Processing

For many years vision researchers have been investigating how the human visual system analyzes images. An important initial result was the discovery of a limited set of visual properties that are detected very rapidly and accurately by the low-level visual system. These properties were initially called *preattentive*, since their detection seemed to precede focused attention. We now know that attention plays a critical role in what we see, even at this early stage of vision. The term *preattentive* continues to be used, however, since it conveys an intuitive notion of the speed and ease with which these properties are identified.

Typically, tasks that can be performed on large multielement displays in less than 200 to 250 milliseconds (msec) are considered preattentive. Eye movements take at least 200 msec to initiate, and random locations of the elements in the display ensure that attention cannot be prefocused on any particular location; yet viewers report that these tasks can be completed with very little effort. This suggests that certain information in the display is processed in parallel by the low-level visual system.

A simple example of a preattentive task is the detection of a red circle in a group of blue circles (Figure 3.18). The target object has a visual property "red" that the blue distractor objects do not (all nontarget objects are considered distractors). A viewer can tell at a glance whether the target is present or absent. In Figure 3.18 the visual system identifies the target

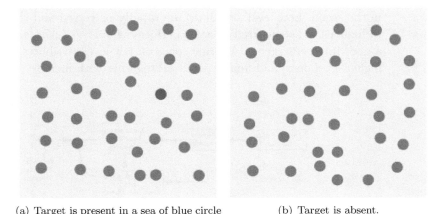

(a) Target is present in a sea of blue circle distractors.

(b) Target is absent.

Figure 3.18.   An example of searching for a target red circle based on a difference in hue.

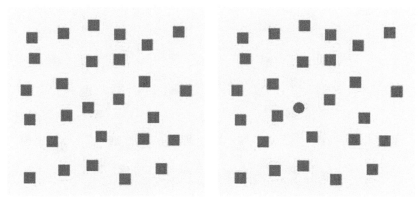

(a) Target is absent in a sea of red square distractors.

(b) Target is present.

Figure 3.19.   An example of searching for a target red circle based on a difference in curvature.

through a difference in hue, specifically, a red target in a sea of blue distractors. Hue is not the only visual feature that is preattentive. In Figure 3.19 the target is again a red circle, while the distractors are red squares. As before, a viewer can rapidly and accurately determine whether the target is present or absent. Here, the visual system identifies the target through a difference in curvature (or form).

A unique visual property in the target (e.g., a red hue in in Figure 3.19(a) or a curved form in Figure 3.19(b)) allows it to "pop out" of a display. A target made up of a combination of nonunique features (a *conjunction target*) normally cannot be detected preattentively. Figure 3.20 shows an example of conjunction search. The red circle target is made up of two features: red and circular. One of these features is present in each of the distractor objects (red squares and blue circles). This means the visual system has no unique visual property to search for when trying to locate the target. If a viewer searches for red items, the visual system always returns true, because there are red squares in each display. Similarly, a search for circular items always sees blue circles. Numerous studies have shown that this target cannot be detected preattentively. Viewers must perform a time-consuming serial search through the displays to confirm its presence or absence.

If the low-level visual system can be harnessed during visualization, it can be used to draw attention to areas of potential interest in a display. This cannot be accomplished in an ad hoc fashion, however. The visual features assigned to different data attributes (the data-feature mapping)

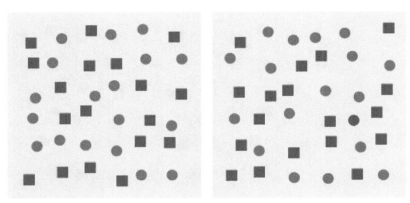

(a) Target is absent in a sea of red square   (b) Target is present.
and blue circle distractors.

Figure 3.20.   An example of a conjunction search for a target red circle.

must take advantage of the strengths of our visual system, must be well-suited to the analysis needs of the viewer, and must not produce visual interference effects (e.g., conjunction search) that could mask information in a display.

The following lists some of the visual features that have been identified as preattentive: length, width, size, curvature, number, terminators, intersection, closure, hue, intensity, flicker, direction of motion, binocular luster, stereoscopic depth, 3D depth cues, and lighting direction.

The key perceptual attributes associated with the above include luminance and brightness, color, texture, and shape. *Luminance* is the measured amount of light coming from some place. *Brightness* is the perceived amount of light coming from a source. Perceived brightness is a nonlinear function of the amount of light emitted by the source, typically a power function $S = a^i$, where S = sensation and i = intensity. Note that these look very different on a screen versus on paper. *Texture* is the characteristic appearance of an area or surface. Whereas texture applies to multiple sensory objects (the texture of a music, the texture of a fabric), *shape* is strictly a geometric attribute.

Experiments in psychology have used these features to perform the following preattentive visual tasks:

Target detection. Users rapidly and accurately detect the presence or absence of a "target" element with a unique visual feature within a field of distractor elements (Figures 3.18, 3.19, and 3.20);

Boundary detection. Users rapidly and accurately detect a texture boundary between two groups of elements, where all of the elements in each group have a common visual property;

Region tracking. Users track one or more elements with a unique visual feature as they move in time and space; and

Counting and estimation. Users count or estimate the number of elements with a unique visual feature.

3.3.2 Theories of Preattentive Processing

A number of theories have been proposed to explain how preattentive processing occurs within the visual system. We describe four well-known models: *feature integration theory, texton theory, similarity theory,* and *guided search theory.* We also discuss briefly the phenomenon of *postattentive vision,* which shows that prior exposure to a scene does not help a viewer answer questions about the content of the scene.

Feature Integration Theory. Anne Treisman was one of the original researchers to document the area of preattentive processing. She provided important insights into this phenomenon by studying two important problems. First, she tried to determine which visual properties are detected preattentively [420, 421, 423]. She called these properties *"preattentive features"* [422]. Second, she formulated a hypothesis about how the human visual system performs preattentive processing [419].

Treisman ran experiments using target and boundary detection to classify preattentive features. For target detection, subjects had to determine whether a target element was present or absent in a field of background distractor elements (Figures 3.18 and 3.20). Boundary detection involved placing a group of target elements with a unique visual feature within a set of distractors to see if the boundary could be preattentively detected (Figure 3.21).

Treisman and other researchers measured preattentive task performance in two different ways: by response time and by accuracy. In the response time model-viewers are asked to complete the task (e.g., target detection) as quickly as possible while still maintaining a high level of accuracy. The number of distractors in a scene is repeatedly increased. If task completion time is relatively constant and below some chosen threshold, independent of the number of distractors, the task is said to be *preattentive.* If the task were not preattentive, viewers would need to search serially through each

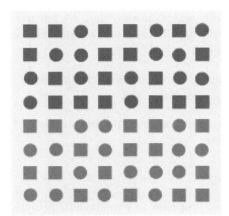 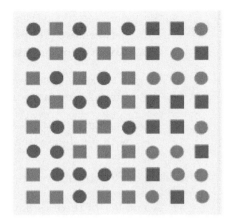

(a) A boundary defined by a unique feature hue (red circles and red squares on the top, blue circles and blue squares on the bottom) is preattentively classified as horizontal.

(b) A boundary defined by a conjunction of features (red circles and blue squares on the left, blue circles and red squares on the right) cannot be preattentively classified as vertical.

Figure 3.21.   An example of a boundary detection, from Treisman's experiments.

display to confirm a target's presence or absence. Increasing the number of elements in the display would therefore produce a corresponding increase in the time required to report on the target.

In the *accuracy model*, the display is shown for a small, fixed exposure duration, then removed from the screen. Again, the number of distractors in the scene varies (i.e., increases) across trials. If viewers can complete the task accurately, regardless of the number of distractors, the feature used to define the target is assumed to be preattentive. A common exposure duration threshold is 200 to 250 msec, since this allows subjects only "one look" at the scene. The human visual system cannot decide to change where the eye is looking within this time frame.

Treisman and others have used their experiments to compile a list of visual features that are detected preattentively, as mentioned above. It is important to note that some of these features are asymmetric. For example, a sloped line in a sea of vertical lines can be detected preattentively. However, a vertical line in a sea of sloped lines cannot be detected preattentively. Another important consideration is the effect of different types of background distractors on the target feature. These factors must often be addressed when trying to design display techniques that rely on preattentive processing.

To explain the phenomenon of preattentive processing, Treisman proposed a model of low-level human vision made up of a set of feature maps

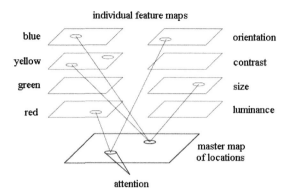

Figure 3.22. Treisman's feature integration model for early vision; individual maps can be accessed to detect feature activity; focused attention acts through a serial scan of the master map of locations.

and a master map of locations (see Figure 3.22). Each feature map registers activity in response to a specific visual feature. Treisman suggested a manageable number of feature maps, including one for each of the opponent color primaries (green, red, yellow, and blue), as well as separate maps for orientation, shape, texture, and other preattentive features.

When the human visual system first sees an image, all the features are encoded in parallel into their respective maps. A viewer can access a particular map to check for activity, and perhaps to determine the amount of activity. However, the individual feature maps give no information about location, spatial arrangement, or relationships to activity in other maps.

This framework provides a general hypothesis that explains how preattentive processing occurs. If the target has a unique feature, one can simply access the given feature map to see if any activity is occurring. Feature maps are encoded in parallel, so feature detection is almost instantaneous. A conjunction target cannot be detected by accessing an individual feature map. Activity there may be caused by the target, or by distractors that share the given preattentive feature. To locate the target, one must search serially through the master map of locations, looking for an object with the correct combination of features. This use of focused attention requires a relatively large amount of time and effort.

In later work, Treisman has expanded her strict dichotomy of features being detected as being either in parallel or in serial [420, 423]. She now believes that *parallel* and *serial* represent two ends of a spectrum. "More" and "less" are also encoded on this spectrum, not just "present" and "absent." The amount of differentiation between the target and the distractors for a given feature will affect search time. For example, a long vertical line can be detected immediately among a group of short vertical lines. As the length of the target shrinks, the search time increases, because the target is harder to distinguish from its distractors. At some point, the target line becomes shorter than the distractors. If the length of the target continues to decrease, search time decreases, because the degree of similarity between the target and the distractors is now decreasing.

Treisman has also extended feature integration to explain certain cases where conjunction search is preattentive. In particular, conjunction search tasks involving motion, depth, color, and orientation have been shown to be preattentive by Nakayama and Silverman [304], Driver et al. [99], and Wolfe et al. [465]. Treisman hypothesizes that a significant target-nontarget feature difference would allow individual feature maps to ignore nontarget information contained in the master map. For example, consider a search for a green horizontal bar within a set of red horizontal bars and green vertical bars. This should result in a conjunction search, since horizontal and green occur within each of the distractors. In spite of this, Wolfe et al. [465] showed that search times are independent of display size. If color constituted a significant feature difference, the red color map could inhibit information about red horizontal bars. Thus, the search reduces to finding a green horizontal bar in a sea of green vertical bars, which can be done preattentively.

Texton Theory. Bela Julesz was also instrumental in expanding our understanding of what we "see" in an image. Julesz's initial investigations focused on statistical analysis of texture patterns [209–212, 214]. His goal was to determine whether variations in a particular order statistic were seen (or not seen) by the low-level visual system. Examples of variations in order statistics include *contrast* (a variation in a texture's first-order statistic), *orientation* and *regularity* (a variation of the second-order statistic), and *curvature* (a variation of the third-order statistic). Unfortunately, Julesz's results were inconclusive. First-order variations were detected preattentively. In addition, some (but not all) second-order variations were also preattentive, as were an even smaller set of third-order variations.

Based on these findings, Julesz modified his theory of how preattentive processing occurs. He suggested that the early visual system detects a group of features called *textons* [213–215]. Textons can be classified into three general categories:

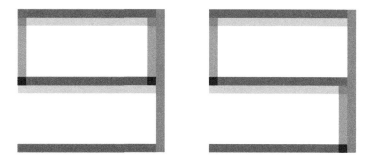

Figure 3.23.   Two simple textons, easily differentiable.

- elongated blobs (e.g., line segments, rectangles, ellipses) with specific properties such as hue, orientation, and width;

- terminators (ends of line segments);

- crossings of line segments.

Julesz believed that only a difference in textons or in their density can be detected preattentively. No positional information about neighboring textons is available without focused attention. Like Treisman, Julesz suggested that preattentive processing occurs in parallel and focused attention occurs in serial. Figure 3.23 provides an example of textons that appear different in isolation, but have the same size, number of terminators, and join points. This shows that even when each appear very different in isolation, it may be difficult, if not impossible, to differentiate any pattern when in a texture or grid.

Julesz used *texture segregation*, the task of locating groups of similar objects and the boundaries that separate them, to demonstrate his theory (other researchers, including Treisman, also used this type of task, for example, identifying the orientation of the boundary between groups of common elements in Figure 3.21). Figure 3.24 shows an example of an image that supports the texton hypothesis. Although the two objects look very different in isolation, they are actually the same texton. Both are blobs with the same height and width. Both are made up of the same set of line segments, and each has two terminators. When both are oriented randomly in an image, one cannot preattentively detect the texture boundary between the target group and the background distractors.

Similarity Theory. Some researchers do not support the dichotomy of serial and parallel search modes. Initial work in this area was done by Quinlan

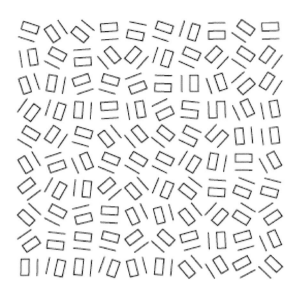

Figure 3.24.   A target group of b-textons is difficult to detect in a background of a-textons when a random rotation is applied.

and Humphreys [325]. They investigated conjunction searches by focusing on two factors. First, search time may depend on the number of items of information required to identify the target. Second, search time may depend on how easily a target can be distinguished from its distractors, regardless of the presence of unique preattentive features. Treisman addressed this second factor in her later work [420]. Quinlan and Humphreys found that Treisman's feature integration theory was unable to explain the results they obtained from their experiments. Duncan and Humphreys developed their own explanation of preattentive processing. Their model assumes that search ability varies continuously, depending on both the type of task and the display conditions [101, 102, 299]. Search time is based on two criteria: T-N similarity and N-N similarity. *T-N similarity* is the amount of similarity between the targets and nontargets. *N-N similarity* is the amount of similarity within the nontargets themselves. These two factors affect search time as follows:

1. As T-N similarity increases, search efficiency decreases and search time increases.

2. As N-N similarity decreases, search efficiency decreases and search time increases.

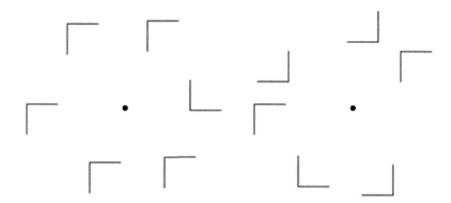

(a) High N-N (nontarget-nontarget) similarity allows easy detection of target L.

(b) Low N-N similarity increases the difficulty of detecting the target L.

Figure 3.25. Example of N-N similarity affecting search efficiency for a target shaped like the letter L.

3. T-N similarity and N-N similarity are related (see Figure 3.25); decreasing N-N similarity has little effect if T-N similarity is low; increasing T-N similarity has little effect if N-N similarity is high.

Treisman's feature integration theory has difficulty explaining the results of Figure 3.25. In both cases, the distractors seem to use exactly the same features as the target, namely oriented, connected lines of a fixed length. Yet experimental results show displays similar to Figure 3.25 on the left produce an average search time increase of 4.5 msec per additional distractor, while displays similar to Figure 3.25 on the right produce an average search time increase of 54.5 msec per additional distractor.

In order to explain the above and other search phenomena, Duncan and Humphreys proposed a three-step theory of visual selection. The visual field is segmented into structural units. Individual structural units share some common property (e.g., spatial proximity, hue, shape, motion). Each structural unit may again be segmented into smaller units. This produces a hierarchical representation of the visual field. Within the hierarchy, each structural unit is described by a set of properties (e.g., spatial location, hue, texture, size). This segmentation process occurs in parallel.

Because access to visual short-term memory is limited, Duncan and Humphreys assume that there exists a limited resource that is allocated among structural units. Because vision is being directed to search for particular information, a template of the information being sought is available. Each structural unit is compared to this template. The better the match, the more resources are allocated to the given structural unit, relative to other units with a poorer match.

Because units are grouped in a hierarchy, a poor match between the template and a structural unit allows efficient rejection of other units that are strongly grouped to the rejected unit. Structural units with a relatively large number of resources have the highest probability of access to the visual short-term memory. Thus, structural units that most closely match the template of information being sought are presented to the visual short-term memory first. Search speed is a function of the speed of resource allocation and the amount of competition for access to the visual short-term memory.

Given these three steps, we can see how T-N and N-N similarity affect search efficiency. Increased T-N similarity means that more structural units match the template, so competition for visual short-term memory access increases. Decreased N-N similarity means that we cannot efficiently reject large numbers of strongly grouped structural units, so resource allocation time and search time increase.

Guided Search Theory. More recently, Jeremy Wolfe has suggested a visual search theory that he calls *"guided search"* [463, 465, 469]. He hypothesized that an activation map based on both bottom-up and top-down information is constructed during visual search. Attention is drawn to peaks in the activation map that represent areas in the image with the largest combination of bottom-up and top-down influence.

Like Treisman, Wolfe believes that early vision divides an image into individual feature maps (see Figure 3.26). In his theory, there is one map for each feature type (e.g., one map for color, one map for orientation, and so on). Within each map, a feature is filtered into multiple categories. For example, in the color map there might be independent representations for red, green, blue, and yellow. Wolfe had already found evidence to suggest that orientation is categorized into steep, shallow, right, and left [467]. The relationship between values within a feature map is different than the relationship between values from different maps (the relationship between "red" and "blue" is different than the relationship between "blue" and "shallow").

Bottom-up activation follows feature categorization. It measures how different an element is from its neighbors. Differences for each relevant feature map are computed and combined (e.g., how different are the elements in terms of color, how different are they in terms of orientation?) The

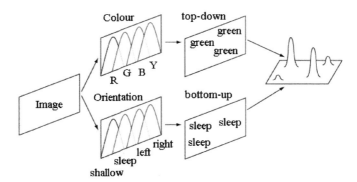

Figure 3.26.   Framework for guided search, the user wants to find a green steep target; image is
filtered into categories for each feature map. Bottom-up and top-down activation
"mark" regions of the image; an activation map is built by combining bottom-up
and top-down information, attention is draw to the highest "hills" in the map [174].

"metrics" used to measure differences in each feature map are still being
investigated.

Top-down activation is a user-driven attempt to find items with a specific
property or set of properties. For example, visual search for a blue element
would generate a top-down request that activates "blue" locations. Previous work suggests subjects must specify requests in terms of the categories
provided by each feature map [464, 467]. Thus, subjects could search for
"steep" or "shallow" elements, but not for elements rotated by a specific
angle. Obviously, subjects should pick the category that best differentiates
the target from its distractors. Finding the "best" category is often nonintuitive, however. Wolfe suggests this might explain cases where subjects'
performance for a task improves over time.

The activation map is a combination of bottom-up and top-down activation. The weights assigned to these two values are task dependent. A conjunction search would place priority on top-down information, since bottom-
up results are, in essence, useless. A search for a target with a unique feature
would assign a high weight to bottom-up activation. Hills in the activation
map mark regions that generated a relatively large amount of bottom-up or
top-down influence. There is no information in the activation map about
the source of a hill. High activation from a color map looks exactly the same
as high activation from an orientation map. A subject's attention is drawn
from hill to hill in order of decreasing activation.

Wolfe's theory easily explains traditional "parallel" visual search. Target elements produce the highest level of activation, regardless of the number of distractor elements. This causes the target to "pop-out" of the scene in time independent of the number of distractors. This also explains Duncan and Humphreys' similarity theory results. Low N-N similarity causes distractors to report higher bottom-up activation, since they now differ from their neighbors. High T-N similarity causes a reduction in the target elements' bottom-up activation. Moreover, guided search also provides a possible explanation for situations where conjunction search can be performed preattentively [304, 465, 466]. User-driven top-down activation may permit efficient searching for conjunction targets.

Postattentive Vision. Preattentive processing asks in part: "What visual properties draw our eyes, and therefore our focus of attention, to a particular object in a scene?" An equally interesting question is: "What happens to the visual representation of an object when we stop attending to it and look at something else?" Jeremy Wolfe addressed this question in his work on postattentive vision [468]. The intuitive belief that a rich visual representation accumulates as we look at more and more of a scene appears not to be true. This provides important insight into why the low-level visual system performs the way it does. The results also act as a bridge between preattentive processing and the new area of change blindness, which shows that people are often "blind" to significant variations that occur between glances at a scene.

Attention to different objects may allow a viewer to learn what is in a scene (if the objects are familiar and recognizable), but it does not allow the viewer to see the scene in a different manner. In other words, the preattentive visual representation of an object after a viewer studies it and looks at something else appears to be identical to its representation before the viewer studied it. No additional information is "saved" in the visual system after the focus of attention shifts to a new location.

Wolfe argues that if multiple objects are recognized simultaneously in the low-level visual system, it would involve a search for links between the objects and their representation in long-term memory (LTM). LTM can be queried nearly instantaneously, compared to the 40–50 msec per item required to search a visual scene. Preattentive processing can help to rapidly draw the focus of attention to a target with a unique visual feature (e.g., little or no searching is required in the preattentive case). To remove this assistance, Wolfe designed targets with two critical properties (Figure 3.27):

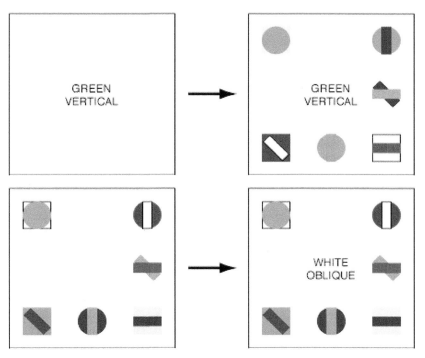

Figure 3.27.   Examples of search for color-and-shape conjunction targets, both with and without a preview of the scene: (top) no preview of the scene is shown (although text identifying the target is shown prior to the search)—in this case, the green vertical target is present; (bottom) a preview of the scene is shown, followed by text identifying the target; in this case, a white oblique target is not present.

- The targets were formed from a conjunction of features (e.g., they could not be detected preattentively).

- The targets were arbitrary combinations of colors and shapes (e.g., they were not objects that could be semantically recognized and remembered on the basis of familiarity).

Wolfe initially tested two search types. In both cases, viewers were asked to answer as quickly as possible while maintaining a high level of accuracy (e.g., a response-time search):

Traditional search. Text on a blank screen was shown to identify the target. This was followed by a display containing 4, 5, 6, 7, or 8 potential target objects in a 3 × 3 array (formed by combinations of seven colors and five shapes (Figure 3.27 (top)).

Postattentive search. The display to be searched was shown to the user for a
specific duration (up to 300 msec). Text identifying the target was then
inserted into the scene (Figure 3.27(bottom)). Results showed that
the postattentive search was as slow (or slower) than the traditional
search, with approximately 25–40 msec per object required for the
target present trials. This implies that previewing the scene provides
no advantage to the viewer for finding a conjunction target. In order
to explore further, Wolfe studied a number of different search scenarios
to test for any benefit from previewing the scene.

These scenarios include:

Repeated search. Viewers were asked to search the same display five times
for five different targets. The display was shown with target text, and
after an answer was provided (target present or absent), the target
text changed to identify a new target. This experiment tested whether
additional exposure to the display improved search performance.

Repeated search with letters. Viewers searched in a manner identical to repeated search, but with displays containing letters rather than combinations of colors and shapes. This experiment tested whether the type
of target used affected search performance.

Repeated search versus memory search. Viewers were asked to search a group
of five letters 350 times for a target letter. Half the viewers were shown
the five letters. The other half were required to memorize the five
letters prior to the target queries. This experiment tested whether a
prolonged exposure to a set of objects improved search performance.
It also tested to see how visual search and short-term memory search
performance differed.

In each case, viewers continued to require 20–50 msec per object to complete the search. Wolfe's conclusion was that sustained attention to the
objects tested in his experiments did not make visual search more efficient.
This has a significant potential impact for visualization design. In most
cases, visualization displays are novel, and their contents cannot be com-
mitted to long-term memory. This means that studying a display may offer
no assistance in searching for specific data values. In this scenario, methods that draw attention to areas of potential interest within a display (i.e.,
preattentive methods) would be critical in allowing viewers to rapidly and
accurately explore their data.

3.3.3 Feature Hierarchy

Based on our understanding of low-level human vision, one promising strategy for multidimensional visualization is to assign different visual features to different data attributes (e.g., building a data-feature mapping that maps data to a visual representation). This allows multiple data values to be shown simultaneously in a single image. One key requirement of this method is a data-feature mapping that does not produce visual interference. Interactions between different visual features hide or mask information in a display. Obviously, we want to avoid this situation during visualization. One simple example of visual interference is the conjunction search shown in Figure 3.20. If we want to search rapidly for combinations of data values, care must be taken to ensure that the resulting combinations contain at least one unique feature for the visual system to cue on.

Other types of visual interference can also occur. An important type of interference results from a feature hierarchy that appears to exist in the visual system. For certain tasks, the visual system seems to favor one type of visual feature over another. For example, during boundary detection, researchers have shown that the visual system favors color over shape (Figures 3.28 and 3.29). Background variations in color interfere with a viewer's ability to identify the presence of individual shapes and the spatial patterns they form [57]. If color is held constant across the display, these same shape patterns are immediately visible. The interference is asymmetric:

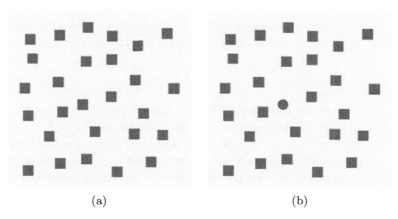

(a)   (b)

Figure 3.28.   An example of hue-on-form feature hierarchy: (a) a horizontal hue boundary is preattentively identified when form is held constant; (b) a vertical hue boundary is preattentively identified when form varies randomly in the background.

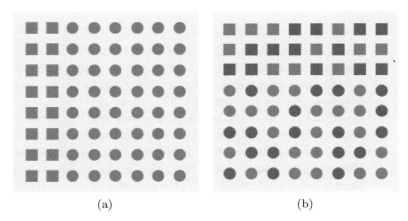

(a)   (b)

Figure 3.29.   Another example of hue-on-form feature hierarchy: (a) a vertical form boundary is preattentively identified when hue is held constant; (b) a horizontal form boundary cannot be preattentively identified when hue varies randomly in the background.

random variations in shape have no effect on a viewer's ability to see color patterns.

Callaghan also documented a luminance-on-hue preference during her experiments [55, 56]. More recently, a hue-on-texture interference has been shown to exist [175, 176, 387, 422]; random variations in hue interfere with the identification of texture patterns, but not vice versa. These hierarchies suggest that the most important data attributes (as defined by the viewer) should be displayed with the most salient visual features, if possible. The data-feature mapping should avoid situations where the display of secondary data values masks the information the viewer wants to see.

3.3.4   Change Blindness

Recent research in visualization has explored ways to apply rules of perception to produce images that are visually salient [448]. This work is based in large part on psychophysical studies of the low-level human visual system. One of the most important lessons of the past twenty-five years is that human vision does not resemble the relatively faithful and largely passive process of modern photography [323, 420, 422, 468, 469]. The goal of human vision is not to create a replica or image of the seen world in our heads. A much better metaphor for vision is that of a dynamic and ongoing construction project, where the products being built are short-lived models of the external world that are specifically designed for the current visually guided

Figure 3.30.   Only one image of many examples of change blindness, each image shows a frame
                   from a sequence which contains a significant variation from the other frame; the
                   animations are available on the book's web site. All sequences courtesy of Ron
                   Rensink; see his discussion of change blindness for additional resources [333]. See
                   also the famous basketball example.

tasks of the viewer [106, 282, 334, 382]. There does not appear to be any
general-purpose vision. What we "see" when confronted with a new scene
depends as much on our goals and expectations as it does on the array of
light that enters our eyes.

   These new findings differ from one of the initial ideas of preattentive
processing, that only certain features in an image are recognized without
the need for focused attention, and that other features cannot be detected,
even when viewers actively search for these exact features. More recent
work in preattentive vision has presented evidence to suggest that this strict
dichotomy does not hold. Instead, "visible" or "not visible" represent two
ends of a continuous spectrum. Issues like the difference between a target's
visual features and its neighbors' features, what a viewer is searching for, and
how the image is presented, can all have an effect on search performance.
For example, Wolfe's guided search theory assumes both bottom-up (e.g.,
preattentive) and top-down (e.g., attention-based) activation of features in
an image [463, 465, 469]. Other researchers have also studied the dual effects
of preattentive and attention-driven demands on what the visual system
sees [421, 423]. Wolfe's discussion of postattentive vision also points to the
fact that details of an image cannot be remembered across separate scenes,
except in areas where viewers have focused their attention [468].

   New research in psychophysics has shown that an interruption in what is
being seen (i.e., a blink, an eye saccade, or a blank screen) renders us "blind"

to significant changes that occur in the scene during the interruption. This change blindness phenomenon can be illustrated using a task similar to a game that has amused children reading the comic strips for many years [282, 334, 382]. Figure 3.30 shows a pair of images from a series of movies dealing with change blindness; each movie is made up of two separate images, with a short blank interval separating them. A significant change occurs between the two images. Run the movies on the book's web site and try to locate the change. Many viewers have a difficult time seeing any difference and often have to be coached to look carefully to find it. Once they discover it, they realize that the difference is not a subtle one. Change blindness is not a failure to see because of limited visual acuity; rather, it is a failure based on inappropriate attentional guidance. Some parts of the eye and the brain are clearly responding differently to the two pictures. Yet this does not become part of our visual experience until attention is focused directly on the objects that vary.

The presence of change blindness in our visual system has important implications for visualization. The images we produce are normally novel for our viewers, so prior expectations cannot be used to guide their analyses. Instead, we strive to direct the eye, and therefore the mind, to areas of interest or importance within a visualization. This ability forms the first step toward enabling a viewer to abstract details that will persist over subsequent images.

Dan Simons offers a wonderful overview of change blindness in his introduction to the *Visual Cognition* special issue on change blindness and visual memory [382]. We provide a brief summary of his list of possible explanations for why change blindness occurs in our visual system. Interestingly, none of these explanations by themselves can account for all of the change blindness effects that have been identified. This suggests that some combination of these ideas (or some completely different hypothesis) is needed to properly model this phenomenon.

Overwriting. One intuitive suggestion is that the current image is overwritten, either by the blank between images, or by the image seen after the blank. Information that was not abstracted from the first image is lost. In this scenario, detailed change can only be detected for objects the viewer focuses on, and even then, only abstract differences may be recognized.

First Impression. A second hypothesis is that only the initial view of a scene is abstracted. This is plausible, since the purpose of perception is to rapidly understand our surroundings. Once this is done, if the scene is not perceived to have changed, features of the scene should not need to be re-encoded. This means that change will not be detected, except for objects in the focus of attention. One example of this phenomenon is an experiment conducted by Simons and Levin [380, 381]. Subjects were asked to view a short movie. During a cut scene in the movie, the central character was switched to a completely different actor. Subjects were not told to search for any unexpected change in the movie (i.e., they were naive to the presence of the change). After viewing the movie, subjects were asked if they noticed anything odd. Nearly two-thirds of the subjects failed to report that the main actor was replaced. When queried, 70% of the subjects who failed to see the change described the central character using details from the initial actor, and not the replacement. This suggests that their first impression of the actors was the lasting one.

Nothing Is Stored. A third explanation is that after a scene has been viewed and information has been abstracted, no details are represented internally. This model suggests that the world itself acts as a memory store; if we need to obtain specific details from the scene, we simply look at it again. A somewhat weaker form of this model suggests that some detail is preserved between scenes (e.g., the details of the objects in the viewer's focus of attention). In this way, we are blind to change unless it affects our abstracted knowledge of the scene, or unless it occurs where we are looking in the scene.

Everything Is Stored, Nothing Is Compared. Another intriguing possibility is that details about each new scene are stored, but cannot be accessed until an external stimulus forces the access. For example, if a man suddenly becomes a woman during a sequence of images, this discontinuity in abstracted knowledge might allow us to access the details of past scenes to detect the change. Alternatively, being queried about particular details in a past scene might also produce the stimulus needed to access this image history. In one study, an experimenter stops a pedestrian on the street to ask for directions [382]. During this interaction, a group of students walks between the experimenter and the pedestrian. As they do this, one of the students takes a basketball that the experimenter is holding. After providing the directions, the pedestrian is asked if anything odd or unusual changed about the experimenter's appearance. Only a very few pedestrians reported that the basketball had gone missing. When asked specifically about a basketball, however, more than half of the remaining subjects reported it missing, and many provided a detailed description. For example, one pedestrian reported, "Oh yeah, he did have a ball, it was red and white." Not only was the pedestrian able to recall the presence of the basketball when prompted; he was also able to provide specific details about its unique appearance.

Feature Combination. A final hypothesis is that details from an initial view might be combined with new features from a second view to form a combined representation of the scene. Presumably, viewers would not be aware of which parts of their mental image come from the first scene, and which come from the second. The details being combined must make sense, and must be consistent with the viewer's abstract understanding of the scene; otherwise, the change will be recognized as "impossible" or "out of place."

3.4   Perception in Visualization

Figure 3.31 shows several examples of perceptually motivated multidimensional visualizations:

1. A visualization of intelligent agents competing in simulated e-commerce auctions: the x-axis is mapped to time, the y-axis is mapped to auction (each row represents a separate auction), the towers represent bids by different agents (with color mapped to agent ID), height is mapped to bid price, and width is mapped to bid quantity.

2. A visualization of a CT scan of an abdominal aortic aneurism: yellow represents the artery, purple represents the aneurism, and red represents metal tines in a set of stents inserted into the artery to support its wall within the aneurism.

3. A painter-like visualization of weather conditions over the Rocky Mountains across Utah, Wyoming, and Colorado: temperature is mapped to color (dark blues for cold, to bright pinks for hot), precipitation is mapped to orientation (tilting right for heavier rainfall), wind speed is mapped to coverage (less background showing through for stronger winds), and pressure is mapped to size (larger strokes for higher pressure).

We briefly describe how perceptual properties of color, texture, motion, and nonphotorealism have been used in visualization.

3.4.1   Color

Color is a common feature used in many visualization designs. Examples of simple color scales include the rainbow spectrum, red-blue or red-green

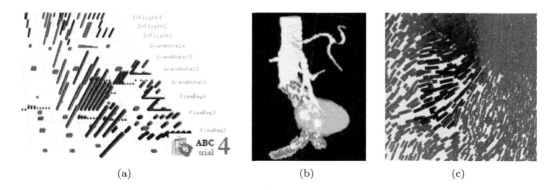

(a)   (b)   (c)

Figure 3.31.   Examples of perceptually motivated multidimensional visualizations: (a) a visu-
                    alization of intelligent agents competing in simulated e-commerce auctions; (b) a
                    visualization of a CT scan of an abdominal aortic aneurism; (c) a painter-like
                    visualization of weather conditions over the Rocky Mountains.

ramps, and the gray-red saturation scale [447]. More sophisticated techniques attempt to control the difference viewers perceive between different
colors, as opposed to the distance between their positions in RGB space.

This improvement allows:

Perceptual balance. A unit step anywhere along the color scale produces a
        perceptually uniform difference in color.

Distinguishability. Within a discrete collection of colors, every color is equally
        distinguishable from all the others (i.e., no specific color is "easier" or
        "harder" to identify).

Flexibility. Colors can be selected from any part of color space (e.g., the
        selection technique is not restricted to only greens, or only reds and
        blues).

Color models such as CIE LUV, CIE Lab, or Munsell can be used to
provide a rough measure of perceptual balance [39, 77, 301]. Within these
models, Euclidean distance is used to estimate perceived color difference.
More complex techniques refine this basic idea. Rheingans and Tebbs plotted
a path through a perceptually balanced color model, then asked viewers to
define how attribute values map to positions along the path [336]. Nonlinear
mappings emphasize differences in specific parts of an attribute's domain
(e.g., in the lower end with a logarithmic mapping, or in the higher end

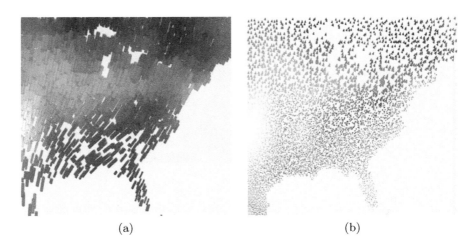

(a)   (b)

Figure 3.32.   Example of color representations for weather maps: (a) a nonphotorealistic visualization using simulated brush strokes to display the underlying data; (b) a
traditional visualization of the same data using triangular glyphs.

with an exponential mapping). Other researchers have constructed rules
to automatically select a color map for a target data attribute [31, 344].
Properties of the attribute, such as its spatial frequency, its continuous or
discrete nature, and the type of analysis to be performed, are used to choose
an appropriate color representation. Ware constructed a color scale that
spirals up around the luminance axis to maintain a uniform simultaneous
contrast error along its length [447]. His solution matched or outperformed
traditional color scales for metric and form identification tasks. Healey and
Enns showed that color distance, linear separation, and color category must
all be controlled to select discrete collections of equally distinguishable colors
[176, 177].

Figure 3.32 shows historical weather conditions over the eastern United
States for March, with color mapped to temperature (blue and green for
cold, to red and pink for hot), luminance mapped to wind speed (brighter
for stronger winds), orientation mapped to precipitation (more tilted for
heavier rainfall), size mapped to cloud coverage (larger for more cloudy),
and frost frequency mapped to density (denser for higher frost).

Healey's color selection technique combines different aspects of each of
these methods. A single loop spiraling up around the Laxis (the luminance
pole) is plotted near the boundary of our monitor's gamut of displayable
colors in CIE LUV space. The path is subdivided into r named color regions

(i.e., a blue region, a green region, and so on). Here, n colors can then be selected by choosing n/r colors uniformly spaced along each of the r color regions. The result is a set of colors selected from a perceptually balanced color model, each with a roughly constant simultaneous contrast error, and chosen such that color distance and linear separation are constant within each named color region (Figure 3.32).

3.4.2 Texture

Texture is often viewed as a single visual feature. Like color, however, it can be decomposed into a collection of fundamental perceptual dimensions. Researchers in computer vision have used properties such as regularity, directionality, contrast, size, and coarseness to perform automatic texture segmentation and classification [168, 329, 330, 404]. These texture features were derived both from statistical analysis, and through experimental study. Results from psychophysics have shown that many of these properties are also detected by the low-level visual system, although not always in ways that are identical to computer-based algorithms [6, 89, 209, 210, 212, 215, 387, 423, 469].

One promising approach in visualization has been to use perceptual texture dimensions to represent multiple data attributes. Individual values of an attribute control its corresponding texture dimension. The result is a texture pattern that changes its visual appearance based on data in the underlying data set. Grinstein et al. visualized multidimensional data with "stick-figure" icons whose limbs encode attribute values stored in a data element [161]; when the stick-men are arrayed across a display, they form texture patterns whose spatial groupings and boundaries identify attribute correspondence. Ware and Knight designed Gabor filters that modified their orientation, size, and contrast, based on the values of three independent data attributes [446]. Healey and Enns constructed perceptual texture elements (or *pexels*) that varied in size, density, and regularity [175, 176]; results showed that size and density are perceptually salient, but variations in regularity are much more difficult to identify. More recent work found that 2D orientation can also be used to encode information [457]; a difference of 15 degrees is sufficient to rapidly distinguish elements from one another. A follow-on to these studies showed that certain 3D orientation properties can also be detected by the low-level visual system [275].

Interrante, Kim, and Hagh-Shenas have studied the use of different texture types and orientations for showing the shape of an underlying 3D object. Initial experiments investigated textures that varied in luminance (e.g., grayscale patterns) [201, 202, 241]. More recent work has studied the use of relief textures. The textures were arrayed over the surface using orientations that were either *isotropic* (e.g., all following a common direction), or *anisotropic* (e.g., following different directions based on a property at that point on the surface). Preliminary results suggest that anisotropic textures that follow both the first or second principal curvature directions produce surface perception that is as good or better than either principal direction alone, or than other orientation rules [240].

3.4.3 Motion

Motion is a third visual feature that is known to be perceptually salient. The use of motion is common in certain areas of visualization, for example, the animation of particles, dye, or glyphs to represent the direction and magnitude of a vector field (e.g., fluid flow visualization). Motion transients are also used to highlight changes in a data set across a user-selected data axis (e.g., over time for a temporal data set, or along the scanning axis for a set of CT or MRI slices). As with color and texture, our interest is in identifying the perceptual dimensions of motion and applying them in an effective manner. Three motion properties have been studied extensively by researchers in psychophysics: flicker, direction of motion, and velocity of motion.

For visualization purposes, our interest is in flicker frequencies F (the frequency of repetition measured in cycles per second) that are perceived as discrete flashes by the viewer. Brown noted that frequency must vary from 2–5% to produce a distinguishable difference in flicker at the center of focus ($1.02 \leq \Delta F \leq 1.05$), and at 100% or more for distinguishable difference in flicker in the periphery ($\Delta F \geq 2.0$) [50, 142, 298].

Tynan and Sekuler showed that a decrease in a target object's velocity or an increase in its eccentricity increased identification time [428], although in all cases viewers responded rapidly (200–350 msec for targets in the periphery, 200–310 msec for targets in the center of focus). In addition, van Doorn and Koenderink confirmed that higher initial velocities produce a faster response to a change in the velocity [190, 288, 433, 434]. They claim this is due to the need for the target to traverse a "critical distance" before it can be detected. For a baseline velocity V_1 and a target velocity $V_2 = 2V_1$, approximately 100 msec is needed to see the velocity change from V_1 to V_2 for slow V_1 ($1°$ per second) and approximately 50 msec for faster V_1 ($2°$ per second or higher).

Researchers in psychology have used properties of motion to extend a viewer's ability to perform basic exploration tasks. Nakayama and Silverman showed that coherent motion or stereoscopic depth can be used to separate elements into coherent groups, allowing viewers to search each group independently [304]. For example, consider searching for a red circle in a background of red squares and blue circles, a situation that normally produces a time-consuming serial search for the target. If the red elements are animated to move up and the blue elements are animated to move down, however, the target is immediately visible. Applying different motion patterns to the red and blue groups allows a viewer's visual system to separate them and search them independently, producing the rapid search for a curved element (a red circle) in a background of linear elements (red squares). Similar results can be achieved by displaying the red and blue elements on different stereoscopic planes. Driver et al. showed that oscillation can also be used to separate elements into independent visual groups, but only if the oscillation pattern is coherent [99]. For example, a viewer could identify a red circle in a set of red squares and blue circles if all the red items oscillate up and down in lock step, and all the blue elements oscillate left and right in lock step. If the elements oscillate "out of phase" (i.e., some red elements start moving down while others are still moving up), however, viewers are forced to revert to serial search. More sophisticated motion patterns have also been analyzed, although with less success in terms of achieving high-speed search performance. Braddick and Holliday studied both divergence (e.g., squares increase or decrease in size over a period of time, then snap back to their original size) and deformation (e.g., rectangles deform from tall and skinny to short and wide, then snap back to their original shape) [43]. Although the basic motion properties being shown can be rapidly identified in isolation, the combinations that form deformation and divergence were not detected by the low-level visual system. See also the iconic extensions to pixels called *moxels* [483].

Properties of motion have been extended to visualization design. Animated motion is used in flow visualization to show the direction and speed of different flow patterns (e.g., by Kirby [243]). Kerlick proposed the use of animated glyphs to visualize 2D and 3D multidimensional data sets [237]. He designed a set of *"boids"* to encode attribute values at specific locations in the data set, for example, a sphere boid to query data values at a user-selected location, or pyramid and dart boids that animate over a vector field to visualize its shape. Bartram et al. studied the use of variations in color, shape, and motion to "notify" viewers while they were engaged in a separate, attention-demanding task [25]. Results showed that applying motion to a static glyph significantly eased recognition, compared to changing the glyph's color or shape. This finding held both when the glyph was near the center of focus and when it was located on the periphery of the viewer's gaze. The authors also studied how distracting a secondary motion cue was judged to be. Flicker was the least distracting, followed by oscillating motion, then divergence, and finally movement over long distances. Related work by Bartram et al. confirmed that different motion paths can be used to perceptually group glyphs in a manner similar to the work of Nakayama and Silverman [304] or Driver et al. [26]. The groups can then be searched independently for a target feature.

3.4.4 Memory Issues

Three types of memory are relevant to our study of perception in visualization:

Sensory memory. Sensory memory is high-capacity information storage. It is effectively preattentive eye filters. Large quantities of information are processed very fast (less than 200 msec). Such learning is physical and can be harnessed by repeated actions. This explains the importance, for example, of positional learning in typing or playing piano (it feels almost as if the memory is in the hand and fingers).

Short-term memory. Short-term memory analyzes information from both sensory and long-term storage. It has limited information capacity. It occurs at a high level of processing, but the time span is limited typically to less than 30 seconds. It represents the beginning of thinking. It can be harnessed by grouping and repetition, by not requiring users to remember too many things, and by chunking. The chunks are grouped objects remembered as a unit, with the number limited to 5 to 9 (see Section 3.5).

Long-term memory. Long-term memory is complex and theoretically limitless, much like a data warehouse. This storage is multicoded, redundantly stored, and organized in a complex network structure. Information retrieval is a key problem and access is unreliable and slow. It can be harnessed by using association mnemonics and chunking.

The following was distributed as an example highlighting how memory supported the quick scanning of words in a document, showing that not all letters are needed.

Rinadeg Oedrr

*Aoccdrnig to a rscarhee at Cigdmabre Uinervtisy, it deosn't mte-
tar in waht oredr the ltteers in a wrod are, the olny iprmoatnt
tihng is taht the frist and lsat ltteer be at the rghit pclae. The
rset can be a taotl mses and you can sitll raed it wouthit porbelm.
Tihs is bcuseae the huamn mnid deos not raed ervey lteter by
istlef, but the wrod as a wlohe.*

This is not quite correct as reordering internal letters slows the reading
process and more complex word structures cannot be discerned. Consider

*Anidroccg to crad cniyrrag lcitsiugnis planoissefors at an ue-
mannd, utisreviny in Bsitirh Cibmuloa, and crartnoy to the duoibus
cmials of the ueticnd rcraeseh, a slpmie, macinahcel ioisrevnn
of ianretnl cretcarahs araepps sneiciffut to csufnoe the eadyrevy
oekoolnr*

Two- and three-letter words do not change. Four-letter words can only
have the internal two letters switched. Longer words have many more possibilities.

In the next section we will see how memory can play a part in studying
a visualization.

3.5   Metrics

How many distinct line lengths and orientations can humans accurately perceive? How many different sound pitches or volumes can we distinguish without error? What is our "channel capacity" when dealing with color, taste,
smell, or any other of our senses? How are humans capable of recognizing
hundreds of faces and thousands of spoken words? These and related issues
are important in the study of data and information visualization. When
designing a visualization, it is important to factor in human limitations to
avoid generating images with ambiguous, misleading, or difficult-to-interpret
information. Many efforts have been made to try and ascertain these limits,
using experiments that test human performance on measuring and detecting
a wide assortment of sensed phenomena. This section presents an overview
of some early seminal work on measuring perceptual capabilities and relate
it to current work in data visualization. The sorts of questions we would like
to be able to answer include:

- What graphical entities can be accurately measured by humans?

- How many distinct entities can be used in a visualization without confusion?

- With what level of accuracy do we perceive various primitives?

- How do we combine primitives to recognize complex phenomena?

- How should color be used to present information?

The answers to these and other questions will enable us to design more effective visualizations, and to have a better understanding of how accurately we are communicating information with the visualization.

3.5.1 Resource Model of Human Information Processing

To be able to measure and compare human perceptual performance on various phenomena, one needs a *metric*, a gauge or yardstick that can reliably evaluate performance and associate numbers with the results of testing a group of subjects. George Miller, in 1956 [295], borrowed the concept of *channel capacity* from the field of information theory. Suppose that we assume the human being is a communication channel, taking input (perceiving some phenomena) and generating output (reporting on the phenomena). The overlap between input and output is the information about the phenomena that has been perceived correctly, and is thus the amount of transmitted information.

For each primitive stimulus, whether it be visual, auditory, taste, touch, or smell, we measure the number of distinct levels of this stimulus that the average participant can identify with a high degree of accuracy. The results will follow an *asymptotic* behavior, e.g., at a certain point, increasing the number of levels being used causes an increase in the error rate, and no additional information will be extracted from the source stimulus. Miller called this level the *"channel capacity"* for information transfer by the human. He measured it in bits (borrowing again from information theory), depending on the number of levels that the average human could measure with high accuracy. Thus if errors routinely begin when more than 8 levels of a phenomenon are tested, the channel capacity for this phenomenon is 3 bits.

As in all experiments involving human subjects, it is important to establish controls, so that only the single isolated phenomenon is being tested.

Training time must therefore be limited, as some individuals can fine-tune their perceptual abilities much faster than others. For the same reason, we need to avoid including the results from *specialists*. Clearly, a musician will likely be more able to accurately perceive sound pitches than the average subject, and a cartographer or navigator will be able to identify spatial features more readily than someone who does spatial analysis less frequently. Related to this is the aspect of *context*; it is very important to design perceptual experiments to be as context-free as possible, as we don't want to bias the results via associations and factors that have little to do with perception. Finally, the experimental data should be free of error and noise; while real data and phenomena are rarely noise-free, it is difficult to obtain accurate measurements from data of variable quality.

There are many other guidelines for the design of perceptual experiments. This section, and the contents of the rest of the chapter, are merely meant to illustrate the general procedure for conducting this sort of analysis. Those wishing to understand the process in more detail are directed to the literature in perceptual psychology, social sciences, and human factors analysis.

3.5.2 Absolute Judgment of 1D Stimuli

A large number of experiments have been performed over the years to ascertain the ability of humans to judge absolute levels of different stimuli. In this section, we summarize a number of these experiments (from [295]) in terms of the number of bits in the channel capacity of humans, as defined earlier. For each, we provide the name of the researcher, the experimental setup, and the number of levels that could, on average, be accurately measured.

1. *Sound pitches (Pollack)*: Subjects were exposed to sets of pitches at equal logarithmic steps (from 100–8000 cps). The result was that the average listener could reliably distinguish 6 pitches. Varying the range didn't change the results appreciably; subjects who correctly classified 5 high pitches or 5 low pitches could not accurately classify 10 when combined. This is a channel capacity of 2.5 bits.

2. *Sound loudness (Gardner)*: In another auditory experiment, the loudness of a sound was varied between 15–110 dbs. On average, 5 levels were accurately discerned, for a capacity of 2.3 bits.

3. *Salinity (Beebe-Center)*: Taste perception had similar results. By varying salt concentrations from 0.3 to 34.7 gm per 100 cc water, subjects

were found to be able to distinguish just under 4 levels, on average, corresponding to a capacity of 1.9 bits.

4. *Position on a line (Hake/Gardner)*: In an experiment much more relevant to data visualization, this experiment varied the position of a pointer located between two markers. Participants attempted to classify its position either from a list of possibilities or on a scale of 0 to 100. Most subjects were able to correctly label between 10 and 15 levels, though this increased with longer exposure. This corresponds to a channel capacity of 3.25 bits.

5. *Sizes of squares (Eriksen/Hake)*: In another graphics-related experiment, the size of squares was varied. Surprisingly, the capabilities of humans to accurately classify the sizes was only between 4 and 5 levels, or 2.2 bits.

6. *Color (Eriksen)*: As color is often used to convey information in visualizations, it is important to understand how well this attribute is perceived. In experiments that varied single color parameters, it was found that users could correctly classify 10 levels of hue and 5 levels of brightness, or 3.1 and 2.3 bits, respectively.

7. *Touch (Gelard)*: In this unusual experiment, vibrators were placed at different locations on the chest area. Several parameters were varied individually, including location, intensity, and duration. The results estimated the capacity at 4 intensities, 5 durations, and 7 locations.

8. *Line geometry (Pollack)*: Lines have many attributes that can be used to convey information. In this experiment, line length, orientation, and curvature were tested. The results were: 2.6–3 bits for line length (depending on duration), 2.8–3.3 bits for orientation, and 2.2 bits for curvature with constant arc length (while only 1.6 bits for constant chord length).

To summarize these experiments, there appears to be some built-in limit on our capability to perceive and accurately measure 1D signals. The average from these experiments was 2.6 bits, with a standard deviation of .6 bits. This means that if we want users of our visualization systems to be able to extract more than 6 or 7 levels of a data value with accuracy, we must look at other means.

3.5.3   Absolute Judgment of Multidimensional Stimuli

One solution to the dilemma regarding this limitation on the number of levels of a data value that can be accurately measured is to use more than one stimulus simultaneously. A logical assumption would be that if we combine stimulus A, with a channel capacity of C_A bits (or 2^{C_A} levels), and stimulus B, with a channel capacity of C_B bits (or 2^{C_B} levels), we should get a resulting capacity of approximately $C_A + C_B$, or the product of the two numbers of levels. Unfortunately, experiments have shown otherwise:

1. *Dot in a square (Klemmer/Frick)*: Given that a dot in a square is actually two position measurements (vertically and horizontally) we should get a capacity that is twice that of gauging the position of a marker on a line (6.5 bits), but it was measured at 4.6 bits.

2. *Salinity and sweetness (Beebe-Center)*: In an experiment that combined sucrose and salt solutions, the total capacity should have been twice that of measuring salinity alone, or 3.8 bits. However, it was measured at 2.3 bits.

3. *Loudness and pitch (Pollack)*: The combination of two auditory channels should have produced a capacity equal to the sum of the results for pitch and loudness in isolation, or 4.8 bits, but it was measured at 3.1 bits.

4. *Hue and saturation (Halsey/Chapanis)*: Combining hue and saturation should have resulted in a capacity of 5.3 bits, but it was measured at only 3.6 bits.

5. *Size, brightness, and hue (Eriksen)*: In an experiment combining geometry and color, the size, hue, and brightness of shapes were varied. The sum of the individual capacities is 7.6 bits, but a capacity of only 4.1 bits was observed.

6. *Multiple sound parameters (Pollack/Ficks)*: In a very ambitious experiment, 6 auditory variables (frequency, intensity, rate of interruption, on-time fraction, duration, and location) were varied. As individual stimuli, each had a capacity of 5 values, so the results should have been 15,600 combinations that could be accurately discerned. However, the results were only 7.2 bits of channel capacity, or 150 different combinations.

To summarize, combining different stimuli does enable us to increase the amount of information being communicated, but not at the levels we might hope. The added stimuli resulted in the reduction of the discernibility of the individual attributes. With that said, however, having a little information about a large number of parameters seems to be the way we do things. This agrees with linguistic theory, which identifies 8 to 10 dimensions, where each can only be classified in two or three categories.

We now look at strategies for improving the information content of data visualizations by taking advantage of alternative perceptual skills.

3.5.4   Relative Judgment

William Cleveland and his colleagues have performed a number of experiments in graphical perception to better understand the ways information can be communicated via images [80]. Their emphasis, rather than on *absolute measurement* (classification), was on *relative judgment*. Thus, the task they were interested in was the detection of differences, rather than extracting a numeric value. In Figure 3.33, it is much easier to detect and gauge the change in heights when the bars are surrounded by a box (a relative change).

They studied how well humans gauge differences using the following 10 graphical attributes (shown in Figure 3.34):

1. angle;

2. area;

3. color hue;

4. color saturation;

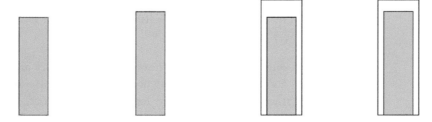

Figure 3.33.   The boxes on the left are not the same size, but it is difficult to estimate the magnitude of the difference. The same boxes are shown on the right. The encapsulating frame makes it easier to gauge the relative difference between them.

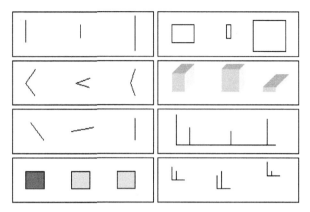

Figure 3.34.   Examples of graphical attributes used in perceptual experiments. Left column (from top): length, angle, orientation, hue. Right column: area, volume, position along a common scale, position along identical, nonaligned scales.

5. density (amount of black);

6. length (distance);

7. position along a common scale;

8. position along identical, nonaligned scales;

9. slope;

10. volume.

Their experiments showed errors in perception ordered as follows (increasing error):

1. position along a common scale;

2. position along identical, nonaligned scales;

3. length;

4. angle/slope (though error depends greatly on orientation and type);

5. area;

6. volume;

7. color hue, saturation, density (although this was only informal testing).

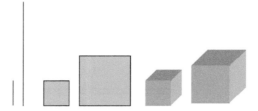

Figure 3.35.   Illustration of Stevens' Law. The size ratio for each pair is 1:4. This magnitude
                    is readily apparent in the lines, but it is easily underestimated in the squares and
                    cubes.

This seems to support the idea that bar charts and scatterplots are effective tools for communicating quantitative data, as they both depend on position along a common scale. It also suggests that pie charts are probably not as effective a mechanism, as one is either judging area or angles.

Two important principles came into play with these experiments. The first, named *Weber's Law*, states that the likelihood of detecting a change is proportional to the relative change, not the absolute change, of a graphical attribute. Thus, the difference between a 25-centimeter line and a 26-centimeter line should be no easier to perceive than the difference between a 2.5- and a 2.6-centimeter line. This means that simply enlarging an object or otherwise changing the range of one of its attributes will not, in general, increase its effectiveness at communicating information.

A second useful principle, known as *Stevens' Law*, states that the perceived scale in absolute measurements is the actual scale raised to a power. For linear features, this power is between 0.9 and 1.1; for area features, it is between 0.6 and 0.9, and for volume features it is between 0.5 and 0.8. This means that as the dimensionality of an attribute increases, so increases the degree at which we underestimate it. This implies that using attributes such as the volume of a three-dimensional object to convey information is much less effective and much more error-prone than using area or, better yet, length (see Figure 3.35).

3.5.5   Expanding Capabilities

The experiments described in the previous three sections indicate that our abilities to perceive various stimuli, and graphical phenomena in particular, is fairly limited. If we need to communicate information with a higher capacity, we must investigate strategies for expanding our capabilities. One way, as illustrated in the previous section, is to try and reconfigure the communication task to require relative, rather than absolute, judgment. Thus, in many cases, we can supplement a visualization so that the viewer just needs to gauge whether an item's attribute is greater than, less than, or equal to some other item's attribute. This is why adding grid lines and axis tick marks is a useful and powerful addition to a visualization.

We can also increase capacity by increasing the dimensionality, as seen in the experiments on multiple stimuli. In most cases, adding another stimulus will lead to larger bit rates. However, there is likely to be a limit to the number of dimensions that can be reasonably managed. This *span of perceptual dimensionality*, according to Miller [295], is hypothesized to be about 10. Another problem with this solution is that in graphics there are a limited number of parameters that we can use (color, size, position, orientation, line/fill style, and so on), although when we discuss *glyphs* in Chapter 8 we will examine efforts to pack many more dimensions into the components of a composite graphical entity.

Another potential strategy is to reconfigure the problem to be a sequence of different absolute judgments, rather than simultaneous stimuli. In this manner, we might be able to overcome some of the loss of capacity that was shown in the experiments on measuring multiple stimuli. If the viewer is directed to examine a sequence of visualizations and compose the measurements from each, we may be able to achieve an improved communication rate. This leads to the analysis of immediate memory.

3.5.6 The Relationship to Immediate Memory

Many studies have examined human memory performance. *Immediate (short-term) memory* is used for very short-term recall, often immediately after a stimulus has been received. Many games have been devised that are based on one's immediate memory skills. Studies have shown the span of immediate memory to be approximately 7 items. In other words, people, in general, can remember with accuracy a sequence of 7 or so stimuli. One question that might arise is whether this is related to our span of absolute judgment, as the capacities are similar.

The answer is that they are unrelated. Absolute judgment is limited by the amount of information, while immediate memory is limited by the number of items, no matter how complex. Thus, they are measurements at different granularities; absolute judgment is measured in *bits* corresponding to distinct levels, while immediate memory involves *chunks* of varying size or complexity. Several experiments involving binary digits, decimal digits, letters, syllables, words, and mixtures have shown that the number of chunks that can be remembered is relatively constant. An interesting observation is that we can remember 6 or so monosyllabic words, but also 6 or so multisyllabic words.

It is conjectured that we "chunk" things at the largest logical unit. But what is that logical unit? Can we increase its complexity to increase our capacity? This process is known as *recoding*.

3.5.7   The Role of Recoding

Recoding is the process of reorganizing information into fewer chunks, with more bits of information per chunk. For example, in the process of learning Morse code, one starts by connecting patterns of dots and dashes into letters, and then longer patterns into words. This process is also found in other avenues of learning, including music and dance. A similar concept, known as *compilation*, can be found in the artificial intelligence field as a form of machine learning.

Many experiments have been designed to study the ability of humans to recode information in this manner. Experiments in recalling long strings of binary digits show nearly linear improvement with chunk size. In other words, remembering a sequence of N individual binary digits is comparable to the effort of remembering a sequence of N binary digit chunks of length 2 or 3.

One problem is that the way we perform recoding differs from person to person. We remember events by creating a verbal recoding of what we saw, and then elaborate from this coded version. This accounts for variations in witness testimonies to a crime or accident; in the recoding process, different aspects are chunked together, and depending on the complexity of the chunks, it may be difficult to recall exact details (we are convinced that our particular decoding is a very accurate depiction of what took place). It also explains how people can change their appearance fairly dramatically (make a major change in hair style, switch from glasses to contacts, gain or lose significant weight) and have it go unnoticed by friends and colleagues. As long as the new attributes fit within the decoded memories, the change may not be detected.

3.5.8 The Role of Focus and Expectation

Related to the use of multiple data coding attributes and sequences of decisions is the work reported by Chapman [67], who observed that in images with multiple attributes, but with observers only reporting on one, prior notification of focus resulted in significantly better results than postselection of focus. This may seem obvious, but it is important, as it indicates that people do better when focusing on a single attribute at a time. Recall from the experiments on judging multiple stimuli that the performance was worse (often much worse) than the combination of the capacities of the individual stimuli. Chapman's work indicates that if the user can focus attention on a small set of attributes (or one attribute), he or she can reduce the influence of the attributes that are outside of the focus group. Thus, if viewers can be trained to look for certain features in isolation and have forewarning as to what those features should be, their performance can be improved. If users are uninformed as to the features containing the most relevant information, it is less likely that they will be able to extract the desired information at the desired accuracy.

This seems directly related to change blindness, an attempt to probe the types of visual representations being built when looking at a scene. The visual system makes assumptions to fill in details outside of the focus of attention. For example, if no motion transient is seen, the visual system may assume that the scene is static. This explains why one can "miss" a big change in a location not being focused on during an eye saccade.

If this theory is accurate, prefocusing the viewer on a particular feature or feature-value would help, as one would only need to build one Boolean map to search for and/or identify what is being looked for (the target). Without prefocusing, one would build maps with some other priority, possibly building and discarding multiple maps until one hits on the right one.

3.5.9 Summary on Metrics

Many factors are involved in communicating information via the human perceptual system. The span of absolute judgment and immediate memory limits our ability to perceive information accurately. We can expand this ability by reformatting into multiple dimensions or sequences of chunks. We can also take advantage of the fact that our ability to perform relative judgment (detection) is more powerful than our absolute (measured) judgment abilities.

In terms of the implications to data visualization, for applications where absolute judgment is required, the best we can do with a single graphical attribute is between 4 and 7 values. To get a larger range of recognizable levels, we must repose the problem in multiple dimensions, do a sequence of simple decisions, or perform some type of chunking.

Alternatively, we could redefine the problem in such a way that relative, rather than absolute, judgment could be used to focus attention, with a second, more quantitatively accurate, stage following the initial focus of attention.

3.6   Cognition

Patterson et al. [314] have defined a human cognition framework for information visualization that makes direct contact with the underlying cognitive processes discussed earlier and thereby enables the induction of insight, reasoning and understanding. They define leverage points that cannot just harness and influence but also measure human cognition in visual analysis. They are exogenous and endogenous attention, chunking, reasoning with mental models, analogical reasoning, and implicit learning.

A rough overview of human cognition can be seen in Figure 3.36, which extends the visualization pipeline presented in Chapter 1.

3.7   Related Readings

Parts of the section on metrics came from the excellent article by George Miller, "The Magic Number Seven, Plus or Minus Two: Some Limits on our Capacity for Processing Information" [295].

More recent work on graphical perception is from the chapter entitled "Graphical Perception" in William S. Cleveland, *The Elements of Graphing Data* [80].

Work on AI and cognition include, Kurzweil, *The Age of Spiritual Machines* [260] and Looks et al., "Novamente: An Integrative Architecture for Artificial General Intelligence" [277]. Stephen Few provides great details on how to develop simple and effective visualizations, focusing on their interface [125].

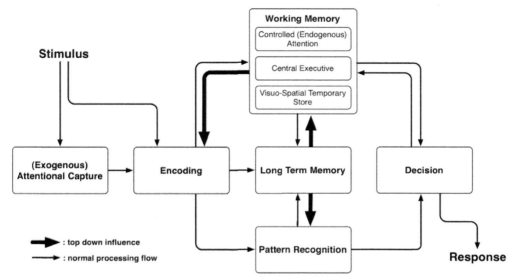

Figure 3.36. Overview of human cognition based on a dual-process framework for reasoning and decision making, which forms the backbone of our human cognition framework information visualization. The flow of information proceeds from left to right, beginning with an impinging stimulus on the left and ending with a decision being made on the right. Various components of human cognition are shown, namely encoding, working memory, pattern recognition, long-term memory, and decision making.

3.8 Exercises

1. List the features you believe you use in recognizing a friend by sight and/or by sound. How might you use related features to communicate a data set?

2. Design an experiment that would integrate an eye-tracking study with a target discovery test.

3. Design an experiment to identify which is better for visualizing a linear pattern in a large data set: a simple point plot, or a point plot where the points are circular, rectangular, colored, or vibrating. Guess at the outcome.

4. Since about 8% of males are color deficient [271] (with less than 1% for females) mostly in the red and green ranges, how would you deal with color in the display of a scatterplot?

5. Explore cultural differences on illusions or visualizations. See, for example, *The Influence of Culture on Visual Perception*, by Marshall H. Segall, Donald T. Campbell and Melville J. Herskovits (1966).

6. How would you measure cognition? How would you measure it over time?

3.9   Projects

1. Take the scatterplot code you've written. Consider some perceptual attribute you've read about and are interested in. Generate a display for a perceptual study, say a target (one objector or a pattern) to be identified within an area of distractors. Ask a few classmates if they can easily identify the target.

2. Write a program to reproduce one of the perceptual experiments, varying either a single graphical attribute or multiple ones. Start with two or three values for a given attribute, and increase this number until you (or a willing friend) start making errors over a short sequence of samples. Describe what feature you are testing, whether you are testing for absolute or relative judgment, and what your results are.

3. Using any graphics package at your disposal, design an experiment for some of the perceptual features described in this chapter.

4. Write a program that will measure a user's memory of a visualization. Describe which features of the visualization and which leverage point you are targeting.

Visualization Foundations

We have now covered the start and the end of the visualization pipeline (see Figure 4.1), namely getting data into the computer, and, on the human side, how perception and cognition help us interpret images. We have looked at one fundamental visualization, namely the scatterplot. There are many other visualization techniques and systems (see some examples in Table 4.1). To make sense of them we need to organize methods into categories or taxonomies. This is necessary for us to structure our study of the field. We first review the visualization pipeline and then discuss various ways to view the multitudes of techniques and systems that have been developed to date.

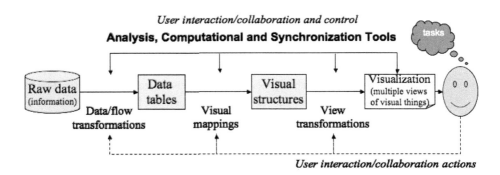

Figure 4.1.   Our reference visualization pipeline. (Image modified from [59].)

Apt	Graphviz	Parallel coordinates	Star Coordinates
Attribute Explorer	gViz	Parallel sets	Tableau
Bifocal display	H3Viewer	Perspective wall	Tablelens
Chat circle	Heatmaps	Photomesa	Tag cloud
Chernoff faces	Hyperbolic trees	Piccolo	Tango
Cone trees	Informational mural	Polka	Tarantula
Cviz	Inxight	PV-WAVE	Textarc
Data mountain	ITK	Radvis	Thebrain
Dendrograms	Jigsaw	Scatterplot matrix	ThemeMap
Disk tree	Kohonen maps	Second life	Tilebar
Document lens	Lifelines	Seeit	Treemap
Excentric labeling	Magic lens	Seenet	Trellis
Film finder	Map of science	Seesoft	VIBE
Fisheye views	Occulus	Sequoia view	VTK
Fluid text	Omniviz	Spotfire	WebBook
Galaxy	OpenDX	Star plot	XmdvTool
GGobi	Palantir	Sunburst	UVP

Table 4.1. Visualization tools, packages, and systems (not a complete list).

4.1 The Visualization Process in Detail

Let's review the steps that need to be taken to define a visualization of data. Figure 4.1 is our reference visualization process. Most visualization pipelines and systems map easily to these stages. Any transformation or computation can be placed at any of the stages. We selected this as the simplest representation of the process. We also note two key points: user interaction ideally takes place at any point in this pipeline (nodes and links), and each link is a many-to-many mapping. For example, many visualization systems have multiple visualizations at the same time on the screen, and thus have multiple representation mappings and corresponding renderings. We now focus on the transformations and processes that alter the data.

Data preprocessing and transformation. The starting point is to process the raw data into something usable by the visualization system. The first part is to make sure that the data are mapped to fundamental data types for computer ingestion. The second step entails dealing with specific application data issues such as missing values, errors in input, and data too large for processing. The data may be simulated or sampled. Missing data may require interpolation. Large data may require sampling, filtering, aggregation, or partitioning.

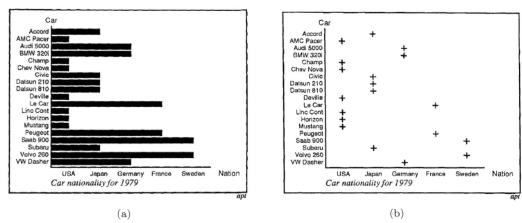

Figure 4.2.   (a) Poor use of a bar chart. (b) Better use of a scatterplot.

Mapping for visualizations. Once the data are clean, we can decide on a specific visual representation. This requires representation mappings: geometry, color, and sound, for example. It is easy to simply develop a nonsense visualization, or one that conveys the wrong information. Figure 4.2(a) shows an improper use of a bar chart. By having the bars extend over each of the x-coordinate tick marks, there is an implication that the x-coordinate is involved, when no such association occurs. For example, the Volvo, second row from the bottom, cuts across several x-values (USA, Japan, Germany, ...) until it gets to Sweden. A better representation is the one in Figure 4.2(b), but even that one can be significantly improved.

Crucial influences on the visualization of data sets are expressiveness and effectiveness. It is an interesting exercise to develop measures or metrics for expressiveness and effectiveness; after all, we do use them as measures.

Rendering transformations. The final stage involves mapping from geometry data to the image. This includes interfacing with a computer graphics Application Programmer's Interface (API). We need to select the viewing parameters, shading technique if 3D, device transformations (for display, printers, ...). This stage of the pipeline is very dependent on the underlying graphics library. In Appendix C and on the book's web site, we have provided examples using OpenGL, Processing, Java, and Flex. There are many others.

We have already precisely defined measures and distance metrics. We now define two measures of visualizations mathematically. Such measures and modifications can actually be applied at all stages of the pipeline. This is becoming increasingly important as we want to measure information transfer. The measures of visualization are:

Expressiveness. An expressive visualization presents all the information, and only the information. Expressiveness thus measures the concentration of information. Given information that we actually display to the user, we can define one measure of expressiveness as the ratio M_{exp} of that information, divided by the information we want to present to the user. We have $0 \leq M_{\mathrm{exp}} \leq 1$. If $M_{\mathrm{exp}} = 1$, we have ideal expressiveness. If the information displayed is less than that desired to be presented, then $M_{exp} < 1$. If $M_{\mathrm{exp}} > 1$, we are presenting too much information. Expressing additional information is potentially dangerous, because it may not be correct and may interfere with the interpretation of the essential information. Such a measure of expressiveness may be extended to include various sets of information, in which case it becomes a function on sets (see projects).

Effectiveness. A visualization is effective when it can be interpreted accurately and quickly and when it can be rendered in a cost-effective manner. Effectiveness thus measures a specific cost of information perception. We can define a measure of effectiveness M_{eff} as some ratio similar to that for expressiveness. However, it is a bit more complex. What we want is a measure such that for small data sets we measure interpretation time (since rendering is usually very fast) and when that time increases, either due to the increasing complexity or the size of the data set, M_{eff} decreases, emphasizing the rendering time. We define

$$M_{\mathrm{eff}} = 1/(1 + \mathrm{interpret} + \mathrm{render}).$$

We then have $0 < M_{\mathrm{eff}} \leq 1$. The larger M_{eff} is, the greater the visualization's effectiveness. If M_{eff} is small, then either the interpretation time is very large, or the rendering time is large. If M_{eff} is large (close to 1), then both the interpretation and the rendering time are very small.

Figures 4.3(a) and 4.3(b) show displays for which E_{exp} can be considered very close, if not identical, for the task of presenting the car prices and mileage for 1979; both display all the information, and only the information, and both can be rendered quickly (there's very little data to be displayed). However, E_{eff} is different. The information in Figure 4.3(b) can

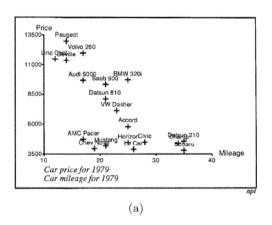
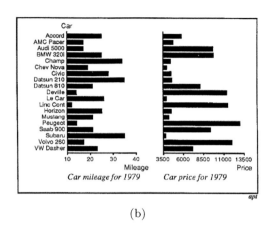

(a)   (b)

Figure 4.3.   (a) Scatterplot using plus as symbol provides good query-answering capabilities, but is slower for simple one-variable queries. (b) Bar charts clearly display cost and mileage, but don't provide as much flexibility in answering some other queries.

be interpreted more accurately or more quickly than that in Figure 4.3(a) for some questions. For example, which car has the best mileage? However, if we ask which car has the best mileage under $11,000, Figure 4.3(b) is less efficient.

4.2   Semiology of Graphical Symbols

We consider a visual object called a *graphical symbol*. Figure 4.4(a) is an example. Such symbols are easily recognized. They often make up parts of visualizations (arrows, labels, ...). We will look at how a graphical object or representation can be well designed, and how it is perceived. The science of graphical symbols and marks is called *semiology*. Every possible construction in the Euclidean plane is a graphical representation made up of graphical symbols. This includes diagrams, networks, maps, plots, and other common visualizations. Semiology uses the qualities of the plane and objects on the plane to produce similarity features, ordering features, and proportionality features of the data that are visible for human consumption.

There are numerous characteristics of visualizations, of images, or of graphics made up of symbols. We describe some of these in the following sections.

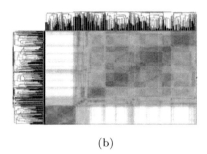

(a)   (b)

Figure 4.4.   (a) Symbol with obvious meaning. (b) Representation with complex meaning.

4.2.1 Symbols and Visualizations

Figure 4.4(a) contains an image that is universally recognizable (yield sign). Such images become preattentively recognizable with experience. Figure 4.4(b), on the other hand, requires a great deal of attention to understand; the first steps are to recognize patterns within that figure.

Figure 4.4(a) is perceived in one step, and that step is simply an association of its meaning. Figure 4.4(b) takes two steps for understanding. The first identifies the major elements of the image, with the second identifying the various relationships between these. With attentive effort, the symbols are perceived (transferred from long-term memory). Patterns, mostly subsets of groups or information having perceptual or cognitive commonality, are extracted from the overall image. The last step is identifying the most interesting things (such as the most interesting point clusters, genes, countries, or products), that is, those having the most interesting or special features.

Important: Without external (cognitive) identification, a graphic is unusable. The external identification must be directly readable and understandable. Since much of our perception is driven by physical interpretations, meaningful images must have easily interpretable x-, y-, and z-dimensions and the graphics elements of the image must be clear.

Discovery of relations or patterns occurs through two main steps. The first is a mapping between any relationship of the graphic symbols and the data that these symbols represent. In other words, any pattern on the screen must imply a pattern in the data. If it does not, then it is an artifact of the selected representation (and is disturbing). This can happen. Similarly, any perceived pattern variation in the graphic or symbol cognitively implies such a similar variation in the data. The same is true for ordering. Any perceived order in graphic symbols is directly correlated with a perceived

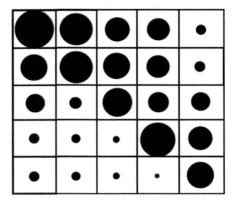

Figure 4.5.   Matrix representation of a set of relationships between nodes in a graph. The size
                   represents the strength of the relationship.

corresponding order between the data, and vice versa. If some order pops
out visually and such an order is not present in the data, we are misled. In
summary:

- similarity in data structure ⟺ visual similarity of corresponding
  symbols;

- order between data items ⟺ visual order between corresponding
  symbols.

4.2.2   Features of Graphics

Graphics have three (or more) dimensions. Figure 4.5 shows a matrix with
points of various sizes within each cell. Every point of the graphic can be
interpreted as a relation between a position in x and a position in y. The
points vary in size, providing a third dimension or variable to interpret.
In effect, this can be considered a value in z. This produces a one-to-one
correspondence between a 3D view with height and a 2D view with size,
thus different interpretations for the z value. Several relationships pop out,
such as the size of the circles along the diagonal (the circles in the upper
right are larger than those in the lower left). The set of all points either in
the 2D or 3D image represents the totality of the relations among the three
dimensions x, y, and z, and any patterns present imply a pattern in the
data.

Figure 4.6.   We identify the tree as the dominant feature of this image, rather than the individual parts that make up the tree.

When looking at Figure 4.6, we immediately see two tree branches. The eye sees either branch independent from the number of its leaves. The graphic can contain a very large number of single data items, themselves graphics, with the only possible limitations being technical ones, such as making sure that the various graphic symbols are distinguishable from each other. But even then, perhaps the texture resulting from the en masse number of symbols may produce an object of interest. The eye can preattentively see the various distributions of symbols. As we saw in Chapter 3, the eye can be directed toward specific elements or groups of elements in an image, while registering spontaneously the three levels of information.

Rules of a graphic. All graphics are represented on the screen. All objects will be interpreted as flat (in 2D) or as physical objects (in 3D). As we saw in Chapter 3, any perceptual interpretation of the data will assume that the graphic represents parts of a 3D scene. So 3D is the medium by which we need to interpret the graphic.

We can identify some fundamental rules:

1. The aim of a graphic is to discover groups or orders in x, and groups or orders in y, that are formed on z-values;

2. (x, y, z)-construction enables in all cases the discovery of these groups;

3. Within the (x, y, z)-construction, permutations and classifications solve the problem of the upper level of information;

4. Every graphic with more than three factors that differs from the (x, y, z)-construction destroys the unity of the graphic and the upper level of information; and

5. Pictures must be read and understood by the human.

Analysis of a graphic. In Chapter 3, we discussed perception and cognition. When analyzing a graphic, we first perceive groups of objects (preattentively). We then attempt to characterize these groups (cognitively). Finally, we examine special cases not within the groups or relationships between the groups (combination of both). This process can be done at many levels and with many different visualizations. Supporting analysis plays a significant role (for example, we can cluster the data and show the results of the computation, hence speeding up the likely perception of groups).

4.3   The Eight Visual Variables

The application of graphics to communicate information requires an understanding of graphic primitives and their properties. For the most part, all graphic primitives will be termed *marks*. One way to encode data for display is to map different data values to different marks and their attributes. However, marks by themselves do not define informative displays, since all the marks would simply obscure all previously drawn marks; it is only through the spatial arrangement of marks that informative displays are created. The positioning of marks within a display space provides a means to map or reveal additional properties of the underlying data, including similarity and distributions. Once the layout and types of marks are specified, then additional graphical properties can be applied to each mark. Marks can vary in size, can be displayed using different colors, and can be mapped to different orientations, all of which can be driven by data to convey information.

    In total there are eight ways in which graphical objects can encode information, i.e., *eight visual variables*: position, shape, size, brightness, color, orientation, texture, and motion. These eight variables can be adjusted as necessary to maximize the effectiveness of a visualization to convey information. Nonetheless, when defining a visualization, it is important to remember that the result will be an image that is to be interpreted by the human visual system and that is subject to all the perception rules and problems identified in Chapter 3.

4.3.1 Position

The first and most important visual variable is that of *position*, the placement of representative graphics within some display space, be it one-, two-, or three-dimensional. Position has the greatest impact on the display of information, because the spatial arrangement of graphics is the first step in reading a visualization. In essence, the maximization of the spread of representational graphics throughout the display space maximizes the amount of information communicated, to some degree. The visualization display with the worst case positioning scheme maps all graphics to the exact same position; consequently, only the last-drawn graphic is seen, and little information is exchanged. The best positioning scheme maps each graphic to unique positions, such that all the graphics can be seen with no overlaps. Interestingly, for the standard computer screen with a resolution setting of 1024 by 768, the maximum number of individual pixels is only 786,432; hence, if each data representation is mapped to a unique pixel, we are still not able to display a million values. And since most graphics employed to represent data take up considerably more visual real estate than a single pixel, the actual number of displayable marks diminishes rapidly. Example displays are shown in Figure 4.7.

The selection of variables used to organize data within a display can answer a variety of questions. First, where do most of the data values fall? Does the data fit any well-known statistical distribution? Are there visible trends in the data? Furthermore, through the use of perception and the relationships of proximity, symmetry, and other Gestalt principles described in Chapter 1, are there clusters and structures within the data?

In addition to selecting appropriate variables to organize the display space and to present values with representative graphics, scales can be applied to variables to remap values to reveal structures. Although scaling is generally not necessary, there are times when it must be used. The first type of scale is the *linear scale*; in this case, the mapping is simply an offset, and a stretching or shrinking of the range. The second type of scale is the

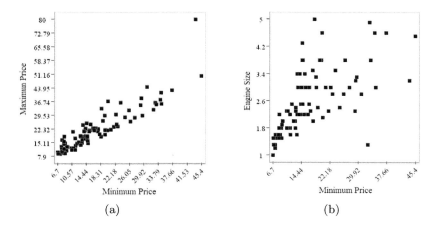

Figure 4.7. Example visualizations: (a) using position to convey information. Displayed here is the minimum price versus the maximum price for cars with a 1993 model year. The spread of points appears to indicate a linear relationship between minimum and maximum price; (b) another visualization using a different set of variables. This figure compares minimum price with engine size for the 1993 cars data set. Unlike (a), there does not appear to be a strong relationship between these two variables.

logarithmic scale that is used to map exponentially increasing variables into more compact ranges.

Although linear and logarithmic scales are applied to a single data variable, there are times when two-dimensional based mappings need to be applied, especially for cartography and the generation of maps. The mapping of two or more variables is more correctly termed a *projection* from one data space to another, the second generally of a lower dimensionality. Various projections used for defining maps are presented in Chapter 6. Many of these projection techniques can also be used for nonspatial data, as described in Chapter 8.

In addition to displaying representational graphics and using various scales or projections, when working with one, two, or three variables, it is common to add supplementary graphics to describe the space. *Axes* are graphical elements that provide additional information for understanding how the visual space is defined. Axes typically contain tick-marks indicating intervals of the data range, and text labels that provide data values. An axis title usually contains the name of the data variable being mapped.

Figure 4.8.   Several examples of different marks or glyphs that can be used.

4.3.2 Mark

The second visual variable is the *mark* or shape: points, lines, areas, volumes, and their compositions. Marks are graphic primitives that represent data. For example, both visualizations in Figure 4.7 use the default point to display individual values. Any graphical object can be used as a mark, including symbols, letters, and words (see Figure 4.8). When working purely with marks, it is important not to consider differences in sizes, shades of intensity, or orientation, as these are additional visual variables that will be described later.

When using marks, it is important to consider how well one mark can be differentiated from other marks. Within a single visualization there can be hundreds or thousands of marks to observe; therefore, we try not to select marks that are too similar. For example, a set of marks that provides easy reading is shown in Figure 4.8 and used in a scatterplot in Figure 4.9.

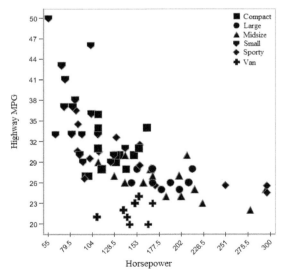

Figure 4.9.   This visualization uses shapes to distinguish between different car types in a plot comparing highway MPG and horsepower. Clusters are clearly visible, as well as some outliers.

Figure 4.10.   Example sizes to encode data.

Another is the set (T and L) or (+ and −), that harnesses our perceptual systems (see examples in Chapter 3). The goal is to be able to easily distinguish between different marks quickly, while maintaining an overall view of the projected data space. Also, different mark shapes in a given visualization must have similar area and complexity, to avoid visually emphasizing one or more of them inadvertently.

4.3.3   Size (Length, Area, and Volume)

The previous two visual variables, position and marks, are required to define a visualization. Without these two variables there would not be much to see. The remaining visual variables affect the way individual representations are displayed; these are the graphical properties of marks other than their shape.

The third visual variable and first graphic property is *size*. Size determines how small or large a mark will be drawn (see Figure 4.10). Size easily maps to interval and continuous data variables, because that property supports gradual increments over some range. And while size can also be applied to categorical data, it is more difficult to distinguish between marks of near similar size, and thus size can only support categories with very small cardinality.

A confounding problem with using size is the type of mark. For points, lines, and curves the use of size works well, in that size provides a relatively quantifiable measure of how marks relate, as illustrated in Figure 4.11. However, when marks are represented with graphics that contain sufficient area, the quantitative aspects of size fall, and the differences between marks becomes more qualitative.

4.3.4   Brightness

The fourth visual variable is *brightness* or *luminance*. Brightness is the second visual variable used to modify marks to encode additional data variables. While it is possible to use the complete numerical range of brightness values, as discussed in Chapter 3, human perception cannot distinguish between all pairs of brightness values. Consequently, brightness can be used

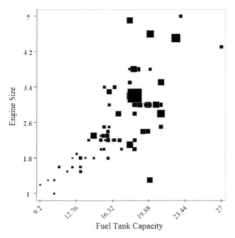

Figure 4.11.   This is a visualization of the 1993 car models data set, showing engine size versus fuel tank capacity. Size is mapped to maximum price charged.

to provide relative difference for large interval and continuous data variables, or for accurate mark distinction for marks drawn using a reduced sampled brightness scale, as shown in Figure 4.12. Furthermore, it is recommended that a perceptually linear brightness scale be used, which defines a step-based brightness scale that maximizes perceived differences. An example visualization using brightness to display information is shown in Figure 4.13.

4.3.5   Color

The fifth visual variable is *color*; see Chapter 3 for a detailed discussion of color and of how humans perceive color. While brightness affects how white or black colors are displayed, it is not actually color. Color can be defined by the two parameters, hue and saturation. Figure 4.14 displays Microsoft's color selector with hue on the horizontal axis and saturation on the vertical axis. Hue provides what most think of as color: the dominant wavelength

Figure 4.12.   Brightness scale for mapping values to the display.

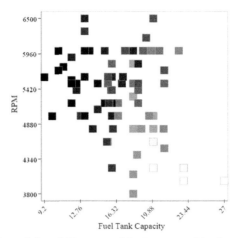

Figure 4.13.   Another visualization of the 1993 car models data set, this time illustrating the use of brightness to convey car width (the darker the points, the wider the vehicle).

Figure 4.14.   Microsoft hue/saturation color selector.

from the visual spectrum. Saturation is the level of hue relative to gray, and drives the purity of the color to be displayed.

The use of color to display information requires mapping data values to individual colors. The mapping of color usually entails defining color maps that specify the relationship between value ranges and color values. Color maps are useful for handling both interval and continuous data variables, since a color map is generally defined as a continuous range of hue and saturation values, as illustrated in Figure 4.15 and Figure 4.16. When working with categorical or interval data with very low cardinality, it is generally acceptable to manually select colors for individual data values, which are se-

Figure 4.15.   Example color map that can be used to encode a data variable.

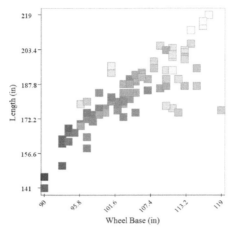

Figure 4.16.   A visualization of the 1993 car models, showing the use of color to display the car's length. Here length is also associated with the y-axis and is plotted against wheelbase. In this figure, blue indicates a shorter length, while yellow indicates a longer length.

lected to optimize the distinction between data types. Many books and articles have been written on color selection for effective communication [45,271]. An excellent web resource for color selection is www.colorbrewer2.org. Figure 4.17 shows examples of popular color maps for visualization.

4.3.6 Orientation

The sixth visual variable is *orientation* or direction. Orientation is a principal graphic component behind iconographic stick figure displays, and is

Figure 4.17.   Some common color maps: standard linear grayscale, rainbow, heated, blue to cyan, and blue to yellow.

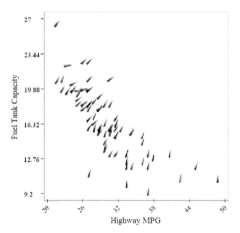

Figure 4.18.   Example orientations of a representation graphic, where the lowest value maps to
                 the mark pointing upward and increasing values rotate the mark in a clockwise
                 rotation.

tied directly to preattentive vision (see Chapter 3). This graphic property
describes how a mark is rotated in connection with a data variable. Clearly,
orientation cannot be used with all marks; for instance, a circle looks the
same under any rotation. The best marks for using orientation are those
with a natural single axis; the graphic exhibits symmetry about a major
axis. These marks can display the entire range of orientations. For example, Figure 4.18 displays a mark that looks like an elongated triangle, which
clearly defines a single major axis. While this figure limits the range or orientation to 90 degrees, this mark could easily map to the entire 360-degree
circle, as used within flow fields. Figure 4.19 displays a sample visualization
that uses this triangle-based mark.

Figure 4.19.   Sample visualization of the 1993 car models data set depicting using highway miles-
                 per-gallon versus fuel tank capacity (position) with the additional data variable,
                 midrange price, used to adjust mark orientation.

Figure 4.20.   Six possible example textures that could be used to identify different data values.

4.3.7 Texture

The seventh visual variable is *texture*. Texture can be considered as a combination of many of the other visual variables, including marks (texture elements), color (associated with each pixel in a texture region), and orientation (conveyed by changes in the local color). Dashed and dotted lines, which constitute some of the textures of linear features, can be readily differentiated, as long as only a modest number of distinct types exist. Varying the color of the segments or dots can also be perceived as a texture.

Texture is most commonly associated with a polygon, region, or surface. In 3D, a texture can be an attribute of the geometry, such as with ridges of varying height, frequency, and orientation. Similarly, it can be associated with the color of the graphical entity, with regular or irregular variations in color with different ranges and distributions (see Figures 4.20 and 4.21). In fact, geometric textures can be readily emulated with color textures, with

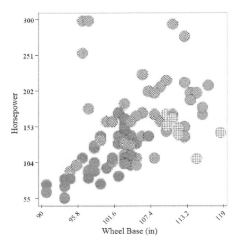

Figure 4.21.   Example visualization using texture to provide additional information about the 1993 car models data set, showing the relationship between wheelbase versus horsepower (position) as related to car types, depicted by different textures.

color variations similar to those obtained via lighting effects. Finally, the distribution and orientation of marks themselves can form regions of texture.

4.3.8   Motion

The eighth visual variable is *motion*. In fact, motion can be associated with any of the other visual variables, since the way a variable changes over time can convey more information. One common use of motion is in varying the speed at which a change is occurring (such as position change or flashing, which can be seen as changing the opacity). The eye will be drawn to graphical entities based not only on similarities in behavior, but also on outliers. The other aspect of motion is in the direction; for position, this can be up, down, left, right, diagonal, or basically any slope, while for other variables it can be larger/smaller, brighter/dimmer, steeper/shallower angles, and so on. As conveying this concept is difficult on the static page, we've included some examples on the book's web site.

4.3.9   Effects of Visual Variables

Different visual variables can serve different purposes. We can categorize these purposes in a variety of ways. Below, we give one such categorization, provide some examples, and indicate which visual variables are effective for the purpose.

Selective visual variables. After coding with such variables, different data values are spontaneously divided by the human into distinguished groups (e.g., for visualizing nominal values).

- Size (length, area/volume);
- Brightness;
- Texture;
- Color (only primary colors): varies with the brightness value;
- Direction/orientation.

Associative visual variables. All factors have same visibility (e.g., for visualizing nominal values).

- Texture (see Figure 4.22(a));
- Color (see Figure 4.22(b));

Figure 4.22.   Example associative variables: (a) textures; (b) colors; (c) direction; (d) shape.

- Direction/orientation (see Figure 4.22(c));
- Shape (see Figure 4.22(d)).

Ordinal visual variables. After coding with such variables, different data values are spontaneously ordered by the human (e.g., for visualizing ordinal and quantitative data).

- Texture;
- Size (see Figure 4.24 right);
- Brightness (see Figure 4.24 left).

Proportional visual variables. In addition, these variables obtain a direct association of the relative size (e.g., for visualizing ordinal and quantitative data).

- Size (length, area/volume);
- Direction/orientation;
- Brightness.

Separating visual variables. All elements are visible (the rest are not visible).

- Texture (see Figure 4.23);
- Color;
- Direction/orientation;
- Shape.

Figure 4.23.   Example of separating texture.

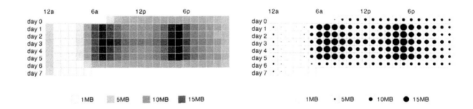

Figure 4.24.   Examples of ordinal visual variables. Image courtesy of Michael Barry.

4.4 Historical Perspective

Although many examples of the various visualization techniques can be found, we still lack a comprehensive language to describe our graphical creations. The art of visualization, the principles of graphics and their comprehension, is generally understood. But as a science, we have yet to define a consistent formalism for general visualizations, or even just for the class of data visualizations. Researchers are now starting to look into such an idea through the development of various models; Robertson first proposed this need for formal models as a foundation for visualization systems [341]. In this section, we look at a number of efforts over the years to formalize the field of visualization. The following section contains descriptions of some taxonomies of visualization techniques.

4.4.1   Bertin (1967) Semiology of Graphics

In 1967, Jacques Bertin, possibly the most important figure in visualization theory, published his *Sémiologie Graphique* [34]. This was the first rigorous attempt at defining graphics and its application to the portrayal of information. Bertin presents the fundamentals of information encoding via graphic representations as a semiology, a science dealing with sign systems. His first key point is the strict separation of content (the information to encode) from the container (the properties of the graphic system). To fully comprehend a sign system, one must first completely understand the primitive elements that define such a system. Consequently, Bertin embarks on defining a graphical vocabulary.

Bertin's graphical vocabulary, shown in Table 4.2, identifies some very specific graphical primitives that correspond to perceptual attributes, graphic qualities that are perceptually identifiable. A graphic is defined as a combination of plane properties (*implantation* plus *imposition*) and *retinal variables* (visual variables above the plane).

Bertin notes that the plane "is so familiar that its properties seem self-evident, but the most familiar things are often the most poorly understood"; he goes on to define the plane as homogeneous with two dimensions. It is important here to remember that the plane for Bertin is a plain sheet of white paper of a standard size, "visible at a 'glance.'" The plane is marked by *implantations*, classes of representations that constitute the elementary figures of plane geometry: points, lines, and areas. These three types of figures are organized in the two planar dimensions by the *imposition*, dividing graphics into four groups: diagrams, networks, maps, and symbols. With the *implantations* and an *imposition*, a visualization is specified.

The third and final component is the graphic representations utilizing *retinal variables*, graphic variations designed for visual perception. These variations affect the *implantations* and are depicted "above" the graphic plane. There are six *retinal variables* identified by experimental psychology: *size* (height, area, or number), *value* (saturation), *texture* (fineness or coarseness), *color* (hue), *orientation* (angular displacement), and *shape*. Bertin then defines various levels of organization specifying how these variables can be combined (see [34] for further explanations).

Marks	Points, lines, and areas
Positional	Two planar dimensions
Retinal	Size, value, texture, color, orientation, and shape

Table 4.2.   Bertin's graphical vocabulary.

4.4.2 Mackinlay (1986) APT

Mackinlay introduced a design for an automated graphical presentation designer of relational information, named APT (A Presentation Tool) [284]. APT was designed to extract some information from a database and to render a graphical design that presented this information. A graphical design is an abstract description of the graphical techniques encoding information. Like Bertin, Mackinlay focused his research on static two-dimensional presentations, such as bar charts, scatterplots, and connected graphs; however, Mackinlay went on to describe graphical languages, defining graphical presentations as sentences of these languages:

> A graphical sentence s is defined to be a collection of tuples: $s \subset \{<o, l >: o \in O \wedge l \in L\}$, where O is a set of graphical objects and L is a set of locations. Each tuple, which is called a *located object*, indicates the placement of an object at a given location. The syntax of a *graphical language* is defined to be a set of well-formed graphical sentences. [284]

Two graphic design criteria were then identified for these languages: first, the *expressiveness criterion*, stating that the graphical languages must express the desired information; and second, the *effectiveness criterion*, requiring for any given situation that the graphical languages must effectively utilize the display medium and the human visual system. Mackinlay based these criteria on the perceptual experiments of Cleveland and McGill [79].

The important aspect of Mackinlay's work pertains to his *composition algebra*, a collection of primitive graphic languages and composition operators that can form complex presentations. Mackinlay mentioned that his idea for this composition algebra occurred to him after looking at a particular diagram and "realizing that many presentations could be described as compositions of a set of primitive languages." Starting with a modified graphical vocabulary from Bertin (see Table 4.3), (although three-dimensional positions and temporal properties are not discussed), Mackinlay defined the *basis set* of primitive graphical languages (see Table 4.4). This basis set is then transformed into syntactical structures.

Marks	Points, lines, and areas
Positional	1D, 2D, and 3D
Temporal	Animation
Retinal	Color, shape, size, saturation, texture, and orientation

Table 4.3. Mackinlay's graphical vocabulary, extended from Bertin.

Encoding Technique	Primitive Graphical Language
Retinal-list	Color, shape, size, saturation, texture, orientation
Single-position	Horizontal axis, vertical axis
Apposed-position	Line chart, bar chart, plot chart
Map	Road map, topographic map
Connection	Tree, acyclic graph, network
Misc. (angle, contain, ...)	Pie chart, Venn diagram, ...

Table 4.4.   Mackinlay's basis set of primitive graphical languages.

Three principles are defined for composing two presentations by merging graphics that encode the same information. First is the *double-axes composition*: the composition of two graphical sentences that have identical horizontal and vertical axes. Second is the *single-axis composition*, which aligns two sentences that have identical horizontal or vertical axes. Third is the *mark composition* for merging mark sets by pairing each and every mark of one set with a compatible mark of the other set. Mackinlay then goes on to define various properties of these compositions, and finally the implementation within his APT system.

4.4.3   Bergeron and Grinstein (1989) Visualization Reference Model

The Visualization Reference Model by Bergeron and Grinstein defines an abstraction of the visualization problem, which establishes a mapping from the underlying data space to a physical representation [30]. Based on the conventional graphics system's viewing pipeline, the model is represented by a conceptual visualization pipeline. This pipeline is organized into four stages. The first stage identifies the source and provides appropriate information about the data structure. Standardized data from the previous stage enters the model transformation stage which defines appropriate projections of the source data space to a usable representation data space. Next, the view specification stage identifies the appropriate mappings from the transformed data space to visual representations. Finally, an association stage performs the generation of graphics defined by the representations and encoded with the data, resulting in the perceptual stimulation of the data, including both graphic and sound representations.

4.4.4   Wehrend and Lewis (1990)

Wehrend and Lewis also defined a mechanism for automatically defining visualizations [456]. They constructed a large catalog of encoding techniques and their effective uses. The catalog is arranged as a two-dimensional matrix classified as *objects* and *operations*. The objects identify the problems and are grouped together based on their target domains, while the operations identify groups of similar goals. The catalog is filled with problems (tasks to perform) and solutions (visualization techniques that provide answers). The resulting catalog matches domain tasks and desired goals with appropriate visualization techniques. Wehrend and Lewis surveyed numerous encoding techniques described in the literature and identified suitable cells for each within the matrix. Although the ideas for an automated system were never implemented, Beshers points out that the catalog would prove especially useful as a visualization knowledge base for such a system [36].

4.4.5 Robertson (1990) Natural Scene Paradigm

The Natural Scene Paradigm introduced by Robertson aims to visually display data represented by identifiable properties of realistic scenes [343]. Robertson reasoned that people have highly developed skills for analyzing multiple aspects of natural scenes, and aimed to exploit these skills for multivariate analysis. *Natural scene views* are defined as two- or three-dimensional spatial surfaces with spectral and temporal variables. Visual properties such as surface height, material, density, phase, and wetness are defined and ranked, based on perceptual characteristics. To these characteristics, data variables are matched appropriately to generate data views that match interpretation requirements. The matching procedure takes into consideration the priority ordering of the interpretation aims, and selects corresponding natural scene representations to maximize the desired aims.

4.4.6 Roth (1991) Visage and SAGE

Roth et al. created Visage [349], a prototype user-interface environment for exploring information, which incorporates SAGE, a knowledge-based automatic graphic design tool, and extends the ideas of Mackinlay for general two-dimensional graphics [348]. The primary contribution of Visage is its "information-centric" approach, where the central focus of user interaction is connected directly to the data elements (graphic representations). The whole environment is based on two basic object types: *elements* and *frames*. The elements are the various data representations, the graphic objects of a visualization. The frames serve as the containers for marks.

Data Objects	Position	Axis, table, keys, network nodes
	Labels	Size, color, length
Correspondence Objects	Points, bars, links, lines, and spatial offsets	

Table 4.5.   SAGE's graphical objects.

As part of Visage, SAGE adds a knowledge-based automatic system for intelligent graphics presentation. Although SAGE is designed with two primary components, graphics and natural language, we are only interested in the specification of visualizations, the graphical support for explanations. SAGE defines two types of graphical objects that encode either the elements of data sets or the correspondence between pairs of elements in two sets (see Table 4.5). The data representations are encoded via positions and retinal variables. Marks and their offsets define the correspondence objects.

As with the other models, SAGE also implements a number of composition operations. Like APT, SAGE includes the axis and mark compositions defined by Mackinlay. In addition, Sage includes four other operators:

1. for merging display edges;

2. for merging retinal techniques, textural techniques, or gauges;

3. for merging network nodes used to build multirelational graphs;

4. for merging object labels with axis labels or text columns, permitting the alignment of graphical techniques in a table.

4.4.7   Casner (1991) BOZ

BOZ, developed by Stephen Casner, is an automated graphic design and presentation tool to assist in performing specific tasks [63]. The main focus of BOZ is to replace logical task descriptions with perceptually equivalent tasks by encoding logical inferences (mental arithmetic or numerical comparisons) with perceptual inferences (shortest distance and average size), from which solutions can be visually obtained. BOZ can be used to design different presentations of the same information customized to the requirements of different tasks. This framework consists of five components:

1. a logical task description language for describing information-processing tasks;

2. a perceptual operator substitution component for converting logical task descriptions to perceptual operators;

3. a perceptual data structuring component that collects sharable perceptual operators into more complex graphical objects;

4. a perceptual operator selection component for defining detailed perceptual procedures and their accompanying graphics; and

5. a rendering component for displaying the resulting graphical designs.

The logical task description language provides a means of describing the information-processing task to BOZ. It contains two basic components: notation for expressing logical facts, and notation for describing logical procedures that manipulate the logical facts. Logical facts are defined as relational tuples of the form (*attribute, object, value*), where *attribute* names some property of the *object* with the specified *value*. Logical procedures require three parts.

1. A set of domain set definitions specifying the data schema;

2. A set of logical operator definitions that includes an operator name, a list of logical facts, and a single logical fact to compute. Logical operators are one of two types: a search operator for querying, or a computation operator for performing arithmetic or logical processing;

3. The main body of the logical procedure is an ordered sequence of calls to the set of defined logical operators.

The perceptual operator substitution component identifies appropriately equivalent perceptual operators to replace the prescribed logical operators. This component contains a catalog of perceptual operators organized around a set of primitive graphical languages (see Table 4.6), plus a substitution algorithm based on some underlying perceptual operator equivalence classes. A perceptual operator qualifies as a substitute for a logical operator if and only if the logical operator can be categorized in the same equivalence class as the perceptual operator.

Horizontal Position (100)	Area (10)	Line Thickness (3)
Vertical Position (100)	Shading (4)	Line Dashing (2)
Height (50)	Connectivity (8)	Shape (5)
Width (50)	Color (12)	Visibility (2)
Line Length (50)	Labels (∞)	Tabular (∞)

Table 4.6.   Casner's primitive graphical languages. The numbers indicate Casner's original upper limits on the number of distinct values that each primitive can practically encode.

Next, the perceptual data structure component analyzes each logical operator by identifying associated domain sets and their associations with the logical operators. This component produces a perceptual data structure specification that outlines the appropriate visualizations that will be used to support the input task, the information that should appear, and how the information is to be grouped. However, this component does not decide how the information is to be graphically encoded within visualizations. Here, a feature space is introduced, defined by the cross product of the specified input domain sets. Vectors are then defined over this feature space for each logical operator. These vectors are then organized to define the underlying data space of the resulting visualization.

The resulting vector relationships are then used by the perceptual operator selection component. The selection component chooses appropriate perceptual operators to substitute for each logical operator in such a way as to maximize the perceptual gain of the resulting visualization. This procedure assumes that the set of primitive graphical properties has been previously defined to include their appropriateness and effectiveness to render mapped information. Here, Casner uses a two-tier ranking system that is a generalization of the approach used within Mackinlay's APT program [284]. Finally, the rendering component displays the resulting graphical facts onto the computer screen.

4.4.8 Beshers and Feiner (1992) AutoVisual

AutoVisual is an automatic system for designing visualizations within the *n-Vision* visualization system [35, 36]. The n-Vision system implements the *worlds-within-worlds* visualization technique that recursively defines subspace coordinate systems, and is defined as a hierarchy of *interactors* consisting of four components: encoding objects, encoding spaces, selections, and a user interface [119].

AutoVisual supports explore, search, and compare operators using task operators and task selections to define the user's specification. With these task operators, users specify a set of visualization tasks to be performed on a set of data relations. Resulting displays are defined by combinations of "ready-made" graph types, using the worlds-within-worlds technique. Appropriate displays use a modified version of Mackinlay's *expressiveness* and *effectiveness* criteria that supports interactive visualizations.

In support of interactive visualizations, AutoVisual incorporates rendering time information about each encoding technique into the selection process. To ensure interactivity within the environment, encoding techniques that would reduce the resulting interactive performance are excluded from consideration in the encoding process [37].

4.4.9 Senay and Ignatius (1994) VISTA

Senay and Ignatius extended the work of Mackinlay, but focused on scientific data visualization. They developed VISTA (Visualization Tool Assistant), a knowledge-based system for visualization design [370]. Senay and Ignatius, like Bertin and Mackinlay, implement composition rules for the generation of complex visualizations from simple visualization techniques. They start by identifying three sub-processes defining the visualization pipeline: data manipulation, visualization mapping, and rendering. These three transformations process the data into graphic representations that are rendered to a display. From this, they classify system knowledge into five categories: data characterization, visualization vocabulary, primitive visualization techniques, composition rules, and visual perception rules. As in Mackinlay's system, VISTA incorporates human perceptual experimental results, plus heuristic rules defining a visualization's *effectiveness*.

Senay and Ignatius define two types of marks, simple and compound, as defined in Table 4.7. Similar to Bertin and Mackinlay, VISTA's marks encode data using three variation methods: positional, temporal, and retinal. Having defined the vocabulary and primitives of visualizations, five composition rules are defined. Through the application of these rules, pairs of visualization techniques are combined to form composite techniques for displaying multidimensional data. The *mark composition*, Figure 4.25(a), merges marks by pairing each mark of one technique with a compatible set of marks of the other, identical to Mackinlay's mark composition. The second rule, *composition by superimposition*, Figure 4.25(b), merges marks by superimposing one mark set onto the other. The *composition by union*, Figure 4.25(c), combines marks using set union. Fourth, *composition by transparency*, Figure 4.25(d) combines two visualization techniques by manipulating the opacity values of marks belonging to either or both visualization techniques. Finally, *composition by intersection*, Figure 4.25(e), computes the intersection of visualization techniques and then superimposes this intersection onto one of

Simple marks	Points, lines, areas, and volumes
Compound marks	Contour lines, glyphs, flow ribbons, and particles

Table 4.7.   VISTA's visualization marks.

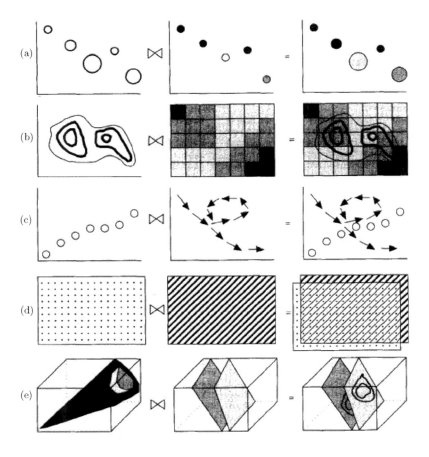

Figure 4.25.   VISTA's composition rules [370, Figure 3]. (Image © 1994 IEEE.)

the components. Rules two and three are similar to Mackinlay's double-axes composition.

4.4.10   Hibbard (1994) Lattice Model

Hibbard presents a *lattice model* for describing visualizations [187]. Unlike the previous graphical models that focused on the graphic primitives, the lattice model focuses on data to display transformations. Hibbard notes, "data objects are approximations to mathematical objects and real displays are approximations to ideal displays" [187]. He considers the process of specifying visualizations as a mathematical transformation from data to displays.

His general idea is to define a data model (a set U of data objects) with a display model (a set V of displays), and a visualization process (a function D: $U \rightarrow V$).

The data model U and the display model V are represented as lattices of data objects and display objects, respectively. These objects are ordered by how precisely they approximate either mathematical data objects or ideal displays. For the display model, Mackinlay's expressiveness criteria are used to order displays according to their information content.

The display model is actually defined as an 8-tuple of graphical primitive values, as specified by Bertin (i.e., two screen coordinates, size, value, texture, color, orientation, and shape) [34]. Specifically, a finite set DS of *display scalars* represents the graphical primitives, and the display model V is defined as the complete lattice of all subsets A of $Y = \{Id : d \in DS\}$, the cross product of the value sets of the display scalars in DS. In addition to Bertin's simple scalars, more complex graphic objects such as icons can be represented via indexing from discrete display scalars. Hibbard then defines general scalar mappings from data lattices to display lattices, based on expressiveness conditions.

4.4.11   Golovchinsky (1995) AVE

AVE (Automatic Visualization Environment) is an automatic graphical presentation system based on a generative theory of diagram design, the construction of diagrams from basic components corresponding to relations present in the data [152]. Diagrams are composed of graphical elements—only rectangles in this implementation—that have attributes and are related to other elements through graphical relations based on the underlying data relations. The resulting graphics are trees and graphs depicting nodes as rectangles and relationships with lines or arrows.

The visualization process within AVE consists of four stages: query, analysis, constraint network generation, and geometric layout. The query stage consists of defining database views that return records of interest, the result of which is a collection of tuples, a domain frame (the set of objects), a slot (a directed arc), and a range frame. The analysis stage groups these tuples into categories based on their relationship type (slot-based relation) and frame type (type-based relation). For example, if the domain type is *person*, the relation (e.g., slot) is place of birth, and the range type is location, then the relation or slot type is a unique mapping. The constraint network generation stage takes the slot-based and type-based relations and maps them to one or more graphical relations. Using a ranked scoring system, multiple potential graphical relations are specified and ranked; the top scoring specification is passed on. The geometric layout stage calculates appropriate object positions that satisfy the constraints of graphical resources (e.g., rectangles with connecting lines or edges), which are then displayed.

4.4.12   Card, Mackinlay, and Shneiderman (1999) Spatial Substrate

For the introduction to Chapter 1 in their book, *Readings in Information Visualization: Using Vision to Think*, Card, Mackinlay, and Shneiderman summarize information visualization research and applications [59]. Of interest here is their section on "mapping data to visual form." Within this section, Card et al. present a *reference model for visualizations* describing three primary transformations for mapping data to visual form that also support human interaction: data transformations, visual mappings, and view transformations.

Their *spatial substrate*, an integral part of the visual structures, deals with the use of spatial positioning for encoding data within the display. As they note, "Empty space itself, as a container, can be treated as if it has metric structure. We describe this structure in terms of 'axes' and their properties" [59]. The authors present four elementary types of axes: *unstructured* (no axis), *nominal* (a region is divided into sub-regions), *ordinal* (the ordering of these sub-regions is meaningful), and *quantitative* (a region has a metric, possibly an interval or ratio or specialized).

Finally, five techniques are described for increasing the amount of information that can be encoded by spatial positions:

1. the composition of axes—orthogonal placement of axes creating a two-dimensional metric space;

2. the alignment of axes—repetition of an axis at a different position in space;

3. the folding of axes—continuation of an axis in an orthogonal dimension;

4. the application of recursion to axes—repeated subdivision of space; and

5. the overloading of axes—reusing the same display space.

4.4.13   Kamps (1999) EAVE

EAVE (Extended Automatic Visualization Engine) by Kamps is an extension of AVE [216]. EAVE takes arbitrary relations as input and generates diagram visualizations. While the diagrams generated by this system primarily depend on data characteristics and graphical knowledge, user preferences are also taken into account. This system only generates traditional types of diagrams that are commonly used in publications. Kamps introduces a language for defining diagrams internal to EAVE.

The automatic design of diagrams is accomplished through a three-phase process: a data classification phase, a graphical resource allocation phase, and a layout phase. The classification phase identifies the specific properties of the given data relation input. The goal of the resource allocation process is to encode the data relations using graphical relations. Finally, the layout phase is responsible for the realization of the design decisions by way of walking down the nested relation's graph and triggering the appropriate procedural layout techniques implemented by the associated graphical relations.

Starting with the definitions for data structures, data types, data objects, and graphical relations, Kamps introduces the general problem of visualizing an object network, the result of a database query. Data relations are visually transcribed by selecting adequate graphical relations and mapping data elements and data tuples into graphical elements and graphical tuples, respectively. An important underlying formalism implemented within EAVE is the application of *formal concept analysis*, an applied mathematical discipline based on a formal notion of concepts and concept hierarchies, allowing the mathematical reasoning of conceptual data analysis and processing [216]. Kamps uses formal concept analysis to define the *relation type lattice* of concepts used to model the binary data relationships and identify logical dependencies between data types.

The next step involves mapping the data relations to graphical relations using a set of specific graphical binary relations; appropriate graphical mappings are defined by matching relation types. The resulting visualization of n-ary relations in general becomes the composition of appropriate graphical binary relations, which implies the designing of a discrete optimization process for selecting those graphical mappings that result in the most expressive display. The final stage involves the layout of the selected graphical binary relations, another optimization process aimed to maximize the readability of the resulting display.

4.4.14   Wilkinson (1999) Grammar of Graphics

Wilkinson's Grammar of Graphics, based on his original Graphics Algebra, specifies the construction of statistical graphics [460]. This grammar of graphics is actually a grammar of statistical visualizations, a subclass of data visualizations readily used for statistical analyses. Each individual component of these graphics is defined as instances of various graphical objects; the combination of individual components defining the resulting display. As with all the other graphical models presented in this section, the grammar of graphics also takes a compositional approach to the generation of complex displays.

There are three primary stages for graphic creation: *specification, assembly,* and *display*. Although the assembly and display of graphics are important for the final visual output of the graphic, Wilkinson's specifications establish the foundation for all visualizations defined by the grammar. The statistical graphic specifications, as Wilkinson put it, form the core of a graphics system, and identify the numerous object transformations and representational mappings that define the display.

The grammar specification is composed of seven parts (see Table 4.8). Data and Trans operate on the data space. Frame, Scale, and Coord define the underlying geometry of the graphic and the arrangement of data variables (dimensions). Graph defines the visual graphic representations for individual data points, and Guide defines individual labels and markers. Just as Bertin, Mackinlay, and others identified graphic marks with retinal variables, Wilkinson's specification defines a collection of primitive *geometric graphs* (Bertin's marks) along with various *aesthetic attributes* (i.e., form, surface, motion, sound, or text properties) (see Table 4.9). Although there are important perceptual considerations when combining aesthetic attributes, this grammar of graphics does not use the effectiveness or expressiveness of graphics as associated with the previously described

Data	a set of data operations that create variables from data sets
Trans	data variable transformations
Frame	a set of variables, related by operators, that define a space
Scale	scale transformations
Coord	a coordinate system
Graph	graph (points) and their aesthetic attributes
Guide	one or more guides

Table 4.8.   Wilkinson's seven specifications [460].

Form	Surface		Motion	Sound	Text
Position	Color		Direction	Tone	Label
stack		hue	Speed	Volume	
dodge		brightness	Acceleration	Rhythm	
jitter		saturation		Voice	
Size	Texture				
Shape		pattern			
polygon		granularity			
glyph		orientation			
image	Blur				
Rotation	Transparency				

Table 4.9.   Wilkinson's aesthetic attributes [460].

graphics models, as this model's only goal is to specify arbitrary data graphics.

There are two primary visualization concepts identified by Wilkinson. First and foremost is the distinction between data points and their visual representations; the graph specification defines mappings from data points to aesthetic objects. Ordinarily, a visualization of data is an empty display without the encoding of the data points by perceptual objects. Second is the formalism of the visualization plane, the algebraic formalism applied to the data variables defining the graphic frame. With the application of an algebra, data variables are combined with operators {blend (+), cross (*), and nest (/)} to define graphic dimensions that are later scaled and mapped to a specific coordinate system specifying the display. More importantly, these algebra operators provide the means to specify complex variable-dimension arrangements. Furthermore, a facet can be defined, enabling the specification of frames within frames. Clearly, Wilkinson captures the important difference between the mathematical underpinning of a visualization and the visible graphic properties enabling a visualization to be perceived.

4.4.15   Hoffman (2000) Table Visualizations

The formal model for Table Visualizations developed by Hoffman was the first attempt at defining a generalized space of data visualizations [189]. The aim was the encapsulation of the primitive-graphic properties that define individual visualization techniques, and then the inference of the space of these techniques as the combination of graphic elements within some geometric layout. This research combined four specific visualization techniques: survey plots, scatterplots, RadViz, and parallel coordinates.

P_1	size of the scatterplot points
P_2	length of the perpendicular lines extending from individual anchor points in a scatterplot
P_3	length of the lines connecting scatterplot points associated with the same data point
P_4	width of the rectangle in a survey plot
P_5	length of the parallel coordinate lines
P_6	blocking factor for the parallel coordinate lines
P_7	size of the RadViz plot point
P_8	length of the spring lines extending from individual anchor points of a RadViz plot
P_9	the zoom factor for the spring K constant

Table 4.10.   Hoffman's dimensional anchor graphical parameters.

Table visualizations are defined as graphic presentations for two-dimensional data tables. The fundamental primitive for this formal model is a *dimensional anchor*, a graphic curve defining a mathematical axis associated with a particular data dimension. The arrangement of some number of dimensional anchors and associated parameters by a specific geometry defines a particular visualization technique.

Each dimensional anchor is associated with a vector containing nine graphic parameters encoding the four visualization techniques (see Table 4.10). Unlike the previously described graphics models, Hoffman's model does not distinguish between marks and their retinal variables. Instead, Hoffman takes a functional approach, where the vector of graphics parameters becomes an input to the visualization's drawing function. Consequently, through the rendering of a visualization, the various types of marks and retinal variables are realized.

By defining individual vectors of parameters with specific geometric layouts, one obtains the four predefined visualizations; and through the linear combination of these parameters for a fixed geometric layout one can generate, as Hoffman puts it, "new visualizations." By implementing the grand tour [22] applied to the vector of graphics parameters, Hoffman graphically demonstrates a subspace of visualizations for data sets used to investigate the mechanism of action for compounds (See the book's web site for a movie).

4.4.16   Summary of the History

In summary, there exists a wide variety of graphics models that formalize the graphical objects used to display information. Primarily, these models characterize graphics by three components: marks, positions, and perceptual variables. Initiated by Bertin and extended by others, the research of these components continues and provides valuable insights into the foundations for a general theory of visualizations. Of all the currently published research, the authors feel that Wilkinson provides the most substantial formalization of statistical graphics, capturing many of the rudimentary elements of most visualization techniques.

4.5 Taxonomies

A *taxonomy* is a means to convey a classification. Often hierarchical in nature, a taxonomy can be used to group similar objects and define relationships. In visualization, we are interested in many forms of taxonomies, including data, visualization techniques, tasks, and methods for interaction. In this section we briefly describe a number of such taxonomies from the literature. Interested readers are directed to the cited papers. Note that many other researchers have defined such taxonomies; this is just a representative sample.

4.5.1 Keller and Keller (1994) Taxonomy of Visualization Goals

Keller and Keller, in their book *Visual Cues* [236], classify visualization techniques based on the type of data being analyzed and the user's task(s). Similar to those identified earlier in this book, the data types they consider are:

- scalar (or scalar field);

- nominal;

- direction (or direction field);

- shape;

- position;

- spatially extended region or object (SERO).

The authors also define a number of tasks that a visualization user might be interested in performing. While some of the tasks seem interrelated, their list is a useful starting position for someone setting out to design a visualization for a particular application. Their task list consists of:

- identify—establish characteristics by which an object is recognizable;

- locate—ascertain the position (absolute or relative);

- distinguish—recognize as distinct or different (identification is not needed);

- categorize—place into divisions or classes;

- cluster—group similar objects;

- rank—assign an order or position relative to other objects;

- compare—notice similarities and differences;

- associate—link or join in a relationship that may or may not be of the same type;

- correlate—establish a direct connection, such as causal or reciprocal.

Given these two lists, they then categorized more than 100 techniques from the literature. While this book is somewhat dated, it can be useful for assessing different visualization techniques and tools.

4.5.2 Shneiderman (1996) Data Type by Task Taxonomy

A related strategy was proposed by Shneiderman [376]. His list of data types was somewhat different from Keller and Keller's, and included more types from the information visualization field. His list of data types consisted of:

- one-dimensional linear;

- two-dimensional map;

- three-dimensional world;

- temporal;

- multidimensional;

- tree;

- network.

For his tasks, Shneiderman looked more at the behavior of analysts as they attempt to extract knowledge from the data. His task set consisted of the following:

Overview. Gain an overview of the entire collection, e.g., using a fisheye strategy for network browsing.

Zoom. Zoom in items of interest to gain a more detailed view, e.g., holding down a mouse button to enlarge a region of the display.

Filter. Filter out uninteresting items to allow the user to reduce the size of a search, e.g., dynamic queries that can be invoked via sliders.

Details-on-demand. Select an item or group and get details when needed, e.g., a pop-up window can show more attributes of a specific object on the screen.

Relate. View relationships among items, e.g., select a particular object that can then show all other objects related to it.

History. Keep a history to allow undo, replay, and progressive refinement, such as allowing a mistake to be undone, or a series of steps to be replayed.

Extract. Extract the items or data in a format that would facilitate other uses, i.e., saving to file, sending via e-mail, printing, or dragging into another application (statistical or presentation package).

Shneiderman suggested that an effective visual exploration tool should support most or all of these tasks in an easy-to-use manner.

4.5.3   Keim (2002) Information Visualization Classification

As shown in Figure 4.26, Keim designed a classification scheme for visualization systems based on three dimensions: data types, visualization techniques, and interaction/distortion methods [234]. His interaction/distortion technique classification has some similarities to Shneiderman's tasks, as do his data types, but his classification of the visualization techniques used is not included in the other taxonomies. The components of each of his classification dimensions are listed below:

Classification of Data Types. 6 types of data exist:

1. *One-dimensional data*—e.g., temporal data, news data, stock prices, text documents

2. *Two-dimensional data*—e.g., maps, charts, floor plans, newspaper layouts

3. *Multidimensional data*—e.g., spreadsheets, relational tables

4. *Text and hypertext*—e.g., new articles, web documents

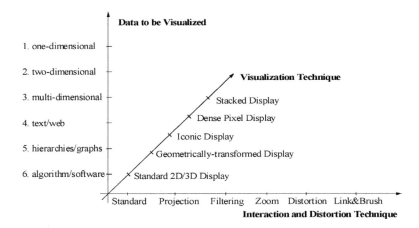

Figure 4.26.   Classification of information visualization techniques [234]. (Image © 2002 IEEE.)

5. *Hierarchies and graphs*—e.g., telephone/network traffic, system dynamics models

6. *Algorithm and software*—e.g., software, execution traces, memory dumps

Classification of Visualization Techniques. 5 classes of visualization techniques exist:

1. *Standard 2D/3D displays*—e.g., x, y- or x, y, z-plots, bar charts, line graphs;

2. *Geometrically transformed displays*—e.g., landscapes, scatterplot matrices, projection pursuit techniques, prosection views, hyperslice, parallel coordinates;

3. Iconic displays—e.g., Chernoff faces, needle icons, star icons, stick figure icons, color icons, tilebars;

4. Dense pixel displays—e.g., recursive pattern, circle segments, graph sketches;

5. Stacked displays—e.g., dimensional stacking, hierarchical axes, worlds-within-worlds, treemaps, cone trees.

Classification of Interaction and Distortion Techniques. 5 classes of interaction techniques exist:

1. *Dynamic projection*—e.g., grand tour system, XGobi, XLispStat, ExplorN;

2. Interactive filtering—e.g., Magic Lenses, InfoCrystal, dynamic queries, Polaris;

3. Interactive zooming—e.g., TableLens, PAD++, IVEE/Spotfire, DataSpace, MGV and scalable framework;

4. Interactive distortion—e.g., hyperbolic and spherical distortions, bifocal displays, perspective wall, graphical fisheye views, hyperbolic visualization, hyperbox;

5. Interactive linking and brushing—e.g., multiple scatterplots, bar charts, parallel coordinates, pixel displays and maps, Polaris, scalable framework, S-Plus, XGobi, XmdvTool, DataDesk.

4.6 Related Readings

Bertin's *Semiology of Graphics* [34] is essential reading for all researchers in visualization. For many years this book was out of print, but recently it has been republished.

Jacques Bertin has another paper that is a useful source for this chapter, namely is his paper "Matrix Theory of Graphics" [33]. According to Bertin, the basic construction of a graphic on a plane is made up of an x position, a y position, and a z position. The z position uses variation through "light energy" to encode the size or value of the third dimension. He outlines that data presented this way is a matrix of data and then goes on to explain that a primary task of understanding data is understanding patterns, and that an initial presentation of data in a matrix may not reveal patterns as well as another presentation. If the x or y values are ordinal, then they may be rearranged to make patterns more easily noticed. He defines this type of matrix as a *reorderable matrix* and goes on to outline several examples of using matrices for graphics, including uses in cartography.

Wilkinson's *The Grammar of Graphics* [460] is an intriguing model for designing visualization techniques and systems. While mostly geared toward statistical graphics, it is applicable to a broader range of applications.

Ed Chi's Data State Reference Model for information visualization [73] has been widely cited, and several visualization packages have been developed based on it. His Ph.D. dissertation [72, 74] is well worth reading.

Another taxonomy relevant to visualization is reported in [267]. The focus of the paper is restricted to graph visualization, and a task-based taxonomy is proposed. The authors decompose complex tasks into a set of low-level tasks, and give examples of many such tasks. Yet another taxonomy [181] is focused on desirable features for visualization tools, and uses existing tools to highlight the features. While the authors admit the taxonomy is not complete, it is a good starting point for those designing new visualization systems.

4.7 Exercises

1. Show that M_{exp} and M_{eff}, as defined earlier, are distance metrics.

2. Extend M_{exp} to deal with different sets of information. For example, suppose A and B are sets of information from some Universe (U). Try to define $M_{\text{exp}}(A \cap B)$, $M_{\text{exp}}(A \cup B)$, $M_{\text{exp}}(U - A)$, and so on.

3. Extend M_{eff} as in Exercise 2.

4. Identify some of the tools, systems, or packages listed in Table 4.1 that are either outdated or no longer available (lots of visualization companies have come and gone!).

5. Identify and describe some currently available visualization tools, systems, or packages that could be added to Table 4.1.

6. Identify and describe 10 or more visualization chart types, such as pie charts and bubble charts. Give examples when possible.

7. Comment on the marks used in Figure 4.8. Are they readily distinguishable? Are they susceptible to bias or occlusion problems?

8. Compare and contrast two or more of the taxonomies or classification schemes described in this chapter. Choose the ones you feel have the most overlap.

4.8 Projects

1. Extend your scatterplot program to enable a third data dimension to be mapped to at least five of the seven remaining visual variables (not counting position).

2. Extend your scatterplot program to enable one of the dimensions to take on nominal values. Test different ways of displaying this dimension using the results of the previous project.

3. Test your program with different data set sizes. Were any mappings better or worse than others?

4. Test your program with variables having different numbers of distinct levels (2–10). Which mappings better enabled users to see subtle differences?

CHAPTER 5

Visualization Techniques for Spatial Data

Spatial data visualization, which corresponds to the field of scientific visualization, assumes that the data has an implicit or explicit spatial or spatiotemporal attribute. This constraint facilitates both the creation and interpretation of the visualization, as there is an intuitive, and often straightforward, mapping of the data attributes to graphical attributes of the entities conveying the information in the visualization. As our visual perception system is constantly receiving and interpreting imagery of the physical phenomena surrounding us, it is quite natural to process the same form of imagery on a computer screen. The main differences are:

- In viewing the world surrounding us, we are not constrained by a two-dimensional, discrete, low-resolution projection.

- On the screen, we can visually explore phenomena (real or simulated) at arbitrary scales.

- On the screen, we can dynamically modify contrast, lighting, resolution, density, and other parameters and aspects of the data.

- On the screen, we can interactively navigate spaces that would be hard to enter in real life.

- On the screen, we can interactively add and remove parts of the data to get more context or remove clutter.

In creating a visualization of spatial data, we must decide what spatial attributes of the data will map to the spatial attributes (locations) on the screen. This can involve many forms of transformation, including scaling, rotation, translation, shearing, and projection. Once the spatial attributes are accommodated, other attributes and values associated with the data must then be mapped to other components of the visualization, whether it is an attribute such as color or texture or the size or shape of a graphical entity.

In this chapter we will survey a wide range of techniques that have been applied to spatial data. We will order the presentation according to the dimensionality of the data, with the implicit assumption that lower dimensional techniques can be used to convey projections or subsections of higher dimensional data. We shall see several examples of this.

5.1   One-Dimensional Data

One-dimensional spatial data is often the result of accumulating samples or readings of some phenomenon while moving along a path in space. For example, a drill-hole sample will contain mineral content and ore grade information based on the distance from the top of the drill-hole. This sort of sampling is often referred to as a *probe* when exploring structures of higher dimensions.

Given a one-dimensional sequence of univariate data (only one value per data item), we can map the spatial data to one of the screen dimensions and the data value itself to either the other screen dimension (to form a *line graph*, see Figure 5.1) or to the color of a mark or region along the spatial axis (to form a *color bar*). The data needs to be scaled to fit within the range of the display attribute (either number of pixels or number of colors). Parts of the display space or color range might be reserved for other aspects of the visualization, such as the axes, labels, and key, so the most general structure for an algorithm to generate such a visualization will use parameters for the bounds of both the data and display spaces.

Assume that $(\text{data}_{\min}, \text{data}_{\max})$ are computed as the minimum and maximum values for the data, and $\text{data}_{\text{count}}$ indicates the number of data points to be displayed (this could be all of the data, or just a selected subset). Also assume the section of the display that will hold the visualization is defined by the rectangle $(x_{\min}, y_{\min}, x_{\max}, y_{\max})$. To generate a line graph from an array called "data," we could use the following code (assuming the drawing command DRAW-LINE exists).

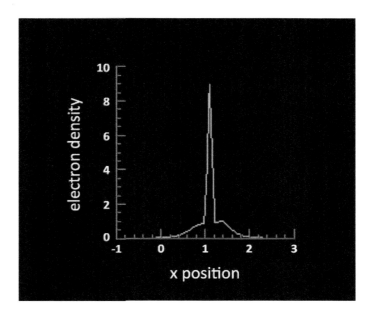

Figure 5.1.   A line graph of a 1D sequence of data values. Image generated with OpenDX [308].

Draw-Line-Graph($data, dataCount, xMin, xMax, yMin, yMax$)

1   $dataMin \leftarrow$ ComputeMin($data, dataCount$)
2   $dataMax \leftarrow$ ComputeMax($data, dataCount$)
3   $xFrom \leftarrow xMin$
4   $yFrom \leftarrow$ WorldToScreenY($data[0], dataMin, dataMax, yMin,$
5   $yMax$)
6   **for** $i \leftarrow 1$ **to** $dataCount$
7   **do** $xTo \leftarrow$ WorldToScreenX($i, dataCount, xMin, xMax$)
8          $yTo \leftarrow$ WorldToScreenY($data[i], dataMin, dataMax,$
9          $yMin, yMax$)
10   DrawLine($xFrom, yFrom, xTo, yTo$)
11        $xFrom \leftarrow xTo$
12        $yFrom \leftarrow yTo$

WorldToScreenX($index, dataCount, xMin, xMax$)
    return $(xMin + index * (xMax - xMin)/dataCount)$

WorldToScreenY($value, dataMin, dataMax, yMin, yMax$)
    return $(yMin + (value - dataMin) * (yMax - yMin)/(dataMax$
    $- dataMin))$

Note that each transformation is a combination of offsets and scaling that we use to convert values in one coordinate system into another. This operation is used heavily in computer graphics, and we will use variants on it numerous times in this book. It is derived based on the observation that a point within a given range can be transformed to a point within a different range by computing the relative position of the point within the range, e.g., what percentage of the distance from one end of the range to the other is the selected point. Mathematically, this is given as:

$$(A_i - A_{\min})/(A_{\max} - A_{\min}) = (B_i - B_{\min})/(B_{\max} - B_{\min}) \qquad (5.1)$$

where A_i is a location in the range $[A_{\min} \to A_{\max}]$ and B_i is the corresponding location in the range $[B_{\min} \to B_{\max}]$.

Also note that the WORLDTOSCREENX function is simpler than the WORLDTOSCREENY function, as we are assuming that the indices in the list of values start at 0. To make it more general and enable the user to select an arbitrary range of values, the function would look as follows:

WORLDTOSCREENX(*index*)
    return $(xMin + (index - indexMin) * (xMax - xMin)/(indexMax - indexMin))$

There are many embellishments to the procedure described above. For example, if the number of data points to be displayed exceeds the number of pixels available in the display range, we might want to sample or average values (see the discussion in Chapter 3 on preprocessing data). Also, we might want to change the data scale to better reveal some structure. For example, using a logarithmic scale can overcome problems with data that have a large range of values. To convert the above to a color bar, we simply replace the line drawing with the drawing of rectangles whose color is proportional to the data value, again transformed into the range of available colors (see the exercises). A *bar graph* is similar to a line graph, except that each data point is replaced by a (colored) rectangle whose height is proportional to the value. The rectangle is usually centered on the spatial attribute of the data, and its width is often uniform.

If the data set is *multivariate*, e.g., it contains more than one variable or value per data entry, we can expand on any of the univariate strategies using either *juxtapositioning* or *superimpositioning*. For line graphs, this would mean that either the visualization would consist of a stack of non-overlapping graphs (most effective if the variables have different scales) or a graph containing plots of two or more variables. In the latter case, different line styles or colors would need to be used to differentiate the variables. Multivariate bar graphs can also be composed in a similar manner, with the possibility to stack the bars on top of each other. Note that it is important to convey the scale of each variable to the user.

5.2 Two-Dimensional Data

Data with two spatial dimensions get visualized predominantly by mapping the spatial attributes of the data to the spatial attributes of the screen. The result can be one of the following visualizations:

1. An *image* results if a single data value at each location is mapped to color and all intermediate pixels are colored via interpolation (see the algorithms in Chapter 2). Figure 5.2 shows an example.

2. A *rubber sheet* results if the data, whether regularly or irregularly spaced, is mapped to the height of a point in three dimensions, with

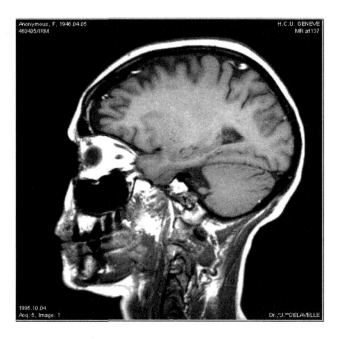

Figure 5.2.   An image from a tomographic data set.

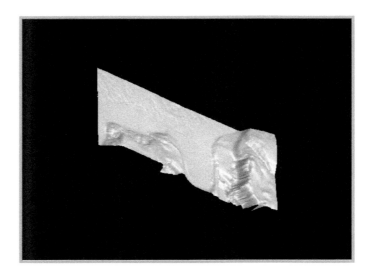

Figure 5.3.   A Rubber Sheet visualization of elevation data for the southeast U.S. (Image generated using OpenDX [308].)

the points triangulated so that a surface can be formed. Figure 5.3 shows sea level and ground elevation for the Florida region.

3. A *cityscape* is formed by drawing three-dimensional objects (generally boxes) at locations on a plane, where the data can control the attributes of the graphical objects (i.e., height and color), such as seen in Figure 5.4.

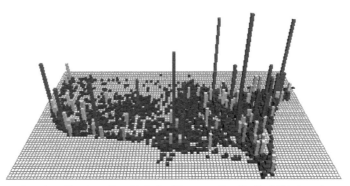

Figure 5.4.   A cityscape showing the density of air traffic over the United States at a particular time period.

4. A *scatterplot* results if, at each location on the plot, the data value(s) control the color, shape, or size of a marker. Note that unlike for images, no interpolation is performed.

5. A *map* results if the data contains linear and area features, as well as point objects. A linear feature, such as a road or stream, is represented as a sequence of connected coordinates, which are plotted as a series of line segments. Area features, such as a lake or political boundary, are generally represented as a closed contour, a set of coordinates where the first and last points are the same. These are generally rendered by converting the data coordinates to screen coordinates (using the mapping discussed in the previous section) and drawing a polygon on the display. This might be filled with a semantically meaningful color, texture pattern, or repeated symbol. In the latter case, the boundary may not be explicitly drawn, such as when depicting land cover or use information. Point features, such as utility poles or schools, are generally represented by a symbol plotted at or near the specified location (this alludes to the complex problem of automated cartography, where objects are positioned in such a way as to be reasonably accurate, while avoiding overlap and excessive congestion on the display). Objects may also have labels associated with them, the placement of which is another complex process. An example is shown in Figure 5.5. More details on geovisualization are presented in Chapter 6.

6. A *contour* or *isovalue* map conveys boundary information extracted from an image depicting a continuous phenomenon, such as elevation or temperature. The term *isovalue* means "single value," and thus a contour on such a map indicates the boundary between points above this value and points below the value. It can be formed by considering two-by-two arrays of adjacent data values as the corners of a rectangle or square, and generating edges across this rectangle when one or more values are on the opposite side of the isovalue from one or more of the others. The actual transition points, which will lie on the edges connecting the corners, can be determined via interpolation (see Section 2.3.5). Each isovalue may generate multiple closed contours. Multiple isovalues may be plotted simultaneously, using color, line thickness, line style, or labels to differentiate values. Figure 5.6 shows several contour lines from a 2D image, using color to encode the isovalue.

For multivariate 2D data, we can expand these techniques as we did with 1D data: via juxtapositioning and superimpositioning. For juxtapositioning,

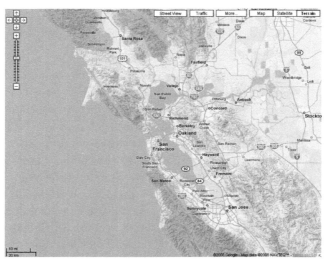

Figure 5.5.   A map of the San Francisco area, generated by Google Maps. (Image © 2008
                   Google Map; data © 2008 NAVTEQ^{TM}.)

this would simply involve stacking several 2D univariate visualizations into a
3D visualization, such as a set of images separated vertically in space. While
it can be difficult to see some features of the data due to occlusion, and detecting correlations between variables may be difficult, this approach does
allow us to get an overview of all data attributes at once. This technique is
also limited in terms of the number of variables that can be readily accommodated, especially when using univariate techniques that already exploit the
third dimension, such as cityscapes and rubber sheets. Superimpositioning
is similarly limited in terms of the number of variables that can be handled.
For example, in cityscapes we can stack blocks of different colors, where each
color represents a data variable, even for 3 to 5 variables, it may become difficult to interpret. With translucent surfaces, one could layer multiple rubber
sheets, and by varying the individual opacities, the different layers could
be revealed. Again, this method would not scale well to large numbers of
variables. Maps are perhaps the most common example of superimposed 2D
data visualization, as a digital map is generally composed of multiple layers of point, linear, and area features. However, excessive overlapping can
make it difficult to extract the individual components. To some extent, this
can be handled by minor adjustments to positions to reduce overlap without
distorting the data too much. An alternate approach when the number of
variables gets too large is to explore the nonspatial multivariate visualization
techniques presented in Chapter 8.

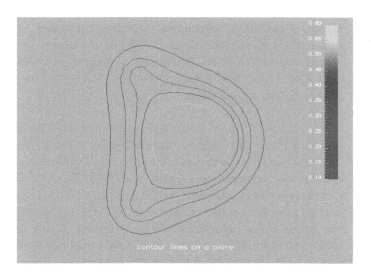

Figure 5.6.   Contour lines from an image slice of a hydrogen molecule. (Image generated using OpenDX [308].)

Probing Two-Dimensional Data

Besides the visualization techniques that display the entire data set, we can also choose to visualize one-dimensional subsets, projections, or summarizations of the data. After reducing the dimensionality in some manner, we are then free to employ any of the techniques described in the previous section. Let us examine some of the projection options in detail.

Frequency histograms. We can summarize data sets of arbitrary dimensionality by computing the frequency at which values or subranges of values occur in the data, and then display this information as a bar graph. Important considerations when using subranges are how to decide the number of subranges to use, and where the breaks between subranges should be. Features of importance in the data might be lost if this is done incorrectly, and it is best performed by someone familiar with the data characteristics. Simply dividing the range into a fixed number of evenly sized subranges, while simple, is rarely an effective strategy.

Row and column aggregations. Visually depicting summarizations of the rows and/or columns of an image is a useful mechanism for localizing the boundaries of features of interest and regions of low or high variability. Many descriptors can be used for this purpose, including the sum, average, median, standard deviation, maximum, or minimum values. The resulting one-dimensional visualization can be viewed separately or, as often the case, placed alongside the two-dimensional visualization as supplemental information. Color bars, line plots, and bar graphs have all been used with success in this type of visualization.

Linear probes. A one-dimensional probe of a two-dimensional data set can be likened to a drill hole for mineral exploration. A line is passed through the data, and the values encountered are visualized using one of the one-dimensional techniques previously described. To accomplish this, we use two mathematical tools already presented in this chapter: parametric equations and bilinear interpolation. We start by creating a parametric equation of our probe using input from the user (either a pair of points or a point and a direction). If we assume that this line was specified as two sets of coordinates, P_1 and P_2, the parametric equation of the line segment joining the points is simply $P(t) = P_1 + t(P_2 - P_1)$, where $0 \leq t \leq 1.0$. We can then get the coordinate of an arbitrary point along this line segment by choosing a value of t within this range. Generally, these are evenly spaced, and the number of samples computed is proportional to the length of the line segment (so that probes that barely clip a corner of the data grid do not get represented by the same number of samples as a probe along the diagonal of the grid). Given the coordinates of the sampled points, we can now use the interpolation procedure to compute values, which can then be visualized as a one-dimensional data set.

5.3   Three-Dimensional Data

As with two-dimensional data, three-dimensional spatial data may be either discrete samples of a continuous phenomenon or a structure best described via vertices, edges, and polygons. In reality, many visualizations of science and engineering data contain a combination of these data representations, such as air flow around a wing or stress attributes of a mechanical part. We will first examine basic visualization techniques for this type of data, and later in the chapter will discuss methods for combining techniques.

5.3.1   Visualizing Explicit Surfaces

An *explicit surface* is one that has been defined in one of two ways:

1. a list of three-dimensional vertices, a list of edges, i.e., connections between the vertices (specified as a pair of indices into the vertex list), and a list of planar polygon patches (usually specified as a fixed or variable length list of indices into the edge list);

2. a set of parametric equations for defining the x-, y-, and z-coordinates of points on the surface, along with an interconnection strategy (e.g., a triangular or rectilinear grid) for computing the edges and patches. The step size of the parameters can be used to control the smoothness of the curved surface.

For example, a unit cube can be represented by the following lists:

```
vertex[0] = (0., 0., 0.)
vertex[1] = (0., 0., 1.)
vertex[2] = (0., 1., 1.)
vertex[3] = (0., 1., 0.)
vertex[4] = (1., 0., 0.)
vertex[5] = (1., 0., 1.)
vertex[6] = (1., 1., 1.)
vertex[7] = (1., 1., 0.)
edge[0] = (0, 1)
edge[1] = (1, 2)
edge[2] = (2, 3)
edge[3] = (3, 0)
edge[4] = (0, 4)
edge[5] = (1, 5)
edge[6] = (2, 6)
edge[7] = (3, 7)
edge[8] = (4, 5)
edge[9] = (5, 6)
edge[10] = (6, 7)
edge[11] = (7, 4)
face[0] = (0, 1, 2, 3)
face[1] = (8, 9, 10, 11)
face[2] = (0, 5, 8, 4)
face[3] = (1, 6, 9, 5)
face[4] = (2, 7, 10, 6)
face[5] = (3, 4, 11, 7)
```

Note that every edge is shared by exactly two faces, and that every vertex is a member of three edges. Also note that edge direction can be an issue; we often try to maintain a consistent orientation in traversing the edges of a face (either clockwise or counter-clockwise, from the outside of the face) to insure that we can compute surface normals correctly, e.g., pointing away from the inside of the object defined by the surface.

The parametric form for a unit cylinder aligned with the y-axis can be defined as follows:

$$y = 1.0, \quad x = \cos\theta, \quad z = \sin\theta, \quad 0.0 \leq \theta \leq 2\pi, \qquad \text{(top)}$$

$$y = 0.0, \quad x = \cos\theta, \quad z = \sin\theta, \quad 0.0 \leq \theta \leq 2\pi, \qquad \text{(bottom)}$$

$$y = h, \quad\quad x = \cos\theta, \quad z = \sin\theta, \quad 0.0 \leq \theta \leq 2\pi, \, 0.0 \leq h \leq 1.0. \quad \text{(sides)}$$

By changing the step size for θ, we can get cylinders with varying smoothness. Note that if we set the step size for h to be 1 and for θ to be $\pi/2$, we get a box with a height of 1 and cross section of 2. Other examples of parametric surfaces, such as B-splines and Bézier curves, can be found in textbooks on computer graphics and geometric modeling.

In general, the visualization of spatial data defined on an explicit surface depends on whether the values to be conveyed are associated with the vertices, edges, or faces. Examples of each are:

- the temperature or stress at a joint (vertex information);

- the strength of attraction for a chemical bond (edge information);

- the ground cover for a map region (face information).

The information to be conveyed in the visualization may be mapped to any of the nonspatial graphical attributes (we assume that the spatial data attributes normally get mapped to the spatial graphical attributes), such as color, opacity, texture, or other surface property. We can also choose to convey *point data*, e.g., data that is associated with a single location and is not to be interpolated in the surrounding neighborhood, using a shape or symbol (often referred to as a *glyph*, *icon*, or *mark*). Examples might be the use of an arrow to depict flow direction (see Section 5.4) or a cylinder whose height, width, and color encode three data dimensions. Remember, as was pointed out in Chapter 3, it is generally not wise to map separate data dimensions to the red, green, and blue components of a color, as most people cannot extract the individual color components and their intensity/proportion with any accuracy.

5.3.2   Visualizing Volume Data

As pixels are to two-dimensional visualization, *voxels*, or volume elements, are to three-dimensional visualization. Volume data is generally a sampling of a continuous phenomenon, and can be either acquired via sensors (e.g., tomographic data sets) or generated via simulations (e.g., computational fluid dynamics). In each case, we have one or more data dimensions with regular or irregular positions, and the goal is to convey to the viewer the structure, patterns, and anomalies within the data.

Most approaches to visualizing volume data fall into one of the following categories [272]:

Slicing techniques. Using a cut plane, either aligned with an axis or arbitrarily oriented, probe the data to extract a two-dimensional slice of the data, and then use one of the two-dimensional spatial data visualization methods.

Isosurface techniques. Given a user-specified value, generate a surface description and visualize it using one of the explicit surface visualization techniques.

Direct volume rendering. Either cast rays into the volume and compute a pixel value based on the data encountered by the ray, or project each voxel onto the projection plane using some method of accumulating effects on pixels.

In all of these approaches, resampling is an essential component. For *isosurfaces* (see the description of the Marching Cubes algorithm below), we need to find the locations where the data matches the selected isovalue, which is almost always between points of the original data set. We saw this process in the discussion of contour map generation in two dimensions. In slicing, especially when the slicing plane is not aligned with an axis, it is essential to resample the data to get an evenly spaced set of pixels. Interpolation is also necessary when dealing with a nonuniform spacing of data points. In direct volume rendering, we need to sample data values along a ray, again using resampling, although with parallel projections along major axes we generally wouldn't need to resample. Thus we see that the resampling process, and coordinate system transformations, are essential tools in the visualization of spatial data.

Slicing Volume Data with Cut Planes. As with two-dimensional data visualization, one strategy we can follow is to probe the three-dimensional data to create a subset of data with a lower dimension. A popular technique for volume data is the use of *cut planes*, where the data block is sliced by a plane with a given orientation and position, and the data that the plane intersects are mapped to the plane for display.

The simplest implementation of this technique is to constrain the orientation of the cut plane so that its normal coincides with one of the data axes. The user then specifies a row, column, or depth in the data block, and the corresponding slice is displayed using one of the techniques described in the section on two-dimensional spatial data visualization. An effective strategy is to animate the slice selection so that the user can form associations between adjacent slices.

For arbitrary orientations, each voxel intersected by the cut plane may influence the value of one or more pixels. We can choose to resample the data volume at locations on a regular grid on the cut plane, or alternatively, we can choose the nearest voxel to a cut plane pixel to represent the volume at the location. Still another approach would be to combine the contributions of the nearest voxels to each element on the cut plane, with weightings inversely proportional to the distance from the center of the voxel to the cut plane. To specify the cut plane, six parameters need to be set: three positional and three for the plane normal. Interactive manipulation of such a surface can be challenging to the user, so often one would first set the orientation and then adjust a slider to indicate the depth along the normal to the plane.

Many variations on this technique exist, and each can provide significant details about the interior of the volume. Some of these include:

- nonplanar slices;

- consecutive slices in varying orientations to remove blocks of the data;

- stacked slices displayed simultaneously;

- orthogonal slices displayed simultaneously.

Isosurface Extraction Using Marching Cubes. Marching Cubes is an algorithm developed by Lorensen and Cline in 1987 [278] for rendering isosurfaces in volumetric data (Wyvill et al. developed a similar strategy a year earlier [475]). The basic notion is that we can define a voxel (cube) by the values at the eight corners of the cube. If one or more corners of a cube have values less than the user-specified isovalue, and one or more have values greater than this value, we know that the voxel must contribute some component of the isosurface. By determining which edges of the cube are intersected by the isosurface, we can create triangular patches that divide the cube between regions within the isosurface and regions outside. By connecting the patches from all cubes on the isosurface boundary, we get a surface representation.

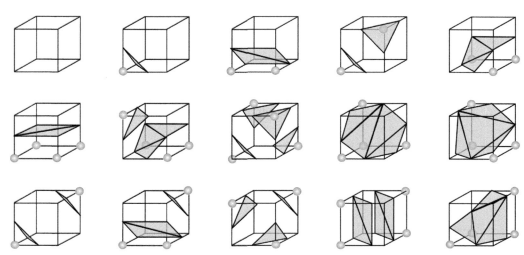

Figure 5.7.   The 15 voxel configurations for Marching Cubes. (Image courtesy Wikimedia Commons.)

Algorithm details.   The following algorithm is based on the description found in [449]. There are two major components of this algorithm. The first is deciding how to define the section or sections of surface that chop up an individual cube. If we classify each corner as either being below or above the isovalue, there are 256 possible configurations of corner classifications. Two of these are trivial; where all points are inside or outside the isovalue, the cube does not contribute to the isosurface. For all other configurations, we need to determine where, along each cube edge, the isosurface crosses, and use these edge intersection points to create one or more triangular patches for the isosurface.

If you account for symmetries, there are really only 15 unique configurations. When there is only one corner less than the isovalue, this forms a single triangle that intersects the edges that meet at this corner, with the patch normal facing away from the corner (see second cube in first row of Figure 5.7). Obviously, there are 8 related configurations of this sort. By reversing the normal we get 8 configurations that have 7 corners less than the isovalue. We don't consider these really unique, however. For configurations with 2 corners less than the isovalue, there are 3 unique configurations (see third and fourth cubes in first row and first cube in the last row of Figure 5.7), depending on whether the corners belong to the same edge, belong to the same face of the cube, or are diagonally positioned relative to each other. For configurations with 3 corners less than the isovalue, there are again 3 unique configurations (see last cube in first row and second and third cube in last row of Figure 5.7) depending on whether there are 0, 1, or 2 shared edges (2 shared edges gives you an "L" shape). There are 7 unique configurations when you have 4 corners less than the isovalue, depending on whether there are 0, 2, 3 (3 variants on this one), or 4 shared edges (see remaining cubes in Figure 5.7).

Each of the nontrivial configurations results in between 1 and 4 triangles being added to the isosurface. The actual vertices themselves can be computed by interpolation along edges, or to simplify computations, by defaulting their location to the middle of the edge. The interpolated locations will obviously give you better shading calculations and smoother surfaces. Figure 5.8 shows a 3D field from a hydrogen atom rendered with a simple version of the Marching Cubes algorithm, using edge midpoints as the triangle vertices. Note the blockiness of the results due to the limited number of unique surface orientations and the small size of the data set. The core of the Marching Cubes algorithm is as follows.

MARCHINGCUBES(*IsoValue*)
1   **for** *EachCell*
2   **do if** *Isosurface Passes through Cell*
3   **then**
4   *Classify each vertex as inside or outside*
5   *Determine index of the* 15 *Cell Types*
6   *Get edge list from table*[*index*]
7   *Interpolate the edge location*
8   *Create Small Polygons for Surface within Cell*

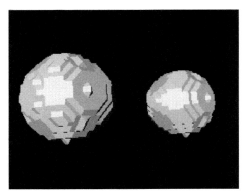

Figure 5.8.   3D hydrogen data rendered with an algorithm based on Marching Cubes.

Now that we can create surface patches for a single voxel, we can apply this process to the entire volume. We can process the volume in slabs, where each slab is comprised of 2 slices of pixels. We can either treat each cube independently, or we can propagate edge intersections between cubes that share the edges. This sharing can also be done between adjacent slabs, which increases storage and complexity a bit, but saves in computation time. The sharing of edge/vertex information, which inspired the name for the algorithm, also results in a more compact model, and one that is more amenable to interpolated shading.

Problems and Alternatives. One obvious problem with Marching Cubes is the amount of memory needed to store the resulting surface. As each boundary cube can generate up to 4 sub-pixel facets, the result can be quite large. We can reduce this somewhat by sharing vertices and edges, or even merging coplanar patches into larger facets. Another solution might be to try to fit parametric surfaces to groups of boundary points, though this may be difficult for complex surface geometries.

Another problem arises when you don't have a filled space of voxels. Depending on how the volume data was acquired, there may be voids that need to be assigned values or circumnavigated in the surface generation algorithm. Any interpolated value used may reduce the validity of the resulting surface.

Direct Volume Visualization Techniques. *Direct volume rendering* means that no three-dimensional polygons are created for use with traditional graphics rendering techniques. Rather, pixels in the resulting image are computed on an individual basis, either by casting rays through the pixel through the volume, or by projecting voxels onto the plane of projection. We shall cover the details of each approach below.

The basic process of rendering a volumetric data set starts by transforming the positions of the voxels into the viewing coordinate system, following the same procedure used in the traditional three-dimensional graphics pipeline. This may or may not include perspective distortion. The viewer must specify a view reference point (the origin of the plane of projection), a view direction (the normal to the plane of projection), the height and width of the image to be projected on the plane of projection, and, for a perspective projection, the distance from the camera to the plane of projection. The reader is referred to textbooks on computer graphics for details of this process.

Once the voxels have been positioned, we have the option of either:

- *forward mapping*—project each voxel onto the plane of projection and determine which pixels will be affected and in what way;

- *inverse mapping*, also called *ray casting*—send a ray from each pixel in the plane of projection through the volume, sampling values along the ray, and determining the resulting value for each pixel.

In forward mapping, we have a number of problems to be resolved (from [272]), including:

1. how to deal with pixels that are influenced by multiple voxels (F1);

2. how to handle pixels to which no voxel directly maps (F2); and

3. how to deal with the fact that voxels usually project to positions between pixels (F3).

For inverse mapping, we have similar problems:

1. how to select the number of points to be sampled along the ray (I1);

2. how to compute the value at these points, which usually fall between voxels (I2); and

3. how to combine the points encountered along each ray(I3).

Problems F2 and F3 can be solved by mapping each voxel to a region of the plane of projection, allowing it to partially influence the value of several pixels adjacent to the location to which it projects. Two common methods for performing this are to weight the voxel's value for each pixel, based on the distance between the pixel and the projected location for that voxel. Generally, at most four pixels would normally be affected. Another approach, known as *splatting*, associates a small texture region with each voxel and projects this region onto the plane of projection.

Problem I1 is readily resolved by determining the spacing between voxels and setting the sampling rate to be less than this distance. In this way, features in the volume cannot be passed over, unless the pixels on the plane of projection are too widely separated. The sampling itself can be accomplished using the resampling/interpolation techniques covered earlier in the chapter.

Problems F1 and I3 are normally solved using a process known as *compositing* in the volume rendering community. While the simplest forms of compositing, such as taking the maximum volume value, or averaging all volume values associated with a pixel/ray, provide some information on the data set contents, a more common approach is to assume that each voxel has an opacity associated with it and integrate all voxels mapped to a given pixel. If we assume that voxel i has color c_i and opacity o_i, its contribution to the final pixel value will be $c_i * o_i * \prod_{j=0}^{i-1}(1 - o_j)$. In other words, we must determine the accumulated transparency (recall that $transparency_i = 1 - o_i$) between the plane of projection and the voxel, and use this to adjust the intensity $(c_i * o_i)$ of the voxel. The final value for the pixel is given by the equation

$$I(x, y) = \sum_{i=0}^{n} c_i * o_i * \prod_{j=0}^{i-1}(1 - o_j).$$

Note that if the accumulated transparency term approaches 0, we can terminate the calculation. Several variations of this formulation have been suggested, including the *back-to-front* process, which simply accumulates the transparency terms from $j = i + 1$ to $j = n$. This results in the same value, but executes more efficiently. However, early termination is not possible.

An important issue in rendering the volume is determining the opacity and color associated with particular data values. This process is often referred to as *classification*, and results in a set of functions defining how the opacity, red, green, and blue channels (or, alternately, hue, saturation, and value) will be set for a given voxel value. These are often referred to as *transfer functions*. Initially, they may be set by analyzing the data and determining the voxel values where significant transitions occur. These make logical points for changes in color, opacity, or both. Alternatively, the user may want to interactively control these functions. This way, regions of interest (where the value of the volume points falls within certain ranges) can be given a different color or more opacity than others, and will thus be emphasized in the resulting image.

Another important problem in direct volume rendering is computing the effects of lighting and shading. As there are no explicit surfaces (and no normals to compute the shading effect), an approximation is made, based on the calculation of *gradients* (rate of change) in each direction. For a given voxel (v_x, v_y, v_z), we can estimate how rapidly the voxel is changing value in, say, the x-direction by examining the voxel's neighbors in that direction, namely (v_{x-1}, v_y, v_z) and (v_{x+1}, v_y, v_z). The simplest gradient is just the difference between the voxel and one of its immediate neighbors. Thus g_x, the x-component of the gradient, would just be $v_x - v_{x-1}$. This is referred to as the *intermediate difference operator*. By computing three subtractions, namely between the voxel and its neighbors in three directions, we arrive at a vector that gives a very coarse estimate of the direction of maximum change in voxel value. This vector can thus be used in place of the normal in our shading calculation. More accurate estimates of this vector

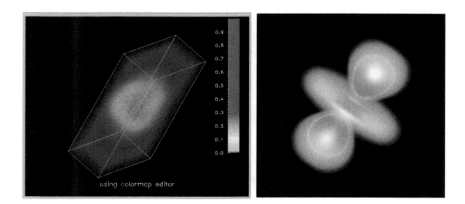

Figure 5.9.   Direct volume visualization. The left image is generated using an emissive model,
                   e.g., all points emit light in a level proportional to their value. No shading calcu-
                   lations are included. (Image generated with OpenDX [308].) The right image uses
                   a texture-based approach and includes diffuse and specular lighting components.
                   (Image from VRVis [439].)

can be obtained by examining a larger neighborhood surrounding the voxel.
The *central difference gradient estimator* uses the points on both sides of the
voxel, rather than the voxel itself. In this case, g_x is computed as $v_{x+1} - v_{x-1}$;
a larger neighborhood is used, but by ignoring the value at (v_x, v_y, v_z) we
can lose some fine detail information. Larger gradient operators, such as
the three-dimensional Sobel operator, use all 26 immediately neighboring
voxels, and it is possible to use even larger neighborhoods. Accurate gradient
estimation can have a significant impact on the visual appeal of the resulting
visualization.

Figure 5.9 shows some examples of direct volume visualization. Each has
strengths and weaknesses in terms of performance and interpretability.

5.3.3   Implicit Surfaces

The typical method of modeling surfaces in computer graphics is using parametric equations to define points on the surface, which can then be connected
to form polygonal meshes. This representation is very useful for performing
transformations and computing surface normals. An alternative method is
the use of implicit representations [41], where the surface is defined as the
zero contour of a function of two or three variables. Implicit representations
have strengths in operations such as blending and metamorphosis, and have

been becoming increasingly popular. They can also be used in data visualization to convey sparse data sets and the field of influence for the data points. They also enable combining clouds of data into higher-level surfaces and solids.

Metaballs, also known as *blobby objects* [475], are a type of implicit modeling technique. We can think of a metaball as a particle surrounded by a density field, where the density attributed to the particle (its influence) decreases with distance from the particle location. A surface is implied by taking an isosurface through this density field—the higher the isosurface value, the nearer it will be to the particle. The powerful aspect of metaballs is the way they can be combined. By simply summing the influences of each metaball on a given point, we can get very smooth blendings of the spherical influence fields.

The key to using metaballs is the definition of the equation for specifying the influence on an arbitrary point from an arbitrary particle. Blinn [40] used exponentially decaying fields for each particle, with a Gaussian bump with height b and standard deviation a. If r is the distance from the particle to a location in the field, the influence of the particle is b^{-ar}. For efficiency purposes, this was changed to the squared distance to avoid computing the square root. The resulting density of an arbitrary location in the field is simply the summation of the contributions from all the particles.

Wyvill et al. [475] simplified the calculations somewhat by defining a cubic polynomial based on the radius of influence for a particle and the distance from the center of the particle to the field location in question. The key is that the influence must be 1.0 when the distance r is 0.0, and 0.0 when the distance is equal to the radius R of influence. A function that satisfies these requirements is $C(r) = 2r^3/R^3 - 3r^2/R^2 + 1$. This equation is a bit slow, due to the square root calculation, so like Blinn, they recast it as a function in r^2 and R^2. By using an additional condition (influence at $R/2 = 0.5$), and for $a = -.444444$, $b = 1.888889$, and $c = -2.444444$, the resulting function is

$$C(r) = ar^6/R^6 + br^4/R^4 + cr^2/R^2 + 1.$$

Given a set of data points, we define a grid and compute the density at each point based on the data in the neighborhood. Once this field is generated, any scalar field visualization technique can be used to render it, such as the Marching Cubes algorithm or direct volume rendering. Figure 5.10 shows a couple of examples of the types of renderings that can be performed

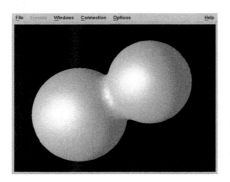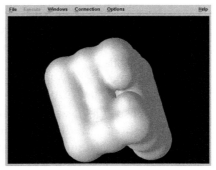

Figure 5.10.   Examples of implicit surfaces. The figure on the left shows two intersecting spheres, while the figure on the right contains a bent grid of 25 spheres with different ranges of influence, where the center sphere is missing.

with implicit surfaces. The first image was generated using just two spheres, with an isovalue of 0.11. Intersecting elements were summed together. Note the smooth transition between the two objects: no discontinuities are visible. The second image contains 24 spheres laid out in an L-shape, with a hole in the middle. The inner spheres were given a smaller radius in an attempt to mimic a cushion that is compressed in the middle. It is important to remember that this moderately complex surface was defined by a total of 24 positions and radii, plus an isovalue.

5.4 Dynamic Data

Flow visualization is the study of methods to display the dynamic behavior in liquids and gases. The field dates back at least to the mid-1400s, where Leonardo Da Vinci sketched images of fine particles of sand and wood shavings that had been dropped into flowing liquids. Since then, laboratory flow visualization has become more and more exact, with careful control of the particulate size and distribution. Advances in photography have also helped extend our understanding of how fluids flow under various circumstances.

More recently, computational fluid dynamics (CFD) has extended the abilities of scientists to study flow by creating simulations of dynamic behavior of fluids under a wide range of conditions. The result of this analysis is usually a 2D or 3D grid of velocity vectors, which may be uniformly or nonuniformly spaced. The goal is then to analyze this vector field to identify features such as turbulence, vortices, saddle points, and other forms of structure.

There are several variations on the structure of the field data that is generated by these experiments. A *static field* is one in which there is only a single, unchanging velocity field. *Time-varying fields* may either have fixed positions with changing vector values or both changing positions and changing vectors (for example, when modeling rotating turbine blades or pitching airfoils). These latter types are referred to as *unsteady*.

5.4.1 Definitions

We provide some definitions that we will need in our discussion of the mathematics of particle advection.

- *pathline*—The trajectory of a particle released into a flow field; it assumes multiple time instances. In experimental visualization, this can be achieved by long-term film exposure.

- *streakline*—Simultaneous positions of a set of particles continuously released from one or more locations.

- *timeline*—Position at an instant of time of a batch of particles that have been released simultaneously.

- *streamline*—A line through the velocity field that is tangent to the velocity field at every point.

- *steady flow*—A flow field that does not change with time. For steady flow, streaklines, pathlines, and streamlines coincide.

- *particle advection*—Computing the motion of particles through a flow field.

- *vorticity*—The curl of the velocity field, giving the magnitude and direction of angular velocity for each particle in the velocity field.

5.4.2 Mathematics of Particle Advection

Below is the pseudocode for computing streaklines in the most general situation, namely where both vectors and grid positions for the field may be changing over time (derived from [263]).

Assume there are N_s seed locations and N_t time steps. Thus there will be s traces, each with a varying number of particles. Each iteration of the outermost loop will compute new positions based on the current time and next time, thus requiring two time steps of flow and grid position data. After each iteration, the next set of flow and position data is read. This procedure looks as follows:

```
Read first 2 time steps of flow and grid data
For t = 1 to Nt-1 do
   Advect_trace(t, t+1)
   Write current traces to file
   Read next time step of flow data
   If moving grid, Read next time step of grid data
   End for
```

For each time step, we look at each trace and each particle within the trace. We compute a new position for each particle, and if it is still within the region associated with the field, we save it. Finally, we start a new particle at the seed location for each trace.

```
For s = 1 to Ns do
   Copy trace s to working trace w
   W_length = Trace_length(s)
   Clear trace s and set Trace_length s to 0
   for i = 1 to W_length do
      p = ith particle of working trace w
      advect_particle(current_time, next_time, p)
      if p within field space
         store p in trace s
         Trace_length(s)++
         End if
      End for
   Release a new particle for trace s at the seed location
   Trace_length(s)++
   End for
```

To advect a particle between two time periods, we need to integrate the point position in small step sizes until either the position falls out of the field space or the ending time is reached. This is usually done using a Runge-Kutta integration based on a predictor-corrector algorithm. This requires a trilinear interpolation of the vector field to compute the velocity at an arbitrary location. The following shows a second-order integration.

```
t = current_time
While (t < next_time AND p inside field) do
   V = Interpolate_velocity(p, t, current_time, next_time)
Adjust:
   h = c/max(V)      /* C is a step size between 0 and 1 */
```

```
        If (t + h > next_time) h = next_time - t
        t = t + h
Predict:
    p_approx = p + h * V
    V_new = Interpolate_velocity(p_approx, t+h, current_time, next_time)
Adapt_step:
    V_total = (V + V_new)/2
    if (h * max(V_total) > c) then
        V = V_total
        t = t - h
        Goto Adjust
        End if
Corrector:
    p = p + h * (V + V_new)/2
End while
```

5.4.3   Visualization Techniques

Many methods for visualizing flows have been developed over the years [21]. The simplest form of flow visualization is to display the velocity field data itself, either as displacement vectors using arrow glyphs (see Figure 5.11) or as magnitude scalar values using image, surface, or volume visualization techniques (mapping values to color, size, or position). The number and placement of the displayed components is a crucial factor in conveying the

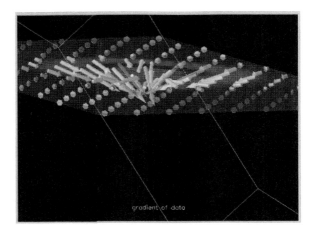

Figure 5.11.   A storm cloud visualization containing glyphs showing wind direction and strength. (Image generated with OpenDX [308].)

important features of the data; showing too many flow field components can lead to significant occlusion, while using too few elements raises the potential for missing features. While the simplest solution is to allow the user to interactively change the density of elements (often specified by a plane or vector in space, along with a sampling rate), recent research has focused on automated placement of the displayed flow field components by analyzing the data and identifying regions where potentially interesting flow is occurring.

The next most common technique is the generation of streamlines based on a static velocity field. The user selects seed locations (often along a line or at two-dimensional grid locations), and computes a path for each seed point through the field, maintaining a continuous tangent to the flow field.

Besides using lines to indicate the streams, we can use planar or solid objects, such as ribbons and tubes. Other attributes of the field, such as magnitude or vorticity, can now be mapped to other attributes of the stream-ribbons or stream-tubes, such as color, size, or twist (see Figure 5.12).

Streaklines are often represented as a continuous stream of particles emanating from a discrete set of points and flowing through the field (see Figure 5.13). Individual points in a given trace (all particles coming from a particular location belong to the same trace) may be identified by color-coding to help distinguish related points that get separated when entering areas of high velocity.

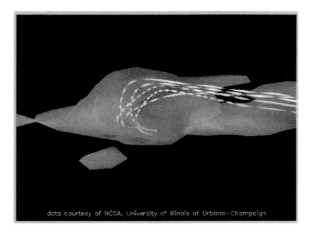

data courtesy of NCSA, University of Illinois at Urbana–Champaign

Figure 5.12.   Flow data visualized using ribbons, with vorticity mapped to twist. (Image generated with OpenDX [308].)

Figure 5.13.   An example of streaklines: Sparks from a Campfire. (Image Courtesy Wikimedia Commons.)

One more recent technique for flow visualization is called a *streamball*, which is based on the use of metaballs or blobby/soft objects [46]. This is an implicit surface based on a field created by computing the influence of seed points on each location in the field. In effect, each seed point will influence a certain part of space, and locations in space can be influenced by multiple points. What this means is that if we use each particle along a streamline or streakline to influence a spherical segment of the field, locations under the influence of multiple particles will have continuous, smooth transitions from one particle to the other. This can form both tubes and surfaces, depending on how close the particles and streamlines are to each other.

Line Integral Convolution. An interesting approach to vector field visualization was developed by Cabral and Leedom in 1993 [54]. The method, called *line integral convolution*, or LIC, uses a random field and a vector field with the same height and width to generate a dense display of flow information (see Figure 5.14). Basically, every pixel in the resulting image is a weighted average of a sequence of adjacent pixels in the random field along a linear path centered on the given pixel and following the streamline going through

Figure 5.14.   The texture field on the left is combined with the vector field in the middle to create the line integral convolution on the right. (Images generated with LicFactory [493].)

the pixel. More formally, we can start at each location (i, j) in the vector field and create two chains of pixels emanating from this location in opposite directions tangent to the vector orientation. The length of the chain is set to $2L$, where L is the distance traveled in each direction. These pixels form a 1-pixel-wide filter kernel. The corresponding pixels in the random field (the authors use white noise) are summed and normalized by the chain length, and the result of the computation is stored at position (i, j) in the result image. The result is that pixels along lines with adjacent similar vectors will have similar sums from the noise texture image.

An improvement on this technique, which defines the actual LIC, is to form the filter by advecting points starting at position (i, j) along the streamline containing the point. The advection, which follows a similar strategy to that presented earlier, takes small steps from the initial position using the initial orientation, and then adjusts the orientation based on the local vector information. A high-level view of LIC is presented below. Many options for the advection and convolution processes exist, and the number of points advected for each position can have a significant impact on the results (a value of 10 is suggested by the authors of the technique [54]).

1. Give a vector field V and a texture image T.

2. Read and store V and T, computing the maximum vector magnitude.

3. For each point (i, j) in the result image:

   (a) Compute, via interpolation, the flow direction and magnitude at this point.

   (b) Advect L points forward and backward, stopping at boundaries. Step size depends on normalized vector magnitude.

(c) Given $2L + 1$ positions, extract corresponding values from T.

(d) Convolve a list of texture points, normalizing based on the shape of the convolution kernel to maintain good range of color/intensity values.

This process continues until the length of the streamline centered on the selected point is equal to $2L$. Again, the texture points are summed and normalized. They may also be weighted using a Gaussian filter to allow a tapering effect at the ends of the filter kernel. The resulting convolution, while much more computationally expensive than the simple straight line version, is much more accurate for flow lines with a small radius of curvature. An interesting effect can be obtained by animating this computation.

5.5   Combining Techniques

Many effective visualizations are actually combinations of two or more of the techniques described above. Each technique has its strengths and weaknesses in terms of the types of information it can or cannot effectively visualize, so a combined visualization, as long as occlusion is minimized, can generate results that are the sum of the strengths. At the same time, more and more problems require the simultaneous analysis of multiple data sets to arrive at an informed result. For example, weather forecasting involves the combination of air and surface temperature, wind speed, relative humidity, and a number of other factors to develop an accurate prediction. In this section we will examine a number of visualizations formed by combining some of the methods previously discussed, highlighting factors important to their successful design and interpretation.

5.5.1   Slice Plus Isosurface

In Figure 5.15, an isosurface from a medical data set is combined with an orthogonal slicing of the same data set, mapping the isosurface to one color and the values in the image resulting from the slice mapped to a separate color ramp. The isosurface is capable of conveying surface structure, which is difficult to obtain from volume slicing, even with animation of the slice position. However, the isosurface only provides information on a single value within the entire volume, with no indication of the distribution of other values or the gradient (rate of change) of the selected value at different locations. The slice provides very detailed two-dimensional information,

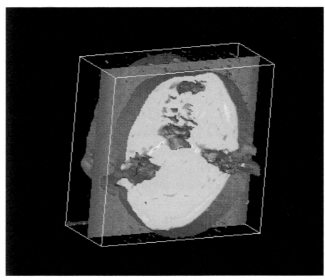

Figure 5.15.   A medical volume data set displayed with an isosurface and a two-dimensional slice. (Image generated with OpenDX [308].)

especially with an appropriate choice of color assignments. It can convey to the user the regions of relative uniformity, as well as those exhibiting significant change. Another advantage is that the image slice can convey nested regions of a particular value range, while the isosurface, in general, will only display the outer-most surface.

Several considerations and capabilities are important when designing and developing this visualization:

- it is critical to support rapid and intuitive modification of the isosurface value;

- the position and orientation (along the three axes) of the slice should be easily controlled by the user, with the option for animating its position as it steps through the volume;

- camera position and orientation control are essential to enable viewing of the surface and slice from different orientations;

- color assignment is crucial, as features of interest in the slice may only be revealed with a carefully chosen color map. Similarly, we might want to choose the color of the isosurface so that it does not appear in the color map used for the slice, to reduce the potential for misinterpretation;

- the user should be able to easily hide either of the two visualization components to make it easier to study the remaining data display. Another option is to allow the user to control the opacity of the components, perhaps using a slider that ranges from hiding the slice entirely to hiding the isosurface.

5.5.2 Isosurface Plus Glyphs

As mentioned in the previous section, isosurfaces are useful for conveying details of three-dimensional surfaces, but, in general, do not incorporate other aspects of the data. Glyphs (described in more detail in Chapter 8), such as the popular arrow glyph, can be used to display the magnitude and direction of change within a data set, either as a gradient in static data or a flow in dynamic data. The glyphs may be positioned in close proximity to the isosurface, since these are known to be positions of interest, or the positions may be controlled separately.

In Figure 5.16, a section of a storm cloud is displayed, with the isosurface indicating water density within the cloud and the arrow glyphs showing the direction and magnitude of the wind field. Additionally, a cut plane is used to show water density details. By moving the starting positions of the arrow glyphs (attached to a movable plane), regions of calm and turbulence can be isolated and investigated. By modifying the isovalue, the shape and position of the cloud may be changed, and interactions with the wind field can be explored.

Many of the design considerations from the previous example pertain to this visualization as well. Interactive control of the parameters of the visualization—the isosurface value, glyph base position, and viewing position and angle—contribute to making this an effective visualization. Other controls are necessary for improving the information content of the glyphs, including:

- varying the density of the glyphs;

- scaling the glyph sizes;

- controlling the color of glyphs to convey additional information or redundantly map to the wind magnitude;

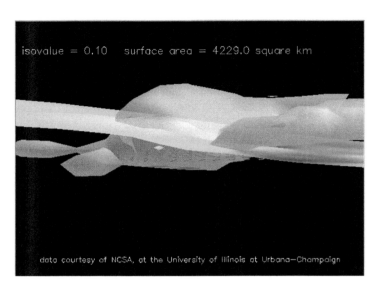

Figure 5.16.   A storm cloud visualization containing an isosurface and cut plane for water density and glyphs showing wind direction and strength. (Image generated with OpenDX [308].)

- computing base positions for the glyphs based on regions of interest in the vector or water density fields.

Other potential enhancements to this visualization would be to use a cut plane or rubber sheet to display variability within one or more fields, taking advantage of the translucent isosurface to maintain context and bearings. Streamlines could also be added to enhance the viewer's understanding of the flow field.

5.5.3   Rubber Sheet plus Contour Lines and Color

We have mentioned several times the benefits of redundant mappings of the same data to different attributes of the visualization. In this example, we start with a rubber sheet to convey a two-dimensional field of values as a height field. This can reveal peaks and valleys found in the data, and by creating a virtual landscape, we can build on the users' intuition about interpreting the data in a topographic manner (see Figure 5.17). We can augment this visualization by mapping color to the elevation, thus making it easier to identify widely separated regions of similar height (see Figure 5.18). Finally, we can superimpose contour lines at certain levels, making

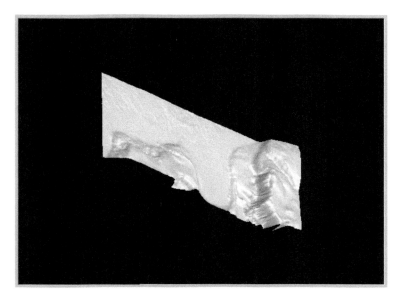

Figure 5.17.   A rubber sheet display of the height above and below sea level for the southeast
United States. (Image generated with OpenDX [308].)

Figure 5.18.   The same data as in Figure 5.17, with color mapped to elevation. (Image generated
with OpenDX [308].)

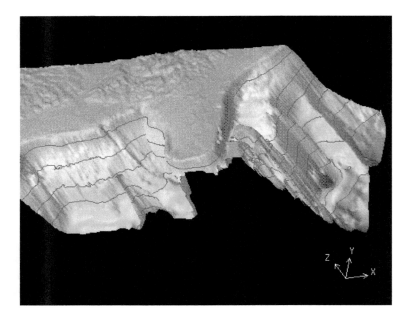

Figure 5.19.   A zoomed-in region of the same data as the previous two figures, with additional contour lines. (Image generated with OpenDX [308].)

the gradient information much more apparent (see Figure 5.19). Note that each addition to the visualization has improved our understanding of the data, yet there is some value to viewing the data in multiple ways. This reinforces our design consideration regarding selective hiding and showing of visualization components to take advantage of their individual strengths while enabling users to incrementally enhance their mental model of the data contents.

5.6   Summary

In this chapter we have surveyed many of the common techniques for visualizing spatio-temporal data, e.g., data with an implicit spatial, and sometimes temporal, dimension. As we progressed through data of increasing dimensionality, we examined several algorithms upon which the visualization techniques are built. As there are many options for visualizing a data set, it is important to understand the benefits and drawbacks of each technique in terms of what data features are clearly presented or potentially hidden.

Indeed, unless the domain area and visualization task are well defined and focused, it is often preferable to support more than one way of visualizing a particular data set. We will reiterate this point in later chapters that focus on the visualization of nonspatial data.

5.7 Related Readings

The book *Introduction to Scientific Visualization* by Helen Wright provides a compact, relatively high-level view of the field of scientific visualization [473]. The author provides software demonstrations of many of the concepts described. The book *Data Visualization: Principles and Practice* by Alexandru Telea provides a more mathematical treatment of the field, and also includes a discussion of information visualization techniques [405]. For those interested in a more in-depth study of scientific visualization, an excellent collection of articles is *The Visualization Handbook* [167], edited by Charles Hansen and Christopher Johnson. A good textbook for algorithms related to scientific visualization is [449]. It includes the basics for several of the algorithms found in this chapter. Other useful books include Lichtenbelt et al.'s book on volume rendering [272] and Bloomenthal and Wyvill's book on implicit surfaces [41]. An interesting article reviewing glyph-based techniques for visualizing spatial multivariate medical data can be found in [346] and an overview of geometric flow visualization can be found in [289]. Many of the algorithms used in spatial data visualization have their roots in image processing and computer vision. Many fine textbooks for these fields exist, including [371] and [153].

5.8 Exercises

1. Discuss the pros and cons of using an isosurface data representation versus slicing a three-dimensional volume. Give two examples where either would be more appropriate than the other.

2. These days, many people carry small, portable display devices with them, such as mobile phones and tablets. Discuss the ramifications of migrating to a small display for the visualization techniques discussed in this chapter. Which mappings maintain most of their benefits when scaling occurs? What strategies might you pursue to allow viewers access to the same or similar resolution of information?

3. Researchers in the visualization field have spent considerable time trying to differentiate classes of techniques, such as scientific versus information visualization, spatial versus nonspatial visualization, and continuous versus discrete data visualization. Describe what you feel are the aspects of the techniques and data discussed in this chapter that seem to be shared. Are there any techniques that don't fit this model as well as others?

4. A new topic called *visual analytics* is now further differentiating the field. Its definition is "the science of analytical reasoning facilitated by interactive visual interfaces" [84]. Describe what you feel are aspects that this new field includes which so far have not been discussed in the chapter.

5. In flow simulation, one often computes a number of different attributes at each time slice and location. Describe at least three distinct ways you could map temperature, pressure, and velocity in a three-dimensional flow field. For each, discuss the accuracy/resolution at which the viewer could attain the data values. Also, discuss the issue of occlusion and the potential for misinterpretation due to partially visible data points.

5.9   Projects

1. Rewrite DRAWLINEGRAPH() to instead draw a color bar, given a color ramp with a range ($color_{\min}, color_{\max}$). You can assume that the number of data points is less than the width of the screen in determining the width of the rectangle. Set the height of the rectangle to some user-specified constant.

2. Write a program that extends DRAWLINEGRAPH() to subsample the data whenever the number of data points $dataCount$ exceeds the number of pixels in the drawing area ($xMax - xMin$).

3. Write a program that reads in a three-dimensional volume data set and displays a user-selected slice. Assume a grayscale color map with 256 intensity levels.

4. Extend the above program to allow the user to specify an orientation for the slice (0 = aligned with x-axis, 1 = aligned with y-axis, and 2 = aligned with z-axis). Note that since the size of the data volume

often differs for each dimension, the selected slice must be confined to a range that depends on the orientation.

5. Extend the above program to allow arbitrary orientation, as specified with a vector normal to the cutting plane plus center point for the cut plane that is within the data volume. Note that this project will require resampling of the data in almost all cases.

CHAPTER **6**

Visualization Techniques for Geospatial Data

Geospatial data is different from other kinds of data in that spatial data describes objects or phenomena with a specific location in the real world. Geospatial data arises in many applications, including credit card payments, telephone calls, environmental records, and census demographics. In this chapter, we provide an overview of the special characteristics and methods that are needed for the visualization of geospatial data, sometimes called *geovisualization*. We introduce the most important basics of geospatial visualization, such as map projections, and discuss visualization techniques for point, line, area, and surface data. Due to the large scope of visualization techniques in geographic information systems (GIS) and cartography, we only provide a basic introduction from a visualization perspective. More details about GIS, spatial visualization, and cartography can be found in [66, 257, 281, 327, 384]. After reading the chapter, the reader should have a general understanding about state-of-the-art visualization techniques for geospatial data and should be able to implement and use them.

6.1 Visualizing Spatial Data

Large spatial data sets can be seen as a result of accumulating samples or readings of phenomena in the real world, while moving along two dimensions in space. Often, spatial data sets are discrete samples of a continuous phenomenon. Nowadays, there exists a large number of applications where it is important to analyze relationships that involve geographic location.

Examples include global climate modeling (e.g., measuring temperature, rainfall, and wind speed), environmental records (e.g., measuring CO_2 and other pollution levels), economic and social measures and indicators (e.g., unemployment rate, education level), customer analysis, telephone calls, credit card payments, and crime data. Because of its special characteristics, the basic visualization strategy for spatial data is straightforward; we map the spatial attributes directly to the two physical screen dimensions, resulting in map visualizations.

Maps are the world reduced to points, lines, and areas. The visualization parameters, including size, shape, value, texture, color, orientation, and shape, show additional information about the objects under consideration. According to the U.S. Geological Survey (USGS), map visualizations are defined as a set of points, lines, and areas, all defined both by position reference to a coordinate system (spatial attributes) and by their nonspatial attributes. MacEachren defines geographic visualization as the use of visual representations to make spatial contexts and problems visible, so as to engage the most powerful human processing abilities, those associated with vision [280].

From the definitions, it becomes clear that we may distinguish spatial phenomena according to their spatial *dimension* or *extent*:

- *point phenomena*—have no spatial extent; they can be termed zero-dimensional and can be specified by a longitude and latitude coordinate pair, along with a set of descriptors or attributes. Examples are buildings, oil wells, aggregated measures, and cities.

- *line phenomena*—have length, but essentially no width; they can be termed one-dimensional and can be specified by an unclosed series of longitude and latitude coordinate pairs for each phenomenon. Examples are large telecommunication networks, roads, and boundaries between countries. Attributes associated with line phenomena might include capacities, traffic levels, and names.

- *area phenomena*—have both length and width; they can be termed two-dimensional and can be specified by a series of longitude and latitude coordinate pairs that completely enclose a region, along with a set of attributes for each phenomenon. Examples are lakes, parks, and political units such as states or counties.

- *surface phenomena*—have length, width, and height; they are termed two-and-half-dimensional and can be specified by a series of longitude, latitude, and height coordinate vectors with a set of attributes for each (longitude, latitude) pair.

Maps can be subdivided into map types based on properties of the data (qualitative versus quantitative; discrete versus continuous) and the properties of the graphical variables (points, lines, surface, volumes). Examples of the resulting maps are

- symbol maps (nominal point data);

- dot maps (ordinal point data);

- land use maps (nominal area data);

- choropleth maps (ordinal area data);

- line diagrams (nominal or ordinal line data);

- isoline maps (ordinal surface data);

- surface maps (ordinal volume data).

Note that the same data may be visualized by different map types. By aggregating point data within areas, a choropleth map may be generated out of a dot map, or a land use map out of a symbol map. We may also generate a density surface from a dot map and display it as an isoline map or a surface map. If we aggregate the point data within areas and map the number of points within the areas to their size, we obtain cartogram visualizations. More details on map types can be found in Chapter 7 of [255].

In exploratory geovisualization, interaction with maps is crucial. In contrast to traditional cartography, the classification and mapping of the data can be interactively adapted by the user, and interactive querying as well as manipulation of the display are possible [16]. A number of techniques and systems have been developed that make extensive use of such interaction capabilities. They allow, for example, a linking of multiple maps or a combination of maps with standard statistical visualizations, such as bar charts and line charts, or even with complex multidimensional visualization techniques such as parallel coordinates or pixel techniques (see Chapter 8). In addition, they usually provide an advanced browsing or querying interface. An example of such as system is the CommonGIS system [14, 15].

6.1.1   Map Projections

In visualizing geospatial data, map projections play a critical role. Map projections are concerned with mapping the positions on the globe (sphere) to positions on the screen (flat surface). A map projection is defined as $\Pi : (\lambda, \varphi) \rightarrow (x, y)$. The data format for degrees of longitude (λ) is fixed to the interval $[-180, 180]$, where negative values stand for western degrees and positive values for eastern degrees. The degrees of latitude (φ) are defined similarly on the interval $[-90, 90]$, where negative values are used for southern degrees and positive values for northern degrees. Map projections may have different properties:

- A *conformal projection* retains the local angles on each point of a map correctly, which means that they also locally preserve shapes. The area, however, is not preserved.

- A map projection is called *equivalent* or *equal area* if a specific area on one part of the map covers exactly the same surface on the globe, as another part of the map with the same area. Area-accurate projections result in a distortion of form and angles.

- A projection is called *equidistant* if it preserves the distance from some standard point or line.

- *Gnomonic projections* allow all *great circles* to be displayed as straight lines. Great circles are the largest circle that can be drawn on a given sphere and cut the sphere into two halves of equal size. Gnomic projections preserve the shortest route between two points.

- *Azimuthal projections* preserve the direction from a central point. Usually these projections also have radial symmetry in the scales, e.g., distances from the central point are independent of the angle and consequently, circles with the central point as center result in circles that have the central point on the map as their center.

- In a *retroazimuthal projection*, the direction from a point S to a fixed location L corresponds to the direction on the map from S to L.

Map projections may also be classified by the type of surface onto which the sphere is projected. The most important surfaces are (see Figure 6.1) as follows:

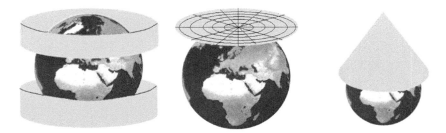

Figure 6.1.   Cylinder, plane, and cone projections.

- *Cylinder projections* project the surface of the sphere on a cylinder that is put around the sphere. Each point of the sphere is projected outward on the cylinder. Cylinder projections allow the entire spherical surface to be visible. Most cylinder projections preserve local angles and are therefore conformal projections. The degrees of longitude and latitude are usually orthogonal to each other. Pseudo-cylindrical projections represent the central meridian and each parallel as a single straight line segment, but not the other meridians.

- *Plane projections* are azimuthal projections that map the surface of the sphere to a plane that is tangent to the sphere, with the tangent point corresponding to the center point of the projection. Some plane projections are true perspective projections.

- *Cone projections* map the surface of the sphere to a cone that is tangent to the sphere. Degrees of latitude are represented as circles around the projection center, degrees of longitude as straight lines emanating from this center. Cone projections may be designed in a way that preserves the distance from the center of the cone. There are also a number of pseudo-conical projections that, for example, retain the distances from the pole, as well as the distances from the meridian.

φ	measured degrees of latitude in radians
λ	measured degrees of longitude in radians
x	horizontal axis of the two-dimensional map
y	vertical axis of the two-dimensional map
$\varphi_0; \lambda_0$	latitude of the standard parallel resp. meridian measured in radians

Table 6.1.   Variables used in map projections.

In the following, we provide the mapping details for a few widely used map projections. A comprehensive list of all map projections support by ArcGIS can be found at [116]. Variables used in map projections are defined in Table 6.1.

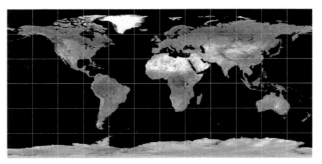

Figure 6.2.   Equirectangular projection.

Equirectangular Cylindrical Projections. The equirectangular projection [164] (see Figure 6.2), one of the oldest and simplest projections, is a cylindrical projection. It maps meridians to equally spaced vertical straight lines and circles of latitude to evenly spread horizontal straight lines. The spherical coordinates are transferred one-to-one to a rectangular surface:

$$x = \lambda, \qquad\qquad y = \varphi.$$

The projection does not have any of the desirable map properties and is neither conformal nor equal area. Because of the distortions introduced by equirectangular projections, it has little use in navigation, but finds its main usage in thematic mapping.

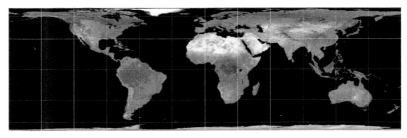

Figure 6.3.   Lambert cylindrical projection.

Lambert Cylindrical Projection. The Lambert cylindrical projection [164] (see Figure 6.3) is an equal area projection that is easy to compute and provides nice world maps. The mapping is defined as

$$x = (\lambda - \lambda_0) * \cos \varphi_0, \qquad\qquad y = \frac{\sin \varphi}{\cos \varphi_0}.$$

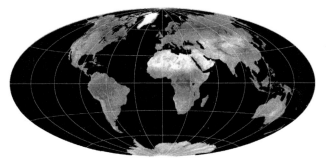

Figure 6.4.   Hammer-Aitoff projection.

Hammer-Aitoff Projection. The Hammer-Aitoff projection [388] is a modified azimuthal projection. The central meridian and the equator are straight lines, with the meridian being half as long as the equator. The other meridians and equator-parallels are unequally spaced curves (see Figure 6.4). The mapping is defined as

$$x = \frac{2\sqrt{2}\cos \varphi \sin \frac{\lambda}{2}}{(1 + \cos \varphi \cos \frac{\lambda}{2})^{\frac{1}{2}}}, \qquad\qquad y = \frac{\sqrt{2}\sin \varphi}{(1 + \cos \varphi \cos \frac{\lambda}{2})^{\frac{1}{2}}}.$$

It is an equal area projection, and its elliptic form gives the viewer a reference to the spherical shape of the earth. Hammer-Aitoff projections are mainly used in thematic world mapping.

Mollweide Projection. The Mollweide projection [388] is an equal-area pseudo-cylindrical projection that represents the earth in the form of an ellipse (see Figure 6.5). All equator-parallels are straight lines, and all meridians except the central meridian are equally spaced elliptical arcs. The Mollweide mapping is defined as

$$x = \frac{2\sqrt{2}(\lambda - \lambda_0)\cos \theta}{\pi}, \qquad y = 2^{\frac{1}{2}}\sin \theta, \qquad 2\theta + \sin(2\theta) = \pi \sin \varphi.$$

In solving these equations, the variable θ is calculated using an interpolation method (Newton). Mollweide projections are mainly used for thematic maps of the entire world.

Figure 6.5.   Mollweide projection.

Cosinusoidal Projection. The Cosinusoidal projection [388] is a simple pseudo-cylindrical equal-area projection that can be quickly computed. It has a unique form and surprisingly good local properties (see Figure 6.6). The mapping is defined as

$$x = (\lambda - \lambda_0) * \cos\varphi, \qquad\qquad y = \varphi.$$

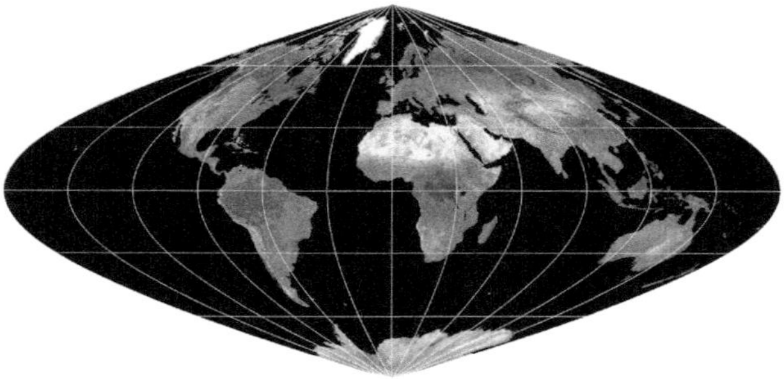

Figure 6.6.   Cosinusoidal projection.

Albers Equal-Area Conic Projection. The Albers equal-area conic projection [164] is an area-accurate cone projection. Its basic idea is to use two standard parallels (defined by β_1 and β_2) to reduce some of the distortions resulting from projection with only one standard parallel. The meridians are equally spaced straight lines intersecting in one point. The equator-parallels are unequally spaced concentric circles. The mapping is

$$n = \frac{\cos\beta_1 + \cos\beta_2}{2}, \quad p = \sqrt{\frac{4}{n} * \sin(\frac{\frac{\pi}{2} - \varphi}{2}) + \frac{4}{n^2} * (\sin\frac{\beta_1}{2})^2 * (\sin\frac{\beta_2}{2})^2},$$
$$x = \frac{p}{\sin(n * \lambda)}, \qquad y = -\frac{p}{\cos(n * \lambda)}.$$

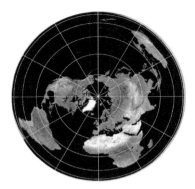

Figure 6.7.   Albers equal-area conic projection.

Neither shape nor distances are correct, but the distortion of these properties is minimized in the region between the two standard parallels. The distances are most accurate in the middle latitudes, and therefore the projection is mostly used for smaller regions with east-west orientation located in the middle latitudes (see Figure 6.7).

6.1.2 Visual Variables for Spatial Data

Maps are used in many different ways: for example, to provide specific information about particular locations, to provide general information about spatial patterns, or to compare patterns in multiple maps. The mapping of spatial data properties to the visual variables must reflect this goal. The visual variables for spatial data are (see Figure 6.8):

- *size*—size of individual symbols, width of lines, or size of symbols in areas;

- *shape*—shape of individual symbols or pattern symbols in lines and areas;

- *brightness*—brightness of symbols, lines, or areas;

- *color*—color of symbols, lines, or areas;

- *orientation*—orientation of individual symbols or patterns in lines and areas;

- *spacing (texture)*—spacing of patterns in symbols, lines, or areas;

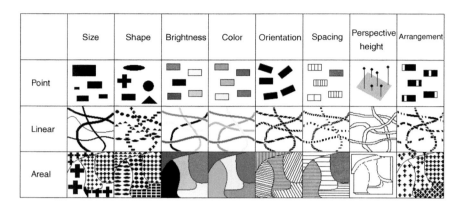

Figure 6.8.   Visual variables for spatial data (Image based on [384].)

- *perspective height*—perspective three-dimensional view of the phenomena with the data value mapped to the perspective height of points,
  lines, or areas;

- *arrangement*—arrangement of patterns within the individual symbols
  (for point phenomena), patterns of dots and dashes (for line phenomena), or regular versus random distribution of symbols (for area phenomena).

Cartographic design has been studied intensively for several decades, and
there are well-established guidelines for map design [281]. All are based on
the results of perceptual research (see Chapter 3), and the same basic mapping principles as discussed in Chapter 4 must be observed. Note that in
spatial data mapping, the chosen class separation, normalization, and spatial aggregation may have a severe impact on the resulting visualization. In
Figure 6.9 (top), for example, two visualizations of the same data are shown.
The only difference is that the class separation chosen has been slightly modified, with a significant impact on the generated map. Figure 6.9 (bottom)
shows the significant change resulting from an absolute versus relative mapping. On the left side, the absolute numbers are shown, while on the right
side, the numbers are displayed relative to the population numbers. Note
that due to the large population differences in some areas, an inverted visual effect results. The visualization also heavily depends on the extent of
the areas for aggregation. Figure 6.10 shows the well-known London cholera
example with different area aggregations, resulting in quite different maps.

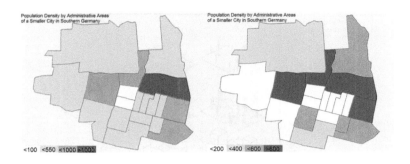

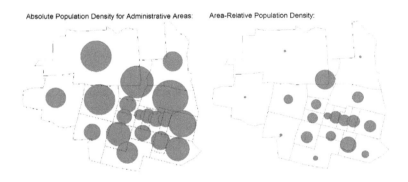

Figure 6.9.   Mapping problems: (top) different class breaks yield different choropleth maps; (bottom) absolute versus relative mappings yield different choropleth maps.

Area Aggregation:

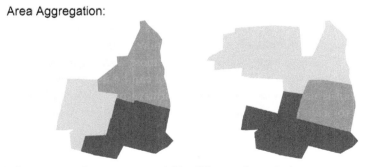

Figure 6.10.   Different spatial aggregation yields different choropleth maps.

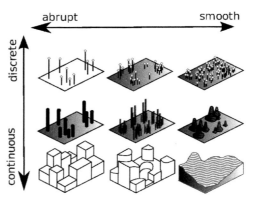

Figure 6.11.   Discrete versus continuous and smooth versus abrupt (based on [281]).

6.2 Visualization of Point Data

The first important class of spatial data is *point data*. Point data are discrete in nature, but they may describe a continuous phenomenon, for example, temperature measurements at specific locations. Depending on the nature of the data and the task, the designer must decide whether to display the data continuously, versus discrete and smooth, versus abrupt. Figure 6.11 show the different options. Discrete data are presumed to occur at distinct locations, while continuous data are defined at all locations. *Smooth data* refers to data that change in a gradual fashion, while *abrupt data* change suddenly.

6.2.1 Dot Maps

Point phenomena can be visualized by placing a symbol or pixel at the location where that phenomenon occurs. This simple visualization is called a *dot map*. A quantitative parameter may be mapped to the size or the color of the symbol or pixel. Circles are the most widely used symbol in dot maps, but squares, bars, or any other symbol can be used as well. If the size of the symbol is used to represent a quantitative parameter, a specific question is how to scale the symbols. Calculating the correct size of the symbols does not necessarily mean that the symbols will be perceived correctly [129]. The perceived size of the symbols does not necessarily correspond to the actual size, due to problems in size perception (see Chapter 3). The perceived size of the symbols depends on their local neighborhood (e.g., the Ebbinghaus illusion [340]), therefore no global formula for perceptual scaling is possible.

If color is used to represent a quantitative parameter, the problems of color perception (see Chapter 3) must be taken into account.

Dot maps are an elegant medium for communicating a wealth of information about the relationships of spatial point phenomena in a compact, convenient, and familiar format. However, when large data sets are drawn on a map, the problem of overlap or overplotting of data points arises in highly populated areas, while low-population areas are virtually empty (see Figure 6.12), since spatial data are highly nonuniformly distributed in real-world data sets. Examples of such spatial data sets are credit card payments, telephone calls, health statistics, environmental records, crime data, and census demographics. Note that the analysis may involve multiple parameters that may be shown on multiple maps. If all maps show the data in the same way, it may be possible to relate the parameters and detect local correlations, dependencies, and other interesting patterns. There are several approaches already in common use for coping with dense spatial data [144]. One widely used method is a 2.5D visualization showing data points aggregated up to map regions. This technique is commercially available in systems such as VisualInsight's In3D [2] and ESRI's ArcView [115]. An alternative that shows more detail is a visualization of individual data points as bars, according to their statistical value on a map. This technique is embodied in systems such as MineSet [437] and AT&T's Swift 3D [253]. A problem here is that a large number of data points are plotted at the same position, and therefore only a small portion of the data is actually visible. Moreover, due to occlusion in 3D, a significant fraction of the data may not be visible unless the viewpoint is changed.

Figure 6.12.   USA dot map: every circle represents the spatial location of an event. Even in the zoomed-in version there is a large degree of overlap. (Image reprinted from [227] with permission of Springer Science and Business Media.)

6.2.2   PixelMaps

One approach that does not aggregate the data, but avoids overlap in the two-dimensional display, is the *PixelMap* approach [230]. The idea is to reposition pixels that would otherwise overlap. The basic idea of the repositioning algorithm is to recursively partition the data set into four subsets containing the data points in four equal-sized subregions. Since the data points may not fit into the four subregions, we must determine new extents of the subregions (without changing the four subsets of data points), such that the data points in each subset can be visualized in their corresponding subregion. For an efficient implementation, a quadtree-like data structure manages the required information and supports the recursive partitioning process. The partitioning process works as follows. Starting with the root of the quadtree, in each step, the data space is partitioned into four subregions. The partitioning is made such that the area occupied by each of the

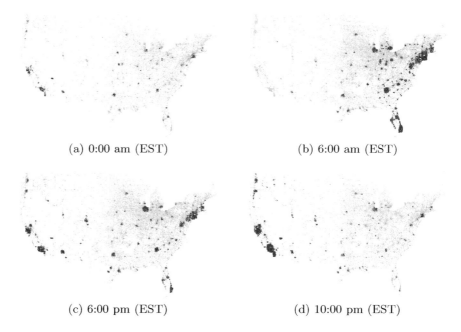

(a) 0:00 am (EST)   (b) 6:00 am (EST)

(c) 6:00 pm (EST)   (d) 10:00 pm (EST)

Figure 6.13.   The figures display U.S. Telephone Call Volume at four different times during one day. The idea is to place the first data items at their correct position and position overlapping data points at nearby unoccupied positions. (Image reprinted from [227] with permission of Springer Science and Business Media.)

subregions (in pixels) is larger than the number of pixels belonging to the corresponding subregion. If—after a few recursions—only a limited number of data points are left in a subregion, the points are positioned by a pixel placement algorithm that positions the first data item at its correct position, and subsequent overlapping data points at nearby unoccupied positions, resulting in a placement that appears locally quasi-random. The details of the algorithm can be found in [230]. A problem of PixelMaps is that in areas with high overlap, the repositioning depends on the ordering of the points in the database. Figure 6.13 presents four time steps of such visualizations, showing the U.S. Telephone Call Volume within a 10-minute interval of the time denoted. The time sequence shows the development of the call volume over time. The visualizations allow an intuitive understanding of the development of the call volume, showing the wake-up from east to west and the drop down in call volume at commuting and lunch time, for example. The visualizations show expected patterns but also reveal unexpected patterns, such as the little dark spots in the Kansas City, KS, and Omaha, NE, areas in the central U.S., which are the locations of call centers with nationwide service during the night (see Figure 6.13(a)).

6.3   Visualization of Line Data

The basic idea for visualizing spatial data describing linear phenomena is to represent them as line segments between pairs of endpoints specified by longitude and latitude. A standard mapping of line data allows data parameters to be mapped to line width, line pattern, line color, and line labeling. In addition, data properties of the starting and ending points, as well as intersection points, may also be mapped to the visual parameters of the nodes, such as size, shape, color, and labeling. The lines do not need to be straight, but may be polylines or splines, in order to avoid clutter in the display. Which mapping is best depends on the application and the task. Note that the choices in visualizing line data are similar to those in graph drawing (see Chapter 9), except that the position of the nodes in the display is fixed in geospatial applications, whereas it is part of the mapping and optimization process in graph drawing applications.

6.3.1   Network Maps

Network maps are widely used in a variety of applications. Some approaches only display the connectivity of networks for understanding their general

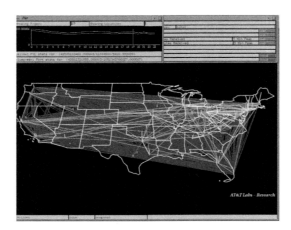

Figure 6.14.   Swift-3D. (Image from [254].)

behavior and structure. Eick, and Wills [107] used functions such as aggregation, hierarchical information, node position, and linked displays for investigating large networks with hierarchies and without a natural layout. They used color and shape for coding node information and color and line width for coding link information. Researchers at NCSA [305] added 3D graphics to their network maps to display animations of Internet traffic packets within the network backbone. Becker, Eick and Wilks [28] describe a system called *SeeNet*, which is motivated by research in dynamic statistical graphics. The basic idea is to involve the human and let him/her interactively control the display to focus on interesting patterns. They use two static network displays to visualize the geographic relationships, and a link matrix, which gives equal emphasis to all network links. Another interesting system for visualizing large network data is AT&T's SWIFT-3D System [224, 253, 254]. This system integrates a collection of relevant visualization techniques, ranging from familiar statistical displays to pixel-oriented overviews, with interactive 3D-maps and drag+drop query tools (see Figure 6.14). The visualization component maps the data to a set of linked 2D and 3D views created by different visualization techniques: statistical 2D visualizations, pixel-oriented 2D visualizations, and dynamic 3D visualizations. In all mentioned approaches, however, the visualization of large networks on maps leads to the overlap problem of line segments in dense areas.

Figure 6.15.   ArcMap. (Image from [87], © 1996 IEEE.)

6.3.2   Flow Maps and Edge Bundling

There are a number of approaches that try to avoid the overlap problem
of traditional network maps by using curved lines instead of straight lines
(see Figure 6.15). While this has been done mostly manually by cartogra-
phers in the past, a number of approaches for an algorithmically generated
visualization of network maps with curved lines have been proposed. Two
prominent examples are Stanford flow maps [318] and Danny Holten's edge
bundling [191].

The *flow map* technique is inspired by graph layout algorithms that minimize edge crossings and node position distortions, while retaining their relative positions. Algorithmically, a hierarchical clustering based on node
positions and flows between the nodes is performed to compute a useful
merging and rerouting of flows. Details can be found in [318]. In comparison to other computer-generated flow maps (Figure 6.16(a)), the results of
the Stanford system show a much clearer picture, with the clutter being
significantly reduced (Figure 6.16(b)).

Edge bundling also aims at reducing the clutter in line drawings. If a
hierarchy is defined on the nodes, the edges can be bundled according to the
hierarchy by using the hierarchy as defining points for B-splines connecting
two nodes. Nodes connected through the root of the hierarchy are maximally
bent, while nodes within the same subhierarchy are only minimally bent.
Hierarchical bundling significantly reduces visual clutter. It is a generic
method that can be used in conjunction with a number of visualization
techniques, including traditional maps, but also standard tree visualizations,
circular trees, treemaps, and many others. The example in Figure 6.17
displays edge bundling being applied to a visualization of IP traffic data. The

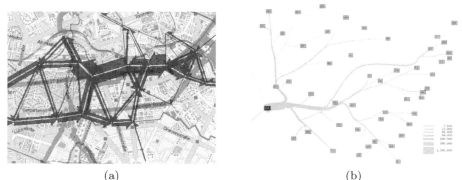

(a)   (b)

Figure 6.16.   Flow maps: (a) flows of tourists in Berlin; (b) produced by the Stanford system showing the migration from California (image from [318], © 2005 IEEE).

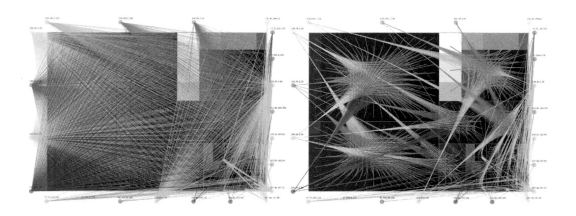

Figure 6.17.   The visualizations show IP flow traffic from external nodes on the outside to internal nodes, visualized as treemaps on the inside. The edge bundling visualization (right side) significantly reduces the visual clutter compared to the straight line visualization (left side). For more details, see [286]. (Image reprinted from [126] with permission of Springer Science and Business Media.)

visualization shows the traffic from external nodes that are on the outside, to internal nodes that are visualized as a treemap (see Chapter 9). The comparison between the standard visualization of the connections by straight lines and the edge bundling visualization clearly shows the advantage of the technique.

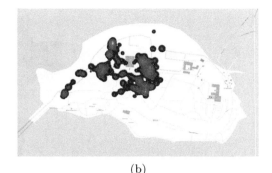

(a)   (b)

Figure 6.18.   Thematic maps: (a) A choropleth map showing U.S. election results of the 2008
Obama versus McCain presidential election. (b) An isarithmic map showing the
number of pictures taken on Mainau Island, using a heatmap, where the colors
range from black to red to yellow, with yellow representing the most photographs.

6.4 Visualization of Area Data

Thematic maps are the main approach to visualizing area phenomena. There
are different variants of thematic maps. The most popular type of thematic
maps are *choropleth maps* (Greek: choro = area, pleth = value), in which
the values of an attribute or statistical variable are encoded as colored or
shaded regions on the map. Choropleth maps (Figure 6.18(a)) assume that
the mapped attribute is uniformly distributed in the regions. If the attribute has a different distribution than the partitioning into regions, other
techniques, such as dasymetric maps, are used. In *dasymetric maps* (Figure 6.19), the variable to be shown forms areas independent of the original
regions, e.g., in contrast to choropleth maps, the boundaries of the areas
derived from the attribute do not need to match the given map's regions. A
third important type of map is an *isarithmic map* (Figure 6.18(b)), which
shows the contours of some continuous phenomena. Widely used examples
of isarithmic maps are contour maps or topographic maps. If the contours
are determined from real data points (such as temperatures measured at a
specific location) the maps are called *isometric maps*; if the data are measured for a certain region (such as a county) and, for example, the centroid
is considered as the data point, the maps are called *isopleth maps*. One of
the main tasks in generating isarithmic maps is the interpolation of the data
points to obtain smooth contours, which is done, for example, by triangu-
lation, or inverse distance mapping. A complex, but less frequently used
mapping technique, is *cartograms*, in which the size of regions is scaled to

Figure 6.19.   A dasymetric map showing the population distribution in Beaverton Creek, Oregon, USA.

reflect a statistical variable, leading to unique distortions of the map geometry. There are different variants of cartograms, ranging from continuous cartograms that retain the topology of the polygon mesh, to noncontinuous cartograms that simply scale each polygon independently to rectangular or circular approximations of the areas.

Note that the area information may also be visualized by displaying discrete points or symbols on the map: for example, by showing symbols that are proportionally sized to the statistical parameter on the map, or by generating a dot map with the regional dot density corresponding to the statistical variable. In the following, choropleth maps and cartograms will be discussed in more detail.

6.4.1 Choropleth Maps

Choropleth maps usually present the area phenomena as shaded polygons that are closed contours of sets of points, where the first and the last points are the same. Examples of closed contours are states, counties, and parks. Choropleth maps are used to emphasize the spatial distribution of one or more geographic attributes. In generating choropleth maps, the normalization of the data (see Chapter 2), as well as color or grayscale mapping (see Chapter 3), are important design decisions. In Figure 6.18(a), a choropleth map showing the 2008 presidential election results is shown.

A problem of choropleth maps is that the most interesting values are often concentrated in densely populated areas with small and barely visible polygons, and less interesting values are spread out over sparsely populated areas with large and visually dominating polygons. Choropleth maps, therefore, tend to highlight patterns in large areas, which may, however, be of lower importance. In the U.S. Census Demographics, for example, such maps tend to highlight patterns in areas where few people live, e.g., the large states in the USA.

6.4.2 Cartograms

Cartograms are generalizations of ordinary thematic maps that avoid the problems of choropleth maps by distorting the geography according to the displayed statistical value. Cartograms are a specific type of map transformation, where the regions are resized according to a geographically related input variable. Example applications include population demographics [412], election results [247], and epidemiology [411].

Several categories of cartogram problems exist. As shown in Figure 6.20(a), *noncontinuous cartograms* can exactly satisfy area and shape

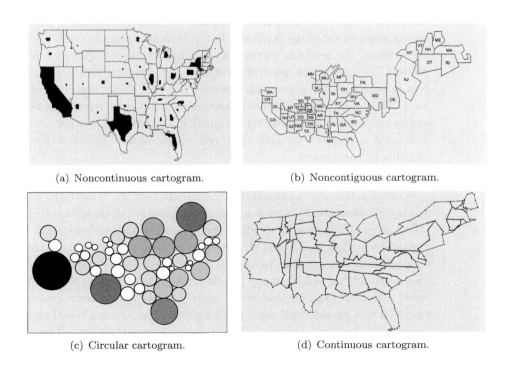

(a) Noncontinuous cartogram.   (b) Noncontiguous cartogram.

(c) Circular cartogram.   (d) Continuous cartogram.

Figure 6.20. Different types of cartograms. (Images from [231], © 2005 IEEE.)

constraints, but don't preserve the input map's topology. Because the scaled polygons are drawn inside the original regions, the loss of topology doesn't cause perceptual problems. More critical is that the polygon's original size restricts its final size. Consequently, you can't make small polygons arbitrarily large without scaling the entire map, so important areas can be difficult to see, and screen usage can be poor. *Noncontiguous cartograms*, shown in Figure 6.20(b), scale all polygons to their target sizes, perfectly satisfying the area objectives. Shapes can be slightly relaxed, so polygons touch without overlapping, and the map's topology is also highly relaxed, because polygons don't retain their adjacency relationships. Noncontiguous cartograms provide perfect area adjustment, with good shape preservation. However, they lose the map's global shape and topology, which can make perceiving the generated visualization as a map difficult. *Circular cartograms*, shown in Figure 6.20(c), completely ignore the input polygon's shape, representing each as a circle in the output. In many cases, area and topology constraints are also relaxed, so circular cartograms have some of the same problems as noncontiguous cartograms. The final category is *continuous cartograms*, shown in Figure 6.20(d). Unlike the other categories, continuous cartograms retain a map's topology perfectly, but they relax the given area and shape constraints. In general, cartograms can't fully satisfy shape or area objectives, so cartogram generation involves a complex optimization problem in searching for a good compromise between shape and area preservation. Although continuous cartograms are difficult to generate, the resulting polygonal meshes resemble the original map more than other computer-generated cartogram variants. The rest of this section therefore focuses on continuous cartograms.

Because cartograms are difficult to make by hand, the study of computer-generated automated methods is of special interest [93, 97, 369, 410, 412, 413]. Cartograms can also be seen as a general information visualization technique. They provide a means for trading shape against area to improve a visualization by scaling polygonal elements according to an external parameter. In population cartograms, more space is allocated to densely populated areas; patterns that involve many people are highlighted, while those involving fewer people are less emphasized. Figure 6.21 shows a conventional map of the 2000 U.S. presidential election, along with a population-based cartogram presenting the same information. In the cartogram, the area of the states is scaled to their population, so it reveals the close result of a presidential election more effectively than the original choropleth map. For a cartogram to be effective, a human being must be able to quickly understand the displayed

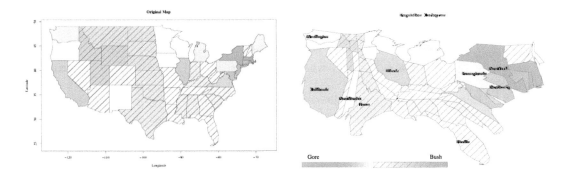

Figure 6.21.   A U.S. state population cartogram with the presidential election results of 2000. The area of the states in the cartogram corresponds to the population, and the color (shaded and not shaded areas) corresponds to the percentage of the vote. A bipolar color map depicts which candidate has won each state. (Image reprinted from [227] with permission of Springer Science and Business Media.)

data and relate it to the original map. Recognition depends on preserving basic properties, such as shape, orientation, and contiguity. This, however, is difficult to achieve, and it has been shown that the cartogram problem is unsolvable in the general case [229]. Even when allowing for errors in the shape and area representations, we are left with a difficult simultaneous optimization problem for which currently available algorithms are very time consuming.

The Continuous Cartogram Problem and the CartoDraw Algorithm. The *continuous cartogram problem* can be defined as a map deformation problem. The input is a planar polygon mesh (map) $\mathcal{P}$ and a set of values $\mathcal{X}$, one for each region. The goal is to deform the map into $\overline{\mathcal{P}}$ so that the area of each region matches the value assigned to it, doing this in such a way that the overall shape of the regions is preserved, and that they all remain recognizable.

Problem (The Cartogram Problem):

Input: A planar polygon mesh $\mathcal{P}$ consists of polygons $p_1, \ldots, p_k$, values $\mathcal{X} = x_1, \ldots x_k$ with $x_i > 0, \sum x_i = 1$. Let $A(p_i)$ denote the normalized area of polygon p_i with $A(p_i) > 0, \sum A(p_i) = 1$.

Output: A *topology-preserving* polygon mesh $\overline{\mathcal{P}}$ consists of polygons $\overline{p}_1, \ldots, \overline{p_k}$, such that the function $f(\overline{S}, \overline{A}) = \omega \cdot \sum_{i=1}^{k} s_i + (1 - \omega) \cdot \sum_{i=1}^{k} a_i$ is minimized with

$$\overline{S} = \{s_1, \ldots, s_k\} \text{ where } s_i = d_S(p_i, \overline{p}_i), \qquad \text{(Shape Error)}$$
$$\overline{A} = \{a_1, \ldots a_k\} \text{ where } a_i = d_A(x_i, A(\overline{p}_i)). \qquad \text{(Area Error)}$$

Here, $\forall j = 1, \ldots, k$ and the weighting factor ω with $0 \leq \omega < 1$.

Intuitively, topology preservation means that the faces of the input mesh must stay the same, e.g., that the cyclic order of adjacent edges in $\mathcal{P}$ must be the same as in $\overline{\mathcal{P}}$. This can be expressed formally by saying that the graphs are *pseudo-duals*.[1]

Even a simple variant of the cartogram problem, which even ignores issues of shape preservation ($\omega = 0$), is likely to be NP-complete. Since it may be impossible to simultaneously fulfill the area and shape constraints, the functions $f(\cdot, \cdot), d_S(\cdot, \cdot),$ and $d_A(\cdot, \cdot)$ model the error of the output cartogram.

There are a number of algorithms to solve the cartogram problem. Most approaches for the automated drawing of contiguous cartograms, however, do not yield results comparable in quality to good hand-made drawings. One reason, first identified by Dent [91, 92], is that straight lines, right angles, and other features are important in human recognition of cartograms. Radial methods such as the conformal maps proposed by Tobler [412], the radial expansion method of Selvin et al. [369], and the line integral method of Guseyn-Zade and Tikunov [410], in many cases do not provide acceptable results, since the shapes of the polygons are often heavily deformed. Likewise, the pseudo-cartograms of Tobler expand the lines of longitude and latitude to achieve a least root mean square area error [413]. Very similar drawings are made by approaching the problem as distortion viewing by nonlinear magnification [62, 218, 220, 303].

Another family of approaches operates on a grid or mesh imposed on the input map. The "piezopleth" method of Cauvin, Schneider, and Cherrier transforms the grid by a physical pressure load model [64]. Dorling's *cellular automaton approach* trades grid cells until each region achieves the desired number of cells [96]. The *combinatorial approach* of Edelsbrunner and Waupotitsch [104] computes a sequence of piecewise linear homeomorphisms of the mesh, which preserve its topology. While the first method is good at preserving the shape of the polygons, the second method allows a very good fit for area but does not account for shape preservation. A synthesis of both approaches was devised by Kocmoud and House, who

---

[1]The *pseudo-dual* of a planar graph is a graph that has one vertex for each face and an edge connecting two vertices if the corresponding faces are adjacent.

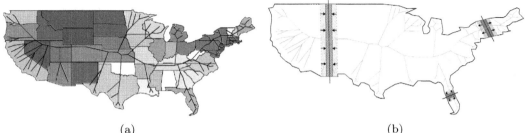

(a)	(b)

Figure 6.22. Medial Axes CartoDraw Algorithm: (a) U.S. map with medial axis and polygons that have to become large and colored red and polygons that have to become smaller and colored blue; (b) medial axes transformation for a few locations. (Images from [231], © 2005 IEEE.)

proposed a force-based model to alternately optimize shape and the area error [247]. Although the results are better than most other methods, this optimization has a prohibitively high execution time for interactive cartogram generation.

Another algorithm that allows explicit control of the shape and area error while retaining interactive performance is the *CartoDraw* algorithm [229, 231]. The basic idea of CartoDraw is to incrementally reposition the vertices of the map's polygons by means of scanlines. Local changes are applied if they reduce total area error without introducing an excessive shape error. The main loop iterates over a set of scanlines. For each scanline, it computes a candidate transformation of the polygons, and checks it for topology and shape preservation. If the candidate transformation passes the tests, it is made persistent; otherwise it is discarded. The order of scanline processing depends on the potential for reducing area error. The algorithm iterates over the scanlines until the area error improvement over all scanlines falls below a threshold.

The input scanlines are arbitrary lines and may be automatically computed (e.g., the medial axes of the overall boundary of the map or of the individual polygons) or interactively entered. The idea for distorting the polygon mesh is to use line segments (called *cutting lines*) perpendicular to scanlines at regular intervals. Consider the two edges on the boundary of the polygon intersected by a cutting line on either side of the scanline. These edges divide the polygon boundary into two connected chains. Now, if the area constraints require that the polygon expand, the algorithm applies a translation *parallel* to the scanline to each vertex of the two connected pieces of the boundary (in opposite directions) to *stretch* the polygon at that point. Similarly, if a contraction is called for, the direction of translation is reversed. Figure 6.22(a) shows the original polygons with the medial axis. Polygons that should be larger are colored red, and polygons that should be smaller are colored blue. Figure 6.22(b) shows how the CartoDraw algorithm works locally. The local shrinking or expanding operations are performed iteratively, until no further improvement is obtained.

The parameters for CartoDraw are a polygon mesh P, a parameter vector X defining the desired size of the polygons ($\tilde{X}$ is the parameter vector X normalized such that the sum of the X_i is 1), and SL is a given set of scanlines (e.g., the medial axes of the overall polygon). Scanline($P, \tilde{X}, s_l$) computes a modified version $\bar{P}$ of the polygon mesh P by changing the polygon mesh in the direction of the desired size as discussed above. If the shape distance ShapeDist($P, \bar{P}$) is smaller than a shape difference threshold ϵ_S and the area distance shows a minimum improvement of ϵ_A, then the changes are made permanent. After all scanlines s_l out of the set of all scanlines SL are processed, it is checked whether the area error is below the acceptable area error threshold $AreaErrorThreshold$, whether the area error still improved significantly (i.e., more than ϵ_A in a whole loop over all scanlines in SL), or whether the maximum number of iterations has been reached.

$CartoDraw(P, \tilde{X}, SL))$

```
1    repeat
2            AreaError = AreaDist(P, X̃);
3            for each (sl ∈ SL)
4                do
5                    P̄ = Scanline(P, X̃, sl);
6                    if ((ShapeDist(P, P̄) < ε_S) AND
7                    (AreaDist(P, X̃) − AreaDist(P̄, X̃) > ε_A))
8                        then P = P̄;
9    until (AreaDist(P, X̃) ≤ AreaErrorThreshold
10           OR AreaError − AreaDist(P, X̃) ≤ ε_A
11           OR IterationCount + + ≥ MaxIterationCount);
```

The Rectangular Cartogram Problem and the RecMap Algorithm. The idea of rectangular cartograms is to approximate familiar land-covering map region shapes by rectangles, and to find a partition of the available screen space where the areas of these rectangular regions are proportional to given statistical values. In order to support the understanding of the information represented by a cartogram, the rectangles are placed as close as possible to their original positions, and as close as possible to their original neighbors.

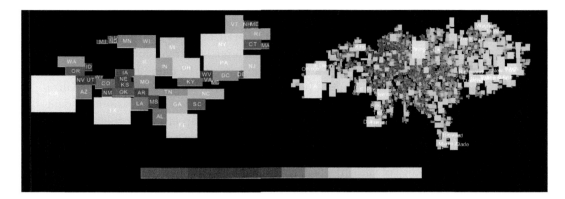

Figure 6.23.   A rectangular U.S. population cartogram on the state and county level. The area
of the rectangles corresponds to the population and the color redundantly encodes
the population numbers. (Image from [184], © 2004 IEEE.)

The problem may be defined as an optimization problem with a number of
constraints and optimization criteria, including the area, topology, relative
polygon position, proportion of the rectangle, and empty space. In defining
a specific instance of the problem, these criteria may be set as required constraints or as a weighted part of the optimization function. For some of the
variants of the rectangular cartogram problem, efficient approximation algorithms such as the RecMap algorithm exist. The RecMap algorithm [184]
uses heuristics and a general optimization procedure to generate multiple
variants on a rectangular cartogram, including space-filling partitions of the
screen space with respect to the given geolocations and one that preserves the
proportion of the individual rectangles. Both variants construct cartograms
where the area of each rectangle exactly reflects the statistical variable to
be shown. Note that the technique performs a fully automatic optimization, with explicit user control, over all constraints. See Figure 6.23 for
examples of a rectangular population cartogram on the state and county
level, generated with the second variant, which exactly represents the statistical variable by the size of the rectangles, preserves their relative propor-
tions, and optimizes all other criteria.

6.5   Other Issues in Geospatial Data Visualization

Prerequisite to generating useful visualizations of spatial phenomena are a
number of well-known techniques from cartography, including map general-

ization and map labeling. *Map generalization* is the process of selecting and abstracting information on a map. Generalization is used when a special-purpose small-scale map is derived from a large-scale map containing detailed information. The goal is to adapt the objects on the map in such a way that the objects of interest may be easily perceived in the resulting visualization. Note that map generalizations are application- and task-dependent, e.g., good map generalizations emphasize the map elements that are most important for the task at hand, while still representing the geography in the most accurate and recognizable way. It is important that the visibility and recognizability of the objects displayed on the map outweigh the lost details of items that are generalized. The goal is to preserve the distinguishing characteristics of what makes the map useful in the particular application.

Examples for typical map generalizations are:

- *Simplify points*—remove or combine points that are not relevant or not separately visible on the small-scale map.

- *Simplify lines*—remove small fluctuations and bends or collapse dual lines to centerlines. Lines that are in danger of touching each other in the scaled version of the map may be removed.

- *Simplify polygons*—remove small fluctuations and bends while preserving the essential shape feature. This includes the removal or simplification of building footprint boundaries while preserving the essential shape and size, as well as the combination of disjoint but adjacent polygons into a new area based on a specified tolerance distance.

Map labeling deals with placing textual or figurative labels close to points, lines, and polygons. This seems to be an easy and straightforward task, but it has been shown to be a difficult problem [95, 131]. There are a large number of label placement algorithms that differ in their effectiveness, e.g., quality of the results, and their efficiency, e.g., speed of calculating the label placement. Map labeling algorithms are based on heuristics, and in most cases use a rule-based label placement followed by an optimization algorithm, such as local search, greedy algorithms, simulated annealing, random placement, and genetic algorithms [75]. Two examples of labeling software are Label-EZ [133] by MapText, Inc. and Maplex by ESRI [117].

Many other issues are related to the design of effective *geographic information systems* (GIS). A GIS essentially allows users to create interactive queries for dynamic search and exploration, to compare and edit spatial data on different geographic map layers, and finally to present the results of all these operations. Geospatial data visualization is just a part of GIS. The advance of visualization and other relevant GIS functions could benefit each other to make the whole system more powerful and useful.

In recent years, with the advance of fast-growing web technology and APIs (e.g., Flex, AJAX, and the Google MAP API), as well as public availability of digitized geographic data and various economic, social, environmental measures and indicators data via the Internet, the GIS community has developed a large number of interactive high-performance tools for spatial data visualization. These tools significantly increase the awareness and better understanding of public issues among large populations of people. It turns out that the visualization of geospatial data has become exciting to many people.

For an advanced GIS, there is a trend that the geospatial data visualization needs to integrate with temporal data visualization, such that the system could more easily and systematically track and model the information as it changes over time [309]. As GIS needs sufficiently integrate data from different sources for facilitating interoperability (e.g., comparing data whose metadata might be slightly different) and data is reused among GIS applications, it is important for geospatial visualization to work with associated ontologies, which provide a semantic approach to allow different specifications of the same concepts and relationships in a given domain to work in a uniform workspace [203].

6.6   Related Readings

The third edition of the book *Thematic Cartography and Geovisualization* by Terry Slocum, Robert McMaster, Fritz Kessler, and Hugh Howard [383] provides a comprehensive coverage of the field of geographic visualization. The authors provide a broad coverage of relevant topics and in most cases give the mathematical details to implement the methods. The book *Cartography: Visualization of Geospatial Data* by Menno-Jan Kraak and Ferjan Ormeling [255] provides a more practical treatment of the field, covering all steps necessary for creating map visualizations. The book is easy to read and includes a large number of examples and figures. The book *How Maps Work: Representations, Visualization, and Design* by Alan MacEachren [281] focuses on the cognitive and perceptual aspects of map understanding and design. For those interested in a systematic study of exploratory spatial data analysis, the book *Exploratory Analysis of Spatial and Temporal Data: A Systematic Approach* by Natalia and Gennady Andrienko [16] contains a broad and systematic coverage of data, task, and tools. The Andrienkos provide a mathematical framework and extract a set of general principles. The book also contains many examples from their rich research work. There are also a number of recent books containing paper collections in the area of geovisualization, including *Exploring Geovisualization* [103] and *Geographic Visualization: Concepts, Tools, and Applications* [105].

6.7   Exercises

1. Map projections are used to visualize geospatial data. Why are these projections difficult?

2. Different projection techniques do exist. At which points do the different projections have no distortion?

3. In the R-project distribution (a public-domain statistics tool at http://www.r-project.org) there is a data set called "quakes." Plot this data and interpret the results of the visualization. Where are the two clear planes of seismic activity?

4. Shape files represent polygonal boundaries of regions. Look up their definitions, history, and identify issues that would present themselves in coding maps.

5. Discuss the projection issues in comparing two regions of the world such as Germany and the United States, or even closer ones such as Atlanta and Boston. Note that this issues help explain the distortions we see in a flatland world map.

6. Use the software Weave to explore various measures and indicators data around the U.S. or World. See http://www.openindicators.org or the course web site for how to use the software.

7. Compare and contrast choropleth maps and cartograms. What are the main features of each? What problems do choropleth maps create that cartograms can help with and vice versa?

8. Name different ways that overlap can be reduced in high-density areas using point data on maps. Are these techniques applicable to nongeographic data sets as well as geographic data sets?

9. Find three examples of different types of flow diagrams. What are the strengths and weaknesses of these different types of flow diagrams?

6.8   Projects

1. Use the TIGER-System (Topologically Integrated Geographic Encoding and Referencing), a geographic polygon data set from the U.S. Census (TGR06001.RT2), to write a script that converts the polygon data in the following format (for each polygon):

   $-121764253| + 37160714$
   $-121746453| + 37611800$
   $-121746709| + 37611300$
   NA—NA

   NA—NA marks the end of a polygon. TIGER files can be found at `ftp://ftp2.census.gov/geo/tiger/TIGER2013`.

2. Use the R-project function "polygon" to draw the extracted polygons of Project 1.

3. Write a program to visualize the "quakes" data from Exercise 3 using the Google Maps API. Think about how to visualize the attributes of depth, magnitude, and stations for each data point in the map with a suitable glyph visualization.

   Hint: Create an image for each of the three attributes, and scale it according to the data value. Place them side by side on the Google Map, so that they look like one glyph.

   Sources: quakes.xml (10% Sample of the "quakes" data; depth, stations, magnitude are normalized), http://www.google.com/apis/maps/ (Google Maps API).

4. Write a program that distorts map regions along the two Euclidean dimensions x and y. The distortion operations should be done by computing a histogram with a given number of bins in the two dimensions x and y to determine the distribution of the geospatial data points in these dimensions. The distortion depends on the number of data points that are geographically located in the bins.

5. The Ramer–Douglas–Peucker Algorithm is a well-known algorithm for line simplification. It takes a polyline as an input and simplifies it up so some threshold distance by taking the following steps:

$\mathrm{RDP}(start, end, polyline)$

```
1   repeat
2               dist = 0.0
3               index = pos = start
4               for each (pos > start AND pos < end)
5                   do
6                           td = PtLinedist(start, end, pos);
7                           if td > dist
8                               do dist = td
9                                   index = pos
10
11                          pos + +;
12
13              if dist ≥ epsilon
14                  do RDP(index, end, polyline);
15                      RDP(start, index, polyline);
16
17      until ((end − start) ≤ 2 OR dist < ε)
18
```

Implement this algorithm in a language of your choice. Assume that the input line is entered as a list of pairs [(x1, y1) (x2, y2) ...] and that the output of your program should be the simplified list of pairs. For extra credit, apply this algorithm to a data set containing political or country boundaries.

6. Write a program that implements two or more of the projections described in this chapter using the country boundaries data set found on the book website (world_countries.shp). SHP files are a standard representation used by many geographic information systems to represent shapes.

CHAPTER 7

Visualization Techniques for Time-Oriented Data

Guest Authors: Wolfgang Aigner, Silvia Miksch, Heidrun Schumann, and Christian Tominski

In this chapter we elaborate on visualization techniques for time-oriented data. We organized and structured this chapter according to our book [5]. Therefore, we first motivate the importance of handling the temporal dimension explicitly by an example. Second, we define the needed concepts and aspects of time and time-oriented data. The basic data foundations are covered already in Chapter 2. Here, we focus particularly on the characteristics of time. Third, we give an overview of different temporal data visualization techniques. Fourth, we briefly explain TimeBench, a data model and software library for visualization and visual analytics of time-oriented data. We conclude with an assessment of our categorization according to the visualization techniques presented, introduce the TimeViz Browser, which is an interactive repository to support researchers and practitioners in finding appropriate visualization techniques, followed by related readings, exercises, and projects.

Significant parts of this chapter have been taken from and are based on [5].

7.1 Introduction

Time itself is an inherent data dimension that is central to the tasks of revealing trends and identifying patterns and relationships in the data. Time and time-oriented data have distinct characteristics that make it worthwhile to treat such data as a separate data type [5, 16]. Due to the importance of time-oriented data, its structure has been studied in numerous scientific publications (e.g., [5, 38, 132]).

The following example illustrates the importance of time. Figure 7.1 shows three different visual representations of the same time-oriented data set, which contains the daily number of cases of influenza that occurred in the northern part of Germany during a period of three years. The data exhibit a strong cyclic pattern. The leftmost image of Figure 7.1 uses a simple line plot to visualize the data. Although peaks in time can be recognized easily when examining this representation, the cyclic behavior of the data, however, can only be guessed and it is hard to discern which cyclic temporal patterns in fact do exist. In contrast, the middle and the right image in Figure 7.1 show a circular representation that emphasizes cyclic characteristics of time-oriented data by using a spiral-shaped time axis [453]. For the left spiral, the cyclic pattern is not visible. This is due to the fact that the cycle length has been set to 24 days, which does not match the pattern in the data. The right spiral representation in Figure 7.1 is adequately parameterized with a cycle length of 28 days, which immediately reveals the periodic pattern present in the data. The significant difference in the number of cases of influenza reported on Sundays and Mondays, respectively, are quite obvious. We would also see this weekly pattern if we set the cycle length to 7 or 14 days, or any (low) multiple of 7.

This example comprehensibly demonstrated that observing the particular characteristics of time can significantly improve the expressiveness of visual representations. Hence, it is vital to (1) chose a visual representation that fits the data characteristics (cyclic time in this case) and to (2) parameterize the visual representation accordingly in order to be able to detect patterns hidden in the data.

In the next section, we investigate the characteristics of time and time-oriented data, which need to be considered and tackled to select appropriate visualization techniques for time-oriented data.

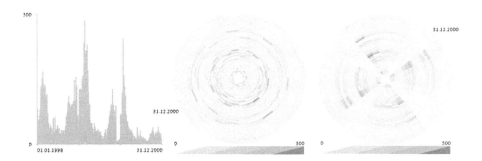

Figure 7.1.   Time characteristics: linear vs. cyclic representation of time: different insights can be gained from visual representations depending on whether linear or cyclic character of the data is emphasized. (Source: Generated by the authors.)

7.2 Definitions: Characterizing Time-Oriented Data

This section covers the main aspects to characterize time and time-oriented data. It is important to make a clear distinction between the physical dimension time and a model of time in information systems. When modeling time in information systems, the goal is not to perfectly imitate the physical dimension time, but to provide a model that is best suited to reflect the phenomena under consideration and support the analysis tasks at hand. Moreover, as Frank [132] states, there is nothing like a single correct model or taxonomy of time—there are many ways to model time in information systems and time is modeled differently for different applications depending on the particular problem. Extensive research has been conducted in order to formulate the notion of time in many areas of computer science, including artificial intelligence, data mining, simulation, modeling, databases, and more [166]. We adapted the works of Frank [132] and Goralwalla et al. [154], where principal orthogonal aspects are presented to characterize different types of time. The basic data foundations are covered in Chapter 2; we focus on the characteristics of time and time-oriented data in particular. These aspects will be described in detail next.

7.2.1 Characteristics of Time

The characteristics of time can be divided into general aspects required to adequately model the time domain as well as the hierarchical organization of time and definition of concrete time elements.

The *general aspects* are scale, scope, arrangement, and viewpoints.

1. *Scale: ordinal vs. discrete vs. continuous.* As a first perspective, we look at time from the scale along which elements of the model are given. In an *ordinal* time domain, only relative order relations are present (e.g., before, after, during). In *discrete* domains, temporal distances can also be considered. Time values can be mapped to a set of integers, which enables quantitative modeling of time values (e.g., quantifiable temporal distances). Discrete time domains are based on a smallest possible unit (e.g., seconds, minutes) and they are the most commonly used time model in information systems. *Continuous* time models are characterized by a possible mapping to real numbers, i.e., between any two points in time, another point in time exists (also known as dense time).

2. *Scope: point-based vs. interval-based.* Secondly, we consider the scope of the basic elements that constitute the time domain. *Point-based* time domains can be seen in analogy to discrete Euclidean points in space, i.e., having a temporal extent equal to zero. Thus, no information is given about the region between two points in time. In contrast to that, *interval-based* time domains relate to subsections of time having a temporal extent greater than zero. This aspect is also closely related to the notion of granularity, which will be discussed later. For example, the time value May 1, 2014 might relate to the single instant May 1, 2014 00:00:00 in a point-based domain, whereas the same value might refer to the interval [May 1, 2014 00:00:00, May 1, 2014 23:59:99] in an interval-based domain.

3. *Arrangement: linear vs. cyclic.* As the third design aspect, we look at the arrangement of the time domain. Corresponding to our natural perception of time, we mostly consider time as proceeding *linearly* from the past to the future, i.e., each time value has a unique predecessor and successor. In a *cyclic* organization of time, the domain is composed of a set of recurring time values (e.g., the seasons of the year). Hence, any time value A is preceded and succeeded at the same time by any other time value B (e.g., winter comes before summer, but winter also succeeds summer).

4. *Viewpoint: ordered vs. branching vs. multiple perspectives.* The fourth subdivision is concerned with the views of time that are modeled. *Ordered* time domains consider things that happen one after the other.

On a more detailed level, we might also distinguish between totally ordered and partially ordered domains. In a totally ordered domain, only one thing can happen at a time. In contrast to this, simultaneous or overlapping events are allowed in partially ordered domains, i.e., multiple time primitives at a single point or overlapping in time. A more complex form of time domain organization is the so-called *branching* time. Here, multiple strands of time branch out and allow the description and comparison of alternative scenarios (e.g., in project planning). In contrast to branching time where only one path through time will actually happen, *multiple perspectives* facilitate simultaneous (even contrary) views of time. Examples for this are eyewitness reports that describe the same situation, each of which being slightly different, various statements of a disaster reported in different countries and time zones, or stochastic multirun simulations.

The *hierarchical organization of time and concrete time elements* is determined based on granularity, time primitives, and determinacy.

1. *Granularity and calendars: none vs. single vs. multiple.* To tackle the complexity of time and to provide different levels of granularity [38], useful abstractions can be employed. Basically, *granularity* can be thought of as a (human-made) abstraction of time in order to make it easier to deal with time in everyday life (such as minutes, hours, days, weeks, months). More generally, granularity describes mappings from time values to larger or smaller conceptual units. If a granularity and calendar system is supported by the time model, we characterize it as *multiple* granularity. Besides this complex variant, there might be a *single* granularity only (e.g., every time value is given in terms of milliseconds) or *none* of these abstractions are supported (e.g., abstract ticks).

2. *Time primitives: instant vs. interval vs. span.* These time primitives can be seen as an intermediary layer between data elements and the time domain. Basically, time primitives can be divided into anchored (absolute) and unanchored (relative) primitives. *Instant* and *interval* are primitives that belong to the first group, i.e., they are located on a fixed position along the time domain. In contrast to that, a *span* is a relative primitive, i.e., it has no absolute position in time. Instants are a model for single points in time (sometimes also referred as time point, e.g., May 10, 2014), intervals range between two points in time

(from May 10, 2014 to May 16, 2014), and spans are durations (of intervals) without a fixed position (e.g., 6 days).

3. *Determinacy: determinate vs. indeterminate.* Uncertainty is another important aspect when considering time-oriented data. If there is no complete or exact information about time specifications or if time primitives are converted from one granularity to another, uncertainties are introduced and have to be dealt with. Examples of this are inexact knowledge (e.g., "time when the earth was formed"), future planning data (e.g., "it will take 2–3 months"), or imprecise event times (e.g., "one or two days ago"). Notice that temporal indeterminacy as well as the relativity of references to time are mainly qualifications of statements rather than of the events they denote. Indeterminacy might be introduced by explicit specification (e.g., earliest beginning and latest beginning of an interval) or is implicitly present in the case of multiple granularities. Consider, for example, the statement "Activity A started on May 14, 2014 and ended on May 17, 2014"—this statement can be modeled by the beginning instant "May 14, 2014" and the end instant "May 17, 2014" both at the granularity of *days*. If we look at this interval from a granularity of *hours*, the interval might begin and end at any point in time between 0 a.m. and 12 p.m. of the specified day. Therefore, the *determinacy* of the given time specification needs to be considered. A determinate specification is present when there is complete knowledge of all temporal aspects.

In the next part we explore and define time-oriented data more precisely.

7.2.2   Characteristics of Time-Oriented Data

Like the characteristics of time, the data have a major impact on the design of visualization approaches. Let us briefly reiterate the key criteria for data that are related to time:

1. *Scale: quantitative vs. qualitative*—Quantitative data are based on a metric scale (discrete or continuous). Qualitative data describe either unordered (nominal) or ordered (ordinal) sets of data elements.

2. *Frame of reference: abstract vs. spatial*—Abstract data (e.g., a bank account) have been collected in a non-spatial context and are not per se connected to some spatial layout. Spatial data (e.g., census data) contain an inherent spatial layout, e.g., geographical positions.

3. *Kind of data: events vs. states*—Events, on the one hand, can be seen as markers of state changes (e.g., the departure of a train) whereas states, on the other hand, characterize the phases of continuity between events (e.g., the train is on the road).

4. *Number of variables: univariate vs. multivariate*—Univariate data contain only one data value per temporal primitive, whereas in the case of multivariate data each temporal primitive holds multiple data values.

These primary categories form a basis for finding an expressive, appropriate, and effective visualization technique for time-oriented data. For basic data foundations we refer to Chapter 2.

7.2.3   Relating Data and Time

Aspects regarding time dependency of data have been extensively examined in the field of temporal databases. Here, we adapt the notions and definitions developed in that area [274, 397]. According to them, any data set is related to two temporal domains: (1) internal time and (2) external time.

Internal time is considered to be the temporal dimension inherent in the data model. Internal time describes when the information contained in the data is valid. Conversely, *external time* is considered to be extrinsic to the data model. The external time is necessary to describe how a data set evolves in (external) time. Depending on the number of time primitives in internal and external time, time-related data sets can be classified as followed:

1. *Static non-temporal data*—If both internal and external time are each comprised of only one temporal element, the data are completely independent of time. This kind of data is not addressed in this chapter.

2. *Static temporal data*—If the internal time contains more than one time primitive, while the external time contains only one, then the data can be considered dependent on time. Since the values stored in the data depend on the internal time, static temporal data can be understood as an historical view of how the real world or some model looked at the various elements of internal time. Common time-series are a prominent example of static temporal data. Most of today's visualization approaches that explicitly consider time as a special data dimension address static temporal data.

3. *Dynamic non-temporal data*—If the internal time contains only one, but the external time is composed of multiple time primitives, then

the data depend on the external time. To put it simply, the data change over time, i.e., they are dynamic. Since the internal time is not considered, only the current state of the data is preserved; an historical view is not maintained. There are fewer visualization techniques available that explicitly focus on dynamic non-temporal data. However, since internal time and external time can usually be mapped from one to the other, some of the known visualization techniques for static temporal data can be applied to dynamic non-temporal data as well.

4. *Dynamic temporal data*—If both internal and external time are comprised of multiple time primitives, then the data are considered to be bi-temporally dependent. In other words, the data contain variables depending on (internal) time, and the actual state of the data changes over (external) time. Usually, in this case, internal and external time are strongly coupled and can be mapped from one to the other. An explicit distinction between internal and external time is usually not made by current visualization approaches, because considering both temporal dimensions for visualization is challenging.

Figure 7.2 summarizes all these above perspectives and their corresponding aspects.

7.3   Visualizing Time-Oriented Data

Data and time was elaborated on in Section 7.2, however, we also have to consider the design issues at the level of visual representations. Communicating the time-dependence of data primarily requires a well-considered placement of the time axis. The large variety of visual techniques covers very different approaches. To abstract from the subtle details of this variety, we concentrate on two fundamental criteria:

1. *Mapping of time*—There are two options for mapping time: the mapping of time to space and the mapping of time to time. When speaking of a mapping from time to space, we mean that time and data are represented in a single coherent visual representation. This representation does not automatically change over time, which is why we call such visualizations of time-oriented data *static*. In contrast to that, *dynamic* representations utilize the physical dimension of time to convey the time dependency of the data, that is, time is mapped to time. This results in visualizations that change over time automatically (e.g., slide

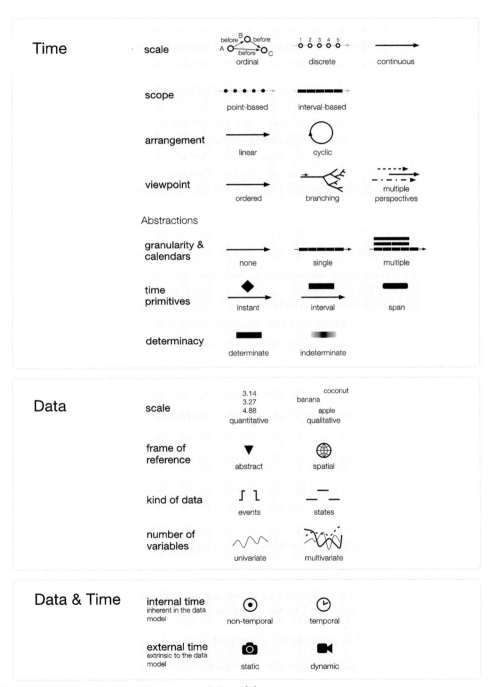

Figure 7.2.   Design aspects of time-oriented data [5].

shows or animations). Note that the presence or absence of interaction facilities to navigate in time has no influence on whether a visualization approach is categorized as static or dynamic.

2. *Dimensionality of the presentation space*—We can differentiate between 2D and 3D presentations of time-oriented data. Visualization approaches that use a 2D presentation space have to ensure that the time axis is emphasized, because time and data dimensions often have to share the two available display dimensions. In the case of 3D representations, a third display dimension is allocatable. In fact, many techniques utilize it as a dedicated dimension for the time axis, clearly separating time from other (data) dimensions.

7.3.1 Categorization

To facilitate a nonambiguous categorization and to keep the categorization of visualization techniques simple, we focus on the core aspects of data, time, and visualization. With various visualization examples, we will illustrate their applicability and demonstrate the functionality of these visualization techniques.

- **data**
    - *frame of reference*—abstract vs. spatial
    - *variables*—univariate vs. multivariate
- **time**
    - *arrangement*—linear vs. cyclic
    - *time primitives*—instant vs. interval
- **vis**
    - *mapping*—static vs. dynamic
    - *dimensionality*—2D vs. 3D

To structure the various visualization techniques for time-oriented data, three questions need to be answered:

1. *What* is presented? *Time and data*

2. *Why* is it presented? *User tasks*

3. *How* is it presented? *Visual representation*

In this chapter, we mainly elaborated about time, data, and visual representations, but neglected the user tasks to keep the chapter as simple and understandable as possible. Supporting visualization techniques requires an understanding of what particular tasks need to be carried out during the exploration and visualization process. While there are a number of task taxonomies and typologies such as [44, 367, 376], there are only a few taxonomies available specifically for time-oriented visual data analysis [16, 281]. MacEachren [281] proposed a low-level task description specifically addressing the temporal domain. The tasks are defined by a set of important questions that users might seek to answer with the help of visual representations, such as the *existence of data element:* does a data element exist at a specific time? or *rate of change:* how fast is a data element changing over time? The task typology by Andrienko et al. [16] distinguishes between elementary and synoptic tasks on the first level. *Elementary* tasks address individual data elements. This may include individual values, but also individual groups of data. *Synoptic* tasks, on the other hand, involve a general view and consider sets of values or groups of data in their entirety. For example, elementary tasks are *direct lookup:* what is the value of glucose on March 1, 2014? or *direct comparison:* compare the value of glucose and the activity level on March 1, 2014. An example of synoptic tasks is *relation seeking:* find two contiguous months with opposite trends in the values of glucose.

In the next section, we will give examples demonstrating each of the above-mentioned categories. More examples of spatial and geospatial data were already covered in Chapters 5 and 6.

7.3.2   Data: Frame of Reference—Abstract

KronoMiner [488] is a multipurpose time-series exploration tool providing rich navigation capabilities and analytical support (see Figure 7.3). Its visualization is based on a hierarchical radial layout, allowing users to drill into details by focusing on different pieces. The data pieces can be rotated, dragged, stretched, or shrunken in a facile manner, supporting various kinds of time-series analysis and exploration tasks. KronoMiner also introduces two analytical techniques: (1) MagicAnalytics Lens, which shows the correlations between two parts of the data pieces when overlapped and (2) Best Match mode, in which an arc shape is displayed indicating the matching parts of two data pieces under a specific similarity measure.

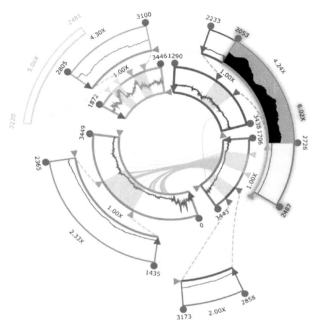

Figure 7.3.   KronoMiner [488]. KronoMiner is a multipurpose time-series exploration tool pro-
               viding rich navigation and analytical support. (Source: Generated with the Kro-
               noMiner software by Jian Zhao.)

7.3.3   Data: Frame of Reference—Spatial

Tominski and Schulz [415] introduce a visualization technique for spatio-
temporal data that refers to 2D geographical space and 1D linear time.
The idea is to construct a non-planar slice—called the *Great Wall of Space-
Time* (Figure 7.4)—through the 3D (2D+1D) space-time continuum. The
construction of the wall is based on topological and geometrical aspects
of the geographical space. Based on a neighborhood graph, a topological
path is established automatically or interactively. The topological path is
transformed to a geometrical path that respects the geographic properties
of the areas of the map. The geometrical path is extruded to a 3D wall,
whose third dimension can be used to map the time domain. Different
visual representations can be projected onto the wall in order to display
the data. Examples illustrate data visualizations based on color-coding and
parallel coordinates. The wall has the advantage that it shows a closed path
through space with no gaps between the information-bearing pixels on the
screen.

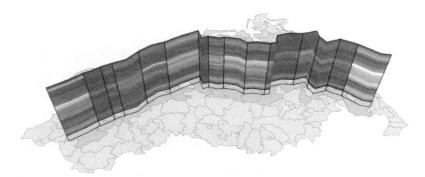

Figure 7.4. Visualization of human health data using the Great Wall of Space-Time [415]. A path through space has been created. Along this path, the wall shows 24 months of data for each area crossed. Dark colors indicate low data values, light colors stand for high values. The figure shows the number of cases of influenza. (Source: Generated by Christian Tominski.)

7.3.4 Data: Number of Variables—Univariate

GROOVE (Granularity Overview OVErlay) visualizations [262] extend pixel-based visualizations by overlaying several aggregation levels with one or more of three methods: (1) color-based overlay, (2) opacity overlay, or (3) spatial overlay. The aggregation levels result from different time granularities. The overlay allows micro and macro readings and avoids eye movements between the overview and detail representations. For illustration purposes, we have kept the arrangements shown here simple and the amount of visualized data low. Empty space emerges due to the irregularities imposed by having to combine the granularities week and month.

First, color components can be employed with color-based overlay (see Figure 7.5). This figure plots traffic data for several weeks, each block depicting one week. The hue varies from blue to red for lower or higher weekly averages. In Figure 7.5 (a), only the weekly values are shown. The lightness for a particular day is higher in case the traffic of that day is higher. In Figure 7.5 (c), only the daily values are shown. In Figure 7.5 (b), the color overlay is shown.

Second, opacity overlay (see Figure 7.6) applies interactive crossfading between the overview and the detail display. Our second example figure shows turnover data from a shop for one year and employs recursive pattern layout [223]. Columns and rows of larger blocks are combined with a pixel arrangement within blocks for the detail structure. Different arrangements

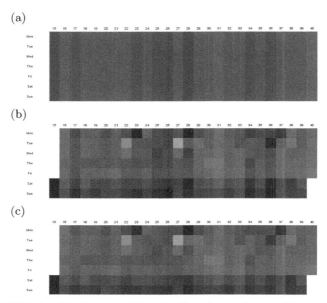

Figure 7.5.   GROOVE [262] visualizations combine detail and overview readings and use regu-
                  lar layouts based on time granularities. The example shows data from the Dodgers
                  Loop Sensor data set [195] which is publicly available. Here a color-based overlay
                  is plotted: (a) Average weekly traffic on a highway ramp (week of year 15 to 40) is
                  mapped to hue from blue over purple to red. (c) Average daily traffic on the high-
                  way ramp is mapped to lightness. (b) Color overlay of both granularities. (Source:
                  Generated with the GROOVE modules for TimeBench [339].)

can be chosen (e.g., row-by-row, back-and-forth). Each block depicts one
month and the blocks are arranged with one row for every quarter. Inside
the blocks, the pixels are arranged with one row for every week, and one
pixel for every day, as in a calendar sheet.

Third, spatial overlay can be used by showing the average values as borders around the detail values, which is possible for more than two aggregation levels. Spatial overlay can be combined with the other two methods. It
can also be applied using interaction by expanding and collapsing areas on
demand.

7.3.5   Data: Number of Variables—Multivariate

The *TimeWheel* [417] is a technique for visualizing multiple time-dependent
variables. The TimeWheel (see Figure 7.7) consists of a single time axis and

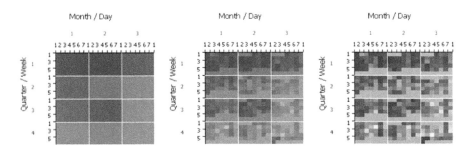

Figure 7.6.   GROOVE [262] visualizations with opacity overlay: Here, data is plotted for daily turnover from a shop for one year; each block depicts one month: dark red represents low and light yellow represents high values. In this example, a monthly overview is combined with daily details using various opacities. (Source: Generated with the GROOVE prototype software.)

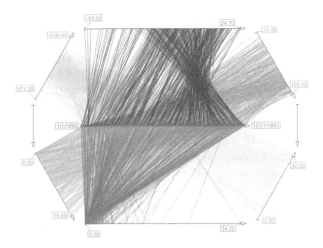

Figure 7.7.   The TimeWheel's [417] central axis represents time. The axes in the periphery represent time-dependent variables; eight different variables of meteorological data are plotted. In the center, the red lines show the average temperature, which is increasing in the beginning and decreasing in the end. The blue lines are rainfall. There are some outliers with high rainfall, but moderate rainfall during the whole year. (Source: Generated with the VisAxes prototype software.)

multiple data axes for the data variables. The time axis is placed in the center of the display to emphasize the temporal character of the data. The data axes are associated with individual colors and are arranged circularly around the time axis. In order to visualize data, lines emanate from the time axis to each of the data axes to establish a visual connection between points in time and associated data values. These lines form visual patterns that allow users to identify positive or negative correlations with the time axis, trends, and outliers. Such patterns can be best discerned for those data axes that are parallel to the time axis. To bring data axes of interest into this focus, users can rotate the TimeWheel. Focused data axes are further emphasized by stretching them, effectively providing them with more drawing space. Data axes that are perpendicular to the time axis are more difficult to interpret and are, therefore, attenuated using color fading and shrinking. Interactive exploration, including navigation in time, is supported through different types of interactive axes.

7.3.6   Time: Arrangement—Linear

One of the most straightforward ways of depicting time-series data is using a Cartesian coordinate system with time on the horizontal axis and the corresponding value on the vertical axis (see Chapter 8). A point is plotted for every measured time-value pair. This kind of representation is usually called a *point plot*, *point graph*, or *scatterplot*. Harris [170] describes it as a 2-dimensional representation where quantitative data aspects are visualized by distance from the main axis. Many extensions of this basic form, such as 3D techniques (layer graph) or techniques that use different symbols instead of points, are known. This technique is particularly suited for emphasizing individual values. Moreover, depicting data using position along a common scale can be perceived most precisely by the human perceptual system.

The *line plot* extends point plots by linking the data points with lines, which emphasizes their temporal relation. Consequently, line plots focus on the overall shape of data over time. This is in contrast to point plots where individual data points are emphasized. Different styles of connections between the data points such as straight lines, step lines (instant value changes), or Bezier curves, can be used depending on the phenomenon under consideration. However, what has to be kept in mind is that one cannot be sure in all cases about the data values in the time interval between two data points, and that any kind of connection between data points reflects an approximation only. A further point of caution is missing data. Simply connecting subsequent data points might lead to false conclusions regarding the data. Therefore, this should be made visible to the viewer, for instance by using dotted lines. There are many extensions or subtypes, such as fever graphs, band graphs, layer line graphs, surface graphs, index graphs, or control graphs (see [170]).

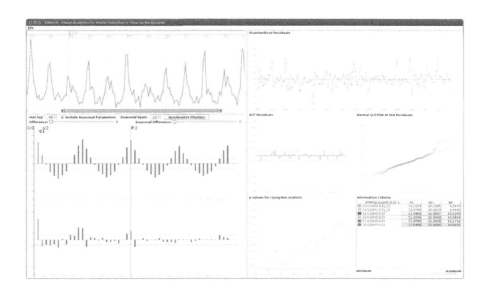

Figure 7.8.   TiMoVA [42]. The interface shows the time series plot as line plot (input data; on the upper left), the model selection toolbox, and various other views to guide the model selection process. (Source: Generated with the TiMoVA prototype software.)

Different kinds of point and line plots as well as other visual plots and cues (e.g., bar charts) are used in *TiMoVA (Time series analysis, Model selection, applies Visual Analytics methods)* [42]. Statistical time series analysis is a challenging task performed by experts in different domains, for example, a public health official may want to predict the number of people that need to be treated because of cardiovascular reasons in the next year. Usually, model selection is a cumbersome task. TiMoVA [42] provides an interactive exploration environment to guide users in the time series model selection processes. TiMoVA enables the domain expert to (1) select the model order interactively via the visual interface, (2) give the domain expert immediate visual feedback of the model results while selecting the model order, and (3) help domain experts with the visualization of the model transitions to decide whether or not the model improves (Figure 7.8). TiMoVA was evaluated by usage scenarios with an example data set from epidemiology and interviews with two external domain experts in statistics [42]. It could be shown that the appropriate line and point plots as well as an interactive visual exploration environment with short feedback cycles supports the model selection tasks in an expressive way.

7.3.7 Time: Arrangement—Cyclic

Tominski and Schumann [416] apply the enhanced two-tone color-coding by Saito et al. [354] to visualize time-dependent data along a spiral. Each time primitive is mapped to a unique segment of the spiral. Every segment is subdivided into two parts that are colored according to the two-tone coloring method. The advantage of using the two-tone approach is that it realizes the overview+detail concept by design. The two colors used per spiral segment allow users to quickly recognize the value range of that segment (overview). If the value range is of interest, the proportion of the two colors indicates the particular data value more precisely (detail). The *enhanced interactive spiral* can be adjusted interactively in various ways. The number of time primitives, the number of cycles, and additional geometrical parameters influence the shape of the spiral and thus the mapping of the time domain. The data representation is mainly controlled by the color scales applied and parameters such as the number of colors, the direction of the mapping, and the mapping function (linear vs. logarithmic). Navigation in time is possible via direct manipulation of the spiral.

This section and Figure 7.9 illustrate an enhanced spiral with two-tone color-coding, the following pseudo-code example will indicate how to draw a simple spiral where color and width of line segments visualize data values (compare the middle and right image in Figure 7.1). The input parameters are *data[]*, an array of n non-negative data values with *max* as the maximum value. The center coordinate of the spiral is denoted by *cx* and *cy*. The inner radius and the outer radius of the spiral are given by the parameters *inRad* and *outRad*. The number of data items that are to be visualized in one full spiral cycle, i.e., the number of line segments per cycle, is given by the parameter *cycLen*.

```
drawSpiral(data[], n, max, cx, cy, inRad, outRad,
        cycLen) {

    // Compute increments
    radiusIncr = (outRad − inRad) / n;
    angleIncr = 2 * Pi / cycLen;

    // Start radius and angle
    radius = inRad;
    angle = 0;

    // Compute coordinate of first point
```

```
x0 = cx + cos(angle) * radius;
y0 = cy + sin(angle) * radius;

// Loop over all data values in array
for (i = 0; i < n; i++) {

        // Increment radius and angle
        radius += radiusIncr;
        angle += angleIncr;

        // Compute second point of line segment
        x1 = cx + cos(angle) * radius;
        y1 = cy + sin(angle) * radius;

        // Compute normalized data value
// (0 <= t <= 1)
        t = data[i] / max;

        // Compute visual attributes line
// width and color
                lineWidth = computeLineWidth(t);
                lineColor = computeLineColor(t);

        // Draw line from (x0,y0) to (x1,y1)
        drawLine(x0, y0, x1, y1, lineWidth,
          lineColor);

        // Update point for next iteration
        x0 = x1;
        y0 = y1;
        }
}
```

7.3.8   Time: Time Primitives—Instant

CareCruiser [163] is a visualization system for exploring the effects of clinical actions on a patient's condition. To this end, CareCruiser visualizes details of treatment plan application in combination with patient parameters with particular respect to time-oriented processes. It supports exploration via aligning, color-highlighting, filtering, and providing focus and context information. Aligning clinical treatment plans vertically supports the comparison of the effects of different treatments or the comparison of different effects of

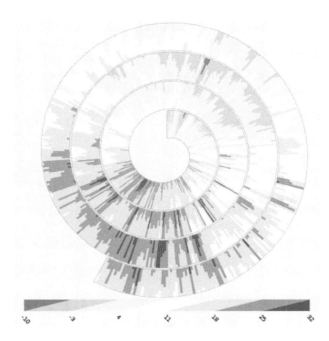

Figure 7.9.   Enhanced Interactive Spiral [416]. The enhanced spiral shows three and a half years
                   of weather data. Each cycle visualizes 365 values of the daily average temperature
                   in the city of Rostock. We can see that the most recent winter (outer cycle)
                   was milder than the previous winters. (Source: Generated with the enhanced
                   interactive spiral display tool.)

one treatment plan applied on different patients. Moreover, aligning all instances of an applied clinical action (e.g., the repeated administration of
a certain drug) facilitates the comparison of the effects this clinical action
has on the patient's condition. Three different color schemes are provided
to highlight interesting portions of the development of a parameter: highlighting the distance of the actual values to the intended value helps to
identify critical values; highlighting the progress of the actual values relative
to the initial values shows to what extent the applied treatment plan has
the intended effect; and highlighting the slope of a value helps to explore
the immediate effects of applied clinical actions. A range slider is provided
to filter the color highlighting for selected events (see Figure 7.10, top) and
a focus window that grays out the color information outside its borders is
used to support a focused investigation of a region of specific interest (e.g., a
certain time section after applying a clinical action). Slightly darker regions

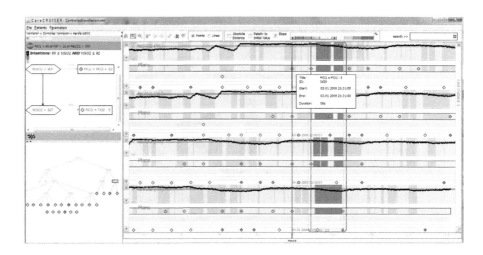

Figure 7.10.   CareCruiser [163]. The temporal view (on the right-hand side) arranges patient
                parameters together with applied clinical actions (the little diamonds below the line
                charts) along a horizontal time axis. The logical and hierarchical views capturing
                the treatment plans are shown on the left-hand side. In the selected area on the
                right, a delayed drop of the patient's $tcSO_2$ values after applying a specific clinical
                action is revealed. *Generated with the CareCruiser prototype software.*

outside the focus window indicate extreme curve events, thus maintaining
some context information.

7.3.9   Time: Time Primitives—Interval

The *SpiraClock* [98] visualizes time by using the clock metaphor. The visual
representation consists of a clock face and two hands indicating hour and
minute. The interior of the clock shows a spiral that extends from the
clock's circumference toward its center. Each cycle of the spiral represents
12 hours, with the current hour shown at the outermost cycle and future
hours displayed in the center (about nine future hours in Figure 7.11). Time
intervals (e.g., meetings) are represented as thick segments along the spiral
shape. These segments show when intervals start and end. Users can also
see if certain appointments are in conflict because they *overlap*, or if the
agenda is too tight, because many appointments *meet*). As time advances,
the spiral is constantly updated and future intervals gradually move outward
until they are current. Past intervals gradually fade out. In this sense, the
SpiraClock enhances classic clocks with a preview of the near future and a

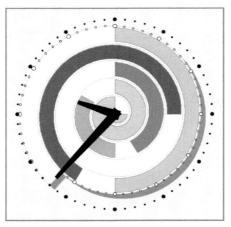

Figure 7.11.   The SpiraClock [98] builds upon the clock display. The minute hand currently
                points to a meeting that has already started. Future appointments are aligned
                along a spiral on the clock face. (Source: Generated by the authors.)

brief view to the past. The SpiraClock allows users to drag the clock hands
to visit different points in time, and intervals of interest can be highlighted
and corresponding textual annotations can be displayed.

7.3.10   Visualization: Mapping—Static

PostHistory [438] visually uncovers different patterns of e-mail activity (e.g.,
social networks, e-mail exchange rhythms) and the role of time in these patterns (see Figure 7.12). PostHistory is user-centric and focuses on a single
user's direct interactions with other people through e-mail. The social patterns are derived from analyzing e-mail header information. So, not the
content of messages, but the tracked traffic is used as the basis for the analysis of people's e-mail conversations over time. Basically, the user interface
visualizes a full year of e-mail activity and is divided into two main panels:
a calendar panel on the left and a contacts panel on the right. The calendar
panel shows the intensity of e-mail activity on a daily basis whereas a square
represents a single day and each row of squares represents a week. The size
of a square is determined by the quantity of e-mail received on that day and
its color represents the average directedness of messages, i.e., whether a mail
was received via TO, CC, or BCC. The brighter the color, the more directed
the messages are that are present on that day. The contacts panel is used
for displaying the names of people who sent messages to the user.

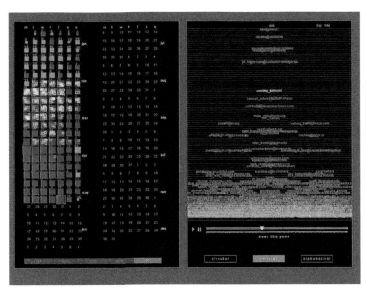

Figure 7.12.   PostHistory [438]. The calendar panel on the left shows e-mail activity on a daily
basis, where the number of e-mails and their average directedness are mapped to
box size and color, respectively. The contacts panel on the right displays the names
of people who sent messages to the user. (©2004 IEEE.)

7.3.11   Visualization: Mapping—Dynamic

Stock market data change dynamically during the day as prices are constantly updated. Vande Moere [436] proposes to visualize such data by
means of information *flocking boids*. The term *boids* borrows from the simulation of birds (bird objects = boids) in flocks. In order to visualize stock
market prices, each stock is considered to be a boid with an initially random
position in a 3D presentation space. Upon arrival of new data, boid positions
are updated dynamically according to several rules. These rules attempt to
avoid collisions of boids, to move boids at the same speed as their neighbors
in the flock, to move boids toward the flock's center, to keep similar boids
close to each other, and to let boids stay away from boids that are dissimilar.
The visual representation is inherently dynamic and aims at the users' capability to perceive emergence of patterns as the visualization updates. To this
end, boids and corresponding traces are visualized as animated curves, as
shown on the left in Figure 7.13. This 3D visual representation is enhanced
by enclosing boids within implicit surfaces, which help users recognize the
spatial structure of the flock (see Figure 7.13, right). The flocking boids

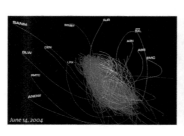 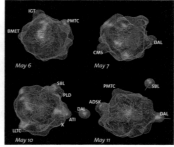

Figure 7.13.   Flocking Boids [436]. Stock market data are represented as flocking boids that move in a three-dimensional presentation space. Left: boids leaving the flock indicate that the corresponding stock price behaves differently than the majority of prices; right: implicit surfaces surrounding boids help users to recognize the spatial structure of the flock. (©2004 IEEE.)

visualization can be useful for detecting various patterns in the data such as the emergence of clusters, the separation of boids from the main flock, or a general chaotic behavior of boids.

7.3.12   Visualization: Dimensionality—2D

VisuExplore [338] is an interactive visualization system for exploring a heterogeneous set of medical parameters over time. It uses multiple views along a common horizontal time axis to convey the different medical parameters involved. VisuExplore provides an extensible environment of pluggable visualization techniques and its primary visualization techniques are deliberately kept simple to make them easily usable in medical practice: line plots, timeline charts, bar graphs, Horizon Graphs [331], event charts, line plots with semantic zoom, and document browsers (see Figure 7.14, top). Furthermore, data might also be presented as textual tables to augment the visual representations. VisuExplore's interactive features allow physicians to get an overview of multiple medical parameters and focus on parts of the data. Visualizations can be added showing one or more additional variables. Users may add, remove, resize, and rearrange visualization views. VisuExplore provides rich interaction to add, remove, organize, and adapt views. Additionally, a measurement tool is integrated that makes it possible to determine time spans between user selected points of interest; this works not only within one but also across different views.

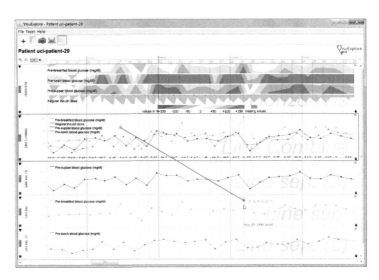

Figure 7.14.   VisuExplore [338]. Simple and easy-to-understand visual representation methods using line plot, bar chart, event chart, timeline chart, horizon graphs, and line plots with semantic zoom. Here, the measure tool is illustrated: A metaphorical tape measure for the time interval between two items (also across multiple diagrams). (Generated with the VisuExplore prototype software.)

7.3.13   Visualization: Dimensionality—3D

3D ThemeRiver [197] (see Figure 7.15) is a 3D variant of the ThemeRiver technique [172] (see Figure 7.16). The 3D approach inherits the basic visual design from its 2D counterpart: multiple time-oriented variables are encoded to the widths of individually colored currents that form a river flowing through time along a horizontal time axis. In the 2D variant, only one data variable can be visualized per current, namely, by varying the current's width. Imrich et al.'s extension addresses this limitation. By extending the design to the third dimension it is possible to use an additional visual encoding: the height (in 3D) of a current can be varied to encode further information. This design is particularly suited to visualizing ternary covariate trends in the data. Imrich et al. [197] conducted user tests to evaluate the usefulness of the 3D encoding, and indeed got positive results that indicate that the 3D variant has advantages over the 2D variant. Specifically, the availability of appropriate interactive 3D navigation tools is highlighted as an important factor contributing to the success of the 3D ThemeRiver.

Figure 7.15.   The 3D ThemeRiver [197]. Distinctly colored currents form the overall shape of
                the 3D ThemeRiver. The width and additionally the height of currents is varied to
                visualize time-oriented data. In this figure, width encodes the overall distribution
                of 17 clusters of aerosol data and height indicates the incidence of zinc. (Used with
                permission of authors.)

Table 7.1 provides an overview of all techniques that are included in this
chapter along with their categorization. This table might also be used to
search for techniques that fulfill certain criteria.

7.4   TimeBench: A Data Model and Software Library for Visual Analytics of Time-Oriented Data

Time-oriented data play an essential role in many visualization and visual
analytics scenarios, such as extracting medical insights from collections of
electronic health records or identifying emerging problems and vulnerabili-
ties in network traffic. However, many software libraries for visualization and
visual analytics treat time as a flat numerical data type and insufficiently
tackle the complexity of the time domain such as calendar granularities and
intervals. Therefore, developers of advanced visualizations and visual analytics techniques need to implement temporal foundations in their application
code over and over again.

| | data | | | | time | | | | vis | | | |
| | frame of reference | | variables | | arrangement | | time primitives | | mapping | | dimensionality | |
	abstract	spatial	univariate	multivariate	linear	cyclic	instant	interval	static	dynamic	2D	3D
KronoMiner	■			■	■		■		■		■	
Great Wall of Space-Time		■	■		■		■		■			■
GROOVE	■		■		■	■	■		■		■	
TimeWheel	■			■	■		■		■		■	
Line Plot	■		■		■		■		■		■	
Enhanced Interactive Spiral	■		■			■	■		■		■	
CareCruiser	■			■	■		■		■		■	
SpiraClock	■		■			■		■		■	■	
PostHistory	■			■	■	■	■		■		■	
Flocking Boids	■			■	■		■			■		■
VisuExplore	■			■	■		■	■	■			
3D ThemeRiver	■			■	■		■		■			■

Table 7.1: Overview and categorization of visualization techniques.

TimeBench [339] is a free and open source software library that provides foundational data structures and algorithms for time-oriented data in visualization and visual analytics (http://timebench.org). Its expressiveness and developer accessibility have been evaluated through application examples demonstrating a variety of challenges with time-oriented data and long-term developer studies conducted in the scope of research and student projects. Figure 7.16 shows seven different application examples developed with the TimeBench library.

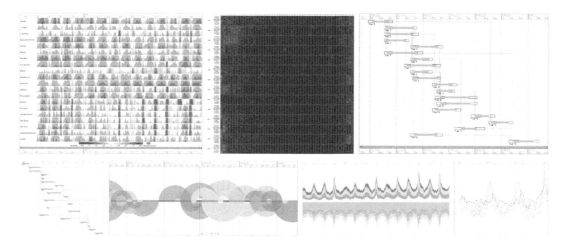

Figure 7.16.   TimeBench [339]. Application examples built using TimeBench: (1) Monthly
                 health data of 20 cities over 14 years in a horizon graph [331]; (2) 14 years of
                 daily health data in a GROOVE visualization [262]; (3) a project plan using
                 the PlanningLines metaphor [4]; (4) a project plan as a Gantt chart [170]; (5)
                 an arc diagram [451] showing relationships between events of three categories;
                 (6) a ThemeRiver visualization [172]; (7) multiple line plots with indexing [34].
                 Health data from the NMMAPS study [316] is used in (1), (2), (5), (6), and (7).
                 (http://timebench.org).

7.5   Summary

In this chapter we have explored concepts and methods for visualizing time
and time-oriented data. We demonstrated how these characteristics are used
in various visualization techniques for time-oriented data. Our characteristics cover data, time, and visual representations (see Section 7.3.1). Since
there are observable balances and imbalances with regard to our categorization, it is worth taking a closer look at possible explanations.

Data: frame of reference. In our survey [5], we mainly focus on abstract data.
Showing time-oriented data in a spatial frame of reference significantly increases the design efforts because more information has to be packed into
the visual mapping. Particularly, the disciplines of cartography and geovisualization, which are established, independent fields of research, have developed approaches to combining the visualization of temporal and spatial
aspects of data [16, 17, 256]. Furthermore, spatial and geospatial data are
already covered in Chapters 5 and 6.

Data: variables. The number of techniques for univariate and multivariate data are almost balanced in [5]. While classic techniques often consider simpler univariate data, modern approaches take on the challenge of dealing with multiple variables.

Time: arrangement. Most of the techniques in our survey [5] support linear time; the approaches with cyclic time are significantly fewer. Reasons for this might be that users are usually interested in trends evolving from past, to present, to future, rather than in finding cycles in the data.

Time: time primitives. Instants in time are the most commonly used time primitive in our survey [5]. This seems natural because data are often measured at a particular point in time. Intervals occur less often and mostly in planning scenarios.

Vis: mapping. Apparently, the static pages of a book are better suited for showing static techniques. In this sense, the selected visualization techniques are a bit biased containing only static approaches. However, dynamic techniques are equally important and often it is the first solution offered when time-oriented data have to be visualized.

Vis: dimensionality. 2D visual representations are often preferred over 3D ones, because they are more abstract and thus easier to understand. Again, our selected visualization techniques are biased mostly towards 2D approaches. Especially, techniques developed in the early days tend to stick with 2D simply due to the limited computing power available then. However, modern technologies have made it easier both for visualization designers to implement 3D visualization, and for visualization users to navigate and explore virtual 3D visualization spaces. This is particularly useful when data with spatial references have to be visualized.

TimeViz Browser. We have built an interactive repository (http://survey. timeviz.net) that helps researchers and practitioners in finding available approaches that fit the categorization explained in Section 7.3.1 (see Figure 7.17). This is achieved via faceted browsing where characteristics of time, data, and visual representation can be specified interactively and a number of applicable techniques is shown. We were inspired by Keller and Keller [236] in structuring our survey on a per-page basis. This allows easy access when a quick reference to a particular technique is sought. Each page briefly describes the background, explains the main idea and concepts, and indicates the application of a particular technique. The description is accompanied by a reference to the original publication or a list of references in the case that multiple publications propose or make use of the same approach.

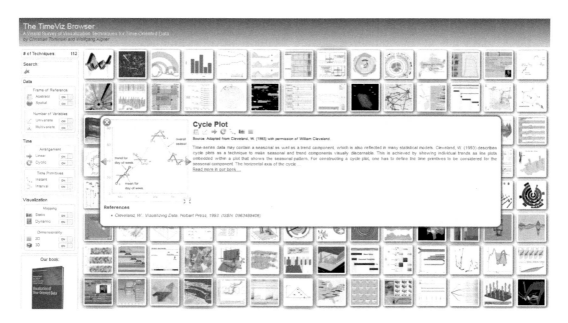

Figure 7.17.   TimeViz Browser. An interactive repository of visualization techniques for time-
                 oriented data (http://survey.timeviz.net) [5].

TimeViz Browser is a great tool to search for appropriate visualization techniques according the three above-mentioned aspects.

7.6   Related Readings

The most comprehensive source about various visualization techniques is
the book we compiled recently [5]. The associated TimeViz Browser (http:
//survey.timeviz.net) is a more up-to-date repository where characteristics
of time, data, and visual representation can be specified interactively and
suitable examples are shown. More formal definitions of the characteristics of time can be found in TimeBench [339] as well as in the classical
approaches [16, 17, 38, 132]. A short introduction to our user-data-task design principle is given in [292]. A recently published book gives a very
good introduction to the theory of time-oriented multivariate network visualizations and their application in software engineering, social nets, and life
science [238].

7.7 Exercises

1. For each of the following plot types, describe at least one solution where you would choose this plot over the other.

   (a) Line plot
   (b) Point plot
   (c) Cycle plot

2. Which of the following visualization techniques are suited to represent medication history for a patient (medication type, dose, start and end of drug administration)? Explain your reasons for selection.

   (a) Cycle plot
   (b) TimeWheel
   (c) Timelines

3. Which of the following visualization techniques emphasize cyclic characteristics of time?

   (a) Horizon graphs
   (b) SpiraClock
   (c) Cycle plot

4. The information that the winter semester starts on Oct. 1st and ends on Jan. 31st can by modeled by:

   (a) an instant
   (b) an interval
   (c) a span

7.8 Projects

1. Implement the function *computeLineWidth* und *computeLineColor* of the pseudo-code illustrating how to draw a spiral (compare Section 7.3.7).

2. A health insurance institution is collecting vast amounts of data related to physician consultations of patients, prescriptions, medications, medical tests, examinations, and lab results, including additional parameters (e.g., hospital, physician, cost, date and time, or duration). This means that large amounts of time-oriented data of different types are available. The insurance institution wants to query, explore, and

analyze these data visually according to different tasks and groups of insured persons.

Your duty is to support this institution using visualization techniques for time-oriented data (and others).

(a) Describe and specify the following:

Users
Who are the users of the visualization?
What are the specifics of the target group?
(not merely "employee", but a more specific description, such as analyst or manager in a specific department, including details of the characteristics of the respective user group)

Data
What kind of data is to be visualized?
Which variables/parameters?
What data types?
Which structure?
Any additional specifics?
(Note: Apart from the above listed attributes, others might be added.)

Tasks
What do the users want to do with the data and which insights do they want to gain?

(b) Sketch a proposed solution in terms of visual representation, interaction, and data analysis methods.

(c) How you would evaluate the proposed solution?

3. Write a program to generate a ThemeRiver representation of traffic accident data where the individual currents represent different road types. Order the currents in a way that smaller values and variations are in the center of the river. [Data set: UK Road Safety Data, http://data.gov.uk/dataset/road-accidents-safety-data]

CHAPTER **8**

Visualization Techniques for Multivariate Data

In this chapter we discuss techniques for the visualization of data that does not generally have an explicit spatial attribute. We organize the presentations based on the graphical primitive used in the rendering, namely, points, lines, or regions, followed by techniques that combine two or more of these types of primitives. We conclude with a section on issues common to all multivariate visualization techniques.

8.1 Point-Based Techniques

Point plots are introduced as visualizations that project records from an n-dimensional data space to an arbitrary k-dimensional display space, such that data records map to k-dimensional points. For each record, a graphical representation, mark, or other aesthetic entity is drawn at its associated k-dimensional point. Individual visualization techniques identified as point plots define appropriate data projections and specific visual representations. Point plots can be defined to display individual records or summary records, and can be structured by various projection techniques. Several popular point-based methods are described in this section. Others may be found in the suggested readings.

8.1.1 Scatterplots and Scatterplot Matrices

As described in Chapter 1, scatterplots are one of the earliest and most widely used visualization techniques in data analysis. Both 2D and 3D scatterplots can be found in most packages designed to support data and information analysis. Their success stems from our innate abilities to judge relative position within a bounded space. As the dimensionality of the data increases, the choices for visual analysis consist of:

- *dimension subsetting*—allowing the user to select a subset of the dimensions to display, or to develop algorithms to find the dimensions containing the most useful information for the task at hand.

- *dimension reduction*—using techniques such as principal component analysis or multidimensional scaling to transform the high-dimensional data to data of lower dimension, while attempting to preserve as best as possible the relationships among the data points.

- *dimension embedding*—mapping dimensions to other graphical attributes besides position, such as color, size, and shape (though there are limits to how many dimensions can be included this way).

- *multiple displays*—showing, either superimposed or juxtaposed, several plots, each of which contains some of the dimensions.

For the case of multiple displays, the most common approach is to use a *scatterplot matrix*. This consists of a grid of scatterplots, with the grid having N^2 cells, where N is the number of dimensions. Thus, every pairwise plot will be shown twice, differing by a 90 degree rotation. The ordering of the dimensions is usually the same for the horizontal and vertical orientations, resulting in symmetry along the diagonal. The diagonal plots, which would normally plot a variable against itself, are often used to convey the names of the dimensions in the corresponding rows/columns, or sometimes to show a histogram of a given dimension. Figure 8.1 shows an example of a scatterplot matrix.

8.1.2 Force-Based Methods

Many techniques for projecting high-dimensional points into 2D or 3D display space have been developed. The key goal is to attempt to maintain the N-dimensional features and characteristics of the data through the projection process, e.g., relationships that exist in the original data must also exist after projection. This, however, is not always possible, especially as the dimensionality of the data increases. The projection may also unintentionally introduce artifacts that may appear in the visualization and are not present in the data. In this section, we describe several such projection methods.

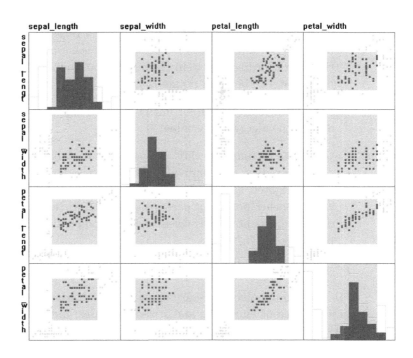

Figure 8.1.   A scatterplot matrix with the diagonal plot showing a histogram of each dimension. Note that the points and histogram regions in red indicate selected data.

Multidimensional scaling (MDS) [259] is an important class of dimension reduction algorithms commonly used in statistical analysis and information visualization. The basic structure of a typical MDS algorithm is as follows:

1. Given a data set with M records and N dimensions, create an M by M matrix, Ds, that contains similarity measures between each pair of data items. For example, one might use Euclidean distance as a measure of similarity.

2. Assuming that you are projecting the data into K dimensions (e.g., for display purposes, K is usually between 1 and 3), create an M by K matrix, L, to contain the locations for the projected points. These M locations can initially be randomly chosen, or techniques such as principal component analysis (PCA) can be used to create reasonable initial positions.

3. Compute an M by M matrix, Ls, that contains the similarities between all pairs of points in L.

4. Compute the value of stress, S, which is a measure of the differences between Ds and Ls. Many such stress measures exist; most assume that the coordinate systems have been normalized so that the maximum distance between points is 1.0.

5. If S is sufficiently small, or hasn't changed significantly in recent iterations, the algorithm terminates.

6. Otherwise, attempt to shift the positions of points in L in a direction that will reduce their individual stress levels. For example, this might be a weighted sum of displacements based on comparing the point with all other points, or perhaps only with its nearest neighbors. The displacement should be scaled such that points don't oscillate between positions.

7. Return to step 3.

As one can imagine, there are many possible variants on this algorithm, including different similarity and stress measures, different initial and termination conditions, and different position update strategies. As in any optimization process, there is the potential to fall into a local minimal configuration that still has a high level of stress. Common strategies to alleviate this include occasionally adding a random jump in the position of a point to see if it will converge to a different location. Figure 8.2 shows an example of the Iris data set, which contains four numeric dimensions, projected using MDS.

As is true for most, if not all, of the projection techniques in this section, there are many common criticisms. Obviously, the results are not unique: minor changes in the starting conditions can lead to dramatically different results. Another problem is that the coordinate system after projection is not *meaningful* to the user in terms of the dimensions of their original data. For example, it is typical to have a data point map to a location high in the display in one running of the algorithm and then map to a low position in a different execution of the algorithm. What is important is relative, not absolute, positions.

RadViz [188] is a force-driven point layout technique that is based on Hooke's Law for equilibrium. For an N-dimensional data set, N anchor points are placed on the circumference of the circle to represent the fixed ends of the N springs attached to each data point. To simplify computations and provide an intuitive feel for the algorithm, these anchors are most commonly placed on a circle of radius 1.0 centered on the origin. Thus,

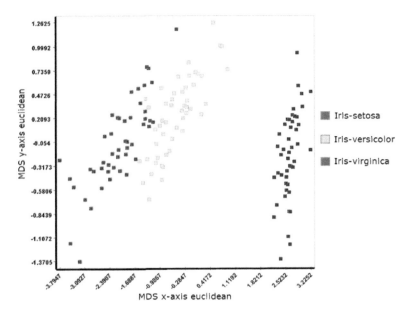

Figure 8.2.   Iris data set projected using MDS.

given a normalized data vector $D_i = (d_{i,0}, d_{i,1}, \ldots d_{i,N-1})$ and a set of unit vectors A, where A_j represents the jth anchor point, we get the following equilibrium equation:

$$\sum_{j=0}^{N-1} (A_j - p)d_j = 0,$$

where p is the vector for the point at equilibrium. Solving for p yields

$$p = \frac{\sum_{j=0}^{N-1} (A_j d_j)}{\sum_{j=0}^{N-1} d_j}. \tag{8.1}$$

Note that different placement and ordering of the anchors will give different results, and that points that are quite distinct in N dimensions may map to the same location in 2D. However, this is a problem common to all projection and dimension reduction techniques. In the case of RadViz, a simple solution is to provide interactions such as moving and reordering the anchors and observing the changes in the visual layout. Relationships in the data can often be teased out in this manner, especially if the changed positions of points are animated along with the anchor movement (see Figure 8.3). Another approach is to implement search algorithms, similar to

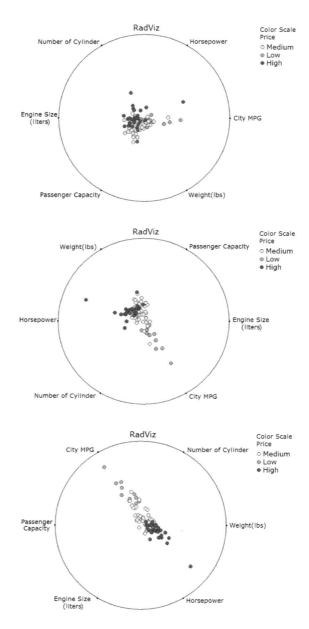

Figure 8.3.   Different views of the same data set in RadViz, using manual reordering of dimen-
               sions. Cars are color-coded according to their cost (low, medium, and high), and
               the goal is to find attributes of cars that can best predict which cost range a car
               is likely to fall into.

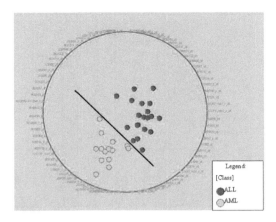

Figure 8.4.   This figure shows a class-discrimination algorithm that selects the dimensions providing the most spread in the data in a RadViz display. By placing the genes
expressed in acute lymphoblastic leukemia (ALL) patients close to each other and
the genes expressed in acute myeloblastic leukemia (AML) close to each other, the
AML patients were separated from the ALL patients.

projection pursuit, that try to find dimension layouts that result in the
maximum spread, such as shown in Figure 8.4.

Vectorized RadViz, or VRV, constructs multiple dimensions from individual dimensions by a flattening process, breaking each dimension into
many [372]. For example, the dimension representing the number of cylinders can be broken down into 5 new dimensions: having 1 or 2 cylinders,
having 3 or 4 cylinders, having 5 or 6, having 7, or having 8. The number
of new dimensions can be determined algorithmically or manually. This is
similar to identifying bins in data (such as the grouping of low, medium,
and high for prices of cars). Each original dimension is thus represented by
a vector of new dimensions, with each new coordinate in that vector having
the value 0 or 1, namely, whether the record has the value corresponding to
that dimension or not. Thus, for each record, each new vector of dimensions
has exactly one dimension with the value 1, and all the others have value
zero. An example of VRV is shown in Figure 8.5.

Barycentric displays [320] are similar in appearance to RadViz. However, instead of assigning positions based on springs connected to anchor
points, coordinates are considered as weighted sums of the anchor positions. While closed form solutions for small numbers of anchors have been
developed, generalizing these displays to arbitrary numbers of anchors is
still a research problem (although a recent patent claims to have solved the
general case).

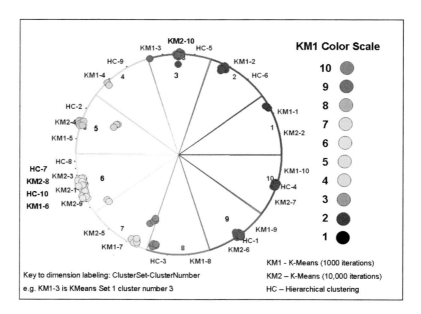

Figure 8.5.   Vectorized RadViz, formed by splitting each dimension into multiple dimensions to create a binary representation for each data record. In this case, each cluster set is separated into multiple dimensions, where each dimension represents a cluster in each cluster set [372].

8.2   Line-Based Techniques

Point-based methods represent each data value or record with a small mark. In line-based methods, points corresponding to a particular record or dimension are linked together with straight or curved lines. These lines not only reinforce the relationships among the data values, but also convey perceivable features of the data via slopes, curvature, crossings, and other line patterns. We describe a couple of techniques within this class of methods.

8.2.1   Line Graphs

A line graph is a univariate visualization technique where the vertical axis represents the range of values for the variable and the horizontal axis represents some ordering of the records in the data set. Most univariate visualization techniques can be extended to multivariate data by either superimposing or juxtaposing the visual representations of individual variables. A commonly used method of this sort is via line graphs. For a modest number

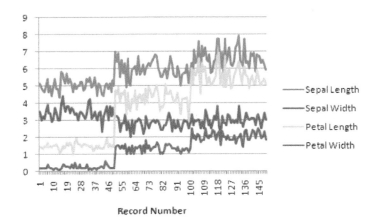

Figure 8.6. An example of a multivariate line chart, in this case, the four-dimensional Iris data set. Note that the modest separation between dimensions makes it easy to identify trends and outliers.

of data dimensions, the line plots can be drawn on a common set of axes, differentiating the dimensions using color, line style, width, or other graphical attributes (see Figure 8.6).

When the number of dimensions increases, or the dimensions have significant overlap in their data ranges, superimposing becomes more problematic. Figure 8.7(a) shows an 8-dimensional data set (AAUP faculty salaries and compensation for different ranks at 100 universities). Clearly, patterns are difficult to perceive. However, a few strategies are possible. Figure 8.7(b) shows a stacked line chart, where instead of using a common baseline, each dimension uses the plot from the previous dimension as a base. While this reduces the number of occlusions, it makes it more difficult to assess actual values of data points. Figures 8.7(c) and 8.7(d) show the effect of another strategy, namely, sorting the records based on one of the dimensions. Patterns in both the regular and stacked versions are easier to identify.

The effectiveness of the examples above is due in large part to the fact that common units exist between the dimensions (e.g., size in one and dollars in the others). When variables have different units, things get more complex. One approach commonly used is to include multiple vertical axes, each labeled and ticked independently. Both the left and right sides of the plot can be used to reduce the clutter. Clearly, if the tick marks are not aligned, it would be unwise to have grid lines on the plot, unless the dimension controlling the grid lines could be readily changed by the user. Another approach is

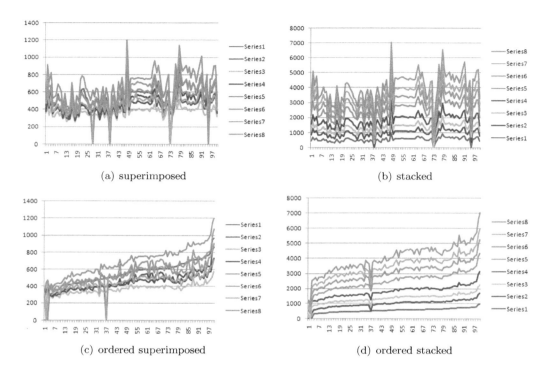

(a) superimposed   (b) stacked

(c) ordered superimposed   (d) ordered stacked

Figure 8.7.   Four versions of line graphs for a subset of the AAUP data set: superimposed, stacked, ordered superimposed, and ordered stacked. Ordering is based on the first dimension, which represents salaries of full professor.

to create a set of plots, one for each dimension, and to stack them vertically (usually after scaling them in the vertical dimension to enable all or most of the plots to be visible simultaneously). Some form of *linked brushing* (see Chapters 11 and 12) can be used to enable users to see the values in other dimensions that correspond to a feature of interest in one of the plots.

8.2.2   Parallel Coordinates

Parallel coordinates, also called ||-coords and PCP (for parallel coordinates plot), were first introduced by Inselberg in 1985 as a mechanism for studying high-dimensional geometry [199]. Since then, numerous researchers have studied and enhanced PCPs for use in multivariate data analysis. The basic idea is that axes, rather than being orthogonal, are parallel, with evenly spaced vertical or horizontal lines representing a particular ordering of the

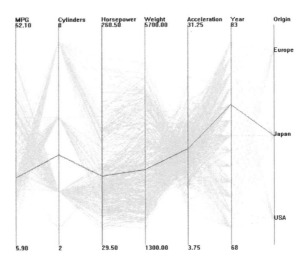

Figure 8.8. An example of a 7-dimensional data set visualized with parallel coordinates. A single data point is represented as the darkened polyline.

dimensions. A data point is plotted as a polyline that crosses each axis at a position proportional to its value for that dimension. Figure 8.8 shows an example. One could consider a PCP as a line graph after rotating the data, since the values of a record are linked together, as opposed to the values of a dimension.

To interpret the plot, one looks for clusters of similar lines (indicating partial correlation between pairs of dimensions), similar crossing points (indicating partial negative correlations), and lines that are either isolated or have a slope that is significantly different from their neighbors (indicating outliers). One problem is that, like scatterplots, parallel coordinates have their strength in showing relationships between pairs of dimensions. To extend this capability, interactive selection and highlighting of records allows users to see relationships that span all dimensions. For example, the lines drawn in dark red in Figure 8.9 were isolated by dragging the mouse along the high values of the MPG coordinate, thus selecting the records falling in that range for the specified dimension. The light grey region identifies the extents of the N-dimensional box that contains the selected points.

Many researchers have extended the capabilities of parallel coordinates over the years. Some of these include:

- hierarchical parallel coordinates that show data clusters rather than the original data [137];

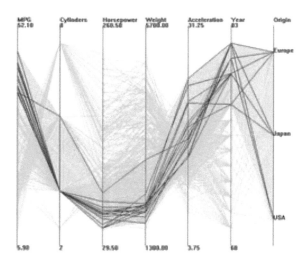

Figure 8.9.   A set of points is selected in the parallel coordinates plot. Selected points are colored dark red, and the subspace containing them is shown in grey.

- using semi-transparent lines to reveal clusters in large data sets [293];

- clustering, reordering, and spacing of axes based on correlation [479];

- reordering axes to reduce visual clutter [317];

- grouping data into cluster bands with special treatment of outliers [307];

- incorporating histograms into the axes to better convey univariate distributions [448];

- fitting curves to the intersection points to better convey continuity across axes [486].

8.2.3   Andrews Curves

Another line-based visualization for multivariate data is the *Andrews curve*, developed by David F. Andrews in 1972 [13]. Each multivariate data point $D = (d_1, d_2, \ldots, d_N)$ is used to create a curve of the form

$$f(t) = \frac{d_1}{\sqrt{2}} + d_2 \sin(t) + d_3 \cos(t) + d_4 \sin(2t) + d_5 \cos(2t) + \ldots.$$

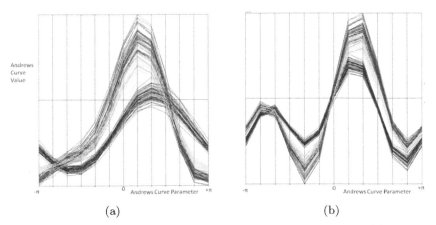

Figure 8.10.   An example of Andrews curves using two different dimension orders: (a) based on
                    the original order of the dimensions (sepal length, sepal width, petal length, petal
                    width); (b) based on the original order of the dimensions in reverse order.

For an odd number of dimensions, the final term is $d_N \cos(\frac{N-1}{2}t)$, while
for an even number of dimensions the final term is $d_N \sin(\frac{N}{2}t)$. As in many
multivariate visualization techniques, the order of the dimensions can have a
significant effect on the resulting Andrews curve. Figures 8.10(a) and 8.10(b)
show the same data with different dimension orders. In particular, outliers
may become more or less perceivable, depending on the ordering.

8.2.4   Radial Axis Techniques

For each of the techniques that orient the coordinate systems horizontally
and/or vertically, there is an equivalent technique that uses a radial orientation. For example, a *circular line graph* is one in which the plotted lines are
offset from a circular base (see Figure 8.11). A long graph can be nested by
dividing it up into equal size segments and mapping each to a base of different radius. This is a potentially useful way to study cyclic events. Variants
on circular line graphs include *radar* and *star graphs*. Many other circular
charts have been developed over the years, including:

- *polar graphs*—point plots using polar coordinates;

- *circular bar charts*—like circular line graphs, but plotting bars on the
  base line;

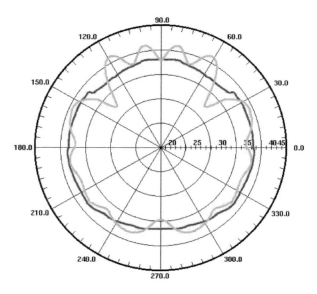

Figure 8.11.   An example of a circular line graph. (Image courtesy http://www.cemframework
                  .com/img/PolarPlot1.png.)

- *circular area graphs*—like a line graph, but with the area under line filled in with a color or texture;

- *circular bar graphs*—with bars that are circular arcs with a common center point and base line (note the difference between these and circular bar charts: in one, the bar is straight and the base is curved, but vice versa for the other).

Any of the techniques that use radial axes and involve more than one cycle can either use concentric rings or a continuous spiral as a layout. For example, Figure 8.12 shows a bar chart with a spiral base. These methods don't suffer from the discontinuity at the end of each cycle that is present in the concentric circle layout. Note that comparisons within and between cycles are fairly easy to perform, especially with the bars all oriented along the vertical axis, rather than perpendicular to the spiral base. Based on our knowledge of human perception, measuring differences between adjacent elements is harder than if we had a common baseline; however, a traditional bar graph would not allow us to easily see patterns between elements in the same position of different cycles.

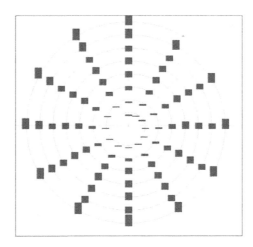

Figure 8.12.   An example of a spiral layout for a bar graph generated by SpiralGlyphics [441].

8.3   Region-Based Techniques

In *region-based techniques*, filled polygons are used to convey values, based on their size, shape, color, or other attributes. Even though it was mentioned in Chapter 3 that our ability to accurately measure area is noticeably worse than our ability to measure attributes such as length, many effective techniques in this category have been developed. For some, the goal is not to show the raw data itself, but rather summaries or distributions of the values. Many of the region-based techniques were initially designed for univariate data, such as pie charts and bar charts. Some, however, have been extended to multiple dimensions.

8.3.1   Bar Charts/Histograms

One of the most common visualizations, in addition to line plots, scatterplots, and maps, is the bar chart, where rectangular bars are used to convey numeric values. As mentioned in Chapter 3, humans have high visual acuity when it comes to comparing the length of linear features. Thus, bar charts are a natural choice for visualizing many kinds of data. Both horizontal and vertical bars are routinely used and are readily interpretable, which means that the visualization designer has some flexibility in the way they are integrated into a given application. If each bar is to receive a text label, it is easier to use horizontally oriented bars, but angling the text for vertical bars can also help to solve the problem of lengthy strings.

One of the critical decisions that needs to be made when using bar charts is deciding how many bars are needed to best represent the data. If the bars represent the state of N variables, then as long as N is not too large, there can be a one-to-one correspondence between variables and bars. If the goal is to represent a summarization or distribution of a data set, we can use a *histogram* to convey the number of occurrences of data values. If the data takes on nominal values or a modest number of distinct integers, the decision is simple—just have the same number of bars as there are different values. For continuous data or integer variables with a large range, we need to divide the data into subranges and assign each subrange to a bar.

If the data is multivariate, there are several options for using bar charts. A common alternative is a *stacked bar graph*, where each bar consists of several shorter bars to represent the values for each dimension (Figure 8.13a). It is common to vary the color, texture, or other attributes of the bars to make them readily distinguishable within a given bar and comparable between bars. Similarly, bars for different variables can be placed next to each other, giving them a common baseline and thus simplifying their interpretation (Figure 8.13b). The choice between these approaches is often based on the number of variables, as well as the number of bars. Stacked bars distribute the burden in two directions, while adjacent bars can demand significant space, unless the bar and dimension counts are modest.

Cityscapes are a 3D version of bar graphs, where 3D boxes are used instead of 2D rectangles. Bars are laid out on a grid using two data dimensions to position the bar on the surface. Other variables control the size and color of the boxes at a given location. Cityscapes get their name

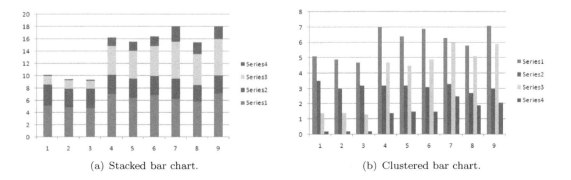

(a) Stacked bar chart.   (b) Clustered bar chart.

Figure 8.13.   Examples of 2D bar graphs for showing multivariate data.

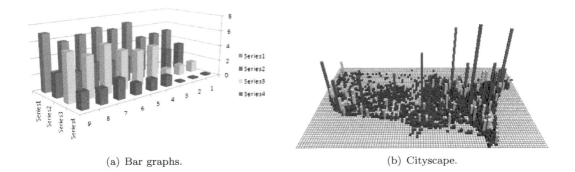

(a) Bar graphs.   (b) Cityscape.

Figure 8.14.   Examples of 3D visualizations for showing multivariate data.

from the fact that the resulting visualization often looks like the buildings of a city. If all cells in the grid are populated, the graph is sometimes called a *3D histogram*. The problem with going to 3D is that there is now the possibility of occlusion (Figure 8.14a). Several strategies exist for reducing or eliminating this occlusion. One is to provide the user the option to rotate the view, thus exposing bars that were previously blocked. Another is to shrink the thickness of the bars to reduce the size of their footprints and therefore reduce the number of bars that a given bar can block. A third approach is to vary the opacity of bars, allowing one to see the bars blocked by those closer to the viewpoint. All of these approaches have shortcomings, but even with their limitations, cityscapes are a popular visualization technique, especially with georeferenced data (Figure 8.14(b)).

8.3.2   Tabular Displays

Multivariate data is often stored in tables, and a number of visualization techniques have been modeled on this structure. These techniques mostly vary in the types of interactions they support.

Heatmaps are created by displaying the table of record values using color rather than text. For this visualization technique, all data values are mapped to the same normalized color space, and each is rendered as a colored square or rectangle. Using different color maps, as well as allowing users to stretch or compress colors to emphasize or deemphasize some value ranges (as we saw in volume rendering using transfer functions), enhances the usefulness of this technique (Figure 8.15).

Permuted Data Matrix

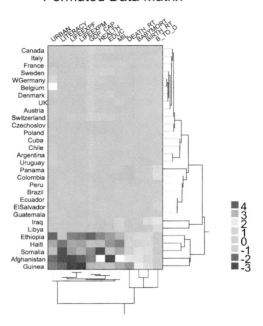

Figure 8.15.   A heatmap showing social statistics for several countries from a U.N. survey. Rows and columns have been reordered via clustering. (Image courtesy Leland Wilkinson [459].)

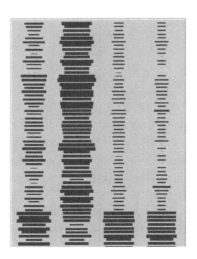

Figure 8.16.   A section of a survey plot as computed by the DataLab tool. Each column is a visual representation of each of the four dimensions of the Iris data set.

Permutation or reorderable matrices are basically heatmaps with the option to reorganize rows and columns to expose features of the data [34]. Columns and rows can be reordered to maximize diagonalization, forming a matrix with higher-valued cells aligned along the diagonal. Other variants reorder to isolate clusters of similar values or patterns of values.

Survey plots create a variant on permutation matrices by varying the size of cells, rather than coloring them and aligning cell centers within individual attributes [276]. This alleviates biases in color perception caused by the effects of adjacent colors. However, because measurement of area is more error-prone than measuring length, this method also has its deficiencies (Figure 8.16).

Finally, table lens combines all these ideas and includes a level-of-detail mechanism for providing panning and zooming capabilities to display whole table views, while still providing some detail through local table lenses [328]. Data can be presented in many ways, depending on how much screen space the user allocates to a particular row or column. Sorting columns helps to quickly identify trends, correlations, and outliers (Figure 8.17).

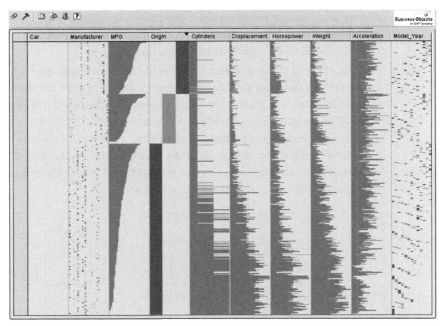

Figure 8.17.   An example of Inxight Table Lens showing the cars data set sorted first by car origin and then by MPG.

8.3.3   Dimensional Stacking

Dimensional stacking is a method developed by LeBlanc et al. [266] for mapping data from a discrete N-dimensional space to a two-dimensional image in a manner that minimizes the occlusion of data, while preserving much of the spatial information. Briefly, the mapping is performed as follows: begin with data of dimension $2N + 1$ (for an even number of dimensions there would be an additional implicit dimension of cardinality one). Select a finite cardinality/discretization for each dimension. Choose one of the dimensions to be the dependent variable. The rest will be considered independent.

Create ordered pairs of the independent dimensions (N pairs) and assign to each pair a unique value (speed) from 1 to N. The pair corresponding to speed 1 will create a virtual image whose size coincides with the cardinality of the dimensions (the first dimension in the pair is oriented horizontally, the second vertically). At each position of this virtual image, create another virtual image to correspond to dimensions of speed 2, again whose size is dependent on the cardinality of the dimensions involved. Repeat this process until all dimensions have been embedded. In this manner, every location in the discrete high-dimensional space has a unique location in the two-dimensional image resulting from the mapping. The concept of the speed of a dimension can best be likened to the digits on an odometer, where digits cycle through their values at different rates.

The value of the dependent variable at the location in the high-dimensional space is then mapped to a color/intensity value at that location in the two-dimensional image. This embedding process is illustrated in Figure 8.18 with a six-dimensional data set, where dimensions d1,..., d6 have cardinalities 4, 5, 2, 3, 3, and 6, respectively. For clarity, we have not displayed the values associated with a dependent variable, which would be the seventh dimension and would dictate the colors in the smallest grid locations. Figure 8.19 is an example of a dimensional stacking visualization.

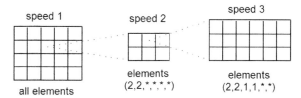

Figure 8.18.   Conceptualization of dimensional stacking; collapsing six dimensions into two dimensions.

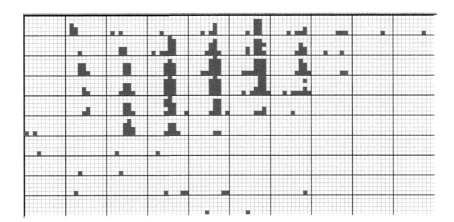

Figure 8.19.   An example of 4D data visualized using dimensional stacking. The data consists of drill-hole data, with three spatial dimensions, and the ore grade as the fourth dimension.

Dimensional stacking is basically a 2D extension of a technique developed by Mihalisin et al. [291], which involves graphing scalar fields in multiple dimensions. Their technique consists of embedding graphs in a recursive fashion, using color and baseline displacement to indicate steps in the slower dimensions. The major differences between the techniques are the use of intensity/color instead of location for the data/graphic mapping (thus permitting a significant increase in information presentation in exchange for a reduction in quantitative perception) and the display of data sets instead of functions. A 3D version of embedded dimensions has also been explored by Feiner and Beshers [119] in a technique referred to as "Worlds within Worlds."

Dimensional stacking can be viewed as an N-dimensional histogram if the color of a cell is set proportional to the number of data values that map to it. The technique nicely captures the occupancy and distribution of a high-dimensional data space, although as the dimensionality or number of bins per dimension increases, the percentage of the space that is empty also increases (the so-called "curse of dimensionality"). Another powerful use of this technique is in presenting the results of simulations involving a significant number of input parameters. By mapping the input parameters to the mapping dimensions and the evaluation metrics to color, an analyst can examine large collections of simulations to ascertain which parameter settings lead to good results. This use of dimensional stacking was reported recently by John Langton and his colleagues [264].

8.4   Combinations of Techniques

In addition to the techniques based on points, lines, or regions, there are a number of hybrid techniques that combine features of two or more of these classes. We describe two of the more popular techniques of this type: glyphs and dense pixel displays.

8.4.1   Glyphs and Icons

In the context of data and information visualization, a *glyph*[1] is a visual representation of a piece of data or information where a graphical entity and its attributes are controlled by one or more data attributes. As an example, the width and height of a box could be controlled by a student's score on the midterm and final exam for a course, while the color could be associated with the gender of the student. This is a rather broad definition for the term, as it can cover such visual elements as the markers in a scatterplot, the bars of a histogram, or even an entire line plot. However, a narrower definition would not be sufficient to capture the wide range of data visualization techniques that have been developed over the centuries and are termed glyphs.

Many authors have developed lists of graphical attributes to which data values can be mapped [34, 80, 81]. These include: position (1, 2, or 3D), size (length, area, or volume), shape, orientation, material (hue, saturation, intensity, texture, or opacity), line style (width, dashes, or tapers), and dynamics (speed of motion, direction of motion, rate of flashing).

In this section, a wide range of possible mappings for data glyphs are discussed, including:

- one-to-one mappings, where each data attribute maps to a distinct and different graphical attribute;

- one-to-many mappings, where redundant mappings are used to improve the accuracy and ease with which a user can interpret data values; and

- many-to-one mappings, where several or all data attributes map to a common type of graphical attribute, separated in space, orientation, or other transformation.

One-to-one mappings are often designed to take advantage of the user's domain knowledge, using intuitive pairings of data to graphical attributes to

---

[1] In some fields, the terms *glyph* and *icon* are synonymous, while in others an icon is a pictorial representation of an object, process, or concept.

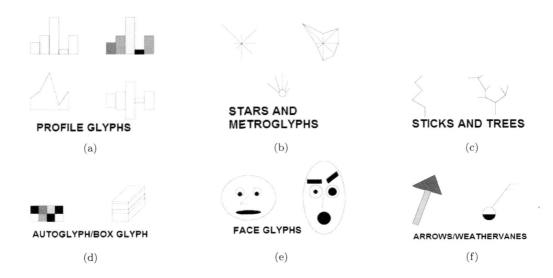

Figure 8.20.   Examples of multivariate glyphs (from [445]).

ease the learning process. Examples include mapping color to temperature, and flow direction to line orientation. Redundant mappings can be useful in situations where the number of data dimensions is low and the desire is to reduce the possibility of misinterpretation. For example, one might map population to both size and color to ease analysis for color-impaired users, and to facilitate comparison of two populations with similar values. Many-to-one mappings are best used in situations where it is important to not only compare values of the same dimension for separate records, but also to compare different dimensions for the same record. For example, mapping each dimension to the height of a vertical bar facilitates both intra-record and inter-record comparison.

The following list (from [445]) contains a subset of glyphs that have been proposed in the literature or are in common use. Some are customized to a particular application, such as visualizing fluid flow, while others are more general purpose.

- profiles [100]—height and color of bars (Figure 8.20(a));

- stars [378]—length of evenly spaced rays emanating from center (Figure 8.20(b));

- Anderson/metroglyphs [11, 149]— length of rays (Figure 8.20(b));

- stick figures [319]—length, angle, color of limbs (Figure 8.20(c));

- trees [246]—length, thickness, angles of branches; branch structure derived from analyzing relations between dimensions (Figure 8.20(c));

- autoglyph [29]—color of boxes (Figure 8.20(d));

- boxes [171]—height, width, depth of first box; height of successive boxes (Figure 8.20(d));

- hedgehogs [245]—spikes on a vector field, with variation in orientation, thickness, and taper;

- faces [71]—size and position of eyes, nose, mouth; curvature of mouth; angle of eyebrows (Figure 8.20(e));

- arrows [462]—length, width, taper, and color of base and head (Figure 8.20(f));

- polygons [365]—conveying local deformation in a vector field via orientation and shape changes;

- dashtubes [139]—texture and opacity to convey vector field data;

- weathervanes [134]—level in bulb, length of flags (Figure 8.20(f));

- circular profiles [290]—distance from center to vertices at equal angles;

- color glyphs [270]—colored lines across a box;

- bugs [76]—wing shapes controlled by time series; length of head spikes (antennae); size and color of tail; size of body markings;

- wheels [76]—time wheels create a ring of time series plots, value controls distance from base ring; 3D wheel maps time to height, variable value to radius;

- boids [237]—shape and orientation of primitives moving through a time-varying field;

- procedural shapes [345]—blobby objects controlled by up to 14 dimensions;

- Glyphmaker [337]—user-controlled mappings;

- Icon Modeling Language [324]—attributes of a 2D contour and the parameters that extrude it to 3D and further transform/deform it;

In using glyphs for information visualization, we need to be aware of the many biases and limitations of the technique. First and foremost are the perceptual biases, depending on what graphical attributes are being used. As discussed in Chapter 3, there are some attributes, such as the length of a line, that we can judge more accurately than others, such as orientation or color. Other issues of bias include the fact that relationships between adjacent graphical attributes are much easier to perceive than those that are more distant, with a few notable exceptions (e.g., comparing two ears on a Chernoff face might be easier than comparing two different, but adjacent, facial features). Similarly, comparing two glyphs that are near each other on the screen is easier than if the glyphs are more separated. Finally, the number of data dimensions and records that can be effectively handled with glyphs is limited.

Once a glyph design is chosen, there are $N!$ different dimension orderings that can be used in the mapping. Which ones are likely to reveal the most interesting features? Several ordering strategies can be imagined:

- Dimensions could be ordered according to their correlation, so that similar dimensions are mapped adjacent to each other. This can help reveal general trends, as well as expose some outliers.

- Dimensions can be mapped in such a way as to promote symmetrically shaped glyphs, which can be easier to perceive and remember. Shapes that are less symmetric than their neighbors will also stand out.

- Dimensions can be sorted according to their values in one record. For example, if the data represents a multivariate time series, sorting the dimensions based on the first record can make the trends over time more pronounced, conveying which dimensional relationships were maintained versus those that changed significantly.

- Dimensions can be manually sorted, based on the user's knowledge of the domain. Thus, semantically similar dimensions can be grouped or used for symmetric glyph features, which can simplify the interpretation.

A final important consideration in designing a glyph-based visualization is the layout of the glyphs on the screen. As described in [445], there are three general classes of layout strategies:

1. *uniform*—glyphs are scaled and positioned with equal space between them to occupy the entire screen. This strategy eliminates overlaps,

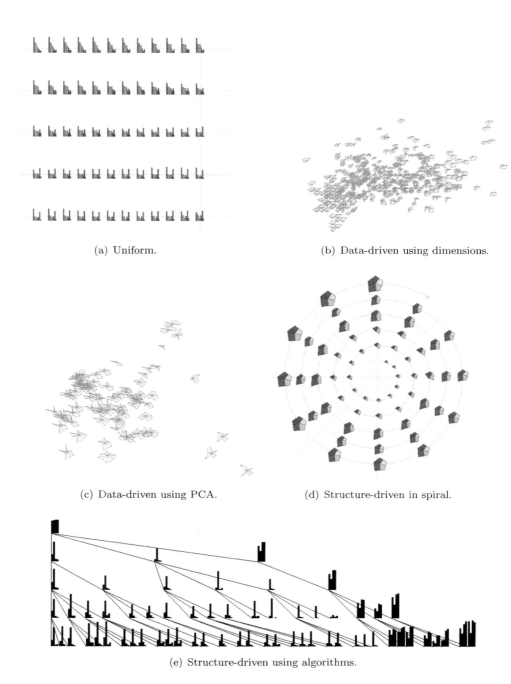

(a) Uniform.

(b) Data-driven using dimensions.

(c) Data-driven using PCA.

(d) Structure-driven in spiral.

(e) Structure-driven using algorithms.

Figure 8.21.   Examples of glyph positioning strategies (from [445]).

while making efficient use of the screen space. Different orderings of records can expose different data features in the same way that different dimension orderings can (Figure 8.21(a)).

2. *data-driven*—data values are used to control the positioning of the glyphs. Two approaches are possible. In the first, two data dimensions (or three for 3D display) are chosen to set the locations (Figure 8.21(b)), while in the second, positions are derived from the data values using algorithms such as PCA (Figure 8.21(c)) or MDS. In either case, we can apply one or more additional passes over the data to reduce overlaps by separating glyphs that are too close.

3. *structure-driven*—if the data has an implicit or explicit structure to it, such as cyclic or hierarchical, this can be used to control the positioning. For example, glyphs may be laid out in a spiral or a grid to emphasize cyclic patterns (Figure 8.21(d)); likewise, any of the multitudes of tree-drawing algorithms (see Chapter 9) can be used to position glyphs to help convey hierarchical relations (Figure 8.21(e)).

8.4.2 Dense Pixel Displays

Dense pixel displays (also known as *pixel-oriented techniques*) are a hybrid between point-based and region-based methods. Pioneered by Keim and his colleagues [221, 233], these techniques map each value to individual pixels and create a filled polygon to represent each data dimension. The displays make maximal use of the screen space, allowing data sets with millions of values to be shown on a single screen. Each data value will control the color for a single pixel; changing the color map used can potentially reveal new features of the data, as we'll see in Chapter 11. Given a data set and a color map, the issues that remain to be resolved are the layout of the data records and their ordering.

In its simplest form, each dimension of a data set will generate a separate subimage within the display. Thus, we can treat each dimension as an independent list of numbers, each of which drives the color of the corresponding pixels. We then need to lay out the elements of this list in a manner that accentuates relationships between points that are close to each other in the list. For example, we might create a subimage where we alternate a left-to-right and right-to-left traversal, shifting down one row when we reach the edge of the subimage. Different shapes of subimages can potentially convey different features of the data. Another approach is to use a spiral layout,

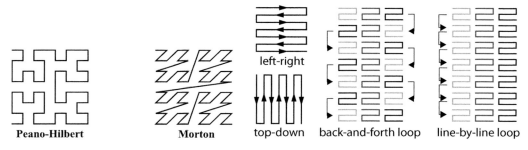

Peano-Hilbert   **Morton**   top-down   back-and-forth loop   line-by-line loop

(a) Examples of screen-filling layouts.   (b) Examples of recursive pattern layouts.

Figure 8.22.   Examples of pixel layout patterns in dense pixel displays. (Right images from [223], © 1995 IEEE.)

where the first data point is centered in the subimage and successive points are laid out in concentric squares. Yet another method is to use one of the many space-filling recursive curves as a layout strategy [223], such as a Peano-Hilbert curve (see Figure 8.22(a)). These curves have the feature that points that are close to each other in the ordered list are near to each other on the screen. Other pixel arrangements are the recursive z-pattern (see Figure 8.22(a)) or the recursive generalization of a line-by-line arrangement, called the *recursive pattern* techniques (see Figure 8.22(b)). A result of the recursive pattern technique arranging the subimages for the different features in a rectangular grid is shown in Figure 8.23(a).

A major issue with pixel-oriented displays is the data ordering. For some data, such as time series, the order is predetermined and fixed. In other cases, however, reordering the records can expose many interesting patterns. For example, if the records are ordered based on one of the dimensions, clusters of values within that dimension will be revealed, as will other dimensions having similar clusters. Another approach is to order the records based on their N-dimensional distance from a selected point. This can expose clusters involving many dimensions at once, rather than one at a time, and by coloring the pixels based on their distance from the selected point, the user gets some insights into the number of clusters in the data, as well as the gaps between them. Figure 8.25 shows the same data with different orderings.

Subimages corresponding to the data for each dimension can be positioned on the screen in a number of ways. The simplest is to create a grid of subimages, which maximizes screen utilization (see Figure 8.23(a)). Differ-

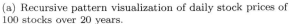

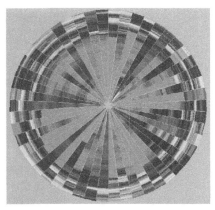

(a) Recursive pattern visualization of daily stock prices of 100 stocks over 20 years.

(b) Circle segments visualization of daily stock prices of 50 stocks over 20 years.

Figure 8.23. Examples of circle segments and recursive pattern visualizations. (Left image from [223], © 1995 IEEE; right image from [18], © 1996 IEEE.)

ent organizations of the grid can be created by changing the dimension order, which can help reveal correlations between dimensions. Another variant is *circle segments* [18], where instead of laying out the pixels in a rectangular subimage, they are instead placed in a circular wedge, starting with the center of the circle and weaving back and forth and outward from the center. Each dimension occupies one N^{th} of a circle, where N is the number of dimensions. Again, reordering the dimensions can help expose similar data characteristics. Figure 8.23(b) presents an example of circle segments. Other approaches to positioning subimages allow overlaps. For example, the *Value and Relation* techniques of Yang et al. [482, 485] use multidimensional scaling to place similar dimensions together on the screen, which can help reveal clusters of dimensions and outliers (Figure 8.24).

The dense pixels may also be positioned on top of a standard bar chart. To make effective use of the screen space, pixel bar charts [225, 226] usually use the bar width instead of the bar height to represent the aggregated data parameter mapped to the bar. In addition, the bars are colored pixel by pixel to show the detailed information about individual values of the data aggregated in the bars. Additional parameters are mapped to the sorting in x- and y-directions which poses an interesting optimization problem, requiring heuristic algorithms to create useful solutions. Figure 8.26 shows multiple pixel bar charts that use the same pixel arrangement (partitioning by month, sorting within bars in the y-direction according to purchase amount and in the x-direction according to the number of visits) within

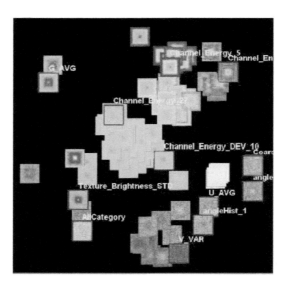

Figure 8.24.   A value-and-relation display using pixel-oriented visualizations with the dimensions positioned based on MDS [482, 485]. (Image © 2007 IEEE.)

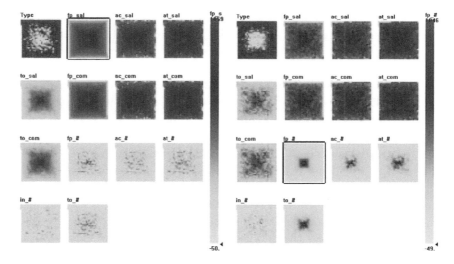

Figure 8.25.   Examples of different orderings of records. In the left image, data is ordered according to full professor salaries. The degree of correlation in other fields seems to drop off with the difference between ranks. In the right image, the data is ordered based on the number of full professors. While there is good correlation with the total number of faculty, there is some disagreement with other ranks.

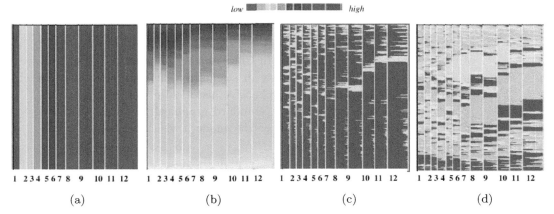

Figure 8.26.   An example pixel bar chart showing 150,000 e-customer purchasing activities (by month): (a) color represents month; (b) color represents purchase amount; (c) color represents number of visits; (d) color represents quantity purchased. (Image from [226], © 1996 Palgrave Macmillan.)

the bars, but that color the corresponding pixel according to different attributes of the web purchase transactions. The visualization allows the user to observe interesting facts about the transactions such as:

- December has the largest number of customers, while February, March, and May have the lowest number.

- The months February to May have the most top purchase amounts.

- The purchase amount in December is mostly in the medium price range.

- In March to June, customers come back more often than in other months. December customers are mostly one-time customers.

- Customers with high purchase amounts tend to come back more frequently and buy more items.

Dense pixel algorithms can also be applied to maps, resulting in PixelMaps [228]. See Chapter 6 for details.

Note that most aspects in the generation of dense pixel displays, including arrangement of pixels, shape of the subimages, and the ordering of the dimensions, require solving complex optimization problems, some of which have been shown to be NP-hard [19]. A more detailed description of the formalization of these optimization problems can be found in [233].

8.5   Related Readings

There are several available sources for general introductions to the subject of multivariate data visualization. In Cleveland's 1985 book, *The Elements of Graphing Data* [80], an overview of standard visualization methods is presented. Tufte provides a comprehensive historical review of graphic approaches [424]. In addition to the standard graphical methods, there are other sources that present many of the modern visualization techniques (e.g., [170]).

8.6   Exercises

1. For each of the following plot types, describe at least one situation where you would choose this plot over the others.

   (a) Line plot

   (b) Area plot (area under line is filled)

   (c) Bar graph

2. Rank the techniques presented in this chapter in order of their ability to effectively display data sets with large numbers of records. Write a brief rationale for your choices.

3. Rank the techniques presented in this chapter in order of their ability to effectively display data sets with large numbers of dimensions/variables. Write a brief rationale for your choices.

4. Rank the techniques presented in this chapter in order of their ability to convey pairwise correlations between dimensions. Write a brief rationale for your choices.

5. Compare the asymptotic upper bounds for parallel coordinates, RadViz, and multidimensional scaling using the "big-O" notation.

6. Display the cars (1993) data set using dense pixel displays.

7. Display the cars (1993) data set using glyphs.

8. Display the cars (1983) data using RadViz.

9. Show how circle segments can be thought of as a transformation of parallel coordinates.

10. Prove that a line in n-dimensional data maps to a line or a point in a RadViz display. Thus lines are invariant in the RadViz transformation. Show that this also applies no matter what the initial positions of the dimensional anchors are (whether on the circumference or even in a grid).

8.7   Projects

1. Write a program to display a data set using a choice of three or more of the glyph types described in this chapter. Test it on a data set with a modest number of records (less than 300) and dimensions (less than 10). Which glyph do you think is most effective? Why?

2. Write a program that will draw multiple line plots (one for each variable of a data set). The program should have two options: juxtaposing the plots (e.g., by slicing the screen horizontally and drawing one plot per slice) and superimposing the plots (e.g., drawn on top of each other). Test it with three color schemes:

   (a) randomly selected hue, saturation, and value

   (b) evenly spaced hues, with full saturation and value

   (c) a perceptually designed color map, such as those described by Cindy Brewer (http://www.colorbrewer.org)

   Comment on the effectiveness of the various color schemes and the two different layouts.

3. Write a program to generate a heatmap from a table of values. Each cell should be a square or rectangle whose color is proportional to the value. Use a standard color ramp, such as grayscale or yellow to red. Make sure you normalize the values first to make best use of the full range of colors. Now write a function for reordering the columns of the table such that the sum of the absolute differences between adjacent columns is minimized (if you have a modest number of dimensions, you can test all possible orderings of columns to find the minimum; otherwise you should use a heuristic search strategy to find a local minimum). Note the patterns that emerge in the final view. What does it tell you about the relationships between dimensions/columns?

4. Extend the previous program to reorder the rows based on the same or similar distance measures and search strategies.

CHAPTER 9

Visualization Techniques for Trees, Graphs, and Networks

While most of the visualization techniques discussed thus far focus on the display of data values and their attributes, another important application of visualization is the conveying of relational information, e.g., how data items or records are related to each other. These interrelationships can take many forms:

- part/subpart, parent/child, or other hierarchical relation;

- connectedness, such as cities connected by roads or computers connected by networks;

- derived from, as in a sequence of steps or stages;

- shared classification;

- similarities in values;

- similarities in attributes (e.g., spatial, temporal).

Relationships can be simple or complex: unidirectional or bi-directional, nonweighted or weighted, certain or uncertain. Indeed, the relationships may provide more and richer information than that contained in the data records. Applications for visualizing relational information are equally diverse, from categorizing biological species, to exploring document archives, to studying a terrorist network.

Typical questions we ask in graphs involve nodes and edges:

- Is there a path from node a to node b?

- What is the shortest path from node a to node b?

- How many paths are there from node a to node b?

- What node is accessible from node a?

- What nodes are connected to both node a and node b?

- How many edges are coming into node a?

- Are these two graphs identical (isomorphic)?

- Is this subgraph of graph A in graph B?

- Is there a cycle in graph A (a non-empty path from a node to itself)?

- Is there a path from node a to node b that goes through exactly one other node (or at least one other node)?

- What are all the nodes with a specific value or range of values?

Note that for graphs that cannot fit into memory, answering some of these questions is very difficult.

In this chapter we will examine a number of techniques that have been developed for visualizing relational information. This presentation, however, will just be the tip of the iceberg, as tree and graph visualization is a well-established field, with its own books, journals, conferences, software packages, and algorithms.

9.1   Displaying Hierarchical Structures

Trees or *hierarchies* (we'll use the terms interchangeably) are one of the most common structures to hold relational information. For this reason, many visualization techniques have been developed for display of such information. We can divide these techniques into two classes of algorithms: *space-filling* and *non–space-filling*. The rest of this section will provide details on implementing algorithms for visualizing this type of data.

9.1.1   Space-Filling Methods

As the name implies, space-filling techniques make maximal use of the display space. This is accomplished by using juxtapositioning to imply relations, as opposed to, for example, conveying relations with edges joining data objects. The two most common approaches to generating space-filling hierarchies are rectangular and radial layouts.

Treemaps [206] and their many variants are an alternative representation of a Venn diagram and are the most popular form of the rectangular space-filling layout. In the basic treemap, a rectangle is recursively divided into slices, alternating horizontal and vertical slicing, based on the populations of the subtrees at a given level. Pseudocode for this process is given in Figure 9.1, and an example is shown in Figure 9.2.

As mentioned, many variants on treemaps have been proposed and developed since they were introduced, including *squarified treemaps* [51] (to reduce the occurrence of long, thin rectangles) and *nested treemaps* [206] (to emphasize the hierarchical structure).

The methods described above are structured using horizontal and vertical divisions to convey the hierarchy. A number of other approaches are possible, however, such as those that divide space radially. *Radial space-filling hierarchy visualizations*, sometimes referred to as *sunburst displays* [393], have the root of the hierarchy in the center of the display and use nested rings to convey the layers of the hierarchy. Each ring is divided based on the number of nodes at that level. These techniques follow a similar strategy to treemaps, in that the number of terminal nodes in a subtree determines the amount of screen space that will be allocated for it. However, unlike treemaps, which assign most screen space to conveying the terminal nodes, radial techniques also show the intermediate nodes. The process is described in pseudocode in Figure 9.3, and an example is shown in Figure 9.4.

For these and other space-filling techniques, color can be used to convey many attributes, such as a value associated with the node (e.g., classification) or it may reinforce the hierarchical relationships, e.g., siblings and parents may have similarities in color, as seen in Figure 9.4. Symbols and other markings may also be embedded in the rectangular or circular segments to communicate other data features.

9.1.2 Non–Space-Filling Methods

The most common representation used to visualize tree or hierarchical relationships is a *node-link diagram*. Organizational charts, family trees, and tournament pairings are just some of the common applications for such diagrams. The drawing of such trees is influenced the most by two factors: the fan-out degree (e.g., the number of siblings a parent node can have) and the depth (e.g., the furthest node from the root). Trees that are significantly constrained in one or both of these aspects, such as a binary tree or a tree with only three or four levels, tend to be much easier to draw than those with fewer constraints.

```
Start: Main Program
  Width = width of rectangle
  Height = height of rectangle
  Node = root node of the tree
  Origin = position of rectangle, e.g., [0,0]
  Orientation = direction of cuts, alternating between horizontal and vertical
  Treemap(Node, Orientation, Origin, Width, Height)
End: Main Program

Treemap(node n, orientation o, position orig, hsize w, vsize h)
  if n is a terminal node (i.e., it has no children)
     draw_rectangle(orig, w, h)
     return
  for each child of n (child_i), get number of terminal nodes in subtree
  sum up number of terminal nodes
  compute percentage of terminal nodes in n from each subtree (percent_i)
  if orientation is horizontal
     for each subtree
        compute offset of origin based on origin and width (offset_i)
        treemap(child_i, vertical, orig + offset_i, w * percent_i, h)
  else
     for each subtree
        compute offset of origin based on origin and height (offset_i)
        treemap(child_i, horizontal, orig + offset_i, w, h * percent_i)
End: Treemap
```

Figure 9.1.   Pseudocode for drawing a hierarchy using a treemap.

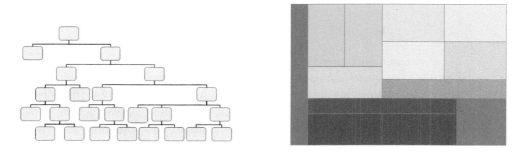

Figure 9.2.   A sample hierarchy and the corresponding treemap display.

```
Start: Main Program
   Start = start angle for a node (initially 0)
   End = end angle for a node (initially 360)
   Origin = position of center of sunburst, e.g., [0,0]
   Level = current level of hierarchy (initially 0)
   Width = thickness of each radial band - based on max depth and display size
   Sunburst(Node, Start, End, Level)
End: Main Program

Sunburst(node n, angle st, angle en, level l)
   if n is a terminal node (i.e., it has no children)
      draw_radial_section(Origin, st, en, l * Width, (l+1) * Width)
      return
   for each child of n (child_i), get number of terminal nodes in subtree
   sum up number of terminal nodes
   compute percentage of terminal nodes in n from each subtree (percent_i)
   for each subtree
      compute start/end angle based on size of subtrees, order, and angle range
      Sunburst(child_i, st_i, en_i, l+1)

End: Sunburst
```

Figure 9.3.   Pseudocode for drawing a hierarchy using a sunburst display.

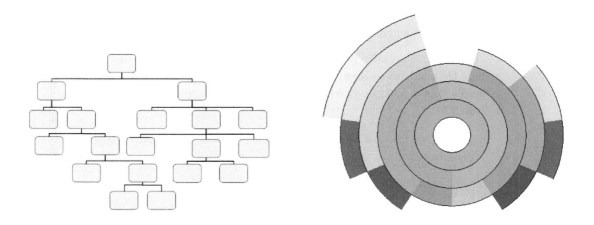

Figure 9.4.   A sample hierarchy and the corresponding sunburst display.

When designing an algorithm for drawing any node-link diagram (not just trees), one must consider three categories of often-contradictory guidelines: drawing conventions, constraints, and aesthetics. Conventions may include restricting edges to be either a single straight line, a series of rectilinear lines, polygonal lines, or curves. Other conventions might be to place nodes on a fixed grid, or to have all sibling nodes share the same vertical position. Constraints may include requiring a particular node to be at the center of the display, or that a group of nodes be located close to each other, or that certain links must either go from top to bottom or left to right. Each of the above guidelines can be used to drive the algorithm design.

Aesthetics, however, often have significant impact on the interpretability of a tree or graph drawing, yet often result in conflicting guidelines. Some typical aesthetic rules include:

- minimize line crossings,

- maintain a pleasing aspect ratio,

- minimize the total area of the drawing,

- minimize the total length of the edges,

- minimize the number of bends in the edges,

- minimize the number of distinct angles or curvatures used,

- strive for a symmetric structure.

For trees, especially balanced ones, it is relatively easy to design algorithms that adhere to many, if not most, of these guidelines. For example, a simple tree drawing procedure is given below (sample output is shown in Figure 9.5):

1. Slice the drawing area into equal-height slabs, based on the depth of the tree.

2. For each level of the tree, determine how many nodes need to be drawn.

3. Divide each slice into equal-sized rectangles based on the number of nodes at that level.

4. Draw each node in the center of its corresponding rectangle.

5. Draw a link between the center-bottom of each node to the center-top of its child node(s).

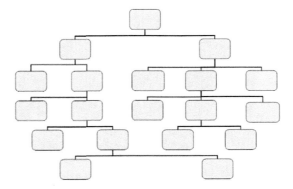

Figure 9.5.   An example of visualizing hierarchies with a simple node-link diagram, using equal spacing per level.

Many enhancements can be made to this rather basic algorithm in order to improve space utilization and move child nodes closer to their parents. Some of these include:

- Rather than using even spacing and centering, divide each level based on the number of terminal nodes belonging to each subtree.

- Spread terminal nodes evenly across the drawing area and center parent nodes above them.

- Add some buffer space between adjacent nonsibling nodes to emphasize relationships.

- If possible, reorder the subtrees of a node to achieve more symmetry and balance.

- Position the root node in the center of the display and lay out child nodes radially, rather than vertically.

For large trees, a popular approach is to use the third dimension, supplemented with tools for rotation, translation, and zooming. Perhaps the most well-known of such techniques is called a *cone tree* [341]. In this layout, the children of a node are arranged radially at evenly spaced angles and then offset perpendicular to the plane. The two parameters critical to this process are the radius and offset distance; varying these influences the density of the display and the level of occlusion. Minimally, they should be set so that separate branches of the tree do not fall into the same section of 3D space. One method to ensure this is to have the radius inversely proportional to

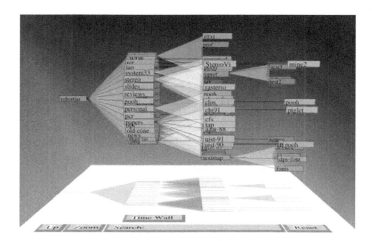

Figure 9.6.   An example of a hierarchy displayed with a cone tree [341]. (Image © 1991 Association of Computing Machinery. Reprinted by permission, courtesy of PARC, Inc.)

the depth of a node in the tree. In this manner, nodes close to the root are significantly separated, and those near the bottom of the tree are closer together. An example is shown in Figure 9.6.

9.2 Displaying Arbitrary Graphs/Networks

Trees are just one type of a more general representation of relations called a *graph*. Technically speaking, a tree is a connected, unweighted, acyclic graph. Clearly, there are many other possibilities, including graphs with weighted edges, undirected graphs, graphs with cycles, disconnected graphs, and so on. Rather than give more algorithms specific to other classes of graphs, which could certainly fill more than a textbook, we will describe some general approaches for visualizing graphs in which the class or structure is not known, which we term an *arbitrary* graph. For our purposes, we will assume that the graph is undirected, though some of the techniques presented are easily extended to directed graphs. We will look at two distinct graph drawing approaches: *node-link diagrams* (building on the material from the previous section) and *matrix displays*. Readers interested in a broader or deeper exposure to graph drawing are directed to the vast amount of literature on this topic, some of which is listed at the end of the chapter.

Some graphs are quite complex [85, 239]. For example, real-world graphs, or networks as they are most often called, have characteristics not often found in simple networks or in random ones. Real-world networks have many disconnected groups of varying sizes, they obey a power law in node degrees, and their diameters are limited compared to similar random graphs with the same number of nodes and edges. [7, 311]. Strogatz [401] describes different ways for graphs to exhibit complexity. These include structural complexity (tangled edges), network evolution (time-evolving network), connection diversity (weight/direction), dynamical complexity (time-varying node states) and node diversity (different node types).

9.2.1 Node-Link Graphs

Force-directed graph drawing methods use a spring analogy to represent the links, with node positions iteratively refined until the overall energy or stress of the system is minimized (see Figure 9.7). For each pair of connected nodes, there are two forces: f_{ij}, the force caused by the spring between them, and g_{ij}, an electrical repulsion force to keep nodes from getting too close. A simple model is to use Hooke's law to represent the spring force and an inverse square law to represent the repulsion force. If $d(i, j)$ is the Euclidean distance between nodes i and j, $s_{i,j}$ is the natural spring length (at rest), and k_{ij} is the spring tension, the x-component of the spring force between two nodes can be computed as

$$f_{ij}(x) = k_{ij} * (d(i, j) - s_{ij}) * (x_i - x_j)/d(i, j).$$

If r_{ij} is the strength of the repulsion between nodes i and j, the x-component of the repulsion force can be computed as

$$g_{ij}(x) = (r_{ij}/d(i, j)^2) * (x_i - x_j)/d(i, j).$$

Thus, one step of the position refinement process would calculate the sum of all the forces on each node (x-, y-, and z-components, as appropriate) and move its position proportional to that force. Clearly, once points have moved, all the forces need to be recalculated and another shift of positions made. To avoid oscillation, it is common to start with movements that are a significant percentage of the force and then use smaller and smaller step sizes to converge on the point where the forces are minimized. Initial positions can be assigned randomly. As it is quite possible to end up in a local, rather than a global, energy minimum, it is common to run the layout algorithm

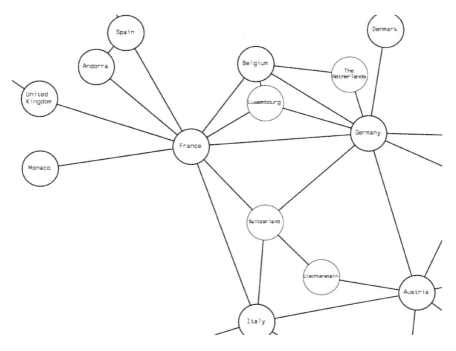

Figure 9.7.   An example of a force-directed graph. The graph, showing relationships between
                   countries of Europe, was generated with aiSee: http://www.aisee.com.

multiple times with different initial configurations to find the best of several
computed configurations. The goodness of the layout can be computed based
on the sum of the magnitude of forces on a given configuration.

Planar graph drawing techniques start with the assumption that the
underlying graph is *planar*, e.g., it has no edge crossings. These algorithms
have gotten a lot of attention, for several reasons. First, as the theory
of planar graphs has a long history, there are many concepts that can be
exploited from the literature. Second, as edge-crossings tend to make graphs
difficult to read, it is a good strategy to minimize or eliminate such crossings.
Finally, planar graphs tend to be sparse; Euler's formula indicates that a
planar graph with n vertices has at most $3n - 6$ edges. Concentrating on
planar graphs is not overly restrictive, as one can eliminate crossings by
inserting dummy nodes at the crossings, perform the layout using a planar
graph algorithm, and then remove the dummy nodes.

We will, in addition, assume that the graph is *connected*, e.g., there is a
path from every node to every other node. Graphs that are not connected can

be separated into subgraphs that can be drawn separately. A subgraph that is maximally connected (all nodes are connected) is a *connected component* of the graph. Other useful definitions include:

- A *face* is a partition of the plane isolated by a set of connected vertices.

- A *neighbor set* is a counter-clockwise listing of the vertices incident to a particular vertex.

- A *planar embedding* is a class of planar graph drawings with the same neighbor sets for each vertex. A planar graph can have an exponential number of such embeddings.

- A *cutvertex* is any node that causes the graph to be disconnected if it is removed.

- A *biconnected graph* is one without a cutvertex.

- A *block* is a maximally biconnected subgraph of a graph.

- A *separating pair* means two vertices whose removal causes a biconnected graph to become disconnected.

- A *triconnected graph* is one without a separating pair. A planar triconnected graph has a unique embedding.

We first need a strategy for determining if a graph is planar. Several such algorithms exist, though efficient ones have a very high degree of complexity and simple ones tend to be computationally expensive. We can start by simplifying the problem a bit. We do this by noting that a graph is planar only if all of its connected components are also planar. Similarly, we can state that a connected graph is planar only if all its biconnected components are planar. Thus, we just need an algorithm that determines if a biconnected graph is planar or not.

The general reasoning of the algorithm is as follows. We will perform a divide-and-conquer approach by noting that if our graph contains a cycle such that no other cycle is present that doesn't contain an edge of the original cycle (e.g., there aren't cycles left when the edges involved in the original cycle are removed), what remain are paths that start and stop on one of the vertices of the cycle (called *attachments*). These *pieces* of the graph can be drawn either within the cycle or outside the cycle. Two such pieces *interlace* if they both start and end on nodes of the cycle, and the two ends of one piece are separated by one end of the other piece. To be drawn in a planar fashion, one of these interlaced pieces would need to be drawn inside the cycle, and the other on the outside. If we now create a graph of all the pieces, with an edge between two pieces if they interlace, as long as this graph is *bipartite* (separable into two sets of vertices such that no edge exists between members of the same set), the original graph is planar. Figure 9.8 shows examples of these components. Note that there are a couple of instances of interlacing among the parts.

If the graph contains more cycles after removing the edges of the original cycle, this means that one or more of the pieces contains a cycle (see the purple piece in Figure 9.8). In this case, we create a subgraph containing this piece and a section of the original cycle connecting the end points of the part, and recursively call the planarity test algorithm. The pseudocode for this algorithm is as follows [27]. Note that a *separating cycle* is one that generates at least two pieces.

Given a biconnected graph G and a separating cycle C:

1. Compute all the pieces of G with respect to C.

2. For each piece P that is not a simple path (e.g., that contains a cycle).

    (a) Create graph G′ consisting of P plus C.

    (b) Create cycle C′ consisting of a path through P plus the section of C joining the ends.

    (c) Apply the algorithm to (G′, C′). If the result is nonplanar, G is nonplanar.

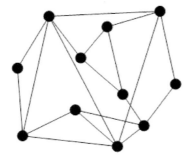

Figure 9.8.   An example of a biconnected graph, a cycle (in black), and the five pieces (in different colors).

3. Compute the interlacement graph I of the pieces of G.

4. If I is not bipartite, G is nonplanar; else G is planar.

If a graph is nonplanar, we can make it planar using the following strategy:

1. Determine the largest planar subgraph of the graph.

2. For the remaining vertices, place each within a face that minimizes the number of edge crossings.

3. For each edge crossing, break the edges into two parts each, and connect the broken ends to a new dummy vertex.

Once a graph has been either determined to be planar or has been augmented to achieve planarity, there are many possible strategies for generating a drawing. One such technique, called the *visibility approach* [27], consists of a two-step process. In the first step, called the visibility step, a *visibility representation* of the graph is formed. In such a representation, each vertex is depicted as a horizontal line segment, and each edge is depicted as a vertical line connecting the corresponding vertex segments. It should be clear that for a planar graph, it is always possible to draw such a representation without crossing edges other than where they meet the vertex segments. Obviously, many possible orderings of the vertex segments are possible; one strategy would be to arrange them to minimize the total length of the vertical connectors.

In the second step, called the replacement step, each vertex segment is collapsed to a single point, and each vertical connector is replaced by a polyline that follows the original edge as much as possible, with a segment at each end connecting the edge to its corresponding vertex. Many options exist for the replacement step, including the location of the nodes and the strategy used to form the connections (e.g., straight versus curved lines, single segment versus multiple segments). An example of the process is shown in Figure 9.9.

Renoust [332] describes an analysis of multiplex networks. He defines a measure of the intertwining of edges (entanglement index) which leads to other measures (e.g., intensity and homogeneity) and finally leads to catalyst interaction network understanding.

Networks are quite varied. Complex networks have been studied for a long time, and their characterization and definition is still the subject of publications [85, 239]. We can, however, admit that a complex network is

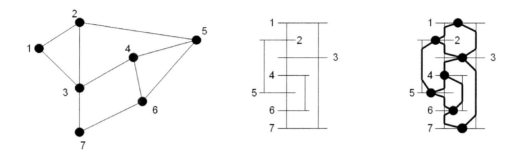

Figure 9.9.   The stages of drawing a planar graph. From left to right: original graph, visibility representation, and replacement step.

a network which presents characteristics we cannot find in simple networks nor in random networks, but that we very often find in real-world networks [452]. More empirically, the literature has uncovered [7] and still uncovers [311] complex network features in many "if not all" real-world networks. Of such characteristics the most famous are [7] a small world appearance—the diameter of the network is rather limited in comparison with one of a random graph with the same number of nodes and edges; a scale-free degree distribution—some observe a long tail in distribution of nodes degree, often referenced as power law; or a high clustering coefficient—the coefficient is much higher for real-world networks than for random networks. A complex network presents at least some of these features—which are not limited to the ones depicted previously [78]. In a real-world graph, we can also observe many disconnected components with a lot of variation in their size (probably induced by some inner scale-free feature as described above). One or more largest components may present most of the features of complex networks. Strogatz in his work [401], defines six different ways for networks to display complexity:

- structural complexity (edges are tangled),

- network evolution (the network evolves over time),

- connection diversity (weights/directions/signs of edges),

- dynamical complexity (node states can vary with time),

- node diversity (different types of nodes),

- meta-complication.

	a	b	c	d	e	f	g	h
a		•	•			•		
b	•			•		•		
c	•				•		•	•
d	•	•				•		
e			•				•	•
f	•	•		•				
g			•		•			•
h			•		•		•	

	p	q	r	s	t	u	v	w
p		•	•	•				
q	•		•	•				
r	•	•		•				
s	•	•	•		•			
t				•		•	•	•
u					•		•	•
v					•	•		•
w					•	•	•	

Figure 9.10.   Two matrix displays of the same graph, using different orderings of nodes. Structure is more clearly present in the matrix on the right.

9.2.2   Matrix Representations for Graphs

An alternate visual representation of a graph is via an *adjacency matrix*, which is an N by N grid (where N is the number of nodes), where position (i, j) represents the existence (or not) of a link between nodes i and j. This may be a binary matrix, or the value might represent the strength or weight of the link between the two nodes. This method overcomes one of the biggest problems with node-link diagrams, namely that of crossing edges, though it doesn't scale well to graphs with large numbers (thousands) of nodes. Bertin [34] was one of the first researchers to investigate the power of this representation, using different reordering strategies to organize the rows and columns to reveal structures within the graph. The importance of the reordering is apparent in Figure 9.10, where each matrix represents the same eight-node graph. The two four-node cliques are clearly apparent in the second display.

There have been numerous algorithms proposed for reordering the rows and columns of the matrix to expose the most structure. Some are primarily user-driven, which would support ordering based on the values in one of the rows or columns as a starting point. Others are purely automatic, which rely on some metric for evaluating a particular ordering and a strategy for generating orders to test. As in any optimization process, there is a good chance that finding the optimal ordering is NP-complete (namely, that no algorithm of polynomial or less complexity can be found). Thus, a number of heuristics have been proposed over the years that generally result in good orderings, especially for certain classes of graphs.

As an example, we can use a simplistic order evaluation strategy, namely to count the number of occurrences of matching elements in adjacent rows or columns. This tends to group nodes that link or don't link to a common node. In Figure 9.10, the left-most matrix has a score of 9 when counting only vertical neighbors, while the right-most matrix has a score of 20. By enumerating all possible orders, we can find the orderings that give the highest match score. For modest numbers of nodes, this would be an acceptable strategy, but since the number of possible orderings is on the order of N!, this approach does not scale well. Ordering of nodes is similar to the traveling salesman problem (TSP), where one tries to find a path that passes through a collection of cities without visiting any city more than once, while at the same time minimizing the total distance traveled. As this is basically the same problem as finding the ordering of the rows or columns of a matrix to minimize some metric, heuristic solutions that have been used for the TSP can also be employed here.

9.3   Other Issues

Once a basic visualization of a tree or graph has been developed, there are a number of additional considerations, primarily addressing the issue of interpretability. Two such important considerations will be elaborated upon in this section: labeling and interaction.

9.3.1   Labeling

Proper labeling of a visualization is crucial to allow a viewer to understand what is being shown. A map would be of little value without some form of labeling; similarly, a color-coded plot would be difficult to understand without some indication of the meaning associated with the colors. In tree and graph drawing, the problem of labeling is compounded, not only because of the potential for many nodes, but also because labels might also be needed for the links between nodes.

If there are only a small number of distinct labels, such as showing the type of link or a class associated with a node, it is best to use nontextual labels, such as the color, size, or shape of a node or the color, thickness, or line style of a link. This does not require much screen space and can usually be interpreted unambiguously even in the presence of modest amount of line crossing and node occlusion. However, if the number of distinct labels exceeds five or six, the likelihood of misinterpretation can become large. A key for interpreting the graphical attribute mapping is essential.

For small graphs, a common strategy for node labeling is to put the labels within the nodes, using rectangular or oval node shapes to accommodate the text. To avoid distorting the perception of the nodes, the size of the nodes should be dictated by the length of the longest label. For situations where the labels can be very long, one option is to use abbreviations or numeric labels, along with a key for interpretation. Viewers will eventually learn the correspondences between the shortened labels and their actual meaning. A similar strategy can be used for edge labeling, placing the labels near the center of the edge. For edges that are predominantly vertical, these should be to the left or right of the edge, while for predominantly horizontal edges, they should be above or below. Using a consistent strategy will reduce the potential for erroneously associating a label with the wrong edge.

At the other extreme, if there are a large number of distinct labels that need to be shown, or the labels themselves are quite long, it becomes readily apparent that simultaneous display of all labels will be ineffective. Several strategies have been developed to cope with this problem. A common solution is to only show labels in a small region of the graph, for example, within a certain radius of the cursor position. If the density of the display is too high, a distortion of the visualization may be required (see the next subsection) to provide more screen space for that section of the graph. An alternate to distortion that sometimes works is to rotate the graph to reduce the overlap between labels (see Figure 9.11). Another interesting solution proposed in [48] is to only show a random subset of the labels for a short period of time, and then switch to showing the labels for a different subset.

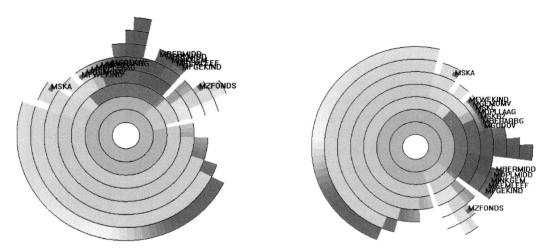

Figure 9.11.   Improving the readability of labels via rotation. (Image from [481], © 2003 Palgrave Macmillan.)

The idea behind this approach is that the viewer's short-term memory will enable recall of a larger number of labels as compared to a static display, especially if this memory is refreshed on a regular basis.

9.3.2   Interactions

Even though Chapters 11 and 12 of this text are dedicated to interactions within visualization environments, there are a few interaction techniques that are most relevant to tree and graph visualization, which will be described in this chapter. Some types of interaction, such as panning and zooming, are common to all types of visualization, and thus will only be briefly mentioned here for completeness. Others, such as focus+context, while applicable to a wide range of visualizations, have been primarily developed in the area of tree and graph visualization and will thus be described in more detail here.

Interactions with the virtual camera. Interactions such as panning, zooming, and rotation can be viewed as simple changes to the virtual camera being used to capture a segment of a scene. These allow the viewer to incrementally build up a mental model of the objects of the scene and their interrelationships. Operations of this type are often manually controlled, though automated techniques such as data-driven fly-throughs and spinning of 3D objects can be automatically derived and presented.

Interactions with the graph elements. Most interactions of this type start with a *selection* operation, where one or more of the components of the graph are isolated for some action, such as highlighting, deleting, masking, moving, or obtaining details. For example, to declutter a graph one might select some nodes and drag them to a less-occupied section of the screen, while maintaining their links. Similarly, one might select and move or change the shape of a link to eliminate a crossing or improve the aesthetics of a graph. Selection may involve a single object, all objects within a specified region or distance, or a set of objects that satisfy a user-specified set of constraints (e.g., all nodes directly connected to a given node). One of the biggest problems with selecting elements in a graph occurs in dense regions of the drawing, where elements are so close together that unambiguous selection is difficult or impossible. This exposes the need for other types of interaction, such as zooming or the distortion techniques described later.

Interactions with the graph structure. There are two classes of interactions that are directed at the graph structure. The first class results in changes to the structure itself. For example, reordering the branches of a tree may expose relationships that were not apparent in the original ordering. Redrawing a graph with different weights on the constraints can generate graphs that make certain tasks easier to perform. Reordering the columns or rows in a matrix visualization can expose new features or relations within the data. Techniques within this class are often very specific to the type of graph being shown.

A second class of interactions associated with the graph structure comprises the so-called *focus+context* techniques, where a selected subset of the structure (focus) is presented in detail, while the rest of the structure is shown in low detail to help the viewer maintain context. These techniques are related to panning and zooming, without the loss of context. The most popular of these distortion techniques are the many variants on a fisheye lens, where the parts of the visualization falling within a focal region are enlarged using a nonlinear scaling, while the parts outside the focal region are proportionally shrunk to maintain their presence in the display. This distortion can be performed either in *screen space* (i.e., based on pixels) or in *structure space* (i.e., based on the components of the graph). It is the latter case that is more interesting in graph visualization, as we might, for example, enlarge one branch of a tree while reducing the size of other branches, or enlarge all links within three connections of a particular node in order to view its neighborhood in more detail. An example of structure space distortion can be seen in Figure 9.12, where the blue subtree of Figure 9.11 has been angularly enlarged to enable easier exploration and interactive selection.

A technique that can be considered related to both of these classes is that of selective hiding or removal of sections of the graph. For example, once a branch of a tree has been thoroughly investigated, the user might want to remove it from the display to provide more space for the unexplored regions. In a sense, this can be seen as changing the structure (deleting a component), or as reducing the level of detail for the branch to its root. The terms *roll-up* and *drill-down* are often used to describe the process of hiding and exposing details in a visualization. Figure 9.12 shows several subtrees that have been rolled up, with the double white band informing the user that details exist under those nodes.

9.4 Related Readings

Robertson et al. [341] and Brian Johnson and Ben Shneiderman [206] introduce the concepts of cone trees and treemaps, respectively. John Stasko and Eugene Zhang [393] describe one of several variants on radial space-filling

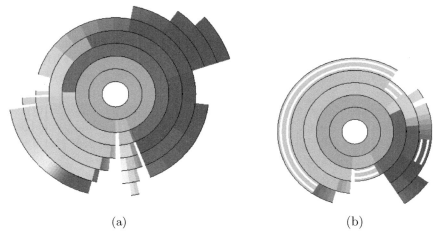

(a)   (b)

Figure 9.12.   Some interaction operations on sunburst displays: (a) the blue subtree has been expanded, while the rest of the tree has been compressed; (b) several subtrees have been rolled up to simplify the display. (Image from [481], © 2003 Palgrave Macmillan.)

techniques for tree visualization. The book, *Graph Drawing: Algorithms for the Visualization of Graphs* [27] is an excellent introduction to the field of graph drawing. *The Semiology of Graphs* [34] by J. Bertin is the seminal work on reorderable matrix representations for graphs. Herman et al. [186] present a survey of graph visualization and interactions with graphs. The paper by Leung and Apperley [268] contains a comprehensive survey of distortion techniques, many of which are applicable to tree and graph visualizations. Renoust [332] deals with multiple graphs. The VAST Challenges provide synthetic data sets that can be used as case studies.

9.5 Exercises

1. Give some examples of how rules for graph drawing can conflict with each other.

2. Compare rectilinear and radial space-filling tree visualization techniques. Under what conditions, or for what tasks, is one better or worse than the other?

3. Compare node-link and matrix graph visualization techniques. Under what conditions, or for what tasks, is one better or worse than the other?

4. What is the smallest node-link graph (e.g., smallest number of nodes and links) that you can devise that is nonplanar?

9.6   Projects

1. Write a program that reads in a graph in the following format:

```
number_of_vertices number_of_edges
edge1_start edge1_end
edge2_start edge2_end
....
edgeN_start edgeN_end
```

Add a very simple drawing function that places the vertices in random positions and connects the vertices based on the edge list. Run the program several times with a data set of your design (it should have more than 10 nodes and 20 edges). What conclusions can you draw from observing the output?

2. Modify the above program to place the vertices at equal angles around a circle. Again, run the program several times and describe your observations. From these observations, can you propose a vertex-ordering algorithm that will generally result in less cluttered displays?

3. Write a program that will determine if a graph entered in the above format is connected, e.g., if there is a path from every node to every other node.

4. Write a program that will determine if a graph entered in the above format is biconnected, e.g., if removal of a single node will not disconnect the graph.

5. Assuming that the input graph represents a tree, and that all links are given in the order of (parent, child), write a program that will draw the tree as in Figure 9.5, where all nodes on the same level are evenly spaced. (*Hint*: in a single pass through the list of links, you should be able to assign each node to a level.)

6. Modify the above program to generate a *radial* layout, e.g., the layers are arranged as concentric circles with a radius proportional to the tree depth.

7. Modify either or both of the above programs to insert extra space between adjacent nonsibling nodes.

8. Write a program that generates the adjacency matrix A using the same data as in Project 1 or some other graph data. Use R-project (or your own code) to compute A^2 and draw it differentiating the values in the matrix using color (note that it may have values larger than 1). Explain what you see and the meaning of the numbers.

9. Design a program that determines if node a is connected to node b in a graph that will not fit into memory.

CHAPTER 10

Text and Document Visualization

We now have huge resources of information; from libraries, to e-mail archives, to all facets of applications running on the World Wide Web. Visualization is a great aid in analyzing such data. We can visualize in many different ways things such as a blog, a wiki, a twitter feed, billions of words, a collection of papers, or a digital library. Since visualizations are task dependent, we can look at what tasks are necessary for dealing with text, documents, or web-based objects. For text and documents, the most obvious tasks are searching for a word, phrase, or topic. For partially structured data, we may search for relationships between words, phrases, topics, or documents. For structured text or document collections, the key task is most often searching for patterns and outliers within the text or documents.

In this chapter we focus on visualization tasks dealing with text, and the various approaches to the visual analysis of text.

10.1 Introduction

We define a collection of documents as a *corpus* (plural *corpora*). We deal with objects within corpora. These objects can be words, sentences, paragraphs, documents, or even collections of documents. We may even consider images and videos. Often these objects are considered atomic with respect to the task, analysis, and visualization. Text and documents are often minimally structured and may be rich with attributes and metadata, especially when focused in a specific application domain. For example, documents have a format and often include metadata about the document (i.e., author, date of creation, date of modification, comments, size). Information retrieval systems are used to query corpora, which requires computing the relevance of a document with respect to a query. This requires document preprocessing and interpretation of the semantics of text.

We can compute statistics about documents. For example, the number of words or paragraphs, or the word distribution or frequency, all can be used for author authenticity. Are there any paragraphs that repeat the same words or sentences? We can also identify relationships between paragraphs or documents within a corpus. For example, one could ask, "What documents relate to the spread of flu?" This is not a simple query; it isn't simply searching for the word *flu*. Why? We can further look for natural connections or relationships between various documents. What clusters are there? Do they represent themes within the corpus? Similarity could be defined in terms of citations, common authorships, topics, and so on.

10.2   Levels of Text Representations

We define three levels of text representation: *lexical, syntactic*, and *semantic*. Each requires us to convert the unstructured text to some form of structured data.

Lexical level. The lexical level is concerned with transforming a string of characters into a sequence of atomic entities, called *tokens*. Lexical analyzers process the sequence of characters with a given set of rules into a new sequence of tokens that can be used for further analysis. Tokens can include characters, character n-grams, words, word stems, lexemes, phrases, or word n-grams, all with associated attributes. Many types of rules can be used to extract tokens, the most common of which are finite state machines defined by regular expressions.

Syntactic level. The syntactical level deals with identifying and tagging (annotating) each token's function. We assign various tags, such as sentence position or whether a word is a noun, expletive, adjective, dangling modifier, or conjunction. Tokens can also have attributes such as whether they are singular or plural, or their proximity to other tokens. Richer tags include date, money, place, person, organization, and time (Figure 10.3). The process of extracting these annotations is called *named entity recognition* (NER). The richness and wide variety of language models and grammars (generative, categorical, dependency, probabilistic, and functionalist) yield a wide variety of approaches.

Semantic level. The semantic level encompasses the extraction of meaning and relationships between pieces of knowledge derived from the structures identified in the syntactical level. The goal of this level is to define an analytic interpretation of the full text within a specific context, or even independent of context.

10.3   The Vector Space Model

Computing term vectors is an essential step for many document and corpus visualization and analysis techniques. In the *vector space model* [356], a term vector for an object of interest (paragraph, document, or document collection) is a vector in which each dimension represents the weight of a given word in that document. Typically, to clean up noise, stop words (such as "the" or "a") are removed (filtering), and words that share a word stem are aggregated together (stemming) [192].

The pseudocode below counts occurrences of unique tokens, excluding stop words. The input is assumed to be a stream of tokens generated by a lexical analyzer for a single document. The *terms* variable contains a hashtable that maps unique terms to their counts in the document.

COUNT-TERMS(*tokenStream*)
1   *terms* ← ∅ ▷ initialize *terms* to an empty hashtable.
2   **for** each token *t* in *tokenStream*
3   **do if** *t* is not a stop word
4   **do** increment (or initialize to 1) *terms*[*t*]
5   return *terms*

We can apply the pseudocode to the following text.

There is a great deal of controversy about the safety of genetically engineered foods. Advocates of biotechnology often say that the risks are overblown. ''There have been 25,000 trials of genetically modified crops in the world, now, and not a single incident, or anything dangerous in these releases,'' said a spokesman for Adventa Holdings, a UK biotech firm. During the 2000 presidential campaign, then-candidate George W. Bush said that ''study after study has shown no evidence of danger.'' And Clinton Administration Agriculture Secretary Dan Glickman said that ''test after rigorous scientific test'' had proven the safety of genetically engineered products.

The paragraph contains 98 string tokens, 74 terms, and 48 terms when stop words are removed. Here is a sample of the term vector that would be generated by the pseudocode:

genetically	said	safety	engineered	study	test	great	deal	controversy	foods
3	3	2	2	2	2	1	1	1	1

10.3.1   Computing Weights

This vector space model requires a weighting scheme for assigning weights to terms in a document. There exist many such methods, the most well known of which is the term frequency inverse document frequency (tf-idf) [355]. Let $Tf(w)$ be the term frequency or number of times that word w occurred in the document, and let $Df(w)$ be the document frequency (number of documents that contain the word). Let N be the number of documents. We define $TfIdf(w)$ as

$$TfIdf(w) = Tf(w) * \log\left(\frac{N}{Df(w)}\right).$$

This is the relative importance of the word in the document, which matches our intuitive view of the importance of words. A word is more important the fewer documents it appears in (lower Df), as well as if it appears several times in a single target document (larger Tf). Said another way, we are more interested in words that appear often in a document, but not often in the collection. Such words are intuitively more important, as they are differentiating, separating or classifying words. Figure 10.1 shows term vectors for a group of documents using tf-idf weights.

id	men	entered	bank	charlotte	missiles	masks	aryan	guns	witnesses	reported	silver	suv	august
seg1.txt	0.239441	0	0.153457	0.195243	0	0.237029	0	0.195243	0.237029	0.140004	0.195243	0.237029	0
seg13.txt	0	0	0	0	0	0	0	0	0	0	0	0	0
seg14.txt	0	0.192197	0	0	0	0	0	0	0	0	0	0	0.172681
seg15.txt	0	0	0	0	0	0	0	0	0	0	0	0	0.149652
seg16.txt	0	0	0	0	0	0	0	0	0	0	0	0	0
seg17.txt	0	0	0	0	0	0	0	0	0	0	0	0	0
seg18.txt	0	0.158432	0	0	0	0	0	0	0	0	0	0	0
seg19.txt	0	0	0	0.197255	0	0	0	0	0	0.141447	0	0	0.155038
seg2.txt	0	0	0	0	0	0	0	0	0	0	0	0	0
seg20.txt	0	0.234323	0	0	0	0	0	0	0	0	0	0	0
seg21.txt	0	0	0	0	0	0	0	0	0	0	0	0	0
seg22.txt	0	0	0	0	0.139629	0	0.127389	0	0	0	0	0	0
seg23.txt	0	0	0	0	0	0	0	0	0.180656	0	0	0	0
seg24.txt	0	0	0	0	0	0	0.117966	0	0.117966	0	0	0	0
seg25.txt	0	0	0	0	0	0	0	0	0	0	0	0	0
seg26.txt	0	0	0	0	0	0	0	0	0	0	0	0	0
seg27.txt	0	0	0.235418	0	0	0	0.214781	0	0	0	0	0	0
seg28.txt	0	0	0	0	0.151753	0	0	0	0	0	0	0	0
seg29.txt	0	0	0	0	0	0	0.129852	0	0	0	0	0	0.142329
seg3.txt	0	0	0	0	0.18432	0	0	0	0	0	0	0	0
seg30.txt	0.078262	0	0	0	0	0	0	0	0	0	0	0	0
seg31.txt	0	0	0.213409	0	0	0	0.194701	0	0	0	0	0	0
seg32.txt	0	0	0	0	0	0	0	0	0	0	0	0	0

Figure 10.1.   An illustration of term vectors for many documents, containing their tf-idf values.

The following pseudocode computes tf-idf vectors for each document in a given document collection. It uses the COUNT-TERMS function in the previous pseudocode example. The first section iterates through all documents, computing and storing term frequencies and document frequencies. The second section computes the tf-idf vectors for each document and stores them in a table.

COMPUTE-TFIDF(*documents*)

```
1   termFrequencies ← ∅ ▷ Looks up term count tables for document names.
2   documentFrequencies ← ∅ ▷ Counts the documents in which a term occurs.
3   uniqueTerms ← ∅ ▷ The list of all unique terms.
4   for each document d in documents
5       do docName ← NAME(d) ▷ Extract the name of the document.
6          tokenStream ← TOKENIZE(d) ▷ Generate document token stream.
7          terms ← COUNT-TERMS(tokenStream) ▷ Count the term frequencies.
8          termFrequencies[docName] ← terms ▷ Store the term frequencies.
9          for each term t in KEYS(terms)
10             do increment (or initialize to 1) documentFrequencies[t]
11                uniqueTerms ← uniqueTerms ∪ t
12
13  tfIdfVectorTable ← ∅ ▷ Looks up tf-idf vectors for document names.
14  n ← LENGTH(documents)
15  for each document name docName in KEYS(termFrequencies)
16      do tfIdfVector ← create zeroed array of length LENGTH(uniqueTerms)
17         terms ← termFrequencies[docName]
18         for each term t in KEYS(terms)
19             do tf ← terms[t]
20                df ← documentFrequencies[t]
21                tfIdf ← tf * log(n/df)
22                tfIdfVector[index of t in uniqueTerms] ← tfIdf
23         tfIdfVectorTable[docName] ← tfIdfVector
24  return tfIdfVectorTable
```

10.3.2 Zipf's Law

The normal and uniform distributions are the ones we are most familiar with. The power law distribution is common today with the large data sizes we encounter, which reflect scalable phenomena. The economist Vilfredo Pareto stated that a company's revenue is inversely proportional to its rank—a classic power law, resulting in the famous 80-20 rule, in which 20% of the population holds 80% of the wealth.

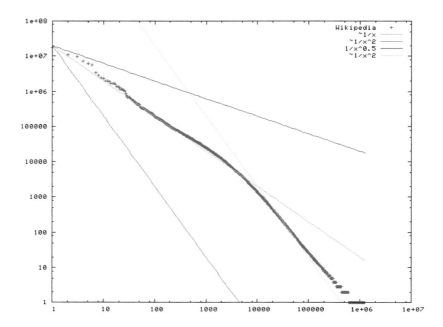

Figure 10.2.   The distribution of terms in Wikipedia, an example of Zipf's Law in action. Term frequency is on the y-axis, and frequency rank is on the x-axis.

Harvard linguist George Kingsley Zipf stated the distribution of words in natural language corpora using a discrete power law distribution called a Zipfian distribution. Zipf's Law [490] states that in a typical natural language document, the frequency of any word is inversely proportional to its rank in the frequency table. Plotting the Zipf curve on a log-log scale yields a straight line with a slope of -1 (see Figure 10.2).

One immediate implication of Zipf's Law is that a small number of words describe most of the key concepts in small documents. There are numerous examples of text summarization that permit a full description with just a few words.

10.3.3   Tasks Using the Vector Space Model

The vector space model, when accompanied by some distance metric, allows one to perform many useful tasks. We can use tf-idf and the vector space model to identify documents of particular interest. For example, the vector space model, with the use of some distance metric, will allow us to answer

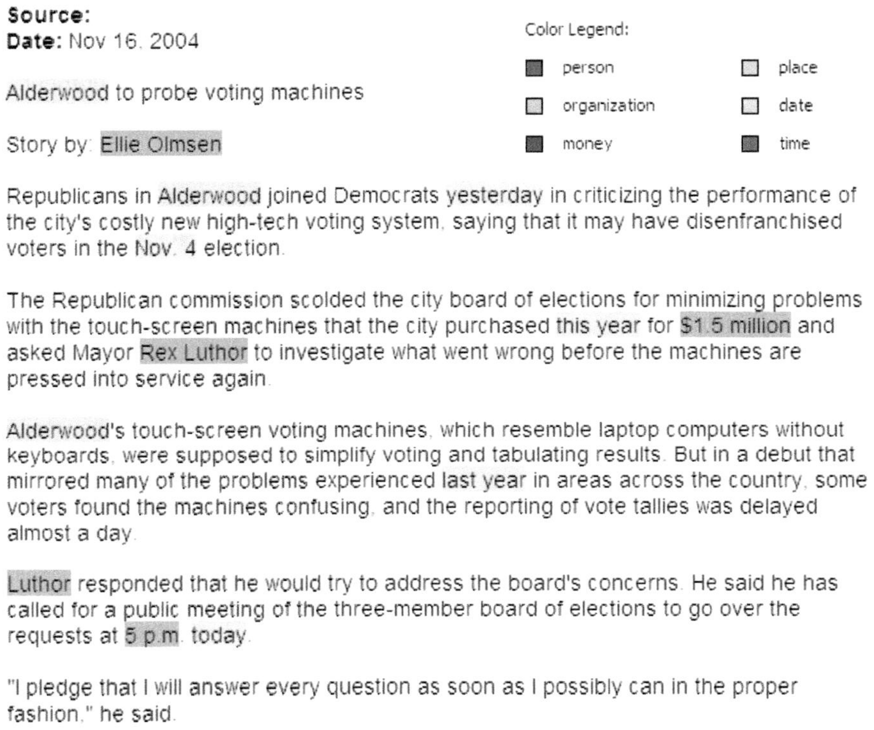

Source:
Date: Nov 16, 2004

Alderwood to probe voting machines

Story by: Ellie Olmsen

Color Legend:

- ■ person
- □ organization
- ■ money
- □ place
- □ date
- ■ time

Republicans in Alderwood joined Democrats yesterday in criticizing the performance of the city's costly new high-tech voting system, saying that it may have disenfranchised voters in the Nov. 4 election.

The Republican commission scolded the city board of elections for minimizing problems with the touch-screen machines that the city purchased this year for $1.5 million and asked Mayor Rex Luthor to investigate what went wrong before the machines are pressed into service again.

Alderwood's touch-screen voting machines, which resemble laptop computers without keyboards, were supposed to simplify voting and tabulating results. But in a debut that mirrored many of the problems experienced last year in areas across the country, some voters found the machines confusing, and the reporting of vote tallies was delayed almost a day.

Luthor responded that he would try to address the board's concerns. He said he has called for a public meeting of the three-member board of elections to go over the requests at 5 p.m. today.

"I pledge that I will answer every question as soon as I possibly can in the proper fashion," he said.

Figure 10.3. A document view in which named entities are highlighted, color-coded by entity type.

questions such as which documents are similar to a specific one, which documents are relevant to a given collection of documents, or which documents are most relevant to a given search query—all by finding the documents whose term vectors are most similar to the given document, the average vector over a document collection, or the vector of a search query.

Another indirect task is how to help the user make sense of an entire corpus. The user may be looking for patterns or for structures, such as a document's main themes, clusters, and the distribution of themes through a document collection. This often involves visualizing the corpus in a two-dimensional layout, or presenting the user with a graph of connections between documents or entities to navigate through. The visualization pipeline maps well to document visualization: we get the data (corpus), transform it into vectors, then run algorithms based on the tasks of interest (i.e., similarity, search, clustering), and generate the visualizations.

10.4   Single Document Visualizations

Here we present several visualizations of a single text document, taken from
the VAST Contest 2007 data set.

Figure 10.4.   A tag cloud visualization generated by the free service tagCrowd.com [396]. The
font size and darkness are proportional to the frequency of the word in the document.

10.4.1   Word Clouds

Word clouds (Figure 10.4), also known as *text clouds* or *tag clouds*, are
layouts of raw tokens, colored and sized by their frequency within a single
document. Text clouds and their variations, such as a Wordle (Figure 10.5),
are examples of visualizations that use only term frequency vectors and some
layout algorithm to create the visualization.

Figure 10.5.   A Wordle visualization generated by the free service wordle.net [118]. The size of
the text corresponds to the frequency of the word in the document.

10.4.2 WordTree

The WordTree visualization [450] is a visual representation of both term frequencies, as well as their context (Figure 10.6). Size is used to represent the term or phrase frequency. The root of the tree is a user-specified word or phrase of interest, and the branches represent the various contexts in which the word or phrase is used in the document.

Figure 10.6. A WordTree visualization generated by the free service ManyEyes [196]. The branches of the tree represent the various contexts following a root word or phrase in the document.

10.4.3 TextArc

We can extend the representation of word distribution by displaying connectivity. There are several ways in which connections can be computed. TextArc [312] is a visual representation of how terms relate to the lines of text in which they appear (Figure 10.7). Every word of the text is drawn in order around an ellipse as small lines with a slight offset at its start. As in a text cloud, more frequently occurring words are drawn larger and brighter. Words with higher frequencies are drawn within the ellipse, pulled by its occurrences on the circle (similar to RadViz). The user is able to highlight the underlying text with probing and animate "reading" the text by visualizing the flow of the text through relevant connected terms.

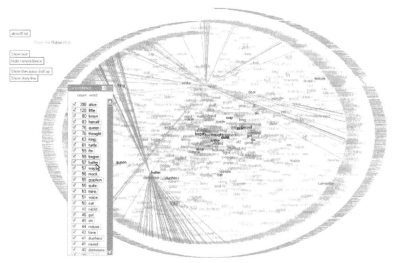

Figure 10.7.   A TextArc visualization that uses the full text of *Alice in Wonderland*. Words
                that occur evenly throughout the document are positioned in the center of the
                display, while words that appear only in specific sections are located closer to the
                circumference. (Image from [312], © 2002 IEEE.)

10.4.4 Arc Diagrams

Arc diagrams [451] are a visualization focused on displaying repetition in
text or any sequence. Repeated subsequences are identified and connected
by semicircular arcs. The thickness of the arcs represents the length of the
subsequence, and the height of the arcs represents the distance between the
subsequences. Figure 10.8 displays Bach's Minuet in G Major, visualizing

Figure 10.8.   An arc diagram visualization of Bach's Minuet in G Major. Repeating sequences
                are connected with semicircular arcs. (Image from [451], © 2002 IEEE.)

the classic pattern of a minuet. It contains two parts, each consisting of a long passage played twice. The parts are loosely related, as shown by the bundle of thin arcs connecting the two main parts. The overlap of the two main arcs shows that the end of the first passage is the same as the beginning of the second.

10.4.5 Literature Fingerprinting

Literature fingerprinting is a method of visualizing features used to characterize text [222]. Instead of calculating just one feature value or vector for the whole text (this is what is usually done), we calculate a sequence of feature values per text and present them to the user as a characteristic fingerprint of the document. This allows the user to "look inside" the document and analyze the development of the values across the text. Moreover, the structural information of the document is used to visualize the document on different levels of resolution. Literature fingerprinting was applied to an authorship attribution problem to show the discrimination power of the standard measures that are assumed to capture the writing style of an author (see Figure 10.9).

10.5 Document Collection Visualizations

In most cases of document collection visualizations, the goal is to place similar documents close to each other and dissimilar ones far apart. This is a minimax problem and typically $O(n^2)$. We compute the similarity between all pairs of documents and determine a layout. The common approaches are graph spring layouts, multidimensional scaling, clustering (k-means, hierarchical, expectation maximization (EM), support vector), and self-organizing maps. We present several document collection visualizations, such as self-organizing maps, cluster maps, and themescapes.

10.5.1 Self-Organizing Maps

A self-organizing map (SOM) [248] is an unsupervised learning algorithm using a collection of typically 2D nodes, where documents will be located. Each node has an associated vector of the same dimensionality as the input vectors (the document vectors) used to train the map. We initialize the SOM nodes, typically with random weights. We choose a random vector from the input vectors and calculate its distance from each node. We adjust the

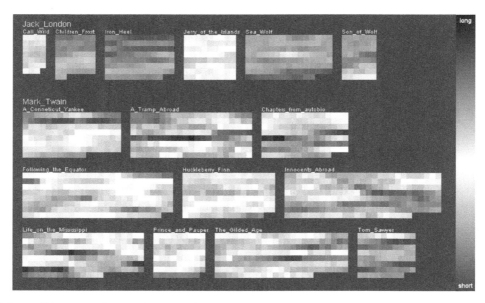

Figure 10.9.   Literature fingerprinting technique. Here, literature fingerprinting is used to an-
                alyze the ability of several text measures to discriminate between authors. Each
                pixel represents a text block, and the pixels are grouped into books. Color is
                mapped to the feature value, in this case to the average sentence length. If a mea-
                sure is able to discriminate between the two authors, the books in the first row
                (written by London) are visually set apart from the remaining books (written by
                Mark Twain). (Image from [222], © 2007 IEEE.)

weights of the closest nodes (within a particular radius), making each closer
to the input vector, with the higher weights corresponding to the closest
selected node. As we iterate through the input vectors, the radius gets
smaller. An example of using SOMs for text data is shown in Figure 10.10
[454], which shows a million documents collected from 83 newsgroups.

10.5.2   Themescapes

Themescapes are summaries of corpora using abstract 3D landscapes in
which height and color are used to represent density of similar documents.
The example shown in Figure 10.11 from Pacific Northwest National Labs
[407] represents news articles visualized as a themescape. The taller mountains represent frequent themes in the document corpus (height is proportional to number of documents relating to the theme).

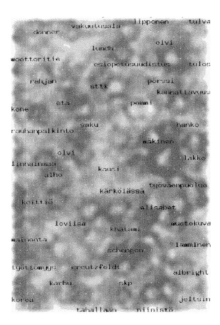

Figure 10.10.   A self-organizing map (SOM) layout of Finnish news bulletins. The labels show the topical areas, and color represents the number of documents, with light areas containing more [454].

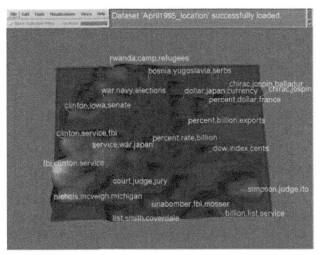

Figure 10.11.   A themescape from PNNL that uses height to represent the frequency of themes in news articles. (Image reprinted from [407] with permission of Springer Science and Business Media.)

10.5.3   Document Cards

Document cards are a compact visualization (Figure 10.12) that represents the document's key semantics as a mixture of images and important key terms, similar to cards in a top trumps game [400]. The key terms are extracted using an advanced text-mining approach based on an automatic extraction of document structure. The images and their captions are extracted using a graphical heuristic, and the captions are used for a semi-semantic image weighting. Furthermore, the image color histogram is used to classify images into classes (class 1: photography/rendered image, class 2: diagram/sketch/graph, class 3: table) and show at least one representative from each non-empty class.

10.6   Extended Text Visualizations

Here we investigate several text visualization techniques that involve metadata or otherwise go beyond the typical term-vector-based visualizations.

10.6.1   Software Visualization

Eick et al. developed a visualization tool called SeeSoft [108] that visualizes statistics for each line of code (i.e., age and number of modifications, programmer, dates). In Figure 10.13, each column represents a source code file with the height representing the size of the file. If the file is longer than the screen, it continues into the next column. In the classic SeeSoft representation, each row represents one line of code. Since the number of lines is too large for one row, each line of code is represented by a pixel in the row. This increases the number of lines that can be displayed. Color is used to represent the call count. The more red a line is, the more often the line is called, and thus is a key hot-spot. A blue line is an infrequently called one. Color can be used to represent other parameters, such as time of last modification or number of modifications. With a 1K × 1K screen, SeeSoft is able to display up to 50,000 lines of code. This figure contains 52 files with 15,255 lines of code. The selected file is file1.c, a block of code with a zoomed-in view of line 408.

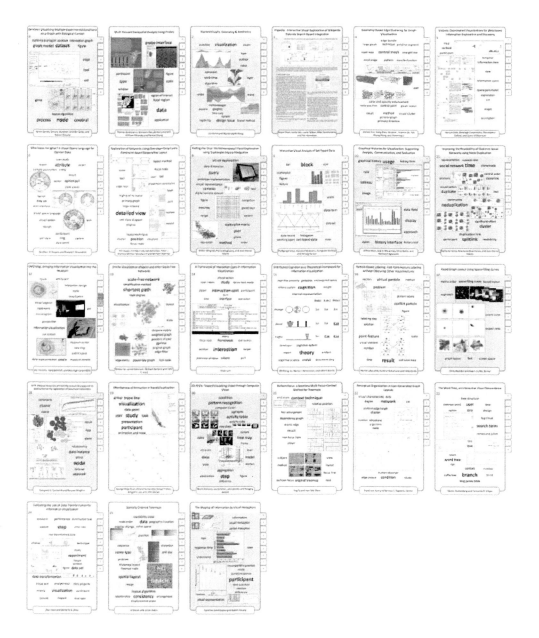

Figure 10.12. The IEEE InfoVis 2008 proceedings corpus, represented by a matrix of document cards. The frequency of the term on each page is shown on the right side of the document card (the more red, the higher the frequency, as can be seen in the first document of row three) [400].

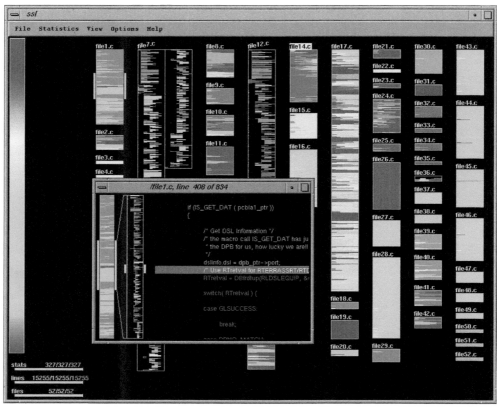

Figure 10.13.   The SeeSoft software visualization. Rectangles represent source code files. The
sizes of the rectangles in each column correspond to the length of the source code
file, and the color of each line represents parameters related to modification. (Image
from [108], © 1992 IEEE.)

10.6.2   Search Result Visualization

Marti Hearst developed a simple query result visualization foundationally
similar to Keim's pixel displays [232] called TileBars [178], which displays
a number of term-related statistics, including frequency and distribution of
terms, length of document, term-based ranking, and strength of ranking.
Each document of the result set is represented by a rectangle, where width
indicates relative length of the document and stacked squares correspond
to text segments (see Figure 10.14). Each row of the stack represents a
set of query terms, and the darkness of the square indicates the frequency
of terms among the corresponding terms. Titles and the first words from

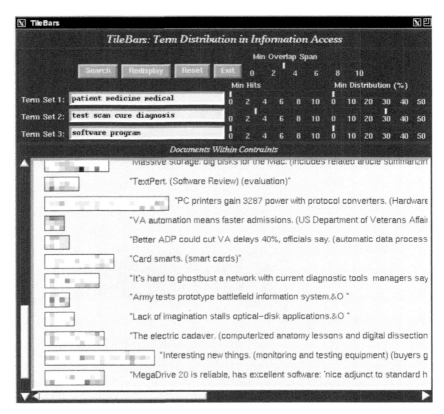

Figure 10.14.   The TileBars query result visualization. Each large rectangle indicates a document, and each square within the document represents a text segment. The darker the tile, the more frequent the query term set. (Image from [178], © 1995 Addison-Wesley.)

the document appear next to its TileBar. Each large rectangle indicates a document, and each square within the document represents a text segment. The darker the tile, the more frequent is the query term set. This produces a representation that is compact and provides feedback on document structure reflecting relative document length, query term frequency, and query term distribution.

10.6.3   Temporal Document Collection Visualizations

ThemeRiver [173], also called a *stream graph*, is a visualization of thematic changes in a document collection over time (Figure 10.15). This visualiza-

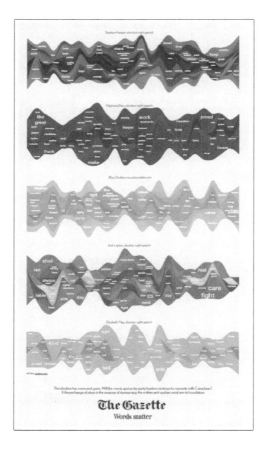

Figure 10.15.   A stream graph (ThemeRiver), depicting the election night speeches of several different candidates for a Canadian election. (Image from [173], © 2002 IEEE.)

tion assumes that the input data progresses over time. Themes are visually represented as colored horizontal bands whose vertical thickness at a given horizontal location represents their frequency at a particular point in time.

Jigsaw is a tool for visualizing and exploring text corpora [155]. Jigsaw's calendar view positions document objects on a calendar based on date entities identified within the text. When the user highlights a document, the entities that occur within that document are displayed (see Figure 10.16).

Wanner et al. developed a visual analytics tool for conducting semi-automatic sentiment analysis of large news feeds [440]. While the tool automatically retrieves and analyzes RSS feeds with respect to positive and

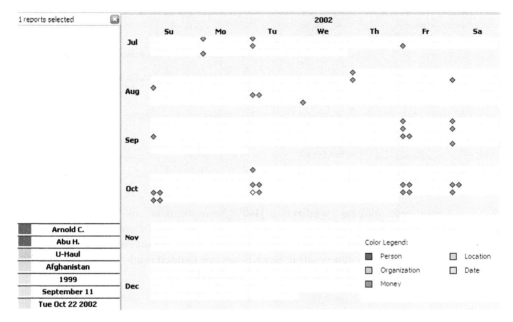

Figure 10.16.   News articles are presented with the Jigsaw calendar view, based on the extracted date entities. (Image from [155], © 2007 IEEE.)

negative opinion words, the more demanding news analysis of finding trends, spotting peculiarities, and putting events into context is left to the human expert. As shown in Figure 10.17, each single news item is represented by one visual object and plotted on a horizontal time axis according to its publication time. The shape and color of an item reveal information about the category it belongs to, and its vertical shift indicates whether it has a positive connotation (upward shift) or a negative one (downward shift).

10.6.4   Representing Relationships

Jigsaw [155] also includes an entity graph view (Figure 10.18), in which the user can navigate a graph of related entities and documents. In Jigsaw, entities are connected to the documents in which they appear. The Jigsaw graph view does not show the entire document collection, but it allows the user to incrementally expand the graph by selecting documents and entities of interest (see Figure 10.19).

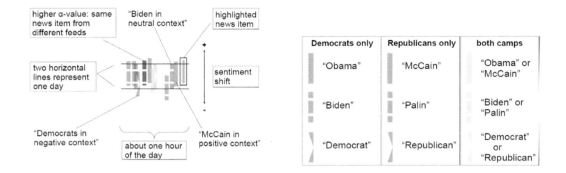

	Democrats only	Republicans only	both camps
	"Obama"	"McCain"	"Obama" or "McCain"
	"Biden"	"Palin"	"Biden" or "Palin"
	"Democrat"	"Republican"	"Democrat" or "Republican"

Figure 10.17.   A sentiment analysis visualization [440]. News items are plotted along the time axis. Shape and color show to which category an item belongs, and the vertical position depends on the automatically determined sentiment score of an item. The visual objects representing news items are painted semi-transparent in order to make overlapping items more easily distinguishable.

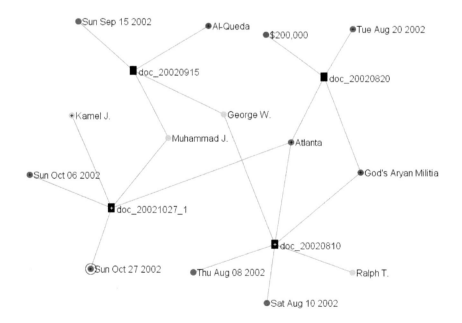

Figure 10.18.   The Jigsaw graph view, representing connections between named entities and documents. (Image from [155], © 2007 IEEE.)

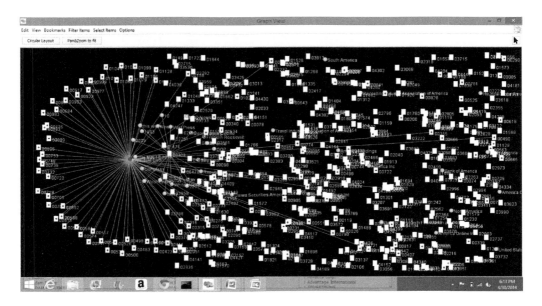

Figure 10.19.   A clustered graph view in Jigsaw that filters for documents having specific entities. Mousing over an entity identifies data about the document. Colors represent token values.

The Jigsaw list view is an alternative to the graph view in that it allows the user to explore relationships between various entity types and documents. As shown in Figure 10.20, when the user selects items of interest, the list view draws connection lines showing their relationships.

10.7 Summary

In this chapter we have explored the fundamental computational approaches to transforming unstructured text into structured data suitable for visualization and analysis. We introduced visualizations such as text clouds and word trees for finding themes and patterns within single documents. Visualizations such as SOMs, map displays, and themescapes are useful for visualizing document collections. For further analysis of document collections with complex relationships and temporal characteristics, we briefly surveyed several visualizations, such as node graphs, ThemeRiver, and Calendar View.

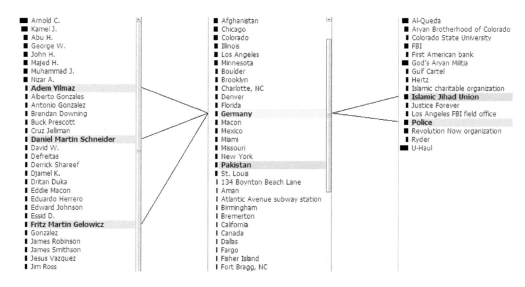

Figure 10.20.   The Jigsaw list view, displaying the connections between people (left), places (center), and organizations (right). (Image from [155], © 2007 IEEE.)

10.8   Related Readings

A wonderful collection of papers originating from a meeting in 2005 to discuss the state of the art in visual information processing and describing integrating text analysis and visualization can be found in the book *Visual Data Mining: Theory, Techniques and Tools for Visual Analytics*, edited by Simoff, Bohlen, and Mazeika [379]. More details on text mining and analysis can be found in Feldman and Sanger's book, *The Text Mining Handbook: Advanced Approaches in Analyzing Unstructured Data* [122]. The book covers the full knowledge-discovery pipeline including visualization. Marti Hearst has a great book entitled *Search User Interfaces* [179] , which includes a very relevant chapter on information visualization for text analysis; the book is also available on line at http://searchuserinterfaces.com/book/.

10.9   Exercises

1. Give examples of the suggested computations required for document analysis for the following applications:

   (a) identifying plagiarism,

   (b) determining papers that discuss a specific topic,

     (c) selecting a Chinese restaurant with good reviews,

     (d) any other of your choosing.

2. What are some advantages and disadvantages of tag clouds?

3. Select a document of your choice and generate a tag cloud.

4. Perform a web search looking for repositories of publicly available text corpora. Retrieve two or three and analyze them in terms of what problems they could be used to solve. What format are they in? What preprocessing is necessary to implement the visualizations given in this chapter?

5. Repeat the above process, using a newspaper as your source. What sorts of data can you extract from the newspaper? What are the data types? What data sets could you derive by processing the information in the newspaper? Try to design at least one data set for each section of the newspaper.

6. The techniques in this chapter could be used with television news. How?

7. Look up Weka (`http://www.cs.waikato.ac.nz/ml/weka/`), an open source data mining library and collection of tools that can be used as a computational engine for preprocessing text for visualization.

10.10 Projects

1. Write a program that determines the distribution of words in a document.

2. Using the above, compute the tf-idf for that same document.

3. Write a program that generates a word cloud.

4. A common task when dealing with data is dividing it into categories, such as *low*, *medium*, and *high*. Write a program that reads in a document and divides the words into three classes: simple, complex, and those in between.

5. Implement the pseudocode of this chapter on a section of text, say one of your reports or on one of the smaller VAST-like data sets available on the book's web site.

6. Explore Zipf's Law on a few documents.

7. Download and install Weka, then use it on one of the smaller VAST-like data sets available on the book's web site or, if you are ambitious, on one of the VAST data sets.

CHAPTER 11

Interaction Concepts

Interaction within the data and information visualization context is a mechanism for modifying what the users see and how they see it. Many classes of interaction techniques exist [487], including:

- *navigation*—user controls for altering the position of the camera and for scaling the view (what gets mapped to the screen) such as panning, rotating, and zooming.

- *selection*—user controls for identifying an object, a collection of objects, or regions of interest to be the subject of some operation, such as highlighting, deleting, and modifying.

- *filtering*—user controls for reducing the size of the data being mapped to the screen, either by eliminating records, dimensions, or both.

- *reconfiguring*—user controls for changing the way data is mapped to graphical entities or attributes, such as reordering the data or layouts, thereby providing a different way of viewing a data subset.

- *encoding*—user controls for changing the graphical attributes, such as point size or line color, to potentially reveal different features.

- *connecting*—user controls for linking different views or objects to show related items.

- *abstracting/elaborating*—user controls for modifying the level of detail.

- *hybrid*—user controls combining several of the above in one technique, for example, increasing the screen space assigned to one or more focus areas to enable users to see details, while showing the other areas of data in a smaller space, in a way that preserves context.

A variety of techniques and tools for performing interactions within data and information visualization systems have been proposed to date. While some of these tools appear quite unrelated, they actually share a number of features and serve a common purpose. As the field of data and information visualization evolves, it is beneficial to try to identify unifying themes and frameworks to help solidify our understanding of the basic building blocks of the field.

In this chapter, we describe such a framework for interaction techniques, identifying distinct classes and shared concepts that will help facilitate discussions and focus future research. We begin by identifying classes of interactive operations and describing them in terms of operators and the operand (the space upon which the operator is applied). Each is described in detail, with references to relevant techniques in the literature. We then define an architecture that combines the different interaction spaces into a single pipeline, along with the interface tools needed by the user to control the process. We conclude with some ideas for future research in the development and assessment of this framework. This chapter draws heavily from a paper written by one of the authors [443] and presented at the 2004 Eurographics Symposium on Visualization.

11.1 Interaction Operators

In this section we describe in more detail a wide range of interaction operations commonly found in data and information visualization. This list is not exhaustive, but it covers many typical interaction tools. Readers interested in more extensive lists of visualization interactions are directed to Keim's classification [234] and Chi's taxonomy [73]. One important note is that interaction operators often can fall into many of the suggested interaction classes, and that almost all operators can be performed interactively or automatically within a visualization. The result can be interpreted as either a modified view or a new view. For example, zooming is available in almost all visualizations; however, it can be thought of as generating a new visualization, especially if different data (such as more roads in a map) need to be displayed.

11.1.1 Navigation Operators

Navigation (also sometimes referred to as *exploration*) is used to search for a subset of data to be viewed, the orientation of this view, and the level of detail (LOD). The subset in question may be one that is recognized by some

Figure 11.1.   Views of the grand tour for the grades data set using GGobi.

visual pattern or one on which further or more detailed exploration is desired. In a typical three-dimensional space, this can be specified using a camera location, a viewing direction, the shape and size of the viewing frustum, and an LOD indicator. In multiresolution visualizations, LOD changes can correspond to drilling down or rolling up hierarchical representations of the data.

Navigation operators can work in absolute or relative coordinates within their particular spaces. Incremental navigation may have different granularities, depending on whether the user wants a small or significant change. Navigation can be user-driven or automatic; a good example of automated exploration is the grand tour [22], where multidimensional data is explored by flying along a path that smoothly covers many or all possible orientations of the data space, as projected onto two dimensions (Figure 11.1). The user can control the step size between views, with the trade-off being smoothness versus the number of projections that need to be inspected. Another automated form of exploration is *projection pursuit* [194], where projections are computationally analyzed and the subset of views that exceed a user's threshold for "interestingness" is displayed.

11.1.2   Selection Operators

In selection, the user isolates a subset of the display components, which will then be subjected to some other operation, such as highlighting, deleting, masking, or moving to the center of focus. Many variations on selection have been developed to date [461], and decisions need to be made on what the results should be for a sequence of selections. For example, should a new selection replace the previous selection or supplement the previous selection? The granularity of selection is also an issue. Clicking on an entity in the display might result in selection of the smallest addressable component (e.g., a vertex or edge) or might target a broader region around the specified location (e.g., a surface, region of the screen, or object).

Selection can be articulated in many different ways. The user may click on entities, paint over a selection of entities (e.g., holding the mouse button down while moving over the entities of interest), or otherwise isolate the entities via techniques such as bounding boxes and lassoes. Finally, selections may be performed in an indirect manner, where the system selects elements that match a user's input set of constraints. An example would be the selection of nodes in a graph that have a user-specified distance from a selected node.

11.1.3   Filtering Operators

Filtering, as the name implies, reduces the volume of data to be visualized by setting constraints specifying the data to be preserved or removed. A good example of such a filter is the *dynamic query specification* described by Shneiderman et al. [375]. One- or two-handled sliders are used to specify a range of interest, and the visualization is immediately updated to reflect the changes made by the user. Range queries are just one form of filtering, however. One might also select items from a set or list to preserve or hide, such as the column hiding operation in Excel. Figure 11.2 shows the effects of filtering on a visualization to simplify the view and ease interpretation.

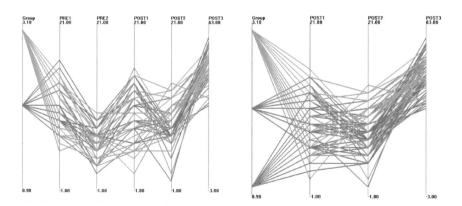

Figure 11.2.   Filtering rows and columns of the grades data set using XmdvTool.

The distinction between filtering and selection followed by deletion or masking is a subtle, but important point. Filtering, in general, is most often done in an *indirect* manner, e.g., the filter specification is not performed on the data visualization itself, but via a separate interface or dialog box. In fact, filtering is often done prior to viewing the data, to avoid overloading the data display. Selection is most often done in a *direct* manner, by indicating objects on the visualization via mouse motions, for example. The operation performed on the selected subset can result in a view that is indistinguishable from a filtering operation.

11.1.4 Reconfiguring Operators

Reconfiguring the data within a particular visualization can often be used to expose features or cope with complexity or scale. By reorganizing the data, say by filtering some dimensions and reordering those that remain, different views are provided to the user. For example, a powerful tool with table-based visualizations is to sort the rows or columns of the data to highlight trends and correlations. Other types of reconfiguration might be to change the dimensions being used to control the x- and y-coordinates of a plotted marker, or even to derive positions based on transformations of the data. Popular instances of this include the use of principal component analysis (PCA) or multidimensional scaling (MDS) to lay out data points so that relationships among all the dimensions are best conveyed in the 2D layout.

11.1.5 Encoding Operators

Any given data set can be used to generate countless different visualizations. Recoding can provide the user a library of possible different types of visualization; features of the data that are difficult or impossible to see with one such mapping might become quite apparent in another. For example, a scatterplot with one axis representing years may have many points that overlap, whereas a parallel coordinate display would represent these uniquely. Many visualization tools today support multiple types of visualization, because no single visualization is effective for all tasks that need to be carried out by the user. Each visualization is most suitable for a subset of data types, data set characteristics, and user tasks. While some work has been done to identify or select the *best* visualization, it is apparent that such guidelines are at best suggestions, and the analyst is most likely to benefit from examining their data using a number of different mappings and views. This is the essence of interactive visualization.

Other forms of encoding operations include those that modify the color map used, the size of graphical entities, and their shape. These can be considered variations within a particular type of visualization, and can be used to emphasize or reveal features of interest. Even limitations of some visualizations can be overcome using variations. The overlapping issue in scatterplots where occluded points are not visible can be overcome by jittering the points or making the size of the points reflect the number of points at that same position. Other attributes of graphical entities that can be controlled include opacity, textures, line or fill style, and dynamic attributes such as fade or flashing rate. Note that these effects can often be mimicked by performing transformations on the data itself, rather than on the graphical entities.

11.1.6 Connection Operators

A frequent use for selection operations is to link the selected data in one view to the corresponding data in other views. While other forms of connection between subwindows of an application exist, such as when opening a new data file, *linked selection* is probably the most common form of communication between windows found in modern visualization tools. Its popularity stems in large part from the fact that each view of one's data can reveal interesting features, and that by highlighting such a feature in one view, it is possible to build a more complete mental model of the feature by seeing how it appears in other views (see Figure 11.3). This can also help reveal relationships between this feature and others in the data set. For example, when examining multivariate spatial data, it is often useful to jump between the spatially referenced view and the dependent variable view, which often does not preserve the spatial attributes.

When the selection data is allowed to be interactively changed, the operator is called *brushing*, in which case the user is continuously changing the selection in one view, and the corresponding linked data in one or more other views is highlighted. The resulting interactive and dynamic display provides information about the changes in values in the linked displays.

Another strength of linked brushing is in specifying complex constraints on one's selection. Each type of view is optimized for conveying certain types of information, as well as for specifying conditions on particular types and with a particular degree of accuracy. Thus, for example, one might specify a temporal constraint using a visualization containing a timeline, a constraint on a name field using a sorted list view, and a geographic constraint using a

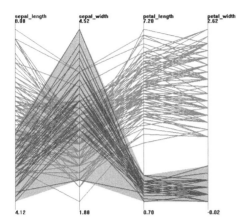 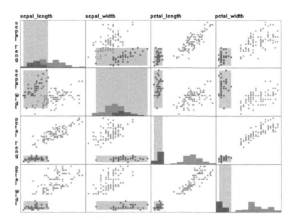

Figure 11.3.   Example of linked brushing. A cluster is isolated in parallel coordinates, with linked selection in the scatterplot matrix. Selected data is dark red, while brush extents are shown as light bands or rectangles.

map. While each is effective as a tool for accurate and intuitive specification of a part of a query, none could be used for the complete query.

In some situations, the user may want to *unlink* some visualizations in order to maintain a given view while exploring a different area of the data or different data set. Some systems allow the user to indicate for each window whether it is transmitting information to other views, and from which other windows it will receive input. A user may also want to constrain the type of information being communicated, as well as its direction. Some types of interaction may be local to a particular window, e.g., zooming in and out, while others are meant to be shared, such as reordering dimensions. Also, in some situations, such as with hierarchically related windows, it may make more sense for the information to move from parent to child, but not the other way. Thus, a fairly rich set of connection and communication options may be needed to maximize flexibility.

11.1.7   Abstraction/Elaboration Operators

In dense data and information displays, it is often desirable to focus in on a subset of the data to acquire details (elaboration) while reducing the level of detail (abstraction) on other parts of the data set. One of the most popular techniques of this type is using distortion operators. While some researchers classify distortion as a visualization technique, it is actually a transformation that can be applied to any type of visualization. Like panning and zooming, distortion is useful for interactive exploration. Many *distortion operators* (also called *functions*) have been proposed in the past [268]. These include methods that distort the entire space being analyzed, and others that have more localized effects. The distortion may take place within the original visualization, or may appear in a separate window. Distortions vary in the features that are preserved and the amount of context maintained. For example, text distortion techniques strive for readability within a small region of interest, with the rest of the text positioned to reinforce document structure, but not generally readable. For other types of distortion, it is important that the undistorted and compressed regions continue to convey useful information, while details are provided in the focus area.

Distortion operators may be linear or nonlinear, with 0th, 1st, or 2nd order continuity (discontinuous operators are also possible). Operators may also operate on structures, rather than on continuous spaces, and thus may be specific to a particular type of operand (see the next section for details). Different operators have different *footprints*, e.g., the shape and extents of the space affected by the transformation. Common footprint shapes include rectangular and circular, and their analogous hyperboxes and hyperellipses for higher dimensional spaces. Extents are usually specified by a distance function within the space being distorted, and are often multidimensional. These extents can be fixed or variable, user-controlled, or driven by the semantics of the information (e.g., page or paragraph extents for text distortion). Finally, operators generally have a variable degree of magnification, depending on the level of detail desired.

11.2   Interaction Operands and Spaces

Parameters of the interaction operators described in the previous section are discussed in more detail later in the chapter. First, however, we present our categorization of the interaction operands, as this will help clarify the role these parameters take in the interaction process and their semantics within the different spaces.

An *interaction operand* is the section of space upon which an interactive operator is applied. To determine the result of an interactive operation, one needs to know within what space the interaction is to take place. In other words, when a user clicks on a location or set of locations on the screen, what entities does he or she wish to indicate? Possibilities include the pixel(s), the data value or record mapped to the location, or even the component of the visualization structure (e.g., an axis) at or near that location. We have identified several distinct interaction spaces. Each is described below, including examples of existing interaction techniques that fall into each class.

11.2.1 Screen Space (Pixels)

Screen space consists of the pixels of the display. Navigation in screen space typically consists of actions such as panning, zooming, and rotation. Note that in each case, no new data is used; the process consists of pixel-level operations such as transformation, sampling, and replication.

Pixel-based selection means that at the end of the operation, each pixel will be classified as either selected or unselected. As previously mentioned, the selection can be performed on individual pixels, rectangles or circles of pixels, or on arbitrarily shaped regions that the user specifies. Selection areas may also be contiguous or non-contiguous. Screen space filtering consists of cropping or masking a region of pixels.

Distortion in screen space involves transformations on pixels, e.g., (x', y') $= f(x, y)$. In order to avoid occlusion, this function should be order-preserving and at least C^0 continuous [220]. The magnification $m(x, y)$ at a particular point is simply the derivative of this transformation, and, in fact, it is useful to be able to switch between transformations and their associated magnifications when controlling the distortion process [220]. Examples of screen space techniques are the fisheye lens [140] and rubber sheet methods [60,360], although the latter techniques could also be placed in the object-space category described below. Figure 11.4 is an example of this type of distortion.

11.2.2 Data Value Space (Multivariate Data Values)

Operations on data space are applied directly to the data, rather than to the screen. Navigating in data value space involves using the data values as a mechanism for view specification. The analogous operations for panning and zooming would be to change the data values being displayed; panning would shift the start of the value range to be shown, while zooming would decrease the size of this range.

Data value space selection is similar to a database query in that the user specifies a range of data values for one or more data dimensions. This can be performed via direct manipulation, as in the data-driven brushing reported in [287] (see Figure 11.5(a)) or via sliders or other query specification mechanisms [375]. Selection may involve a single value, or one or more ranges of values.

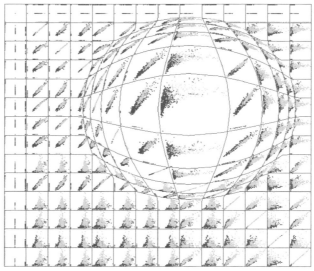

Figure 11.4.   In screen space techniques, pixel regions are enlarged or reduced to provide selective detail. In this scatterplot matrix display, a center of focus has been selected
and magnified using a confocal lens technique. (Image from [443], © 2004 Eurographics.)

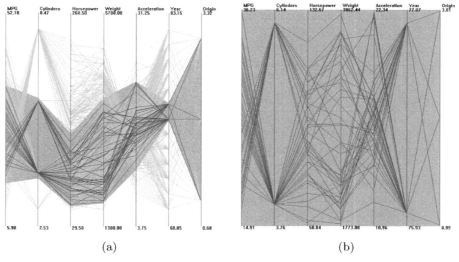

Figure 11.5.   In data value space distortion, transformations are performed according to the
dimensionality of the data. In this example, generated using XmdvTool [137],
an N-dimensional hyperbox is selected via painting over a section of an axis and
scaled in all dimensions (by different amounts) to fill a unit hypercube, which is
then displayed. Animation is used to preserve context. Clusters and anomalies
within the selected region are much easier to see in the zoomed version. (Image
from [443], © 2004 Eurographics.)

Data value space is perhaps the most obvious space in which to perform filtering. When visualizing extremely large data sets, it is common to first reduce the data to a particular region of data space. For spatial data, this is analogous to clipping the data falling outside of a viewing region; for nonspatial data, this involves eliminating some records, dimensions, or both. For example, sampling might be used to examine a representative subset of a large data repository [110] where the visualization might otherwise be too cluttered to discern any useful patterns. Dimensions may also be filtered [480] to allow the user to either examine a subset of dimensions with similar characteristics or select representatives from clusters of related dimensions.

There are many reconfiguring operators for data value space. One of the most powerful is in reordering (e.g., sorting) the records and/or the dimensions. Different ordering functions will expose different subsets of patterns within the data. For distortion in data value space, data values $(d_0, d_1, \ldots, d_n)$ may be transformed via a function $j : (d'_0, d'_1, \ldots, d'_n) = j(d_0, d_1, \ldots, d_n)$ prior to visualization. In fact, each dimension may have its own transformation function $j_i : d'_i = j_i(d_i)$. In its most general case, the function j_i could depend on any number of dimensions, although user control of such a function might be problematic. An example of data value-space distortion is the dimensional zooming found in XmdvTool [137], where each dimension of a selected subset of the data is scaled so that the subset fills the display area (see Figure 11.5).

11.2.3 Data Structure Space (Components of Data Organization)

Data can be structured in a number of ways, such as lists, tables, grids, hierarchies, and graphs. For each structure, one can develop interaction mechanisms to indicate what portions of the structure will be manipulated, and how this manipulation will be manifested. Navigation in data structure space involves moving the view specification along the structure, as in showing sequential groups of records, or moving down or up a hierarchical structure (as in drill-down and roll-up operations). For example, Figure 11.6 shows the difference between a screen space zoom (involving pixel replication) and a data structure space zoom (involving retrieval of more detailed data). A technique presented by Resnick et al. [335] selects subsets of data to be visualized by specifying a focus, extents, and density in a regular grid structure, where the density can be a function of distance from the focus.

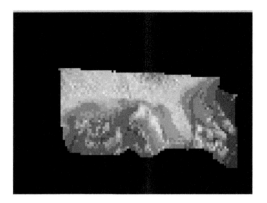 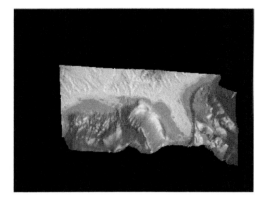

Figure 11.6.   In screen space zooming (left), pixels are replicated to provide selective size, while in data space zooming (right), the data itself can be resampled at the appropriate resolution.

Selection in data structure space generally involves displaying the structure and allowing the user to identify regions of interest within it. This in turn can drive the display of the data corresponding to the selected substructure. For example, structure-based brushing [138] involves controlling the selection of data stored in a cluster hierarchy, with interactions such as highlighting data that fall within a particular branch of the tree (see the example in Figure 15.5). Similarly, *InterRing* is a radial space-filling hierarchy visualization tool that allows semi-automatic selection of nodes, according to the hierarchical structure [478]. Figure 11.7 shows a dimension hierarchy in InterRing, with a subset of terminal nodes automatically selected via a query on their common parent node.

Filtering is often performed in data structure space to reduce the amount of information on the display. For example, in time-series visualization, it is common to identify a range in the time axis (implied by the data ordering) on which to focus one's attention [441]. Examining neighborhoods in a graph visualization often consists of filtering out nodes and links that are greater than a particular number of links away from a focus point, and many techniques for hierarchy visualization allow users to filter based on the level of the hierarchy.

Abstraction/elaboration operators take many forms in data structure space. With a hierarchical structure, abstraction simply means moving up the hierarchy to aggregations or summarizations of the data at the current level, while elaboration implies drilling down into the hierarchy. Abstraction

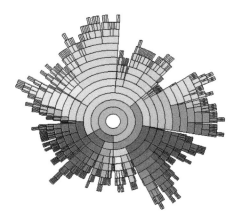

Figure 11.7.   Selection of nodes in a hierarchy via InterRing. Nodes with a red stripe in them have been selected via a user-specified query, rather than one node at a time. The hierarchy consists of nearly 400 nodes (Image from [478], © 2003 IEEE.)

of ordered or grid-based data structures implies either a resampling of the data or some form of aggregation (e.g., averaging). In all cases, there are limits to the degree of abstraction and elaboration, namely a single data record or the complete set. Both operators may be global or only applied to a subspace of the data.

An example of three-dimensional grid distortion is presented by Carpendale et al. [61]. They apply concepts from screen space distortion to elements with three spatial dimensions. Four classes of distortion are defined: *stretch orthogonal, nonlinear orthogonal, nonlinear radial,* and *step orthogonal.* To provide improved visibility to entities within the volume of data, they define a visual access distortion that shifts data to provide a clear line of sight to internal objects.

Distortion of hierarchies is a common practice due to the density of information that can result from broad or deep hierarchies. Several researchers have developed techniques based on radial hierarchy displays, such as Andrews and Heidegger [12], Stasko and Zhang [393], and Yang et al. [478]. Other multiresolution techniques, such as wavelet transforms [470], have been used to visualize details in a focused region of an ordered list of data records.

In each of the cases above, it is the structure holding the data, rather than the data values themselves or the mechanism by which they are visualized, that is the focus of the distortion. Formalization of this procedure is somewhat more complicated than for the other spaces, but we can classify most of these distortions as mapping a vector (D, S), where D is the data and S is the structure holding the data, to (D', S'), where the transformation may modify the data, the structure, or both.

11.2.4 Attribute Space (Components of Graphical Entities)

In *attribute space*, operators are focused on one or more of the attributes associated with the graphical entity being used to convey information. Such attributes could include color, size, shape, or any other of the eight visual variables. Navigation in attribute space is similar to that in data value space; panning involves shifting the range of the values of interest, while zooming can be accomplished by either scaling the attributes or enlarging the range of values of interest. As in data value-driven selection, attribute-space selection requires the user to indicate the subrange of a given attribute of interest. For example, given a visual depiction of a color map, a user can select one or more entries to highlight. Similarly, if data records have attributes such as quality or uncertainty, a visual representation of these attributes, accompanied by suitable interaction techniques, can allow users to filter or emphasize data according to the attributes. Remapping is often done in attribute space, either via selecting different ranges of an attribute to be used in the data to graphic mapping, or by choosing a different attribute to be controlled by the data. For example, in the GlyphMaker system [337], users could select mappings for a given data dimension from a list of possible graphical attributes. Many visualization tools provide an assortment of predefined color scales to be used for the visualization: some perceptually designed, others designed to be compatible with a particular application domain.

Given an attribute A of a graphical entity being used to convey information, we can perform a distortion transformation by applying a function $k : a' = k(a)$. We can assume A can take on values in the range $[a_0 \rightarrow a_1]$, or that A is specified as a vector. For example, distortion of a color map would allocate a wider or narrower range of colors for some subranges than for others, thus enabling fine variations to be more readily perceived (see Figure 11.8). This form of distortion is often used in medical image analysis to identify regions of interest. The size attribute of a data glyph or scatterplot marker, when not used to convey a data dimension, can also be distorted to emphasize or deemphasize selected subsets. Attribute-space techniques can be seen as complementary to data value space methods, since similar effects may be attained through either approach if one or more of the data dimensions is controlling the specified attribute.

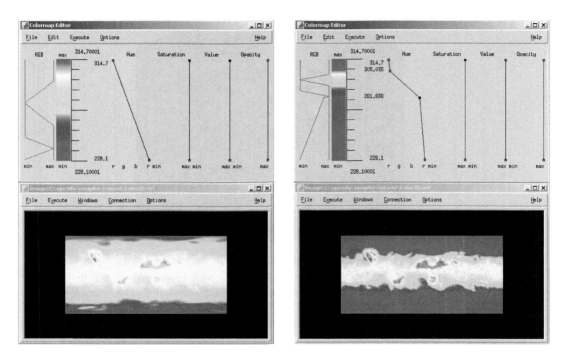

Figure 11.8.   Attribute-based distortion modifies one or more attributes of the graphical objects used to depict the data, as shown in this color map modification, generated using the color map editor in OpenDX. The color map is distorted to allot a greater portion to values in the middle of the data range.

11.2.5   Object Space (3D Surfaces)

In these displays, the data is mapped to a geometric object, and this object (or its projection) can undergo interactions and transformations. Navigation in object space often consists of moving around objects and observing the surfaces on which the data are mapped. The system should support global views of the object space as well as close-up views. The latter may be constrained to enable the user to find good views more quickly. Selection involves clicking anywhere on the object(s) of interest, or indicating target objects from a list.

A typical example of remapping in object space would be changing the object upon which the data is being mapped, such as switching the mapping of geographical data between a plane and a sphere.

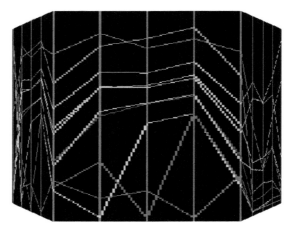

Figure 11.9.   Object-based techniques distort an object upon which data has been projected. In this example, inspired by the perspective wall [283], a parallel coordinates display is projected onto walls, and perspective is used to make a selected wall more readable, while maintaining context with the rest of the data. (Image from [443], © 2004 Eurographics.)

For distortion, examples of this form of interaction are perspective walls [283] (Figure 11.9) and hyperbolic projections [302]. These methods can be envisioned as a variant on screen-based methods, where the object onto which the data is projected encapsulates the distortion function. However, after mapping, the surfaces can undergo additional transformations in 3D, such as rotation, scaling, and perspective distortion. For example, Kreuseler et al. [258] map hierarchies first to a hemisphere, and then adjust the focus by changing the center of projection, resulting in a distortion that enlarges one region while shrinking others. We can represent the process of object-space distortion as a sequence of two functions. The first maps the data (generally parameterized to two dimensions) onto a 3D structure ($(x, y, z) = g(a, b)$), and then this structure is transformed and projected to the screen ($(i, j) = h(x, y, z)$).

11.2.6   Visualization Structure Space

A visualization consists of a structure that is relatively independent of the values, attributes, and structure of data. For example, the grid within which a scatterplot matrix is drawn and the axes displayed in many types of visualizations are each components of the visualization structure, and can be the focus of interactions. Visualization *dashboards*, consisting of a set of tightly or loosely connected visualizations juxtaposed on the screen, have become increasingly popular for monitoring and analyzing complex data environments, such as for business analytics and command-and-control centers.

Examples of navigation in visualization structure space might include moving through pages in a spreadsheet-style visualization tool or zooming in on an individual plot in a scatterplot matrix. For selection, typical operations would include choosing components to hide, move, or rearrange. For example, one might select an axis in parallel coordinates and drag it to a new location to discover different relationships among the data dimensions.

A good example of distortion in this space is the table lens technique [328, 406], which allows users to transform rows and/or columns of a spreadsheet to provide multiple levels of detail. See Figure 11.10 for an example of this process, as applied to a scatterplot matrix.

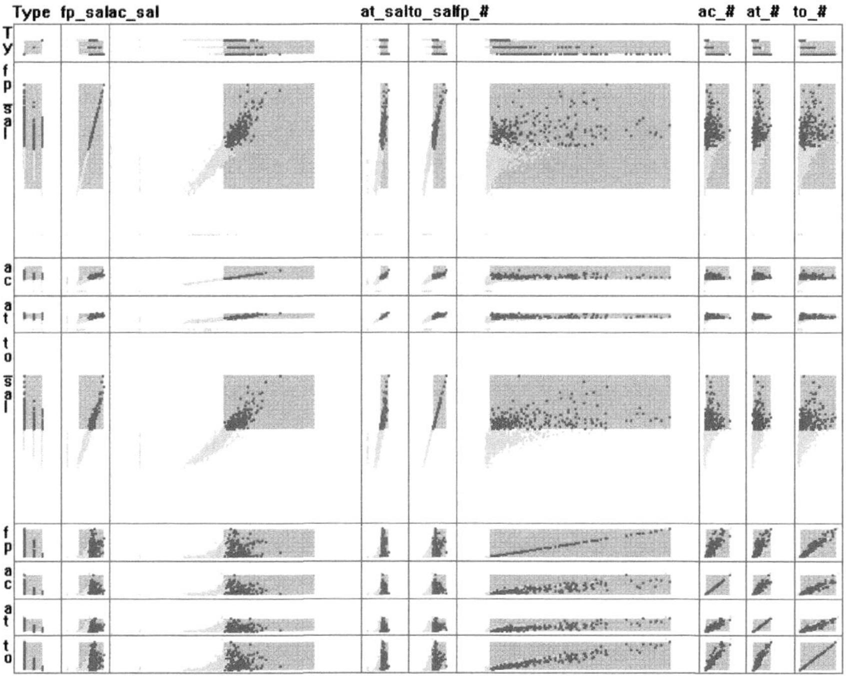

Figure 11.10.   Structure-based distortion modifies the underlying structural elements of the visualization. This example, inspired by TableLens [328], shows a scatterplot matrix with two grid cells (and their corresponding rows and columns) magnified, with a corresponding shrinkage in other cells. (Image from [443], © 2004 Eurographics.)

11.3   A Unified Framework

For each interaction operator to be applied to a specified space/operand, several parameters are required. Some of these may be constants for a given system. The parameters are described below.

Focus. The location within the space at the center of the area of user interest. There may be multiple simultaneous foci, though for navigation this usually requires multiple display windows.

Extents. The range within the space (can be multidimensional) defining the boundaries of the interaction. The metric used for specifying the range is specific to the space; in screen space this would be in pixels, while in structure-space this might be the number of rows in a table or links in a graph.

Transformation. The function applied to the entities within the extents, generally a function of distance or offset from the focus. The shape of this transformation might also depend on the type of information being affected. For example, text distortion is more likely to have a flat peak to the transformation function. Another component of the transformation is the *degree* or scale factor for the transformation, thus allowing varying amounts of the specified action.

Blender. How to handle parts of space touched by more than one interaction. For selection, this operation may include performing logical operations on overlapping entities [287]. For distortion, Keahey and Robertson identify several approaches, including weighted average, maximal value, and composition [219]. Each has advantages in terms of smoothness and ease of interpretation.

In Figure 11.11 we show a pipeline depicting the structure of the generalized distortion process (similar figures can be generated for other forms of interaction). At each stage, the user can control any or all of the operator parameters described above. While no system implemented to date supports all of these pipeline components, most visualization systems support one or more of them, allowing users interactive control over one or more of the operator parameters. It should be noted that the order in which the operations are applied may be modified, although the screen space method is most intuitively placed last. The order of operation presented in Figure 11.11 seems to the authors to progress in an intuitive, progressive fashion, but experiments are needed to verify this hypothesis.

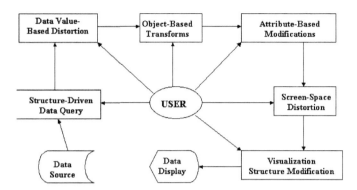

Figure 11.11.   The distortion pipeline. The user interactively controls each stage of the pipeline. Each distortion operation is optional. (Image from [443], © 2004 Eurographics.)

11.4 Summary

In this chapter we presented a framework for enveloping the wide assortment of interaction techniques developed to date for data and information visualization. By identifying the type of the operator (navigation, selection, manipulation, distortion, filtering) and the space of the interaction (screen, data value, data structure, attribute, object, or visualization structure), along with the parameters of the interaction operator (focus, extents, transformation, blender), we can define an extensive assortment of interaction operations. We also described a computational architecture to support interactions within the visualization pipeline.

Most visualization systems developed to date support, at most, a small set of interaction techniques. Future work should involve assessing user reactions to an environment containing a wider range of interaction operators. Questions to be addressed include:

- Given training in the use of individual interaction operations, how readily will users acquire expertise in composing interactions in different spaces?

- What combinations of operations will prove to be most effective, and in what situations?

- What are the best ways to provide users with unambiguous controls of the individual operations?

Initial experiments aimed at combining data value space and data structure space selection, navigation, and distortion within XmdvTool [138] have shown clear advantages to including all types of interaction; users are provided with many alternative ways of viewing and exploring their data sets, which can increase the likelihood of discovering features of interest. No problem in predicting the effects of the composition of operations has been discerned in this environment. We hope to expand this work into the other interaction spaces, and to attempt to answer the questions mentioned above, as well as others that arise during our investigations.

11.5   Related Readings

Several surveys and categorizations of interaction types in information visualization have been published, including the ones by Yi et al. [487] and Ward and Yang [443]. Individual types of interaction have also been the focus of surveys, including Leung and Apperley's excellent taxonomy of distortion techniques [268] and papers on selection by Wills [461], Resnick et al. [335], and Heer et al. [183]. Others have focused on interactions for a particular type of data visualization, such as networks [474] or have tried to identify some of the most difficult challenges for large-scale visual interactions [472]. Most other papers we reference focus on a single interaction operator within a particular visualization technique, though many are readily generalizable to other spaces.

11.6   Exercises

1. Give three examples of interaction operators in two distinct spaces generating identical or very similar results.

2. Give an example of two specific interaction operations in different spaces that are *commutative*, i.e., the results do not depend on the order of application. Give an example where they are *not* commutative. Are there any general rules you can think of for identifying the conditions under which commutativity would hold or not hold?

3. In most situations, the user should be able to control the magnitude of the operator being applied (e.g., magnification of distortion, step size in camera position). However, the initial amount should be set to some default level. Discuss how one might set defaults for different

kinds of interaction operations. Consider techniques that are driven by characteristics of the data as well as those independent of the data.

4. Related to the question above, discuss strategies to set the default *extents* for different kinds of interaction operations.

5. Give examples of distortions with 0th-, 1st-, and 2nd-order continuity. For what reasons might the user choose a particular continuity level?

6. Select a visualization tool with which you are familiar and examine the types of interaction it supports. List the interaction operators and operands, as well as the parameters of the interaction that the user can control.

7. Continuing the previous exercise, identify some interaction operators and operands *not* present in the tool that you feel would be useful additions to the system. Give an example of how they might be used.

11.7   Projects

Programming projects dealing with interaction are included in Chapter 12, which covers details of interaction techniques based on the concepts covered in this chapter.

Interaction Techniques

In this chapter, we discuss algorithm and implementation details pertaining to the interaction concepts described in Chapter 11. We give examples from each of the interaction spaces, and conclude with guidelines for implementing some of the user interaction dialogs needed to specify some of the types of interaction. Note that many of the algorithms discussed here could actually be applied to interactions in multiple spaces.

12.1 Screen Space

Screen-space distortion is a common tool for providing focus+context. We present one example of such a distortion: the fisheye lens [140]. The implementation of a fisheye lens is rather straightforward. One needs to specify a center point for the transformation (c_x, c_y) a lens radius r_l, and a deflection amount d. We then transform the coordinates of our image into polar coordinates relative to the center point. The lens effect is simply a transformation on the radius portion of the coordinates. One popular transformation is

$$r_{\text{new}} = s \log(1 + d * r_{\text{old}}), \tag{12.1}$$

where

$$s = \frac{r_l}{\log(1 + d * r_l)}. \tag{12.2}$$

This ensures that the radius component of points at the edge of the lens maintain their original value. Note that $\frac{1}{r_l} \leq d \leq 0.0$. The overall pseudocode for the algorithm is as follows:

1. Clear the output image.

2. For each pixel in the input image,

    (a) Compute the corresponding polar coordinates.

    (b) If the radius is less than the lens radius,

        i. Compute the new radius;

        ii. Get the color at this location in the original image;

        iii. Set the color of the pixel in the result image.

    (c) Else set result image pixel to that of original image.

Depending on the transformation used in screen space distortion, it is possible to either leave gaps or to cause pixels to overlap on the output image. While the overlaps do not cause much concern (in some implementations, these are averaged), the gaps need to be resolved via interpolation. Different functions give different shapes to the lens; for text visualization, it is common to use a piecewise linear function with a flat top to make reading easier.

12.2 Object Space (3D Surfaces)

One of the methods for navigating large document and data visualizations is via a perspective wall [283], which shows one panel of the view on a surface orthogonal to the viewing direction, with the rest of the panels oriented so they fade into the distance via perspective foreshortening. A simplistic version of the perspective wall can be created by noting that the front wall implements a horizontal scaling on a segment of the 2D image being mapped, while the adjacent segments are subjected to a horizontal and vertical scaling proportional to the distance to the edge of the front wall, along with a shearing transform. Thus if the left, center, and right sections of the original image to be plotted are bounded by $(x_0, x_{\text{left}}, x_{\text{right}}, x_1)$ and the left, center, and right panels of the result image are $(X_0, X_{\text{left}}, X_{\text{right}}, X_1)$, the transformation is as follows:

- for $x < x_{\text{left}}$:

$$x' = X_0 + (x - x_0) * \frac{(X_{\text{left}} - X_0)}{(x_{\text{left}} - x_0)},$$
$$y' = (X_{\text{left}} - x') + y \left(1 - \frac{(X_{\text{left}} - x')}{(X_{\text{left}} - X_0)}\right),$$

- for $x_{\text{left}} <= x < x_{\text{right}}$:

$$x' = X_{\text{left}} + (x - x_{\text{left}}) * \frac{(X_{\text{right}} - X_{\text{left}})}{(x_{\text{right}} - x_{\text{left}})},$$

$$y' = y,$$

- for $x >= x_{\text{right}}$:

$$x' = X_{\text{right}} + (x - x_{\text{right}}) * \frac{(X_1 - X_{\text{right}})}{(x_1 - x_{\text{right}})},$$

$$y' = (x' - X_{\text{right}}) + y \left(1 - \frac{(x' - X_{\text{right}})}{(X_1 - X_{\text{right}})} \right).$$

Given the perspective wall, the user could interact with it by sequential page movements (forward and backward), either one at a time or in a scanning or page-flipping manner. Indexes could also be used to jump to sections of interest, perhaps implemented as a tab sticking out of the top of the page at the start of each section. It might also be useful to have more than one page be in the direct focus, thus trading off some detail for a larger undistorted window on the data.

Other forms of exploration/navigation have similar needs. For example, a fly-through of a medical data set representing the human heart or digestive system would require controls to specify direction and rate of motion, as well as the field of view. However, flying through the vessels at any significant speed might cause problems in terms of staying within the vessel; as anyone who has played with a 3D simulator for a car or airplane can tell you, it can be very challenging to control motion in such a way as to avoid collisions. For visualization fly-throughs, we therefore may want to automate the path of motion, and maybe even to force the user to maintain a fixed orientation (to avoid spinning). For vessels in a volume data set, this would involve finding the central point of each slice of the vessel and linking these positions together between frames. This, however, can lead to a rather jerky flight path, as slices in a volume are not always aligned perfectly, and segmentation of the boundaries of the vessel can introduce inaccuracies from one frame to the next. This can require the introduction of *smoothing* operations.

The smoothing of a path of discrete points can be performed in a number of ways. The simplest method is to perform one or more passes of *neighborhood averaging*, whereby each point on the path is replaced by the average of some number of points before and after it, such as,

$$p'_i = (p_{i-1} + p_{i+1})/2,$$

or
$$p_i' = (p_{i-1} + p_i + p_{i+1})/3.$$

Using larger neighborhoods or multiple passes of averaging can result in increasingly smoother paths, but there is an increased risk of moving outside the vessel, especially in regions of high curvature. Inserting constraints, such as repulsion forces from vessel boundaries, can alleviate this problem, at the cost of more complex processing. Another approach involves fitting the points to a parametric curve, which can then be used to plot a path with arbitrary levels of smoothness. For example, the points could be used as control points for a Bézier curve or B-spline. Additional control points could be added to achieve desired shape properties for the path.

Fully automated navigation techniques have also been explored. One popular method within multivariate statistical graphics is Asimov's grand tour [22], which generates a sequence of projections of high-dimensional data into two or three dimensions for visualization (see Chapter 11 for an example); the path is designed such that every possible projection (constrained only by a step size) will eventually be visited, and adjacent projections differ so slightly in the viewing parameters that smooth motion is perceived. The process is as follows.

For those of you who have studied computer graphics, you know that a rotation of points in 3D around the z-axis is accomplished by multiplying a vector representation of each point by the following matrix:

$$\begin{pmatrix} \cos\alpha & \sin\alpha & 0 & 0 \\ -\sin\alpha & \cos\alpha & 0 & 0 \\ 0 & 0 & 1 & 0 \\ 0 & 0 & 0 & 1 \end{pmatrix}.$$

This extends to an arbitrary number of dimensions by having all diagonal elements set to 1 except for the two dimensions involved in the planar rotation, which are set to the cosine of the angle of rotation. Likewise, the off-diagonal values are all set to 0 apart from the two entries with positive and negative values of the sine for the angle of rotation. Any arbitrary rotation can be specified by multiplying all the transformation matrices for pairwise planar rotation, e.g.,

$$Q(\theta_{0,1}, \theta_{0,2}, \ldots, \theta_{d-1,d}) = R_{0,1}(\theta_{0,1}) * R_{0,2}(\theta_{0,2}) * \ldots * R_{d-1,d}(\theta_{d-1,d}),$$

where $R_{i,j}\theta_{i,j}$ is the rotation matrix for the dimension pair (i, j) for a rotation angle of $\theta_{i,j}$. The total number of rotation angles and matrices required is

$n * (n - 1)/2$, where n is the number of dimensions in the data. Once the rotation is performed on each point, we can project the data to 2D or 3D, depending on the type of display we are using. By sequencing the changes in the angles $\theta_{i,j}$ such that the difference between adjacent angle vectors is small, we can obtain smooth animation. Several algorithms for generating a space-filling sequence of angle vectors have been proposed, such as

$$\theta(t) = (\lambda_0 t, \lambda_1 t, \dots, \lambda_p t),$$

where $(\lambda_0, \lambda_1, \dots, \lambda_p)$ is a sequence of mutually irrational real numbers and $\lambda_i t$ is interpreted modulo 2π [455]. Other techniques allow users to perform partial tours by eliminating changes in some planes or allowing the user to control the speed of change, though at a risk of losing the effect of continuity.

12.3   Data Space (Multivariate Data Values)

Data space transformations are actually quite common in data analysis and visualization. Some typical functions include:

- scaling and translating to fit a particular range of values;

- exponential or log scaling to spread or compress the distribution of the data;

- sinusoidal functions to help study cyclic behavior;

- absolute value transformation to focus on magnitudes of change;

- negating the values so that low values become high, and vice versa.

A key requirement for these and other types of transformations is that the user be made aware that a transformation on the data has occurred. It is all too common that a data set is modified without the viewer being informed of this modification. Clear labeling of axes is essential; augmenting the visualization with a note describing any data transforms that have been applied reduces the chances of misinterpretation. Another key requirement is to translate and scale the resulting data values to fall within an acceptable range for the graphical entities and attributes being rendered. Failure to incorporate this transformation can result in objects being mapped off the display, color wrap-around, negative values for graphical attributes, and other undesirable artifacts.

12.4   Attribute Space (Properties of Graphical Entities)

As mentioned in Chapter 11, a great many interactions on attributes have direct equivalents with interactions in data space. Examples include global or local scaling, boundary enhancement, and color equalization. However, in some situations it makes more intuitive sense to consider the interaction to be simply on the graphical representation of the data, rather than the data itself. Thus, for example, when enlarging a data glyph of interest, the intuition is that you are not changing the data, just modifying the attributes of the glyph. There is also some overlap between the actions in attribute space and those in screen space, as the previous example hints at. If the glyph is not overlapping other glyphs, the enlarging can be based on pixel operations, rather than scaling the drawing primitives. In attribute space, however, you are more likely to avoid blocky artifacts that are typical of pixel-oriented zooming operations.

Perhaps the widest range of attribute space interactions involves modification of the color and opacity attributes. Techniques such as contrast enhancement, color histogram equalization, and others have been designed to make better use of the color space and make features of the data more readily perceived. For example, via controls for contrast and brightness, we can emphasize certain regions of the data to attract the attention of the analyst and make feature detection, classification, or measurement easier (see Figure 12.1).

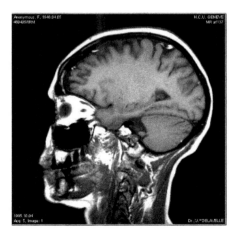 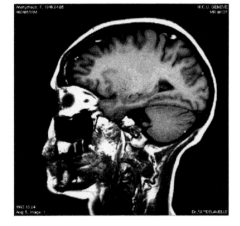

Figure 12.1.   Example of modifying the contrast and brightness of an image to emphasize certain features.

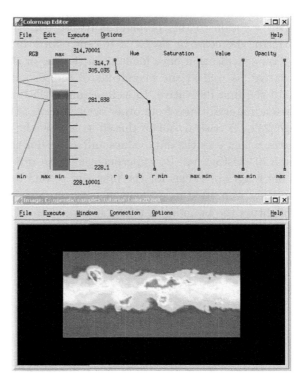

Figure 12.2.　　The interactive color map editor from OpenDX, and the effect of inserting rapid changes in the hue over a small range of data values.

Interactive tools for specifying and modifying transfer functions are widely used in volume rendering to control color and opacity to help reveal structures in volumetric data. In their simplest form, such tools consist of a visual representation of a function plotting data value (horizontal axis) versus opacity or a color component (hue, saturation, value), as shown in Figure 12.2. The user is allowed to insert and move control points, with the resulting function being a piecewise linear plot through adjacent control points. This can be tricky, though, since even small changes in the transfer function can result in significant changes in the visualization. Another problem with such a strategy is that basing the color or opacity strictly on the data value can result in visual artifacts caused by noise or variability within the data. For example, a particular data value might indicate one type of material in a section of the data set, but another type of material in a different section, due to lighting differences.

One solution to this problem is to use more than just the data value to control the color or opacity. Recent efforts in semi-automatic transfer function specification have focused on the use of the magnitude of the first derivative, as well as the magnitude of the second derivative in the direction of the first derivative, to isolate values that correspond to boundaries between material types from other occurrences of the specific value or value range [242]. A critical tool for this effort is what the authors term a *histogram volume*, which uses the data values and values for the first two derivatives to form a 3D histogram. By experimenting with different methods for breaking the ranges of values for the first and second derivatives into histogram bins, they were able to develop opacity functions that proved effective at highlighting the boundaries in the volume data. This also helped filter out spurious occurrences of values that were the same or similar to the values associated with a material of interest, as the signatures of the derivatives would be different than at a material boundary.

12.5   Data Structure Space (Components of Data Organization)

Most of the common structures for data (i.e., ordering, grids, grouping, hierarchies, and networks) have logical operations that users will want to interactively perform. In terms of the implementation, the main decisions to be made are the degree to which the operation can or should be automated, and whether the interactions will be specified directly on the visualization or in a separate dialog box. For automatic techniques, one must evaluate the tradeoffs between thorough, time-consuming techniques versus quick, yet suboptimal methods. In this section we will examine some of the design decisions that need to be made in providing these sorts of interactive operations.

Consider dimension ordering in multivariate data visualization. Fully manual techniques might involve manipulating text entries in a list, either via shifting operations (move up, move down) or drag-and-drop methods. In some visualizations, such as parallel coordinates or scatterplot matrices, direct manipulation of the axes may be possible. In the case of the scatterplot matrix, the movement of one element of the matrix would entail changes to entire rows and columns, in order to preserve the symmetry along the diagonal plots.

Automated dimension reordering requires at least two major design decisions: how do you measure the goodness of an ordering, and what strategy will you use to search for good orderings? Many measures are possible. One commonly used one is the sum of the correlation coefficients between each pair of dimensions. The *correlation coefficient* between two dimensions is defined as follows:

$$\rho_{X,Y} = \frac{\sum(x_i y_i - n\mu_X \mu_Y)}{(n-1)\sigma_X \sigma_Y},$$

where n is the number of data points, X and Y are the two dimensions, x_I and y_i are the values for the ith data point, μ_X is the mean value for X, and σ_X is the standard deviation for X. Other statistical measures of similarity between dimensions include the correlation ratio and the mutual information.

Another measure of goodness could involve the ease of interpretation. Different dimension orders can result in displays with more or less visual clutter or structure [317]. For example, one might conjecture that when using star or profile glyphs to represent data points, simpler shapes would be easier to analyze than complex shapes. Thus, if one could measure the average or cumulative shape complexity, e.g., by counting the number of concavities or peaks in the shape, this could be used to compare the visual complexity of two different dimension orders. An example of this is shown in Figure 12.3.

Once a goodness measure has been selected, the second big challenge is to find an effective and efficient search strategy. Enumerating all possible dimension orders is expensive for situations other than when the number of

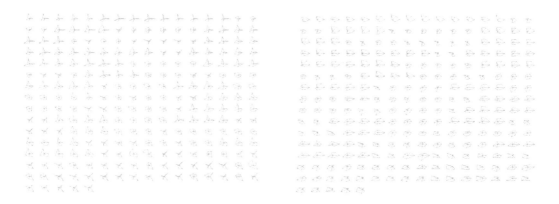

Figure 12.3.   Example of shape simplification via dimension reordering. The left image shows the original order, while the right image shows the results of reordering to reduce concavities and increase the percentage of symmetric shapes. (Image from [317], © 2004 IEEE.)

dimensions is quite small, as there are $N!$ distinct orderings. This can be divided by 2, as one assumes that the inverse of an ordering will have the same goodness measure, but it is still a large number for even a moderate number of dimensions. The typical strategy used in such situations is to explore the field of *optimization* and its extensive range of techniques. As the dimension ordering problem is similar to the *traveling salesman problem* [265], many of the strategies developed for that problem are directly applicable. One of the simplest to implement works as follows.

1. Select two different dimensions at random.

2. Swap their positions and evaluate, using the goodness measure.

3. If this measure is worse than that computed for the original order, undo the swap.

4. Repeat steps 1–3 either a fixed number of iterations, or until some number of tests are performed with no improvement.

Such heuristic approaches, while certainly not optimal, will often find solutions that are reasonable. One can easily envision a hybrid manual-automatic approach where users could set some of the ordering manually based on their knowledge of the data and let the system automatically refine things from that starting position. Likewise, when an automated method gets stuck in a suboptimal peak or valley, the user might insert a change and then resume the automated search. There are many opportunities in visual exploration and design where such optimizations can come in handy, which suggests that students in the visualization field should add algorithms for optimization to their set of useful tools.

12.6   Visualization Structure Space (Components of the Data Visualization)

Several of the techniques described earlier can be readily adapted to work in visualization structure space. For example, the fisheye lens technique in screen space could just as easily be used in any of the visualization structures with sequences or grids of components; we could use the same distortion function to adjust the spacing between axes in parallel coordinates or the size of the grid cells in scatterplot matrices or TableLens. As another example, we might adapt data clustering, filtering, or optimization actions (both manual and automated) to select and organize sets of visualizations on the screen, such as the results of performing volume visualization with hundreds or thousands of different parameter sets. Even drill-down, roll-up operations can be effectively utilized in multi-component visualizations that are hierarchically structured. One key is to make sure the user is aware at all times of the operations that can be done on the structure of the visualization, using consistent icons, labels, and visual representations that the user can quickly learn to use. Another key is to use smooth transitions between visualizations, as is discussed in more detail in the next section.

12.7 Animating Transformations

Virtually all user interactions within visualization systems will result in a change in the image being viewed. Some of these changes will be quite dramatic, such as when opening a new data set. Others may keep some aspects of the view the same, while changing other aspects. In situations where the user needs to maintain context while having his or her attention drawn toward the change, it is best to provide smooth transitions between the initial and final visualizations. Thus, for example, when rotating a three-dimensional object or data set, smoothly changing the orientation is generally better than simply jumping to the final orientation. In some cases, this might involve simply a linear interpolation between the starting and ending configurations, perhaps with the number of intermediate views dependent on the magnitude of the change. In some cases, however, linear interpolation does not result in a constant rate of change (such as moving a camera along a curved path). In addition, in most cases, a more appealing result can be obtained by performing smooth acceleration and deceleration of the change, rather than a constant velocity change. In this section we will discuss the algorithms necessary to achieve this control of changes. Students interested in a detailed exposure to these concepts will find them in textbooks on computer animation, such as [313].

The first step is to get a uniform parameterization of the variable or variables you wish to control during the animation. For some variables, such as position along a straight line, or a scaling transform, linear interpolation does provide consistent changes in successive equal time steps. For others, such as position along a curved path, we need to recast the problem using a new parameter. Assume that the original parameter is a function of t, which goes from 0 to 1. For example, we might use a cubic polynomial to calculate the x- or y-position for different values of t, as in $x(t) = At^3 + Bt^2 + Ct + D$

(a similar function can be used to compute $y(t)$). We can then create a list of positions p_i, for $0 \leq i \leq n$, where n is the number of steps between the initial position and the final position. By dividing t into n equal subintervals, we simply insert the appropriate values of t in the parametric equations above. We can then estimate the arc length A by summing the distances between successive points:

$$A = \sum_{i=1}^{i=n} \text{dist}(p_{i-1}, p_i).$$

Clearly, the smaller the step size between adjacent points, the more accurate the estimate of the arc length.

Note that for most curves, the distances between adjacent points will vary. Thus, if we simply used the positions directly in our animation, the user would perceive the speed as varying, rather than a uniform velocity. While computing the arc length, it is also useful to compute for each point p_i, the corresponding d_i, or the distance from the start of the curve to the point. We can then compute the function

$$A(i) = d_i/A,$$

which is the percentage of the distance traveled at the ith time step. To keep things simple, we use t instead of i, with $0.0 <= t <= 1.0$. We define a new parameter, $s = A(t)$, for use as follows.

We store these results in a table so that for each value of t, we know the value of $A(t)$. We can then use s to generate a uniform velocity by dividing the arc length A into even step sizes, where the number of steps corresponds to the number of frames to be used in the animation. Because it represents the percentage of the arc length, s falls in the range $0.0 \leq s \leq 1.0$. If we divide s into equal steps based on the number of frames, we then can look though the table of percentages of distance traveled to find the values of $A(t)$ that are on either side of the desired percentage. We perform a linear interpolation to estimate the value of t that approximates the desired distance. This value of t will then correspond to the appropriate value for s, or in other words,

$$t = A^{-1}s.$$

The above process is known as *reparameterization*. The parameter s now gives us a mechanism to control velocity. If we plot s versus time, we will get a straight line from the origin $0, 0$ to $(1.0, 1.0)$; in other words, when time starts, we are in the original position, and when time hits 1.0, we are at the end position. The velocity is simply the slope of this line. But what happens if this line is curved, rather than straight? For parts of the curve that have a low slope, the velocity will be low, while a steep slope will indicate high velocity. As long as the start and end points are fixed, we're assured of finishing where we want. There are an infinite number of possibilities, including stopping for some duration along the way. The main assumption is that the curve is monotonically increasing, so that the position can't go beyond the arc length and shouldn't (for now) involve going backward. A commonly used curve for controlling animation involves an *ease-in, ease-out* behavior, where one accelerates from a velocity of 0 to a *cruising speed*, and then decelerates to a speed of 0 when approaching the destination. Segments of a sine wave, with a straight line between them, can be used to approximate this behavior. The key is to maintain a smooth curve. Examples are shown in Figure 12.4.

Sometimes it is easier to specify the movement with a *velocity* curve. As we noted, the velocity is simply the first derivative of the position curve. A velocity curve for the ease-in, ease-out behavior would simply be a straight segment with positive slope starting at 0, a segment with a slope of 0, and then a segment with negative slope ending on 0 (see Figure 12.5). The key to note is that the area under this curve must equal 1.0, so that if the cruising speed is high, the amount of time spent speeding up or slowing down must be larger, to ensure that the ending position is correct. Similarly, it is clear

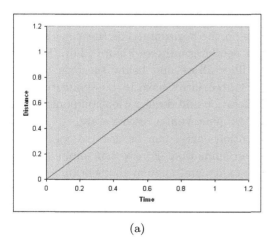

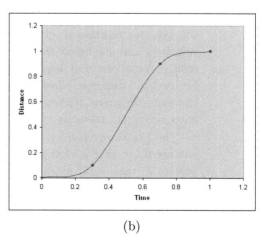

(a)   (b)

Figure 12.4.   Examples of position curves: (a) shows constant velocity; (b) shows ease-in, ease-out behavior.

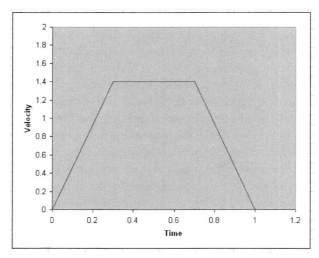

Figure 12.5.   Example of a velocity curve corresponding to the position curve, with ease-in, ease-out movement.

that there is a minimum cruising velocity that must be achieved to reach the ending point within the time allotted.

A third type of curve that is sometimes used to control movement is an *acceleration* curve. This is simply the second derivative of the position curve, or the first derivative of the velocity curve. The shape of the ease-in, ease-out acceleration curve is simply three horizontal line segments, one above the axis (for positive acceleration), one on the horizontal axis (for constant velocity), and one below the access (for deceleration) (see Figure 12.6). The relative positions and lengths of the lines above and below the axis can be used for different effects, and don't necessarily have to be symmetric. However, the areas defined by the acceleration and deceleration components must be equal, to ensure starting and stopping from a resting state.

The position, velocity, and acceleration curves can be used to control any attribute that is changing during an animation. Forces that mimic the physics of real-world motion, such as gravity and angular momentum, can be used in the equations to provide dynamics that ease the interpretation of the changes and maintain continuity over time. This is especially important when occlusion is possible, since the normal expectation would be that motion of unseen objects is consistent with that present when the objects are visible.

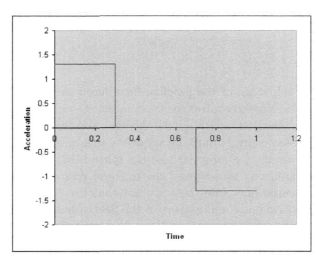

Figure 12.6.   Example of an acceleration curve corresponding to the position curve, with ease-in, ease-out movement.

12.7.1 Animation Pseudocode

The following pseudocode renders a scatterplot of circles that animates over time between two sets of x, y, and r (radius) dimensions using linear interpolation. The *numFrames* argument specifies the number of frames of animation to be used for the transition animation, and *delay* specifies a delay in milliseconds between frames.

SCATTERPLOT-ANIMATE($xDim1, yDim1, rDim1, xDim2, yDim2, rDim2,$
$$cDim, rMin, rMax, numFrames, delay)$$

```
1   for each frame f from 0 to numFrames
2       do for each record i ▷ For each record,
3           do x1 ← NORMALIZE(i, xDim1) ▷ derive first state,
4              y1 ← NORMALIZE(i, yDim1)
5              r1 ← NORMALIZE(i, rDim1, rMin, rMax)
6              x2 ← NORMALIZE(i, xDim2) ▷ derive second state,
7              y2 ← NORMALIZE(i, yDim2)
8              r2 ← NORMALIZE(i, rDim2, rMin, rMax)
9              p ← f/numFrames ▷ compute percent complete,
10             x ← x1 + (x2 − x1) ∗ p ▷ and current state.
11             y ← y1 + (y2 − y1) ∗ p
12             r ← r1 + (r2 − r1) ∗ p
13             MAPCOLOR(i, cDim) ▷ Derive color, then
14             CIRCLE(x, y, r) ▷ draw the record as a circle.
15      SLEEP(delay) ▷ Pause between frames.
```

12.8   Interaction Control

At each stage of the pipeline introduced in Chapter 11, the user requires mechanisms to control the type, location, and level of each interaction as he or she navigates within both the data and the visualization. The realization of these controls must be intuitive, unambiguous, and at a level of detail and accuracy appropriate for the space being operated upon. In particular, the following lists typical controls and reasonable candidates for their implementation. Note these are not the only choices; indeed, there exists an extensive body of literature in the field of human-computer interaction dedicated to design strategies for such interfaces, to which the interested reader is directed.

Focus selection. Selection is most readily accomplished via direct manipulation tools, e.g., using a mouse or other selection device to indicate the focus location. In screen and object space, this can be easily accomplished via normal selection operations. In data space, an n-dimensional location might need to be indicated. Depending on the method of display, this could involve multiple selections (e.g., selecting in a scatterplot matrix only enables simultaneous specification of two dimensions). In attribute and structure space, one first needs a graphical depiction of the structure or the range of the attribute, such as a display of a tree or table, or a curve showing the range of colors in the color map. Finally, the focus can be specified implicitly, by assuming that the focus is the center of the extents of the interaction, which can be specified as outlined below.

Extent selection. Specifying the extents for an interaction is generally dependent on the type of interaction and the space in which the interaction is being applied, and can be done either via direct manipulation or separate interface tools. It may be specified via a single value (e.g., a radius or maximum number of items) or via a vector of values (e.g., a range for each data dimension or a set of constraints). In many systems, the extents are often hard-coded to reduce the effort in performing the operation.

Interaction type selection. Given the many types of interaction possible, and the variety of spaces in which they may be applied, a reasonable interface for this task would be a pair of menus: one to select the space, and the other to specify the general class of the interaction. Icons or buttons in the user interface could also be used, as the number of choices would normally be modest.

Interaction level selection. The degree of interaction is an important control parameter that can be specified by a single value (e.g., the magnitude of scaling that will occur at the focal point). A slider or dial is sufficient for this activity, along with a button to reset the operation to its minimum level. A direct manipulation equivalent would be to associate upward mouse motions with an increased interaction level, perhaps in conjunction with direct manipulation of the extents via horizontal mouse motions.

Blender type selection. If more than one interaction can be simultaneously viewed and manipulated, there must be some mechanism for selecting a strategy for mixing regions of space affected by more than one interaction. As with interaction-type selection, this is best accomplished via a menu of options. Available options might be dependent on both the space in which the interaction is occurring and the type of interaction being used. As interactions in different spaces are applied at different points in the pipeline, it is necessary to consider methods for controlling the combination of interactions involving two or more spaces.

An important feature that should be present in all operations is the animation of interpolated values of the interaction parameters as they are changed. This has been shown to be extremely effective in many implementations of operators for helping users to both preserve context and to obtain a better understanding of the effects of the operation on the data [435]. Rapid changes can lead to confusion and a loss of orientation, especially when interactively exploring large data or information repositories. Related to this, users should have some control over the rate of this animation (the number of frames or steps in the interpolation).

12.8.1 Algorithms for Selection

The following pseudocode derives a set of selected records in a scatterplot based on a selection rectangle created by the user. This could be readily extended to other spaces as well. Hashing or other access/indexing functions could help avoid scanning the entire data set.

SCATTERPLOT-SELECT($xDim, yDim, xMin, xMax, yMin, yMax$)
```
1   s ← ∅▷ Initialize the set of records
2   for each record i ▷ For each record,
3       do x ← NORMALIZE(i, xDim) ▷ derive the location,
4          y ← NORMALIZE(i, yDim)
5          if xMin < x < xMax and yMin < y < yMax
6             do s ← s ∪ i ▷ select points within the rectangle.
7   return s
```

The next pseudocode determines whether a point is in a given polygon. This task is essential in determining, for example, which polygon in a choropleth map or glyph in a scatterplot is under a given mouse location. The code uses the even-odd rule algorithm [130], which counts the number of times a ray coming from the point to be tested intersects faces of the polygon. If the ray intersects the polygon an odd number of times, then the point is inside the polygon.

POINT-IN-POLYGON($xs, ys, numPoints, x, y$)
```
1   j ← numPoints − 1
2   oddNodes ←false
3   for i ← 0 to numPoints − 1
4       do if ys[i] < y and ys[j] >= y or ys[j] < y and ys[i] >= y
5             do if xs[i] + (y − ys[i])/(ys[j] − ys[i]) ∗ (xs[j] − xs[i]) < x
6                   do oddNodes ← not oddNodes
7          j ← i
8   return oddNodes
```

12.9   Related Readings

Theo Pavlidis wrote an excellent book on algorithms for computer graphics [315] that is still being referenced more than 30 years after publication. A good overview of distortion algorithms can be found in an article by Leung and Apperley [268]. For developing efficient indexing structures to access data, Samet's book [357] is a standard reference. Standard textbooks on databases and computational geometry are also useful, both for organizing information and performing some of the computations mentioned in this chapter. A number of researchers have also studied methods to smoothly animate between views in data visualization, including Heer and Robertson [180] and Van Wijk and Nuij [435].

New devices are also leading to new ideas for ways of interacting with visualizations, with multi-touch [363] and gesture recognition [296] as two prime examples.

Many of the success stories in developing interaction techniques in data visualization have their roots in the field of human-computer interaction. Indeed, most modern textbooks in the field dedicate one or more chapters to the design of graphical user interfaces. Some popular texts include *Human-Computer Interaction* [94], *Interaction Design: Beyond Human-Computer Interaction* [373], and *Designing the User Interface: Strategies for Effective Human-Computer Interaction* [374].

12.10 Exercises

1. Describe the spaces and interaction techniques in which you feel the fisheye lens algorithm could be effectively applied.

2. Given a census data set, describe three or more ways you might order the dimensions prior to visualization. What are the strengths and weaknesses of each? You may use the U.S. County Census data set available on the book web site or at the http://www.openindicators.org web page.

3. When animating a given change, the number of frames over which the change takes place can have a significant impact on the user's comprehension and satisfaction. Describe the problems that can occur when changes are too fast or too slow, and describe some of the criteria you would use for automatically determining the duration of the animation.

4. Describe two or more distinct options for animating the shifting of focus on a perspective wall display (*Hint*: just changing the speed is not sufficiently distinct). Indicate what you feel are the strengths and weaknesses of each.

12.11 Projects

1. Implement a screen space distortion that is shaped like a truncated pyramid, e.g., it is flat on top and has linear ramps on the edges. Note that such a distortion would be much more appropriate for viewing text than the more common lens effects.

2. Implement a set of data space transformations for a line plotting program. Make sure the resulting data values fall within the range of your display. Test the program on several 1D data sets.

3. Implement an attribute space transformation that sets the opacity of a glyph or scatterplot element based on how close one of its data dimensions is to a user-specified value. For example, if the value specified is 0.5 and the first data dimension is selected, then points for which that data dimension is at 0.0 or 1.0 should have an opacity of 0.5.

4. Modify the program above to enable a *range of influence* to be specified. This means that the opacity would be set to 0.0 for points whose value is further than the range of influence from the selected value. Thus, distant points would be transparent, unless the range of influence is very large.

5. Choose one type of distortion (i.e., in one of the interaction spaces) and implement it, along with controls for specifying focus, extents, and transformation. Focus can be controlled by the mouse or via a dialog box. Extents should just be one or more sliders that convey a size parameter. Transformation should be a list of possible types of transformation. This implies that you must implement at least two such transforms, so that you can switch among them.

6. Extend the above system so that smooth animation is used between the undistorted and distorted views. The user should be allowed to control the rate of the animation. What range of rates do you think is most effective or aesthetically pleasing?

7. Repeat Projects 5 and 6 in a different interaction space.

8. Repeat Projects 5 and 6 using filtering rather than distortion.

CHAPTER 13

Designing Effective Visualizations

The goal of this chapter is to provide some guidelines for designing successful visualizations. A successful visualization is one that efficiently and accurately conveys the desired information to the targeted audience, while bearing in mind the task or purpose of the visualization (exploration, confirmation, presentation). For any particular set of data there is a myriad of possible methods for mapping data components to graphical entities and attributes. Similarly, there exists a wide range of interactive tools that the user may be provided. Selecting the most effective combinations of techniques is by no means a straightforward process.

A visualization may be ineffective for a number of reasons. It might be too confusing or complex to be interpreted by the intended audience, or some of the data may have been distorted, occluded, or lost during the mapping process. Other signs of deficient visualizations are the lack of support for view modification or color map control. Even aesthetics can influence the success of a visualization; a visually unappealing presentation can affect an audience's willingness to look at the images. In each of the above cases, some component of the visualization is interfering with the delivery of information to the user.

This chapter first presents design considerations for the components that the authors feel are necessary for a good visualization. Following this, we explore some of the common problems found in visualizations and propose some techniques for avoiding these problems. We summarize by revisiting some of the issues presented in Chapter 3 and indicate how they fit into the visualization design process. At a recent visualization conference, it was stated that it is much easier to make bad visualizations than good ones. Hopefully, through reading this chapter, visualization designers will gain some of the skills necessary to make design decisions leading to effective visualizations.

The ideas and techniques presented in this chapter come from not only the authors' experiences, but also from the vast body of literature on designing good visualizations. Readers are encouraged to study one or more of the books on this subject, as listed in the Related Readings section.

13.1 Steps in Designing Visualizations

Creating a visualization involves deciding how to map the data fields to graphical attributes, selecting and implementing methods for modifying views, and choosing how much data to visualize. Additional information regarding the data being shown (e.g., labels) and the mapping (e.g., a color key) are also essential to facilitate interpretation, and must be integrated into the visualization. The final, less tangible, consideration is the overall aesthetics of the resulting display. In this section we present, for each of these design stages, some issues that should be addressed by the visualization designer.

13.1.1 Intuitive Mappings from Data to Visualization

To create the most effective visualization for a particular application, it is critical to consider the semantics of the data and the context of the typical user. By selecting data-to-graphics mappings that cater to the user's domain-specific mental model, the interpretation of the resulting image will be greatly facilitated. In addition, the more consistent the designer is in predicting the user's expectations, the less chance there will be for misinterpretation. Intuitive mappings also lead to more rapid interpretation, as translation time is reduced. For example, in Figure 13.1, images of planets are used to plot the relationship between the distance from the planet to the sun and the duration of its orbit.

Mapping spatial data attributes, such as longitude and latitude, to screen position is perhaps the most common and intuitive mapping found in visualizations. Some of the earliest visualizations took advantage of the ability of humans to correlate position on the drawing medium with position in the three-dimensional world. Likewise, with the advent of animation, it is obvious that displaying temporally related data sets via animation is reasonably intuitive, with the added advantage of allowing time to vary in both speed and direction.

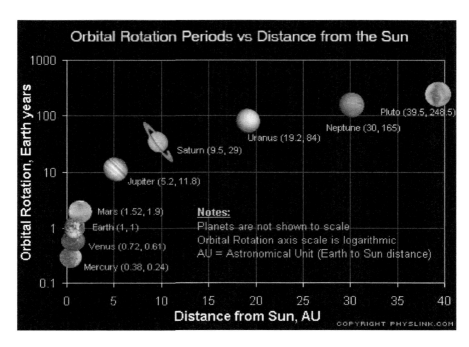

Figure 13.1.   Using intuitive scatterplot symbols to show the distance from planets to the sun versus the duration of a single orbit. (Image from http://www.physlink.com.)

Other mappings become intuitive when associated with a particular context. For example, mapping temperature to color is fairly common, as many cultures associate red or white with high temperatures. Color has specific interpretations in fields such as cartography (land use classification) and geology (stratigraphic layer classification), and thus the application domain for the visualization may dictate the logical use for the color attribute.

Height, or alternatively the length of a line, is another useful mapping for temperature, as we associate temperature with the readout on thermometers. In fact, for medical practitioners, it may be intuitive to use length for displaying pressure or any other scalar value (e.g., the patient readouts in the *Star Trek* sick bay).

One of the important considerations when selecting a mapping is the compatibility between the scale of the data field and that of the graphical entity or attribute. For ordered data attributes (e.g., age), it is not reasonable to select a graphical attribute that is not ordered, such as shape. Similarly, unordered data attributes (e.g., country of origin) should not be mapped to ordered attributes (e.g., length).

With that said, it is, however, sometimes interesting to examine data with nonintuitive mappings, as the resulting image may expose an interesting attribute in the data. For example, mapping time to color along a streakline can reveal variations in particle speeds that might otherwise be difficult to detect. Thus a good rule of thumb is to set the default mappings based on the most intuitive selection according to the typical user, but, especially for exploratory tasks, to permit user customization.

13.1.2 Selecting and Modifying Views

Except for fairly simple data sets, one view is rarely sufficient to convey all the information contained in the data. The key to developing an effective visualization is to be able to anticipate the types of views and view modifications that will be of most use to the typical user, and then provide intuitive controls for setting and customizing the views. Useful views, as mentioned earlier, depend heavily on the type of data being presented, and the task associated with the visualization. Each supported view should be clearly labeled, and selecting a new view should require minimal actions on the user's part.

View modifications fall into a number of categories, and their inclusion as part of the functionality should be considered based on user priorities.

- Scrolling and zooming operations are needed if the entire data set cannot be presented at the resolution desired by the user.

- Color map control is almost always desirable, minimally supporting a set of different palettes, and preferably offering the user control of either individual colors or the complete palette.

- Mapping control allows users to switch between different ways of visualizing the same data. Features of the data that are hidden in one mapping may stand out in others (Figure 13.2).

- Scale control permits the user to modify the range and distribution of values for a particular data field prior to its mapping. Similarly, clipping and other forms of filtering allow the user to focus on data subsets.

- Level-of-detail controls provide the ability to eliminate or highlight detail, supporting views at different levels of abstraction. Depending on the task at hand, a user may need to repeatedly switch between several distinct levels (Figure 13.3).

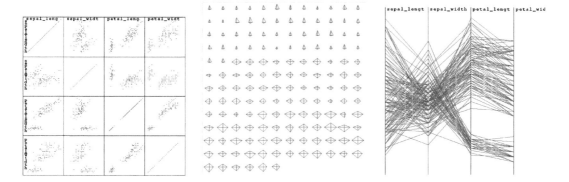

Figure 13.2.   Three views of the Iris data set (scatterplot matrix, star glyphs, and parallel coordinates). (Image from XmdvTool.)

In all cases, it is essential that the view manipulations be implemented in a manner that is easy for the user to remember, and that provides suitable accuracy for the task. If possible, direct manipulation (specifying changes on the image itself rather than a separate control or command line) is generally preferred. For example, mouse motion could be mapped to panning, with button clicks invoking zoom operations (See Chapters 11 and 12).

13.1.3   Information Density—When Is It Too Much or Too Little?

One of the key decisions one makes when designing a visualization is determining how much information to display. This gives rise to two extreme situations. The first, which might be called "gratuitous graphics," occurs when there is very little information to present. Many examples of graphics

Figure 13.3.   Levels of detail in maps. (Images courtesy of Google Maps © 2008 Google; map data © 2008 NAVTEQ™.)

can be found that convey only two or three distinct values, such as the percentage of males and females within a particular sample (this actually can be communicated with one number). Others can be found that "pad" the number of pieces of information by deriving additional quantities, such as showing two numbers, their sum, and their difference. In cases such as these, it is often more effective to simply display the quantitative values as text. This requires much less screen real estate (which in many applications is quite valuable), while still getting the message across. It must be remembered that simply because one *can* create a visualization doesn't imply that one *must* do so.

The other extreme, trying to convey too much information, is also a common problem. Excessive information content can lead to confusion, intimidation, and difficulties in interpretation on the part of the viewer. Important information contained within the data can be lost or deemphasized on a cluttered display, and viewers may have a hard time determining where to focus their attention.

There are many effective solutions to the problem of excessive information content in a visualization. One method is to give the user the option of disabling or enabling different components of the display. In this manner, a user can decide which parts are most important to her, and can have the less important information displayed on demand. Another solution is to use multiple screens, either as disjoint panes or with partial occlusion. This method makes better use of screen space, while making each of the individual pieces of data readily available.

Another common cause of cluttered displays is large or unevenly distributed data sets. As mentioned in the previous section, data sets may be filtered to remove uninteresting data points, allowing the user to concentrate only on the significant parts. Similarly, uneven distributions, which might lead to some parts of the screen being congested, while others are sparsely populated, can sometimes be rectified through scaling of one or more data dimensions.

13.1.4   Keys, Labels, and Legends

A common problem with many visualizations is that insufficient information is provided to the user to allow unambiguous and accurate interpretation. This supporting information should begin with a detailed caption indicating the particular data fields being displayed, and the mappings that were used. Additionally, grid or tick marks should be displayed to convey the ranges and

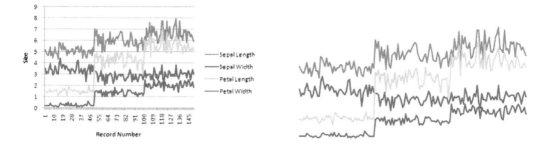

Figure 13.4.   A complex visualization with and without captions/ticks/legends.

values of interest for numeric fields when absolute judgments are important, and all axes should be labeled with appropriate units. If symbols are being used, a key must be provided, either along the border of the display or within a separate widget. Finally, if color has a significance, sufficient information must be available to allow easy interpretation (e.g., via a labeled color bar). Figure 13.4 highlights the importance of this supplementary information.

The use of grid and tick marks can be both a boon and a curse to the visualization. Poor choices of the types of markings and the density used can occlude the data being displayed and lead to a cluttered appearance. Figure 13.5 shows three degrees of markings. Clearly, one should avoid the extremes.

The actual positions of the markings can also have a bearing on how readily the data is interpreted. Based on the semantics of the data, certain gaps between markings may make more sense to the user than others. Unfortunately, the default values used by some visualization tools may make correct interpretation difficult (Figure 13.6).

The designer must also decide which range of values is to be displayed (this decision may have been made in an earlier stage). There is always the risk of misinterpretation when the expected range of values is not shown. For example, when dealing with a percentage, most users would expect the display to range from 0 to 100. However, in many cases this would lead to significant waste of display space and loss of perceptual resolution (e.g., if all percentages were below 10 percent), as can be seen in Figure 13.7. Thus, the range must be carefully chosen and clearly marked to help convey accurate information.

One final rule of thumb pertains to the use of multiple frames or windows. It is important to follow a consistent labeling and gridding scheme. Changing the position of labels and keys or the range of values shown (for the same

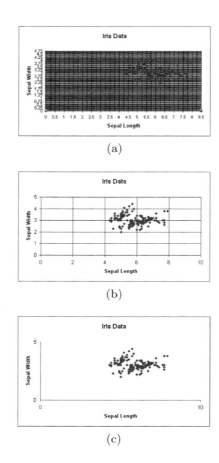

Figure 13.5.   Varying degrees of tick marks: (a) excessive, (b) moderate, and (c) minimal.

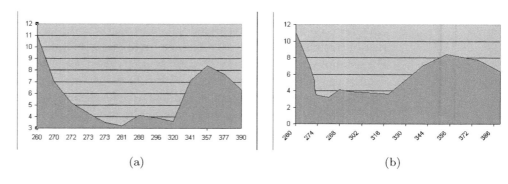

Figure 13.6.   Grid spacings: (a) illogical; (b) logical.

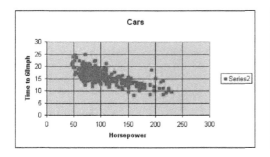 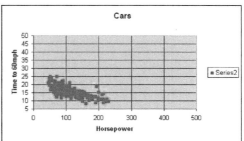

Figure 13.7.   Logical and illogical data ranges.

field) can cause confusion and increase the risk of misinterpretation. If range changes are necessary (e.g., for views that differ in level of detail), the label, as well as the grid markings, should convey the change. Similarly, if different color mappings are necessary, the visualizations must clearly convey this information.

13.1.5   Using Color with Care

One of the most frequently misused parameters in visualization design is that of color. Selecting the wrong color map or attempting to convey too much quantitative information through color can lead to ineffective or misleading visualizations. Also, since color perception is context-dependent (a particular color will appear quite different, depending on adjacent colors), the characteristics of the data itself can influence how the colors are perceived. Finally, it must be remembered that many people are color blind or color confused; it has been determined that as many as ten percent of all males have some form of color deficiency. The following guidelines can assist in the effective use of color in visualization.

1. If the visualization task involves absolute judgment, keep the number of distinct numeric levels low (see Figure 13.8 and Chapter 3 on perception).

2. Use redundant mappings if possible, e.g., map a particular field to both color and size (see Figure 13.9), to improve the chances of the data being communicated accurately.

3. In creating a color map for conveying numeric information, make sure that both hue and lightness are changed for each entry (see Figure 13.10).

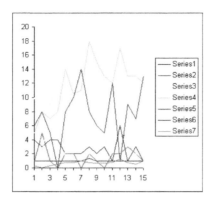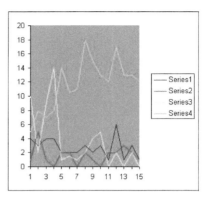

Figure 13.8.   Too many colors versus a moderate number of colors.

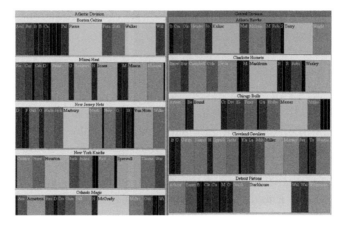

Figure 13.9.   Treemap of basketball statistics, with points per game redundantly mapped to color
                    and size. (Figure generated using Treemap 4.0, from the University of Maryland.)

4. Include a labeled color key to help users interpret the colors (see the previous section).

5. When possible, use semantically resonant colors in the visualization [273]; these will be easier for users to learn and remember.

Color can add significant visual appeal to a visualization, but can also significantly decrease the effectiveness of the communication process. Some

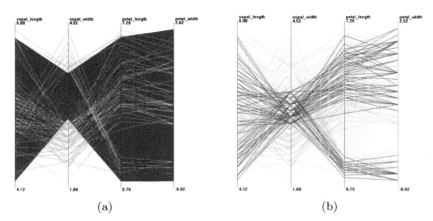

(a)   (b)

Figure 13.10.   (a) Changing hue; (b) changing both hue and saturation.

interface designers advocate an initial design process that only involves the use of grayscales. Once this design has been refined and tested, the addition of color can usually be done in a more effective manner.

13.1.6   The Importance of Aesthetics

Once we have ensured that our designed visualization conveys the desired information to the user (function), the final step is to assess the aesthetics (form) of the results. The best visualizations are both informative and pleasing to the eye. In contrast, a visualization might be so visually unappealing that it detracts from the communication process. An aesthetically pleasing visualization invites the viewer to study it in depth.

There are many guidelines for attractive visualization design that can be drawn from the art and graphic design communities. These include:

Focus. The viewer's focus should be drawn toward the part of the visualization that is most important. If the important components are not sufficiently emphasized, viewers don't have sufficient cues for guiding their inspection (see Figure 13.11).

Balance. The screen space should be used effectively, with the most important components in the center. Emphasis should not be given to any particular border (Figure 13.12).

Simplicity. Don't try to cram too much information in one display (see Section 13.1.3), and don't use graphics gimmicks simply because they are available (e.g., using 3D Phong shaded histograms when a bar or

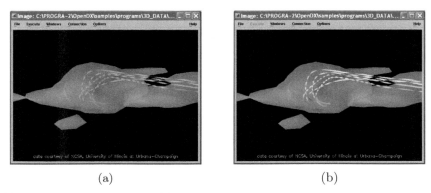

(a)   (b)

Figure 13.11.   (a) Subdued streamlines vs. (b) highlighted streamlines from OpenDX.

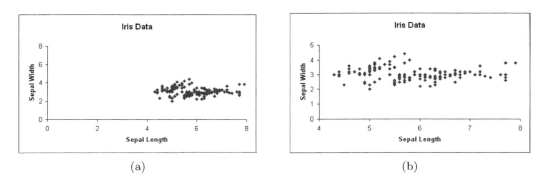

(a)   (b)

Figure 13.12.   (a) Everything to one side vs. (b) balanced between left and right.

line chart could convey the same information). A useful procedure to follow once a visualization has been designed is to iteratively remove features and measure the loss of information being conveyed. Features whose removal results in minimal loss can probably be discarded (see Figure 13.13).

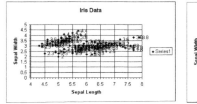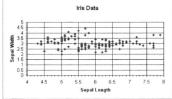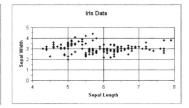

Figure 13.13.   Progression from a cluttered chart to a simplified chart.

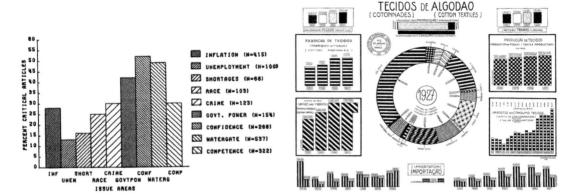

Figure 13.14.   Some ugly visualizations: (a) from Miller et al. [294] and (b) from a Brazilian economic statistics report [200]. In both cases, the cross-hatchings are seemingly random and distracting. Shades of gray would significantly improve the aesthetics of the images.

There are many examples of ugly visualizations in the literature. We reproduce a few of these below (see Figure 13.14). We encourage designers to perform aesthetic assessment on their results prior to presenting them to users, and to seek out and incorporate the extensive literature available on graphics design.

13.2   Problems in Designing Effective Visualizations

In the following sections we examine some of the common problems found in visualizations that can occur even if the steps outlined above are followed. These problems have a deeper root, and relate to decisions regarding what to visualize and what is the most appropriate method to use. Some of the problems involve intentional or inadvertent data distortion, which can lead to misinterpretation. Others involve hiding the real data behind "cleaned" versions or excessive supporting graphics. In all cases, steps can be taken to improve the quality and "honesty" of the visualization.

13.2.1   Misleading Visualizations

One of the foremost rules of visualization is that the image should be an accurate depiction of the data. However, throughout history, there are ex-

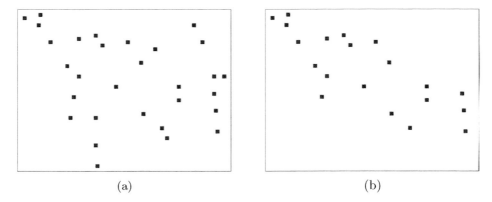

(a)   (b)

Figure 13.15.   The problem with data scrubbing: (a) raw data showing lack of correlation; (b) scrubbed data revealing false correlation.

amples of how visualizations from distorted data have been used to sway opinions and lie to the audience. These so-called "viz lies" can be found everywhere, from the most prestigious journals to company portfolios. In this section, we identify some of the common strategies for creating misleading visualizations, not for the reader to practice, but to try to avoid!

Data scrubbing. Raw data can often be very rough in form, and the temptation when creating a visualization is to remove some of the roughness. Unfortunately, sometimes the selection of which data to remove is biased to eliminate data that does not support a particular point that the author of the data is espousing (see Figure 13.15). Outlier removal is a common tactic in this situation. Unless there is reason to believe that the outliers resulted from flaws in the data acquisition process, they should not be removed without informing the viewer and providing the option for the outliers to be displayed.

Unbalanced scaling. Scaling is a powerful tool in visualization, since careful selection of scale factors can reveal patterns and structures not visible in unscaled views. However, scaling can be used to deceive the viewer into believing that a trend is stronger or weaker than supported by the data. This can lead to what Tufte refers to as the *lie factor* [424], which is the ratio between the raw data change and the change as depicted in the visualization. For example, in Figure 13.16 the size of objects in the background is reduced in width and height by perspective, thus distorting comparison with foreground objects.

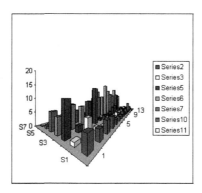

Figure 13.16.   Vis Lies: perspective distorts size in favor of closer objects.

Range distortion. As mentioned in an earlier section, viewers often have an expectation about the ranges for a particular data dimension; by setting this range to be significantly different from this expectation, the user may be deceived into misinterpretation. This is often done by moving an axis so it no longer corresponds with the expected "zero value" (see Figure 13.17). Since relative judgment is such a strong component of our perceptual system, changing the baseline for the relations being portrayed could have a serious effect on how the image is interpreted. The designer may want to give the user the option of moving this baseline to avoid wasting screen space, but it should be made clear what the baseline is, especially if it departs from the established norm.

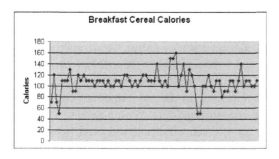
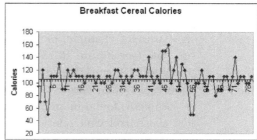

Figure 13.17.   Plotting data with different baselines.

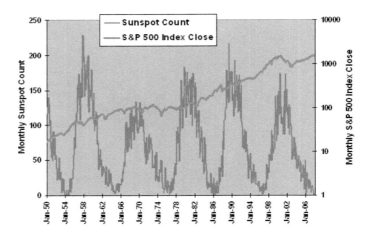

Figure 13.18.   A nonsense plot, showing sunspot occurrence versus the S+P 500 Index. (Image
from http://www.cxoadvisory.com/blog/internal/blog4-07-09/.)

Abusing dimensionality. In Chapter 3 we noted that errors in interpretation
rise with the power of the dimensionality being portrayed. Thus, our
errors in judging volume are much worse than those for area, which
in turn are worse than those for length. Therefore, mapping a scalar
value to a graphical attribute such as volume can dramatically increase
the likelihood of erroneous interpretation. As mentioned earlier, it is
often the case that simpler is better.

13.2.2 Visual Nonsense—Comparing Apples and Oranges

Visualizations are designed to convey information, and it is important that
the information be meaningful. Visualizations are often created by combining data sets from different sources. However, it is easy to combine unrelated components into a single visualization and identify what seems to be
structure; for example, plotting stock market values against occurrences of
sunspots (see Figure 13.18). In this case, coincidental relationships can be
confused with causal relationships. In deciding what data to combine, it is
important to first ensure that there is some logic in the combination. One of
the problems found in analytic pattern recognition/data mining processes is
that these irrelevant relationships are often discovered and reported, which
must then be eliminated by a domain specialist. The visualization designer
should attempt to avoid creating nonsense graphics before they are presented
to users.

Another factor that must be considered is compatibility between temporal and spatial ranges for data being compared. Thus, for example, one (probably) shouldn't compare the sales of a particular product in one year for a particular region of the country with the sales of the same product for a different region and year, unless one is hypothesizing that a migration in interest for the product is occurring.

Compatibility in units also needs to be examined in creating a data set for visualization. For example, food products that are measured in terms of price per volume are often mixed with those measured in price per weight. An effective visualization of this data might normalize them both to price per serving.

Finally, there is often a temptation to perform operations suitable for ordered or continuous data on categorical, unordered data, simply because the mapping process resulted in an ordered graphical representation. An example might be an attempt to fit a line or curve to a sequence of data points that map a company name to a position on the screen. Obviously, this has no semantic meaning, but because the mapping converts the scale of the data, users might feel that it is useful to perform the fitting.

The key point is that some thought must be put into the semantics of the visualization to insure that it makes logical sense.

13.2.3   Losing Data in the Chart Junk

In a previous section we stressed the importance of including labeled grid or tick marks on visualizations that require quantitative assessment. The excessive use of such markings is an example of what Tufte referred to as *chart junk* [424]. Chart junk can be defined as any supplementary (nondata) graphics in a visualization that are not necessary for the accurate interpretation of the data. This additional information can lead not only to visualizations that appear overly complex, but also to occlusion and deemphasis of the actual data.

Deciding the amount of supplementary graphics to put in a visualization is sometimes a difficult process, since the designer might not know the needs of all potential users. However, because we are dealing with a dynamic, customizable medium (unlike Tufte's static charts), the option exists to allow users to adjust the types and density of this supporting information on the display. In some visualization tasks, users can switch between qualitative overviews and quantitative analysis. In the former case, it is usually more important to give viewers a clear view of the data, while in the latter case,

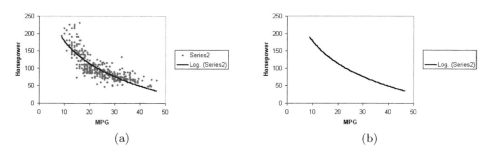

Figure 13.19.   (a) Raw data plot with fitted curve; (b) only fitted curve.

tools to help quantify the elements of the display are much more desirable. Thus, a good rule of thumb is to provide sufficient tools to support the user's quantitative needs, but with the option of disabling them or altering their degree of presence in the visualization.

13.2.4   Raw versus Derived Data

A common practice is to compute an analytic model of the data using curve/-surface fitting to obtain a more visually appealing result. Again, this is distorting the truth, and it may lead to false assumptions and conclusions on the part of the observer. In some visualizations, it is common practice to throw out all of the raw data and only show the smooth approximation derived from that data. This forces the viewer to trust that the approximation is an accurate portrayal of the data, which is often not the case when the designer blindly applies statistical fitting algorithms. It is best to show both the raw data and the fitted model first, and to allow one or the other to be deemphasized or filtered out on demand (see Figure 13.19).

Yet another form of cleaning the data is the process of *resampling*, where raw data positioned either on a sparse grid or randomly are used to create data that are either denser or on a regularly spaced grid. This can result in a much richer visualization, approaching that of continuous sampling, but it again deceives the user into believing the data set is much larger than it actually is. The denser the resampling, the more likely that the user will misinterpret the data, unless the phenomenon being observed has little variability. For example, Figure 13.20 shows the locations of global temperature monitoring stations. Clearly, there are large voids where no stations exist, so resampling could result in many wrong conclusions, such as that the entire northern part of South America would be interpolated by

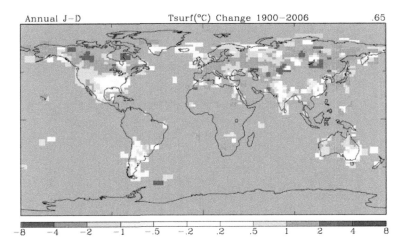

Figure 13.20. Sparse global temperature change data would give erroneous values for most of the planet if interpolated. (Image courtesy [150].)

the readings from four or five stations, with the conclusion being that the region has dropped in temperature over the past century.

Insufficient sampling is another problem. As the images in Figure 13.21 show, a sampling that doesn't look at the data characteristics can miss many important features. The left image is sampled and interpolated uniformly, while the right image uses contour information to add sample points where significant changes occur.

It is critical that the user always have access to the raw data and be informed of any scrubbing/smoothing/resampling operation that has been

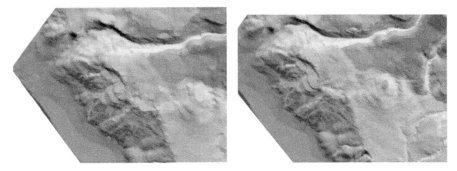

Figure 13.21. Different sampling and interpolation of the same data set. Some of the details in the right image are not seen in the left image. (Image from [185].)

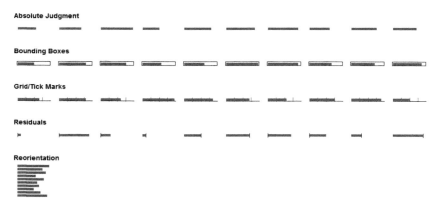

Figure 13.22.   Some examples of absolute versus relative judgment. (Image courtesy of Michael
Barry.)

applied. In some domains, such as radiology, analysts are adamantly opposed to any sort of data smoothing or filtering, as there is danger that an
important signal in the data might be discarded as noise. Thus, views should
be provided that show the raw data set prior to deriving new versions, allowing the user to decide whether the derivation is an accurate representation
of the original data.

13.2.5   Absolute versus Relative Judgment

As mentioned in Chapter 3, humans have a fairly limited ability to make
absolute judgments of visual stimuli. This implies that visualizations that
depend too heavily on users performing accurate measurements of graphical attributes such as position, length, and color will result in problems in
interpretation. One means of combating this human limitation is to design
visualizations that either rely on relative rather than absolute judgment, or
that are restricted to only using a small number of distinct values for each
graphical attribute being used to convey information.

Bounding boxes, grids, and tick marks are all excellent tools for converting an absolute judgment task to one that depends more on relative
judgment. By comparing the length or position of a graphical entity against
a quantified structure, users can more rapidly determine the approximate
value relative to the known levels. Using residuals (e.g., subtracting values
from their means) can also change a measurement task to one of deciding
whether a value is above or below a particular level (see Figure 13.22).

13.3 Summary

In this chapter we have presented a number of design rules for creating effective visualizations. These include:

- use data-graphic mappings that are likely to be intuitive to the targeted audience;

- provide users with multiple views of their data, along with easy-to-use tools for modifying views;

- avoid putting too much information in a given display; rather, provide users with the ability to turn components of the visualization off and on;

- include keys, labels, legends, and grids/ticks to help users interpret the visualization;

- use color with care; color perception is highly context sensitive, and humans are limited as to the number of distinct colors that can be identified with accuracy;

- design your visualizations to be attractive, as well as functional;

- avoid misleading users with unbalanced scales and other visualization lies;

- verify that the visualization has semantic meaning and compatible units;

- use grids in such a way that the data is not overly occluded; too much chart junk can misdirect the user's attention;

- always provide users access to the raw data; it is usually OK to perform some data scrubbing, but the user should be aware of how the resulting data has been derived;

- design visualizations that rely on relative, rather than absolute, judgment, when possible.

None of these rules are hard and fast; there are exceptions to each, and indeed, there are times when one rule conflicts with another. Designers should be prepared to try many alternatives before deciding on a final form, assessing each based on the criteria presented here. However, be strongly advised that there is no substitute for rigorous usability studies with subjects drawn from the anticipated audience (see Chapter 14). Only after this testing has been performed can the designer be reasonably assured that an effective visualization has been created.

13.4   Related Readings

Many books have been written on the design of informative graphics. Notable authors include Edward Tufte [424–427], Stephen Few [123, 124], and Stephen Kosslyn [251, 252]. Their work provided much of the information and concepts in this chapter. A significant percentage of modern HCI textbooks focus on designing effective graphical user interfaces. One early work dedicated to this topic is the book by Mullet and Sano [300], which provides a number of useful rules of thumb.

A number of articles have been written on the subject, with many lists of guidelines, principles, and design patterns, including [3, 58, 69, 112, 370].

13.5   Exercises

1. Identify at least three problems with the visualization shown in Figure 13.23.

2. For each of the visualizations in Figure 13.14, suggest at least three modifications that would improve their effectiveness.

3. Describe four examples of how some of the rules of this chapter may conflict with each other.

4. Assume that you are plotting the exchange rates for 20 different countries. List at least three ways of ordering the names of the countries and describe why each might be useful.

5. Other than the figures used in the exercises, find at least three examples of figures in this book that could be improved using design guidelines described in this chapter. Send suggestions for improvements to the authors (yeah, we can take the criticism!).

6. Examine several visualizations found in different media (newspaper, magazine, company prospectus) and critique the designs. Rank them from best to worst.

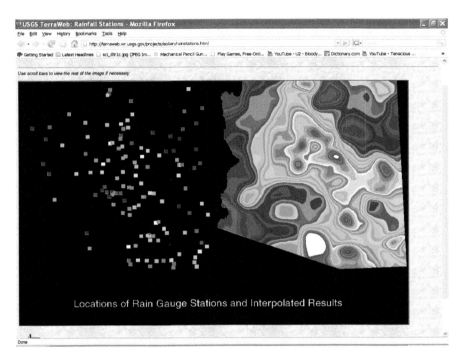

Figure 13.23.	Rainfall data for Arizona from the USGS.

## 13.6	Projects

1. Choose three visualization programs that you've written for this course. For each, try to find at least three ways of improving them, based on the design guidelines of this chapter. Reimplement these programs with the improvements you've identified. Compete with your classmates to see who can create the most attractive, informative visualization.

2. Choose three visualization programs that you've written for this course (they can be the same three as used in the project above). For each, try to find at least three ways of making them *worse* by violating design guidelines of this chapter. Reimplement these programs with the *negative* improvements you've identified. Compete with your classmates to see who can create the ugliest, least informative visualization!

3. Write a scatterplot program that reports the percentage of data that is at least partially occluded. Show how changing the size of the marks or adding random jitter to locations for data points affects this occlusion percent.

4. Write a program for generating a line chart from a time series data set. Experiment with drawing grid lines with varying density, width, brightness, and color. Try variations on the attributes of the plotted line to find good settings (i.e., those that help the user focus on the plotted points).

CHAPTER 14

Comparing and Evaluating Visualization Techniques

A common question from users of visualization tools is "Which visualization technique(s) should I use to solve my problem?" In general, there is no simple answer to this question; many factors go into the evaluation process, such as the specific task or tasks the user wishes to accomplish, the characteristics of the data, and the user's level of experience in using visualization to help solve problems.

Another common problem that is often avoided by developers of visualization techniques is to determine under what conditions their technique is better than existing techniques, or whether a modification made to a particular method improves or makes worse some aspect of the technique or system. Indeed, the degree of formal evaluation for visualization techniques has been limited to date, partly because it is more satisfying on the part of the developer to create new methods and partly because performing rigorous evaluation is difficult and time-consuming.

In this chapter we attempt to identify some of the components and procedures necessary to assess and compare the effectiveness of visualization techniques. We first list the types of tasks a user may wish to perform with the aid of visualization, such as identifying trends or detecting the presence of a known phenomenon. We then define user characteristics, such as level of experience, that can affect the success of a visualization technique. Next, we review the characteristics of data, as presented in Chapter 2, and examine how these features bear on the process of effective visualization. Finally, we describe attributes of visualizations themselves, such as the presence or absence of occlusion, that need to be considered in the evaluation. To conclude the chapter, we outline a procedure for designing a benchmark process that would enable a person charged with comparing two or more visualization techniques to approach the problem in a methodical way.

14.1 User Tasks

To perform a valid assessment of a particular visualization technique, or to compare two or more techniques, it is important to identify the specific actions or tasks one wishes to accomplish with the assistance of visualization. As mentioned in Chapter 4, Keller and Keller [236] identify the following actions that a user might perform with a visualization:

- *identify*—to recognize an object based on the characteristics presented, such as finding a fracture in an x-ray;

- *locate*—to establish the position of an object, such as determining the location of maximal stress in structural analysis;

- *distinguish*—to determine that an object is distinct or different from another, such as separating elevations that exceed a given threshold from those below the threshold;

- *categorize*—to classify objects into distinct types, such as different land cover or material types;

- *cluster*—to group similar objects based on some relationship. A related action is to *segment*, which consists of separating dissimilar objects;

- *rank*—to place a group of objects in an order, such as numerical or chronological;

- *compare*—to examine the similarities and differences between two or more objects where ordering is not possible, such as masking the intersection of two data sets to reveal how they differ;

- *associate*—to draw a relationship between two or more objects, such as linking temperature and location in weather maps;

- *correlate*—to find a causal or reciprocal relationship between two or more objects, such as determining the relationship between interest rates and economic growth.

Each of the above tasks can be performed to varying degrees using visualization. In deciding if a particular visualization technique is useful for accomplishing one or more such tasks, one needs to have a clear vision of the degree of accuracy with which it needs to be accomplished. For example, is it essential to correctly identify *every* occurrence of an object? What rate of classification or ranking error is acceptable? At what resolution is the location of an object needed? How many falsely labeled correlations are acceptable? For what data characteristics is it important that errors be minimized? Thus, we must augment the generic task with specifics dealing with the domain, user, and data, as outlined below.

14.2   User Characteristics

Besides the tasks to be performed, the effectiveness of a visualization technique is tightly associated with the users of the visualization. Users can be classified based on their knowledge and skills. Some of the particular aspects of interest include:

Familiarity with domain. How much expertise does the user have with the domain of the data being explored? Has she studied the field for a long time, or is she relatively new to the field?

Familiarity with task. How much experience has the user had in performing the desired task? Is she an expert or a novice, or somewhere in between? Note that this differs from the previous point, as someone could have significant domain experience, but minimal experience in a particular task.

Familiarity with data. Has the user examined this data previously and formed a reasonable mental model of its contents, or is this her first exposure to it? Is it similar to other data sets she has examined?

Familiarity with the visualization technique. Is this the user's first attempt to interpret the data using this particular kind of visualization, or has she spent considerable time using the technique?

Familiarity with the visualization environment. Has the user employed the particular tool (or a similar one) in the past, or is it her first exposure? This differs from the previous factor, as a visualization technique can be implemented in several different packages, and aspects of the packages themselves can influence the effectiveness of the exploration of the data.

Each aspect can be treated as a continuum, and each can influence the assessment of a visualization. In an ideal evaluation using human subjects, we would want the range of characteristics of the participants to be as similar as possible to the intended audience for the technique, and the results should be evaluated by grouping people with similar characteristics.

14.3   Data Characteristics

In Chapter 3 we discussed many of the attributes of data, from the types of the lowest-level components to its structure. The characteristics of the data being visualized can have a profound influence on the effectiveness of the visualization technique, and they must be considered in the evaluation process. In an ideal assessment, a large variety of data sets should be tested, and they should span the range of characteristics found in the domain for which the visualization is being designed. Some of these tests should include:

Type. In many cases, the data is all of the same type (e.g., floating-point numbers). Often, however, it is a mixture of types, such as text intermingled with numbers. All combinations of types that can occur should be tested.

Size. Data sets in a particular domain can often take on a wide range of sizes, from a few records to thousands or millions of records. Tests should cover the normal size range, as well as extreme values for the size.

Dimensionality. While in many scientific domains the data generally have fixed dimensionality (one, two, or three), it is generally useful to test a visualization with all possible subsets of dimensions (slices or projections), as well as, with the normal dimensionality.

Number of parameters. The normal number of parameters in a data set varies widely from one domain to another. Visualization techniques should be tested with both univariate and multivariate data sets (unless only univariate data exists); indeed, a common test is to ascertain the maximum number of parameters that can be effectively displayed by a technique.

Structure. In a data set, the structure of the data can be simple (e.g., a uniform grid or a table) or complex (e.g., hierarchical). While many domains use a single fixed structure (defined by the data model), others might allow multiple fixed structures or variable structures. Secondary structures may also be derivable from the main structures, such as a hierarchical clustering derived from a list or a multilevel grid. Visualization techniques should be tested using all commonly encountered structures within the domain.

Range. Objects in data sets can take on a wide range of values. Testing should involve exercising the entire range of possible values, including the extremes of the range.

Distribution. Data can be uniformly or nonuniformly distributed, both in values and in attributes (such as spatio-temporal position). Tests should involve data sets that include distributions usually encountered in the domain, as well as some extreme cases.

Real vs. Synthetic. Many researchers perform evaluations using synthetic data, as it allows tight control of the data characteristics. For some types of evaluation* (e.g., size tests) this is fine, but in general it is more convincing to use real data that has the characteristics of typical data found in a particular domain.

As can be seen in this section, data has a large number of characteristics, and thus, to thoroughly evaluate one or more visualizations for a given domain can potentially involve gathering or generating a tremendous number of test data sets. In many domains, however, some of these characteristics are reasonably constrained, which can greatly reduce the number of distinct tests that are needed. Few domains have made concerted efforts to gather large numbers of data sets for testing (nice examples include the machine learning archive at the University of California, Irvine [430] and the StatLib repository at CMU [394]), and fewer still have attempted to classify data sets according to their characteristics to enable testers to gauge the data attributes that should be tested with the data sets. It would be a great service, both to researchers in a given domain and to visualization developers, for such annotated archives to become more available.

14.4 Visualization Characteristics

Once the task, user, and data have been characterized, we can focus on the specific visualization technique(s) to be assessed. There are many aspects of the visualization that can be evaluated. These include the following:

Computational performance. How quickly can the visualization be generated, using data sets of various sizes?

Memory performance. How much computer memory is required to generate the visualization?

Data limitations. What are the upper and lower bounds for the size and complexity of the data that can be visualized with this technique? At what point does the amount of information extractable from the visualization stabilize or decrease with increased data size/complexity? At what point does the error rate for performing the task increase to an unacceptable level?

Degree of occlusion. What is the likelihood that some subset of the data to be displayed will be occluded by other parts of the visualization? How much is normally occluded? How many views does the user need to see the entire data set?

Degree of complexity. What is the normal learning curve for the technique? How many parameters does the user need to set in order to generate views? How much knowledge is needed to set and adjust these parameters in an effective manner?

Degree of usability. How easy is it to perform the task? How intuitive is the interpretation of the visualization? How intuitive are the controls for interactions?

Degree of accuracy. How frequently is the user successful or unsuccessful in performing the desired task with this technique? Under what conditions are errors made, and how bad are the errors (i.e., distance from correctness)?

14.5   Structures for Evaluating Visualizations

Many forms of evaluation for interactive systems have been developed within the field of human-computer interaction, most of which are applicable and have been applied to data and information visualization systems. Some of the most common techniques are detailed below.

Usability tests. These evaluations concentrate on "the Five E's": effective, efficient, engaging, error tolerant, and easy to learn [398]. These tests are usually carried out by observing users attempting to perform tasks, and noting the types of difficulties they are having, the features they commonly use, and their level of comfort/satisfaction with the tool. Often, the evaluation starts with some usability goals or requirements, and the result of the evaluation indicates whether the goal or requirement has been met or not.

Expert reviews. While some forms of evaluation depend on having a significant number of participants, expert reviews can generally be carried out with a small number (three or fewer) of qualified reviewers [418]. These evaluators may be experts in visualization, or they may be domain experts who can thoroughly test the applicability of a tool for a set of specific application tasks. A visualization expert is someone who has studied visualization design and has likely used or developed a number of successful tools. He or she may have a checklist of desirable features for an effective visualization, against which the object of the evaluation is assessed (this is sometimes referred to as *heuristic evaluation*). A domain expert, on the other hand, is generally familiar with the types of data and tasks found within their domain, and will attempt to identify the extent to which the system or technique could accommodate the data and support the tasks.

Field tests. Unlike usability tests, which are often carried out in a controlled environment over a short period of time to better enable measurement, field tests are performed in the natural environment of the typical user and may last for weeks or months [321]. Field tests attempt to assess the degree to which the new technique or tool becomes an integral part of a user's activities once the initial curiosity and learning curve have been overcome. The results of field tests are often qualitative, and may change significantly over time. They can be effective, especially if users are encouraged to submit questions and critiques that can lead to clarifications and improvements in functionality.

Case studies and use cases. Rather than using experts, users, or student volunteers in evaluation, some visualization researchers attempt to validate the effectiveness of their techniques by showing real (or sometimes contrived) examples of how their method can be used in solving a particular problem or performing a given task. The key to this sort of evaluation is to ensure that the case studies are sufficiently realistic so that someone with a particular task to perform can be convinced that at least one of the case studies is sufficiently similar to his or her own task, and that the tool will effectively support it.

14.6   Benchmarking Procedures

Benchmarking is a formal procedure for evaluating the performance of some object or set of objects. A wide assortment of objects can be benchmarked for a variety of attributes, such as the speed of a car or the user-friendliness of an interface. Benchmarks can be quantitative (resulting in a number) or qualitative (resulting in a relative judgment). Qualitative benchmarks generally involve the use of human subjects, while quantitative assessment can be done either with or without the use of human subjects. In general, quantitative benchmarking experiments are easier to set up and execute than qualitative experiments, due to the difficulties of factoring in the variability of users in testing with human subjects. However, the procedures do have similarities, as outlined below:

1. *Formulate a hypothesis.* A benchmark requires a specific statement about one or more attributes of the object being assessed, such as "This algorithm executes faster than that algorithm" or "This technique allows the identification of tumors more easily than other ones." Care must be taken in designing a hypothesis that isn't too general— stating as a hypothesis that system A is "better" than system B is very difficult to prove or disprove. In terms of comparing visualization techniques, a more complete hypothesis would be "System A allows novice users to more easily identify clusters in data sets containing 5–10 dimensions and 1000 to 10000 data points than system B." Note, we have integrated aspects of most of the characteristics described earlier in the chapter: namely, task, user, and data. This degree of specification, while resulting in rather constrained results, is much easier to design, execute, and validate than the more general claims.

2. *Design the experiments.* The key to designing benchmark experiments is to create tests that vary only a single attribute at a time. For example, a test of computational speed for a set of algorithms would require that all experiments be run on the same computer, using the same data, with similar degrees of optimization of the specific implementations. Similarly, a benchmark measuring the usability of a tool would require the subjects to perform identical tasks that exercise only the

usability issue, and not peripheral issues such as the color scheme or the hardware speed.

3. *Execute the experiments.* There are many ways a well-designed experiment can be executed so that little in the way of reliable conclusions will result. Factors such as the training of human subjects are critical; each participant should get a similar amount of instruction on performing the experiments, including identifying the procedure they should follow, the expected format of their responses, and the pace at which they should proceed. The amount of time provided should be reasonably constrained, as users often will respond differently, given differing time constraints. Finally, the audience should be of sufficient size to make the results statistically significant. For testing a single attribute of a visualization, it is best to have at least 15–20 subjects with similar backgrounds.

Similar issues need to be considered for experiments that don't involve human subjects. For example, tests of computational performance should be done on similarly loaded machines at similar times of the day to insure that external influences are reasonably balanced.

4. *Analyze the results and validate the hypothesis.* Given the results of the experiments, it is then necessary to ascertain whether

- the hypothesis is supported,
- the hypothesis is refuted, or
- there is insufficient evidence to support or refute the hypothesis.

Generally, one is looking for results that are statistically significant, e.g., they are far enough from random to indicate credibility. For quantitative variables of the experiments, such as data set size, it is useful to plot results against the variable. For nonquantitative variables, such as the type of task or structure of the data, it is best to analyze each value of the variable separately, and then try to draw conclusions only if there is a dominant trend or clear majority.

14.7   An Example of Visualization Benchmarking

In an article by Ward and Theroux [442], a set of experiments is described for assessing the strengths and weaknesses of three multivariate visualization techniques, namely scatterplot matrices, parallel coordinates, and star glyphs, in performing two distinct tasks: cluster analysis and outlier detection. The structure and results of their experiments are outlined below.

14.7.1   Outlier Detection and Measurement Experiments

Stage 1. The first step was to develop a quantifiable definition for an outlier and create an algorithm capable of labeling data points appropriately. The first part of the algorithm calculated a one-dimensional projection regression that resulted in a measure of fit for each point within each dimension. The standard deviations of the measures of fit for each dimension were then calculated and compared against a threshold standard deviation to determine if the point was an outlier. If the standard deviation for a point was greater than the threshold value, the point was labeled an outlier.

Stage 2. Data sets, both real and simulated, were then acquired or generated that contained outliers, according to the definition in Stage 1. For some data sets, the degree of separation between the outliers and the main bodies of data points were varied to test subject sensitivity (see Figures 14.1 and 14.2). A total of six outlier experiments were designed, and each was repeated three times for the three visualization techniques being tested.

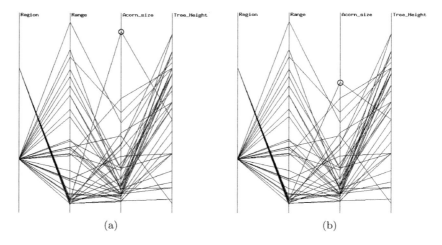

(a)   (b)

Figure 14.1.   Parallel coordinates view of data set describing acorn attributes, with a single outlier (circled, in the acorn size dimension) (a) in its original position and (b) with the distance artificially shortened [442]. (Image © 1997 IEEE.)

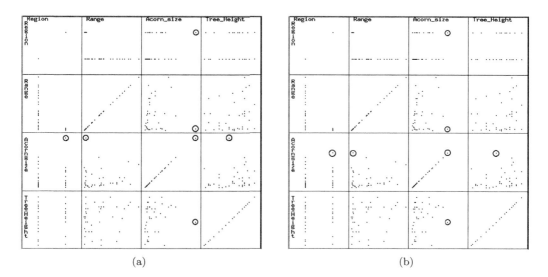

Figure 14.2.   Identifying outliers with scatterplot matrices: same data as previous figure, using scatterplot matrices [442]. (Image © 1997 IEEE.)

Stage 3. After the subjects (19 computer science graduate students with minimal exposure to data visualization) were trained to interpret the visualization technique(s) to be assessed and given examples of data sets with identified outliers (approximately one hour of training), they were shown a set of 18 images of data sets containing between 0 and 6 outliers. The subjects were asked not to spend more than one minute per image. The tasks given to them were:

1. Determine if an image contains one or more outliers.

2. Identify the points believed to be outliers.

3. Estimate the degree of separation of each outlier on a 5-point scale (marginal to extreme).

Stage 4: Given the subject responses, the usefulness of each visualization method tested was assessed in terms of outlier detection and measurement across data sets with different characteristics. The percentages of correctly and incorrectly detected outliers were tallied, as well as the average error in estimating the degree of separation.

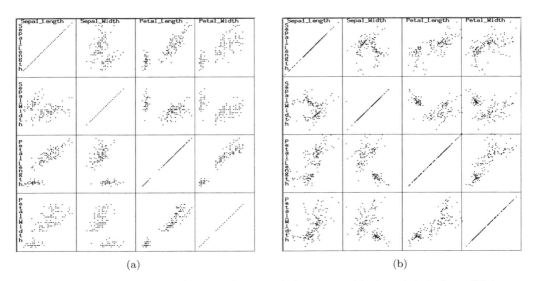

Figure 14.3.   Iris data showing different degrees of clustering: (a) the original data; (b) has a
                    40% added noise factor [442]. (Image © 1997 IEEE.)

14.7.2   Cluster Detection and Measurement Experiments

Stage 1. A quantifiable definition for a cluster was developed and an algorithm capable of labeling data points according to which cluster they belong
to was implemented. The algorithm output gave the probabilities of each
point belonging to each cluster.

Stage 2. Data sets, both real and simulated, were acquired that contained
clusters according to the definition in Stage 1. For simulated data, the
number, size, and orientation of clusters and their relative positions were
varied. Random noise was also added to some of the simulated data sets
(see Figure 14.3). Sixteen distinct experiments were designed, and each was
presented using the three display techniques.

Stage 3. After the subjects (19 computer science graduate students) were
trained to interpret the visualization technique(s) to be assessed and were
given examples of data sets with known clusters (approximately 1 hour of
training), they were given a packet containing 48 images of data sets that
contained between 0 and 4 clusters. The subjects were asked to not spend
more than one minute per image. The tasks given to them were:

1. Determine if an image contains one or more clusters.

2. Highlight the groups of points believed to lie in distinct clusters.

3. Estimate the size of each cluster on a 5-point scale (small to very large).

Stage 4. Given the subject responses, the usefulness of each visualization method tested could be assessed in terms of cluster detection and measurement across data sets with different characteristics. The percentages of correctly and incorrectly detected clusters were tallied, as well as the average error in estimating the size.

14.7.3   Results

In all, over 4000 data points were gathered during the experiments, categorized as cluster identification, cluster size assessment, outlier identification, and outlier separation identification. For both tasks, scatterplot matrices generally fared best, followed by star glyphs positioned by principal component analysis, and lastly by parallel coordinates. Each had measurable strengths and weaknesses, as outlined below.

- Scatterplot matrix

    - less effective for overlapping clusters;
    - less effective in size assessment for large clusters;
    - less effective when outliers fell between clusters;

- Glyphs

    - best for identifying internal outliers (between clusters);
    - poor for differentiating nonoutliers;
    - good for conveying outlier separation;
    - good for overlapping clusters;
    - good for measuring moderate sized clusters;

- Parallel Coordinates

    - good for differentiating nonoutliers.

In some cases, the difference in performance by the different techniques was quite significant. For example, with scatterplots there were only 27 instances of incorrectly identified clusters (false positives), while for glyphs and parallel coordinates there were 126 and 159 occurrences, respectively. On the other hand, there were many circumstances where the performance difference was less striking. For example, there was no major difference in the number of accurately identified clusters among the different visualization methods (78% for scatterplots, 74% for glyphs, and 71% for parallel coordinates).

14.8   Related Readings

Many articles have been written on the evaluation of visualization techniques and systems. Some of these include [68, 109, 162, 165, 235, 297, 321, 358, 359, 368, 418, 432, 492], many of which were presented at a workshop associated with the AVI conference in 2006. Some are specific to one type of visualization (e.g., graphs) or to a specific application area (e.g., bioinformatics), but many of the concepts are more broadly applicable.

The VAST contests and challenges evaluate visualizations and visual analytic systems against benchmark data sets (data sets having embedded ground truth). The summary papers and the archived papers by the participants are a very worthwhile read. See http://vac.nist.gov/index.html.

There is also a growing interest in novel approaches to evaluating visualizations, including pioneering work on eye-tracking [151] and analyzing brain activity [10].

14.9   Exercises

1. Make a table listing the pros and cons of various evaluation strategies for visualization tools (you may need to read some of the recommended literature first). Are there any strategies that are complementary (e.g., the pros of one address the cons of the other)? This might indicate pairings of strategies that together can paint a clearer picture of the effectiveness of a technique, as compared to running only a single type of evaluation.

2. Design a set of experiments for evaluating one characteristic of volume visualization techniques. Be careful to specify in detail the task, data, and user characteristics (if human subjects would be involved) that you would be using for the analysis.

3. Repeat the process using a different task.

4. Repeat the process using a different characteristic of the technique.

5. Repeat the process for 2D flow visualization techniques.

6. Choose a paper from the literature that describes a new visualization technique. Write a summary of what (if any) assessment was performed on the technique, and suggest ways in which further assessment could be performed (you will find that only a small percentage of visualization papers report extensive evaluation).

7. Skim the papers from one information visualization conference and count how many include evaluations. For each one that does include evaluation, identify the type of evaluation performed (e.g., usability test, expert review, field test, case/use study). Which method(s) appear to be most common?

8. In light of the above, look up the VAST Challenge summary papers (http://vac.nist.gov/index.html) and the participants' submissions; determine how the visualizations and even the evaluations could be improved.

14.10   Projects

1. Design and carry out one or more evaluations of one of the visualizations that you implemented for this course. For example, test your visualization using a variety of user characteristics, as outlined in Section 14.2, or data characteristics, as outlined in Section 14.3. If the evaluation requires human subjects, try recruiting people with similar backgrounds (e.g., the students in this class).

2. Implement a minor variation on this visualization, for example, using a different color scheme, default layout, or other easily changed aspect. Design and carry out an evaluation that compares the original and modified versions. If there is a noticeable difference in performance or satisfaction levels, describe what you believe to be the likely cause.

3. Design and carry out an evaluation of a visualization implemented and evaluated by one of your classmates. You should *not* ask people how they evaluated their own program, or what the results were! Once the evaluation has been completed, you should compare the procedures, as well as the results. How were they similar or different? This might expose some biases that we often have when it comes to evaluating our own work—we generally want the results to come out well, while in evaluating the work of others we don't usually have a preference as to how things work out.

CHAPTER 15

Visualization Systems

In this chapter we present an overview of a number of data and information visualization systems and toolkits. We have concentrated primarily on software that is freely available, to enable students interested in exploring further in the field of visualization to try out existing technology. These are only a sampling, however; many fine tools that we have not mentioned are also available, and readers are encouraged to search for and download them. We also mention some commercial packages with functionality that overlaps with the systems we've chosen to describe. Caveat: the URLs given were correct at the time of publication. These may have changed since then, or some of the tools may no longer be freely distributed.

15.1 Systems Based on Data Type

15.1.1 Scientific Data

OpenDX [308,408], which was formerly marketed as IBM Visualization Data Explorer, is an extensible visualization environment primarily used for the analysis of scientific and engineering data. What separates it from most other visualization platforms is the visual programming process used to create custom visualizations. Its Network Editor allows users to drag and drop components onto a canvas and create links between components for communicating data of specified types. The modules fall into several distinct classes, including:

- *import and export*—modules to load and save data in different formats;

- *flow control*—modules to create loops and conditional execution;

- *realization*—modules to map the data to renderable entities, such as isosurfaces, grids, and streamlines;

- *rendering*—modules to control display attributes, such as lighting, cameras, and clipping;

- *transformation*—functions to apply to the data, such as filtering, mathematical functions, and sorting;

- *interactor*—widgets such as file selectors, menus, dials/sliders, and button boxes.

Figure 15.1 shows a typical network. Flow passes along the connectors, and each component is a pure function, e.g., it doesn't store any state information. As each component executes, its color changes in the editor to let users to monitor progress. If flow stops due to some exception condition,

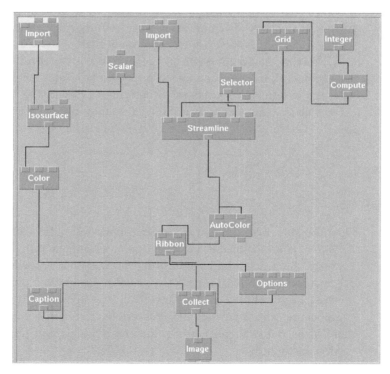

Figure 15.1.   An example of a network in OpenDX. Flow proceeds from the Import modules down to the image. This specific program combines an isosurface, a set of streamlines represented as ribbons, and a caption for the final display.

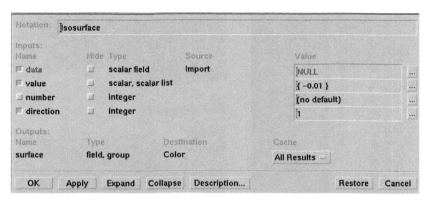

Figure 15.2.   An example of the interface for a module in OpenDX. Some parameters are set
                manually, while others are set by connecting an input or output tab to the input
                or output of another module.

the component where the problem arose is colored to indicate a problem.
Each component has its own interface to set both required and optional
parameters (see Figure 15.2), other than the connections between components, which are set via point-and-click operations. Interactors are widgets
that let people using the program set thresholds, select from menus, modify
color maps, and otherwise control the execution of the program. An iterator
module is provided to enable animating sequences of visualizations.

A large range of existing modules have been developed to date, and visualizations can be created that combine different data and different mappings
into a single visualization (see Figure 15.3). Users can either restrict themselves to using the existing library of components/modules, or they may
write their own, using a software development kit that contains libraries to
access data structures and interface components. In this way, OpenDX can
be customized to new applications with proprietary or nonstandard data
file formats. OpenDX was designed to run on UNIX/Linux systems, but
can run on Windows and Mac platforms using an X-server. The OpenDX
software, including source code, executables, documentation, and sample
networks and data can be downloaded from the OpenDX web site [308].
Systems with overlapping capabilities include AVS [23] (commercial) and
SCIRun [65] (public domain).

15.1.2   Multivariate Data

XmdvTool [477], developed at Worcester Polytechnic Institute (WPI) by
Matthew Ward, Elke Rundensteiner, and their students, is a public domain

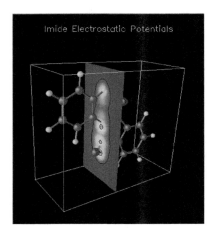
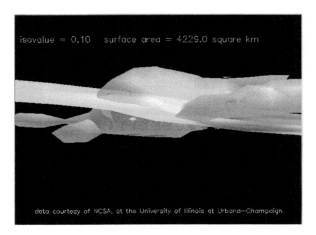

Figure 15.3.   Examples of visualizations that can be created with OpenDX. The first combines
                a slice through a potential field, superimposed on a geometric model, while the
                second combines temperature, moisture levels, and a wind field to see attributes
                of a storm cloud.

visualization software package that integrates five common methods for multivariate data visualization into a single exploration application [287, 444].
This tool includes standard scatterplot matrices, scatterplots of star glyphs,
parallel coordinates, dimensional stacking, and pixel-oriented techniques.
These visualizations are linked together using a simple selection and highlighting mechanism called an N-dimensional brush, which defines a hyperbox
in the data space. Selected data in one view are also selected in other views,
and the resulting selection can be highlighted, masked, deleted, or analyzed
separate from the rest of the data.

Beyond its original inception, XmdvTool has been extended to include
additional architectural features for supporting large data sets. First, Ying-
Huey Fua et al. introduced hierarchical parallel coordinates for the exploration of data sets containing many records [137] (see Figure 15.4). Data
is hierarchically clustered and the results displayed in a summarized parallel coordinates display using variable opacity bands. This was followed
by the addition of a structure-based brush, an associated user interface
for browsing, and brushing within this hierarchical data structure (see Figure 15.5(a)). Jing Yang et al. generalized the application of this hierarchical
data structure to XmdvTool's other visualizations and defined the *interactive hierarchical displays* (*IHD*) framework [480]. Furthermore, XmdvTool
provides a *visual hierarchical dimension reduction* (*VHDR*) framework that

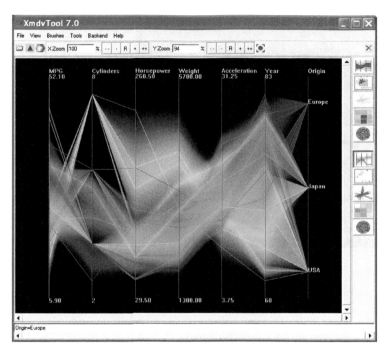

Figure 15.4.   An example of hierarchical parallel coordinates in XmdvTool. Each line represents
the center of a cluster, and the opacity bands around each centerline indicate the
extents of the cluster in each dimension. The opacity near the center conveys the
cluster population. Users can drill-down or roll-up in the data hierarchy, using a
structure-based brush (see Figure 15.5).

groups and organizes the space of dimensions, providing meaningful sub-
spaces of the dimensions for analysis [480] (see Figure 15.5(b)). XmdvTool
also includes the *distance quantification classing* (*DQC*) approach to handle nominal variables [347] and tools to reorder dimensions to reduce visual
clutter [317].

XmdvTool was first released to the public domain in 1994, and at the time
of this writing is in release 7.0. Beyond its native file format, the software
can import data from Excel spreadsheets and Oracle databases. It has been
successfully employed in a wide range of application domains, including earth
and space sciences, bioinformatics, census studies, and network performance
analysis. XmdvTool runs on both Windows and UNIX/Linux platforms;
source code, data sets, executables, and documentation can be found at the
project web site [477].

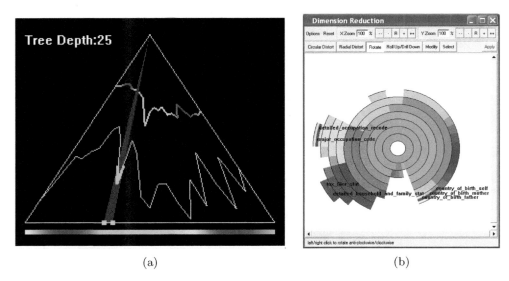

(a)   (b)

Figure 15.5.   Displays of hierarchical structures in XmdvTool: (a) a structure-based brush,
which is used to navigate and select in a data hierarchy; (b) InterRing, which
allows users to cluster dimensions of their data and select subsets or averages of
dimensions for the data display.

Software with overlapping functionality include Spotfire [409] (commercial) and Tableau Software [403] (commercial), though each of these is far
more developed and robust than XmdvTool.

15.1.3   Graph Data

GraphViz [111, 156] is a library of graph layout algorithms developed at
AT&T Research. The architecture and philosophy of GraphViz is rather
unique compared to other visualization tools. It supports a range of graph
specification methods, layout methods, and rendering methods. While some
interactive components have been integrated with the system, it is primarily a script-driven system. One selects a graph description file and feeds
it to a layout engine, along with a desired output format and any other
parameters to the layout technique. The output formats supported are
vast, to enable easy integration of results into documents, web pages, and
applications.

All GraphViz programs accept input files in the DOT language, which is
defined by an abstract grammar. A simple example of a graph specified in
DOT is as follows:

```
digraph G {
size="6,6";
node [shape=circle,fontsize=8];
rankdir=LR;
st9 -> st9 [label="11/1"];
st9 -> st10 [label="10/1"];
st8 -> st8 [label="10/1"];
st8 -> st0 [label="00/-"];
st7 -> st8 [label="10/1"];
st7 -> st7 [label="00/1"];
st6 -> st6 [label="01/1"];
st6 -> st0 [label="00/-"];
st5 -> st6 [label="01/1"];
st5 -> st5 [label="11/1"];
st4 -> st4 [label="01/1"];
st4 -> st0 [label="00/-"];
st3 -> st4 [label="01/1"];
st3 -> st3 [label="00/1"];
st2 -> st9 [label="11/1"];
st2 -> st7 [label="00/1"];
st2 -> st2 [label="01/1"];
st10 -> st10 [label="10/1"];
st10 -> st0 [label="00/-"];
st1 -> st5 [label="11/1"];
st1 -> st3 [label="00/1"];
st1 -> st1 [label="10/1"];
st0 -> st2 [label="01/-"];
st0 -> st1 [label="10/-"];
st0 -> st0 [label="00/0"];
}
```

Each line defines attributes of a graph as a whole, a node, or a link. Both directed and undirected graphs are allowed (just switch -> to - for undirected). The resulting graph is shown in Figure 15.6 using four different layouts. The techniques are:

- *dot*—a layered approach that attempts to aim edges in the same direction;

- *neato*—a spring model based on multidimensional scaling;

- *circos*—a circular layout that is often effective for communications networks;

- *fdp*—a force-directed method that uses multigrid heuristics to enable handling of large graphs.

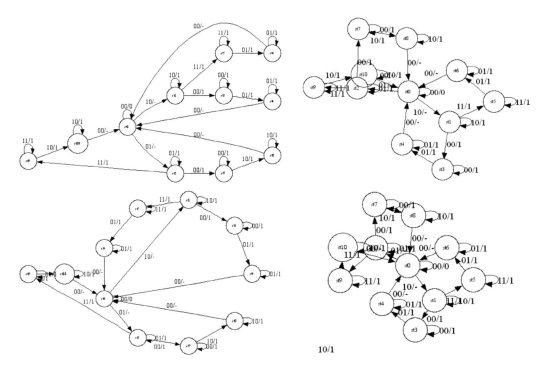

Figure 15.6.   Sample outputs from GraphViz, showing the same graph with four different layouts.

GraphViz runs on all popular platforms (Windows, UNIX, Mac), and is available via the GraphViz web site http://www.graphviz.org. The distribution includes a large number of sample graphs, and the web site contains a significant amount of documentation.

Other visualization tools for graphs include Tom Sawyer Software [414] (commercial).

15.2   Systems Based on Analysis Type

15.2.1   Statistics

GGobi [145] (like its predecessor XGobi) is an interactive tool for multivariate data visualization and analysis developed by Deborah Swayne, Dianne Cook, and Andreas Buja in the early 1990s while they were at Bellcore,

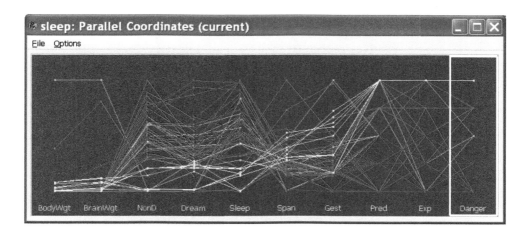

Figure 15.7.   An example of parallel coordinates in GGobi. Color is controlled by the rightmost dimension.

Inc. The system continues to evolve, with many others contributing to its development. It supports a number of different visualizations, including scatterplots, scatterplot matrices, bar charts, graphs, and parallel coordinates (see Figure 15.7). For each visualization, a control panel specific to that view is shown; clicking on any visualization exposes its control panel.

Color is used to link data between multiple views, and the user has a wide range of options for controlling the colors assigned to graphical entities. The user starts by selecting a data dimension to control the color; an interactive histogram can then be used to adjust the ranges of values assigned to each color (see Figure 15.8). Options are available to either use uniform bin width or bin count to create the initial histogram. All views of the data set will then use this color assignment. Linked brushing can then be used to highlight a selected data point in each view.

One of the most powerful tools within GGobi is the ability to generate and view so-called *grand tours* of the data, using a path through projection space to show the data from all views, or from user-constrained subsets of views. Users can change the speed of the movement and pause it to examine features of interest, as well as the viewing parameters that generated the view.

Many other analytic tools have been added to GGobi over the years, including linkage to the R statistics package [83], support for several graph drawing techniques (see Figure 15.9), imputation methods for handling

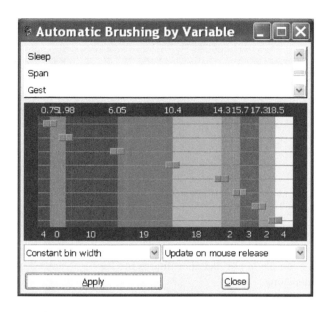

Figure 15.8.   Automated color brushing in GGobi. Users can assign any data dimension to control the color, and can adjust the ranges and colors used.

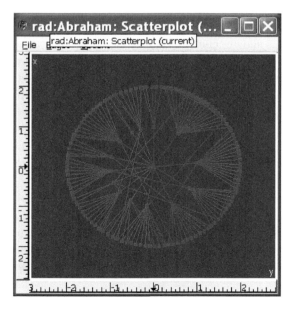

Figure 15.9.   An example of graph drawing in GGobi. Radial layouts are just one of several supported.

missing values, and dimension reduction methods such as PCA and MDS. The software runs on Windows, Mac, and Linux platforms, using the graphics package GTK as its base. Code, executables, documentation, and other support can be obtained from the GGobi web site [145].

Other packages for statistical graphing and analysis include SPSS [392] (commercial) and SAS [361] (commercial), though each of these has far more functionality than just statistical visualization.

15.2.2   Spatio-Temporal

Macrofocus [47, 285] has produced a number of powerful interactive tools for visually exploring data and information. One such tool is *InfoScope*, which links geographic views with several other visual and textual representations of information. A sample of InfoScope's main screen is shown in Figure 15.10. In this example, information compiled by the United Nations on human development can be explored in a wide assortment of ways. The geographic view (Figure 15.11) shows either a global or local view of the geographic components of the data set. A bifocal fisheye lens is used to perform context-preserving zooming by shift-dragging the mouse. The theme view (Figure 15.12) displays data points that have been laid out based on

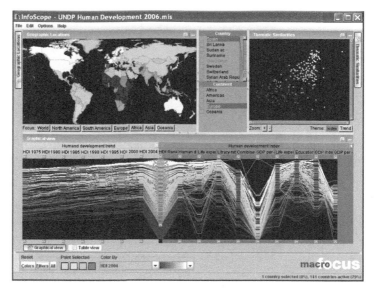

Figure 15.10.   A sample InfoScope screen.

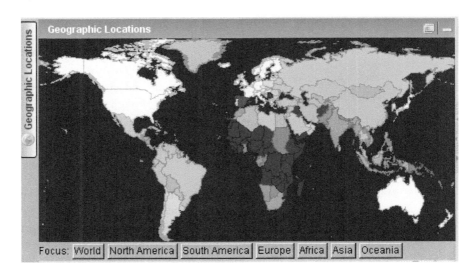

Figure 15.11.   The Geographic View in InfoScope: users can focus by using set buttons, or by shift-clicking on a map location.

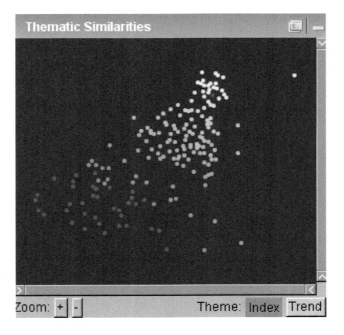

Figure 15.12.   The Theme View in InfoScope: users can select from a number of different layouts that show relations between data records.

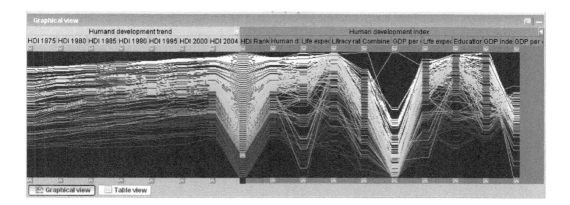

Figure 15.13.   The Graphical View in InfoScope, with a parallel coordinates plot of the data. Lower values on one of the dimensions have been filtered, resulting in dark coloring for those data records in all views.

similarities using an optimized spring-based MDS algorithm. The data view (Figure 15.13) can show the data either as parallel coordinates or in textual tables.

The power of InfoScope lies in its tight linkages between the different views. Brushing in any view will highlight the corresponding data in all views. Up to four brushes can be used to isolate individual records for simultaneous viewing. Data can be filtered by dragging handles at the top or bottom of each parallel coordinates axis to enable users to dim out high or low values. Color can be associated with any of the data variables, so the user can quickly switch between different thematic maps. Mousing over data records causes the labels and/or values to be displayed in all appropriate visualizations.

Animated changes are also used effectively in InfoScope. Zooming operations in each of the displays are performed in a continuous fashion, allowing users to easily maintain context. Dimensions in the parallel coordinates displays can be squeezed or spread out to enable easier analysis. In the theme view, switching between different themes results in a smooth animation of the movement of data points, allowing users to differentiate relationships that are relatively constant between themes versus those that differ significantly based on the theme.

Macrofocus software is not technically freeware; the company distributes executables for free that allow users to explore the several data sets that

Macrofocus provides, but in order to import one's own data, the commercial version of the software is needed. This is available via the company's web site [285] for a modest fee.

Spatio-temporal visualization is a strength of geographic information systems. Many such systems exist, including GRASS [157] (freeware), ArcGIS [116] (commercial), and ERDAS IMAGINE [114] (commercial).

15.3   Text Analysis and Visualization

Jigsaw [198] is a text visualization tool that was developed by John Stasko and his students at the Georgia Institute of Technology. This system explores entities (people, places, dates, money) and the relationships between them. Jigsaw uses several different views to present information to the user, including calendar, list, graph, scatterplot, text, and time line views, shown in Figure 15.14. Each view is presented as a separate window that updates automatically with the results of various queries.

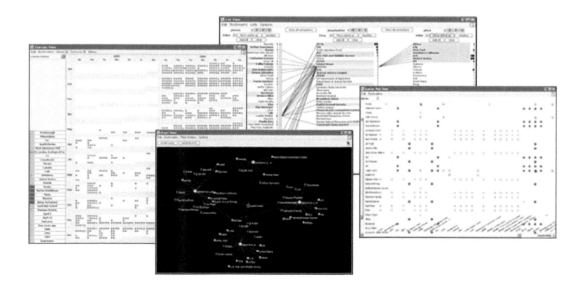

Figure 15.14.   Examples of various views in Jigsaw. Clockwise, starting from the top, you can see the list view, the scatterplot view, the graph view, and the timeline view.

Figure 15.15.   An example of a monitor configuration used with Jigsaw. Since real estate is critical, even this might be insufficient, and a display wall might be recommended.

All views are linked by default to one another, so acting on a document or entity in one view causes all other windows that are listening to update in accordance with that action. Listening can be toggled on or off in any window to preserve its state. It is often helpful to actually witness the views as they update, in order to more easily see how they are changing. One may find that it is necessary to use Jigsaw across four or more screens, as seen in Figure 15.15, to harness the system's full potential.

This tool is especially useful in data exploration involving large collections of data and information. Applications include military intelligence, law enforcement, or journalism, among many others. It is important to point out here that while this tool can help an analyst make sense of a large number of documents, their entities, and the connections between them, it is not a substitute for actually reading the documents. For example, it will help an analyst determine which documents are important and need to be read, saving the time of reading the entire document collection, which may not be feasible, and the hassle of trying to keep all the facts and connections straight.

15.4   Modern Integrated Visualization Systems

Tableau [403] is a commercial software package initially developed by Pat
Hanrahan and his students at Stanford. It is designed with more modern
interactions to aid in data analysis. Tableau allows users to import data
from a wide variety of formats. It provides standard visualizations, such as
graphs, scatterplots, bar charts, and pie charts, as well as maps. Tableau
recognizes data types such as geography, and automatically handles the first
steps in the generation of visualizations. It also supports the export of annotated presentation visualizations in PDF format and provides interactive
dashboards that automatically update from data sources, as well as web
publishing tools.

Figure 15.16 displays a map with merged data: gas field production
changes from 2004 to 2005, and the paths of hurricanes Rita and Katrina

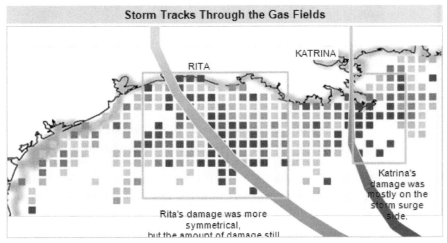

Long (deg) vs. Lat (deg). Color shows sum of Energy. Size shows average of Storm speed (mph).
The data is filtered on Year and Basin. The Year filter keeps 2005. The Basin filter keeps Atlantic.
The view is filtered on Storm Name, which keeps KATRINA and RITA. The marks are labeled by
Storm Name.

Avg. Storm speed (mph)   Sum of Energy
        6.21   15.00   4,913 [   ] 2,460,375
       10.00   ≥ 20.00

Figure 15.16.   An example of linked displays and tables in Tableau with overlaid paths colored
by hurricane strengths. A great deal of attention has been paid to the interface
and perceptual issues.

colored by their strength. Hurricane Rita caused more damage and was more symmetrical around its path, whereas Katrina's damage was more to its right, the surge side. Note the support for presentation visualization (legend, text, annotation).

15.5 Toolkits

15.5.1 Prefuse

Prefuse [32, 182] is a toolkit for building visualization applications. It includes two components, one using Java and the other written in Action-Script. The former provides a set of Java interfaces and classes to help software developers create stand-alone or web-based (Java applet) visualization applications. The latter, Prefuse Flare, enables users to create visualizations and animations for Adobe Flash Player. Prefuse Flare is a relatively new component, whose alpha version was released in October 2007, while the original Java-based toolkit was released in May 2006. (Prefuse is available at its web site [32].) Prefuse can support multiple data structures, visualization, and interaction techniques, as follows:

- table, graph, and tree data structures;

- various layout, color, size, and shape encodings, distortion, and animations;

- common interactive, direct-manipulation operations;

- animation through a general activity scheduling mechanism;

- view transformations, including panning and zooming;

- dynamic queries for interactive filtering;

- integrated text search;

- a physical force simulation engine for dynamic layout and animation;

- multiple views, including "overview+detail" and "small multiple" displays;

- a built-in, SQL-like expression language for writing queries;

- the ability to issue SQL queries to databases and map query results into Prefuse data structures;

- the ability to create custom processing, interaction, and rendering components.

The structure of the Prefuse toolkit is based on the information visualization reference model proposed by Ed Chi [72]. This model breaks up the information visualization process into several discrete steps. Prefuse implemented these steps as shown below:

Data transformations. Raw data is transformed to construct data tables, which are the internal representation of data. Note that data tables can also represent tree or network data, as well as multivariate data, despite the name. Prefuse can handle multiple file formats, such as CSV (comma-separated values), tab-delimited, GraphML, and TreeML files. GraphML and TreeML are two types of XML file formats to represent graph and tree structure data.

Visual mappings. This step aims to create a visual abstraction, a data model including visual features such as spatial layout, color, size, and shape. Prefuse provides filtering, layout, color, shape, and size assignment, distortion and animation for the construction of visual abstractions.

Visual transformations. This step performs the rendering and generates the final views. One visual abstraction can correspond to multiple views to support panning, zooming and "small multiple" displays.

Below are some important packages or classes in the Java-based Prefuse toolkit:

- *Packages data and data I/O*—defining table, tree, and graph data structures and reading or writing the physical files in various formats;

- *Class visualization*—creating the visual abstraction through adding the data that is instanced via Class VisualItem;

- *Class display*—responsible for the final rendering;

- *Package controls*—providing some classes to process mouse and keyboard actions on the display to help developers easily create interactions.

Several pictures from the Prefuse demo package or applications developed using Prefuse are shown below to convey some of the tool's power. Figure 15.17 shows an artificial data set to convey network relationships

g r a p h v i e w

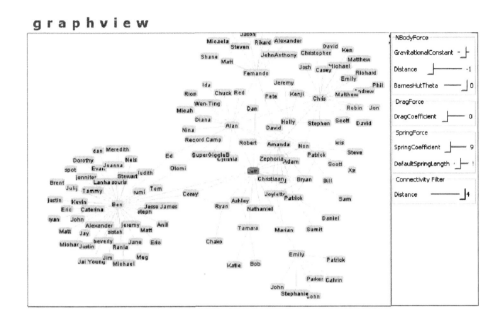

Figure 15.17.   An example of a graph generated with Prefuse.

among different people. Users can use the control panel on the right side to adjust visualization parameters for different exploration tasks. Another example is Data Mountain (see Figure 15.18), which displays thumbnails for a number of objects [342]. Users can drag and drop these thumbnails to visually manage the objects.

DocuBurst is an application developed based on Prefuse [82]. We present it to show the extensibility of Prefuse in developing various types of information visualization applications. Figure 15.19 uses a radial, space-filling tree to represent the hyponymy (IS-A) relationship among the keywords in a document. On the same level, the angular width of a word is proportional to its number of occurrences in this document. At the same time, the nodes having gold borders are the query result for keywords whose spelling starts with "pl."

15.5.2   The Visualization Toolkit

The Visualization Toolkit (*VTK*) [244] is an open source toolkit for building 3D visualizations that include computer graphics, modeling, imaging, and

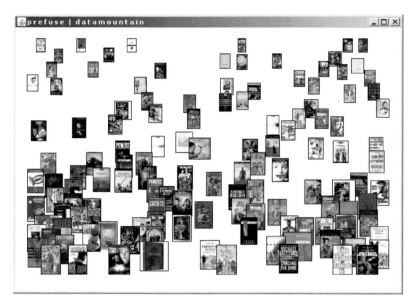

Figure 15.18.   Thumbnail view of a document collection using Prefuse.

Figure 15.19.   Examining keywords of a document and their relationships using Prefuse.

both scientific and information visualizations. It provides a number of UI tools, interaction widgets, annotation support, and even supports parallel computation. It is written in C++, but has a number of wrappers available.

VTK adheres to the classic visualization (and graphics) pipelines. It is based, like OpenDX and AVS, on the data-flow paradigm. Modules are connected into a network, and each performs transformations on data as it flows through the network. The fundamental data sets are polygonal data and structured points, and both structured and unstructured grids. These represent vertices, lines, polygons, and triangle strips (the fundamental primitives supported by graphics hardware of the 1990s), 2D and 3D images as structured points, and grids for finite element analysis.

The programming style is similar to OpenGL. The toolkit consists of numerous classes and is an extremely rich environment for programming, modeling, and the development of 3D graphics-based applications. The toolkit extends the power of OpenGL by providing higher-level functions and controls for the display of 3D data. Whereas programming in OpenGL requires direct dealing with the 3D points, programming with VTK entails dealing with the higher-level structure and higher-level controls, thereby relieving the programmer of low details and making application development more rapid and less error prone. Figure 15.20 displays a VTK interface highlighting the airflow over a delta aircraft using streamlines, and Figure 15.21 shows a computed tomography (CT) scan from the Visible Woman data set, which also includes full magnetic resonance imagery. An isosurface of the skin is clipped with a sphere, uncovering the underlying bones. Volume rendering is also possible (data from Bill Lorensen, while at General Electric Corporate Research and Development).

Examples of applications built by Kitware on top of VTK include

- *ITK*—an open source toolkit for image registration and segmentation;

- *ParaView*—an open source application for the analysis and visualization of data sets using distributed computation;

- *VolView*—an application for interactive volume visualization.

Another toolkit for building visualizations is the InfoVis Toolkit [120] (freeware).

15.5.3   Weave

Weave [266] is an open source modern web-based software visualization toolkit, developed by Georges Grinstein and his students at the Institute for

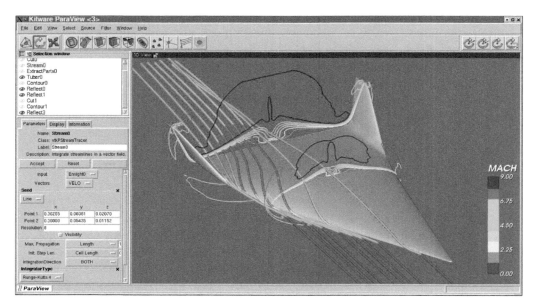

Figure 15.20.   Airflow streamlines over a delta aircraft. (Image from Kitware, http://www.vtk
.org/VTK/project/imagegallery.php.)

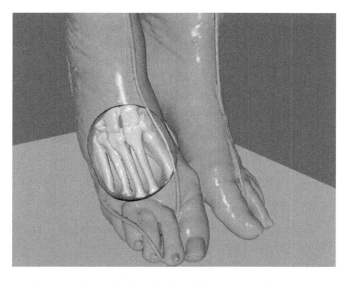

Figure 15.21.   A rendering of a section of the Visible Woman, combining outer skin and
bones from a CT scan. (Image from Kitware, http://www.vtk.org/VTK/project/
imagegallery.php.)

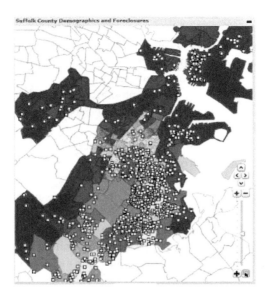

Figure 15.22.   Foreclosures (dots) and black population percentages (colors) in the Boston area,
generated with Weave.

Visualization and Perception Research at the University of Massachusetts
Lowell with seed funding from the Open Indicators Consortium. Weave can
be used with numerous data sources, server-based databases, spreadsheets,
or tables. It works with open data sources such as CKAN and data.gov. It
is available at http://iWeave.org. Weave provides flexible geographic visualization within web pages (see Figure 15.22). It supports a variety of visualizations (including scatterplots, bar or pie charts, line graphs, heatmaps,
RadViz, parallel coordinates and many more) and maps with multiple juris-
dictions (for example, neighborhoods, census tracts, municipalities, voting
districts, and watersheds). The software supports multiple visualizations in
a single browser web page simultaneously or on multiple web pages. There is
a desktop version. Data can be accessed through SQL queries. There is an
R editor and advanced analytics capabilities for large data sets via Parallel
R. Weave also works with Stata and other external tools such as Cytoscape.
Each data provider (i.e., an organization with their own data sets) sets up
their own server with security settings defined. Clients are then able to access this data across the web from a single web application—i.e., a user could
ask to look at both Boston and Atlanta to compare the two (in this case it
downloads Boston data from Boston servers and Atlanta data from Atlanta
servers).

Users can open data sets, view and interact with maps or other visualization tools, collaborate with other users, and review or restart previous sessions. Data that is downloaded is cached on the client side in order to provide (a) faster interactions after the initial download and (b) reduction of bandwidth between client and server. There are three main technologies used to create the client interface: Adobe Flex, JavaScript, and Flex SharedObjects.

The client interface includes visualization and data set navigation tools, session history, storytelling support, annotation, user preference settings, and collaboration features (including awareness, private and public spaces, and voice chatting). Annotations allow users to add their own comments and interpretations to the visualization tools and states they create. User preferences are persistent; any time the user logs in, the preferences are restored. Figure 15.22 shows one example map. Other Weave websites include Metrobostondatacommon.org and Ridatahub.org.

15.6   Libraries

15.6.1   D3.js

D3, Data Driven Documents (see Figure 15.23), was initially developed as a follow on to Protovis by Bostock, Heer, and Ogievetsky of the Stanford Visualization Group and is a framework that provides for the creation and control of interactive forms that run in web browsers. D3 supports a functional coding style. D3 works well with modern browsers and its core library has minimal requirements, namely, JavaScript and the W3C DOM API, Scalable Vector Graphics (SVG), HTML5 and Cascading Style Sheets (CSS) standards. This allows D3 to embed interactive and dynamic visualizations within an HTML page and apply data-driven transformations to the document. Its main goal was to manipulate the document object while improving the compatibility and reusability of the library.

Thus the JavaScript D3.js library allows a programmer to use prebuilt JavaScript functions to select elements, create SVG objects, style them, or add transitions, dynamic effects, or tool tips to them. These objects can also be widely styled using CSS.

Data sets can be bound to SVG objects using simple D3 functions to generate various visualizations. The data can be in various formats, most commonly JSON but as with most other toolkits, JavaScript functions can be written to read other data formats and perform extended functionality.

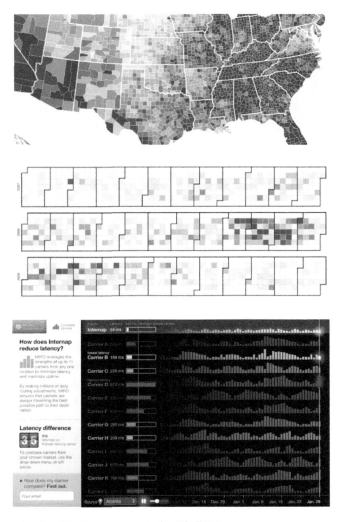

Figure 15.23.   Some example visualizations generated with D3.js.

15.6.2   QGIS

QGIS is an open source geographic information system (GIS) and an official project of the Open Source Geospatial Foundation (OSGeo). It runs on Linux, Unix, Mac OSX, Windows, and Android and supports numerous vector, raster, and database formats and functionality. It provides support for generating maps on the web (see Figure 15.24).

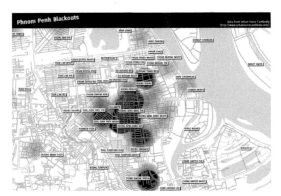
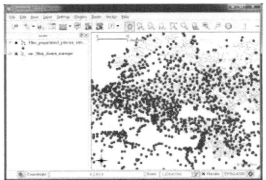

Figure 15.24.   Some example visualizations generated with QGIS.

15.6.3   Google Maps

Google Maps is a web-based application that provides numerous map-related services, including, for example, directions for driving, walking, or mass transit, finding rides, transit and traffic information, street or aerial views, all with interactive capabilities on the layered map (see Figure 15.25). Users can interact with the displayed maps by adding layers, such as traffic and directions, as well as display many different kinds of maps. Although Google Maps is free to use, it is a proprietary application and edits or other uses may require some form of signing on (e.g., a profile or license).

Google Maps provides numerous features that support the building of interesting rich applications. For example, voice-guided navigation, restaurant suggestions based on your current location, identification of landmarks

Figure 15.25.   Some example visualizations generated with Google Maps.

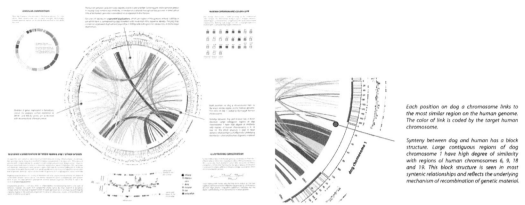

Figure 15.26.   Circos visualization with zoomed in portion (from http://circos.ca/guide/genomic/
img/circos-conservation.png).

or public transportation schedules to those landmarks. This makes Google
Maps very similar to a mashup library whereby users can combine Google
Maps with other data and applications.

15.6.4   Circos

Circos is a radial graph visualization developed by Martin Krzywunski at
Canada's Michael Smith Genomic Sciences Center (see Figure 15.26). Although its initial uses were in displaying genomic data, it has been applied
to numerous other applications domains but its strengths remain in biology.
It displays relationships between records all within a circle. The arcs in the
graph show connections to other points and thus Circos is a visualization
of graphs within a circular domain. With proper ordering, as in RadViz,
groupings may be discerned.

15.7   Related Readings

Several books on visualization contain descriptions of systems in current
use. Some, such as [83, 366, 408], describe a single package, while others,
including [390, 405], have figures and descriptions from many systems.

15.8   Exercises

1. Examine the functionality of two visualization tools that focus on the same type of data, one commercial and one public domain. How would you characterize their major similarities and differences? Under what conditions, and for what reasons, would you choose to use one over the other (besides, of course, the cost)?

2. Search the web for a visualization tool not mentioned in this chapter. Write a summary of the system in a style similar to those presented here. Include links to appropriate web pages and published papers. If you'd like, submit the resulting work to the book web site. Those deemed accurate and well written will be posted for others to read.

3. Choose one of the visualization systems described in this chapter and describe some possible applications for the system. You are encouraged to use the web to identify instances of "real" applications, as well as to use your imagination.

15.9   Projects

1. Download, install, and test at least one of the visualization systems described in this chapter. You should attempt to import a data set into the system from scratch, rather than using the ones provided with the system.

2. Download and install one of the toolkits described in this chapter. Follow the guidelines to create a simple application, such as a scatterplot or line graph, using the toolkit. Write a summary of your experience, including the difficulty/ease of creating an application, and your satisfaction level with the results.

CHAPTER 16

Research Directions in Visualization

Visualization is a sufficiently mature field that many groups of researchers are dedicating time to contemplate and predict the future directions for it. Many such research agendas have been published in recent years, including:

- Chris Johnson's list of top problems in scientific visualization [208];

- Chaomei Chen's list of top unsolved problems in information visualization [70];

- MacEachren and Kraak's report on research challenges in geovisualization [279];

- the NVAC research and development agenda for visual analytics [84];

- the NIH/NSF visualization research challenges report [207];

- the Grand Challenge in Information Visualization panel [160].

In this chapter we will identify and elaborate upon some of the common themes within these and other research agenda reports. Interested readers are directed to the original reports for in-depth descriptions, as well as identification of research areas specific to particular branches of the ever-enlarging field of visualization.

16.1   Issues of Data

Many of the current and proposed future research activities are centered on expanding the characteristics of data that can be effectively visualized. Some of these are discussed here.

Scale. Perhaps the most frequently addressed problem dealing with data is finding solutions for coping with ever-increasing sizes of data sets. For scientific domains, both acquired and simulated data have been growing in orders of magnitude, certainly outpacing Moore's Law. While only a few years ago researchers were focused on data sets of modest size (kilobytes to a few megabytes), it is now common to be looking at problems involving gigabytes and terabytes of data [377]. Solutions such as clustering, sampling, and abstraction are all being actively pursued in areas such as graph visualization [1], genetic sequence analysis, and large-scale flow simulations [429]. Massive data, that which does not fit into memory, is now commonplace.

Static versus dynamic. While most visualization techniques to date have been developed with the assumption that data is static (e.g., in files or databases), a growing interest is in the area of visual analysis of dynamic data [471]. An increasing number of *streaming* data sources are being studied in the database and data mining communities, and efforts to perform visual analysis on this type of data are starting to emerge. The basic concept is that the data is continually arriving, and has to be analyzed in real time, both because of the urgency with which analysis must be performed, as well as the fact that the volume of data precludes its permanent storage. Analysts are interested not only in the values at a particular time period, but also in how the data is changing. Since the data is so large in many cases, the data cannot even be stored as it is streaming.

Spatial versus nonspatial data. A growing number of application areas for visualization include both spatial and nonspatial data, including many scientific and engineering fields. To provide analysts with a powerful environment for studying this data, several recent efforts have focused on the integration of the spatial visualization techniques normally found in scientific visualization with the nonspatial techniques that are common in information visualization. The linkages between these distinct types of views is critical to successful analysis [250].

Nominal versus ordinal. The graphical attributes to which we map data in our visualizations, such as position, size, and color, are primarily quantitative in nature, while it is quite common to have data that is not quantitative, such as the name of a gene or the address of an employee. If this nominal data is to be used in the visualization, a mapping is needed. However, it is also important to ensure that relationships derived from visual analysis are truly part of the data, and not an artifact of the mapping. Some solutions include selecting color schemes and plot symbols that do not impose a perceptual ordering; others attempt to assign a numeric mapping of the nominal variables that preserves similarities and differences implied by the data [347]. For example, in a data set containing statistics about cars, two cars with similar characteristics in their attributes might have similar numbers assigned to the name field.

Structured versus nonstructured. Data can be classified based on the degree to which it follows a predictable structure. For example, tables of numbers would be considered highly structured, while newspaper articles may be regarded as unstructured. In between, we can have semi-structured data, such as an e-mail message that contains both a structured component (sender, time, receiver) and an unstructured part (message body). Key research problems include the extraction of useful information from the unstructured components of data sets and using the structured components as methods to index and organize the data records. Text analysis and visualization have made great progress, but the research is still in its infancy.

Time. Time is a special variable (and attribute of data). Time in dynamic data provides one view: a volume visualization over time deals with a physical representation, and a common interactive visualization uses time as a control. Spatio-temporal databases and queries and the visualization of results are becoming prominent as more data is being made publicly available. Time here can be handled just as in the volume visualization. But one can do more. For example, in a data set involving education and health indicator data, a useful question is how to identify similar patterns involving not just the data, but time as well. This begs a key research question of how to handle time as just another variable, and what are the ramifications.

Variable quality. While most visualization systems and techniques assume the data is complete and reliable, in fact most sources of data do not match these constraints. Often, there are missing fields in the data, often due to acquisition problems (e.g., defective sensors, incomplete forms). The quality of the data itself may also be problematic; out-of-date information can have low certainty associated with it, inaccurate sensors may produce values with significant variability, and manual entry of data can be error-prone. There is a great need for visualization technology that can cope with this data quality issue, this uncertainty, not only in its visualization, but also in keeping the analyst informed, so that the quality information can be incorporated into the decision-making process [351, 476].

16.2   Issues of Cognition, Perception, and Reasoning

Many of the foundational concepts in data and information visualization have their roots in our understanding of human perception, particularly in aspects of selecting effective mappings of data to graphical attributes such as color and size. Much less work, however, has built on our knowledge of human cognition and reasoning processes, with the notable exception being the Gestalt laws to better understand how visual grouping is performed. Thus, a far-reaching research agenda for the visualization field must include the study of how humans do problem solving with support from interactive visual displays, and how we can leverage this knowledge to design even more effective and powerful visual tools.

Part of this effort will be directed at raising the level at which visual tasks are performed. For example, rather than using the visualization to identify a cluster or trend, it might instead be focused on building a mental model of the entire phenomenon being studied. While this task may be comprised of several more primitive subtasks, the visualization tool will need to support the combination and sequencing of these tasks to enable the analyst to cope with the scale and complexity of the data and information being gathered and generated. Tasks such as discovering associated patterns of change in the data will involve not only visualization of the data, but also how the data is changing and how those changes may be associated with other changes taking place. These higher-level discoveries can then be used by the analyst to form, confirm, or refute hypotheses, expand or correct mental models, and provide confidence in decision-making processes [484].

Beyond decision making, we can also envision the expansion of visualization in the process of human learning. Educational opportunities for data and information visualization abound, but it is critical in the design of tools to support education that the theories of how humans learn be components of the design. People vary in the ways in which they learn most effectively: concrete versus abstract, sequential versus random. Different visual tools and mechanisms are likely to be needed to address these very different styles of learning.

In both problem solving and learning activities, we can also imagine using visualizations as a mechanism to expand and support the memory process, which is critical to both activities. Providing visual representations of intermediate results or supporting evidence, as well as structuring these artifacts on the screen, can help people remember facts and relationships in the same way that writing notes to oneself can relieve the human memory system of having to perform accurate recall. The extents to which visualization can be applied to this have yet to be extensively studied and exploited. Finally, and perhaps most importantly, we would like to measure cognitive primitives in the transfer from the data to the screen (easy) and from the screen to the human (hard).

16.3   Issues of System Design

One of the most crucial research challenges in developing visualization tools is determining how best to integrate computational analysis with interactive visual analysis. While many visualization systems support a modest number of computational tools, such as clustering, statistical modeling, and dimension reduction, and similarly many computational analysis systems support some amount of visualization, such as visualizing the analysis results, there have been no systems developed to date that provide a truly seamless integration of visual and computational techniques. Clearly, there are many tasks for which human perception and cognition are the most effective means to a solution; however, there are likely comparable numbers of tasks for which computational solutions are far superior. Indeed, in many situations, one can easily imagine using computational methods to guide the visual exploration, and vice versa. For example, one can use visual overviews of data to decide on appropriate parameters for filtering and clustering algorithms, after which the analyst could examine a resulting cluster to help select a computational model that best fits the characteristics of the data subset. Both visual and computational methods could then be used to ascertain the goodness of fit for the model. Many such scenarios can be easily envisioned.

Another key problem in visualization system design is the development of powerful new interaction paradigms to support the user's tasks. Many researchers believe that existing modes of interaction during visual analysis are ill-suited to the tasks being performed. This is likely due to the fact that while advances in hardware and visualization techniques have been moving by leaps and bounds, interaction methods have expanded at a much slower pace. While exciting and novel interaction tools can be seen in the immersive environment field, these and other types of interactions are either too low-level or are not designed with a particular high-level task in mind. What is needed is a fresh look at how users can interact with their data and information to perform specific tasks, such as determining the underlying phenomena or processes that are generating the data; understanding causal relationships; and designing, executing, and assessing "what if" scenarios. While existing low-level interactions such as point-and-click and drag-and-drop may be parts of the solution, there likely is much more needed to make visual analysis more efficient and effective.

Another issue is that most visualization systems require an expert user. Visualization in the last few years has made its appearance in daily newspapers and television, and interactive visualization is common on the web. These are minimally interactive and often very simple visualizations. Can we develop ones that are engaging and easy to use? This is becoming critical as we are encountering the era of the democratization of data.

Finally, we are still developing visualizations and visualization systems based on experience, pragmatic research, and heuristics. We do not yet have a science of visualization. There have been attempts at automating the process: given data, automatically generate a visualization. It's clear that tasks need to be incorporated into the process. It's just as clear that evaluation and metrics can help solve this complex problem.

16.4   Issues of Evaluation

In the early days of visualization research, rigorous evaluation was rarely performed; the assumption was that some visualization was better than no visualization for many tasks, and that if a new technique were developed, it was sufficient to simply place a couple of sets of images side by side and do a qualitative judgment of the results. More recently, there have been a large number of concerted efforts to incorporate a more formal evaluation process into visualization research, not only to enable quantification of improvements as they occur, but also to validate that visualization has measurable benefits to analysis and decision making [68, 321]. While many strategies have been developed and tested, there are many avenues of research toward improving the overall process. Some unanswered questions include:

- How important are aesthetics in designing visualizations, and how can they be measured?

- How can we use the understanding of human perceptual and cognitive limitations to design and improve visualizations?

- How do we measure the benefits of visual analysis as compared to more traditional computational analysis?

- What quantitative and qualitative measures of usability are most important for different categories (novices versus experts) and domains of users?

- How do we measure the information content, distortion, or loss in a visualization and use this information to produce more accurate and informative visualizations?

- What are the relative benefits of long, longitudinal studies with a small number of users, versus limited tests with a large number of subjects?

- What mixture of domain knowledge and visualization knowledge is needed to design and develop effective tools?

These and other aspects of evaluation will be a topic of discussion and research within the field for many years to come. The numerous competitions, including the VAST challenges, are a step in the right direction. The key point to make is that evaluation is a necessary component in moving a field from ad hoc methods to a real science, and we can learn from and build upon the evaluation strategies used in many other fields, such as human-computer interaction and sociology, to help validate the usefulness and effectiveness of techniques.

16.5   Issues of Hardware

Whenever computer technology advances, the applications that employ this technology must be reassessed to see how the advances can be leveraged. For visualization, there are several technologies that can and will have an impact.

Hand-held displays. Most people these days carry with them at least one form of digital display, whether it be mobile phones, PDAs, portable games, or tablets. While most visualization systems have been designed for desktop (or larger) displays, there are still significant opportunities to deliver interactive representations of information and data on these smaller devices. Examples of potential applications abound. For maintenance of aircraft, ships, and even buildings, having detailed presentations of wiring and plumbing diagrams, sensor output, and access paths can greatly simplify a technician's tasks. For crisis management during an emergency, police, firefighters, medical personnel, and other key players need interactive real-time access to information presented in a clear, unambiguous fashion. For those who monitor border crossings, rapid access to risk assessments, cargo manifests, and travel histories can help prevent entry by unwelcome individuals and material. The key is to develop visual solutions that make effective use of the limited display space and interactivity options.

Display walls. At the other extreme, large-scale displays, often involving multiple panels stretching 10–30 feet in each direction, are becoming more and more common, not only for control centers, but also for investigating large data and information spaces. While directly porting desktop solutions to these large displays is generally straightforward, it is not necessarily the most effective use of the display space. A better solution would be to redesign the visual analysis environment to arrange the displays of different types and different views of information in a way that supports the analysis. In this way, high-resolution displays can always be visible, rather than being covered in a typical desktop solution, thus requiring viewers to just move their head or shift their focus to see different views.

Immersive environments. Virtual and augmented reality systems have been frequently used within the visualization field. Early efforts, such as the virtual wind tunnel [52], enabled active, user-driven studies of the output of computational fluid dynamics experiments. Virtual walk-throughs and fly-throughs have been used in a diversity of fields, including architecture, medicine, and aeronautics. A key problem with this technology is the need to render the visualizations with minimal latency, which has spawned significant research in algorithm optimization. While the "killer application" for virtual environments has yet to be discovered, it will undoubtedly require significant visualization technology. Google glasses and similar devices providing an augmentation to the user's world are creating a number of opportunities for improved interactions and visualizations in dealing with the real world and the projected one.

Graphical processing units. The development of special-purpose graphics hardware has actually exceeded the growth in performance of general purpose CPUs, primarily driven by the computer game industry. There is much active research in the visualization community that focuses on harnessing this computational horsepower [249, 399]. Due to the architecture of a typical GPU, existing algorithms designed for CPUs do not, in general, port directly to the GPU, but require a nearly total redesign. However, as more and more software and hardware engineers become versed in this programming paradigm, it is likely we will see a growing use of this technology, not only for graphics, but also for complex algorithms in general.

Interaction devices. Each new device for user interaction with the computer opens up a wide range of possibilities for use in visualization. Voice/sound input and output have been extensively studied, though they are rarely an integral component of a visualization system. Tactile feedback is another area of great promise. Already, there have been efforts to train surgeons via virtual surgery, using force-feedback devices to mimic the feel of using probes and scalpels in surgical procedures [90]. Another avenue for development is to examine how different controllers used in modern game consoles could be employed to support visualization. The popular Wii input wand could be used for specifying actions via gestures. Other devices, such as head and eye trackers, may have significant potential in the visualization field. Interactive tables improve on the interactions with touch screens that have been used successfully for kiosks, and may lead to larger, less tiring environments. Brain control is another area providing great opportunities for controlling and interacting with visualizations. There are many opportunities for research on interaction metaphors.

16.6 Issues of Applications

Many advances in the field of visualization have been driven by the needs of a particular application domain. These advances are then often generalized to be applicable to many other domains and problems. Thus, research issues can be divided between those specific to a given domain and those involving the extension of techniques into other domains.

Depth-based innovations. To develop truly useful visualization tools for a particular domain, it is very important for the visualization designer to understand the domain and the tasks the domain specialist is trying to perform. Unfortunately, it is often the case that visualization designers just focus on the syntax or format of the data or information to be analyzed, which can easily result in tools that are either not useful/understandable to the domain analyst, or that provide little advantage over existing techniques. In a similar process, when domain experts attempt to design and develop visualization tools for their needs, they often produce tools with poor designs and user interfaces; this is mainly because they are generally unaware of the perceptual and cognitive issues involved in visualization design, as well as being unfamiliar with the range of different visualization techniques that have been developed for other purposes. In contrast, many of the most successful visualization systems have resulted from tight interactions between domain and visualization specialists, focusing on real problems that affect progress in a domain.

A key research challenge is thus to develop strategies to create effective collaborations between the two groups. Many professional meetings and workshops have focused on this issue over the past decade, and much can be learned from the reports that have been produced [207]. This is often difficult, due to issues of time (most active researchers have little in the way of free time), distance (willing collaborators may be in different institutes, cities, states, or even countries), and institutional constraints (collaborations between different schools within a university may be difficult to gain approval or support for). One of the keys to successful collaborative development is to convince domain experts that new visualization technology will improve their productivity, perhaps even allowing them to discover insights into their data that would otherwise be impossible to derive using existing technology. Thus the cost of analyzing the problem domain, designing, implementing, and evaluating solutions, and training the domain experts must be weighed against the potential benefits of the new technology. To improve the chances of success, there are many design considerations, such as ensuring that the technology being developed fits into the existing analysis environment; in general, people prefer to use tools they know, so designing new tools that interact seamlessly with existing tools can greatly improve the chances of acceptance within the domain.

Breadth-based innovations. Another direction of research is to broaden the number of applications in which data and information visualization can be applied. Indeed, it is hard to imagine an area in which visualization would not be applicable, as all areas of society are experiencing a glut of information, while at the same time, display devices have become ubiquitous. In many applications, visual information presentation is rapidly replacing much of the textual communication, such as weather reports, stock market behavior, health statistics, and so on. Daily schedules are often best captured in a graphical presentation of an hourly or daily calendar. Graphs are used to capture complex social networks, organizational charts, process flows, and communication patterns. One key to successful research and development in the broadening of the visualization field is to find the appropriate visual representations and interaction metaphors for new domains and tasks. Another critical problem is the conversion of data and information into a format that is amenable to existing visualization techniques. While many tools now accept input from standard database tables and spreadsheet files, much data and information is still stored either in proprietary formats or as unstructured files. Concerted efforts are needed, both in the visualization of unstructured data, as well as in automatic or semi-automatic conversion of unstructured data into structured forms, to tap into these rich sources of new visualization applications.

16.7 Related Readings

The interested reader is directed to the list of reports given at the start of this chapter for detailed descriptions of potential research directions for the field.

16.8 Exercises

1. Think of three activities you perform on a daily or weekly basis that you currently do without visualization, but that could potentially benefit from the introduction of visual tools. Describe some ideas for displaying the data or information and for interacting with the resulting views.

2. Which area of graphics hardware development do you feel will have the biggest impact on the field of visualization: display technology (i.e., bigger screens, more pixels) or rendering technology (e.g., faster GPUs)? Explain your answer.

3. Give an example of an unstructured data type, and describe what aspects of the data could be visualized.

4. For at least three different types of data (e.g., spatial, multivariate, relational), discuss the impact on typical visualization techniques if the data is dynamic, rather than static.

5. Watch a weather report on television on two separate occasions, once with only the sound, and the other time with only the visuals (no text, either). Describe the quantitative and qualitative information you got out of each report, including the strengths and weaknesses of each technique. How much more information would need to be in the visual presentation to equal the quantitative accuracy of the spoken/written report? How much more information would need to be in the spoken/written report to convey qualitative information seen in the visual presentation? Suggest possible enhancements to each.

6. Choose an application area that currently or potentially uses visualization, and search the web for a published research agenda or list of major unsolved problems. Is visualization mentioned? If so, for what tasks (i.e., exploration, confirmation, presentation)? Try to identify potential uses that were not mentioned.

7. Talk to a friend, colleague, or family member who you feel is an expert in some area other than visualization. Ask them if and how visualization plays a part in carrying out his or her work. Discuss some potential new ways that person might use visualization. Who knows? It may be the start of a beautiful collaboration!

8. What user interface issues come into play for visualization for the masses?

16.9   Projects

1. Write a program that will generate a continuous set of numbers. For example, you could start with a parametric equation and then either randomly perturb the parameters or the values after they are generated. Now write a program that plots these points in real time (you may need to slow down the generator by putting *sleep()* calls in). What do you observe happening? Implement at least two distinct solutions to the scale problem.

2. Take one of the visualization programs you wrote earlier in this course and modify it so that it would work on a small display (e.g., 200×300 pixels). What design changes would be required? What functionality would you need to make to enable effective use of the results? Implement and test some of these changes to see how well you anticipated the effect of reduced scale.

3. Take one of the visualization programs you wrote earlier in this course and modify it so that it would run on a GPU (this will likely involve acquiring a book on GPU programming). Note that you may only be able to perform a subset of the processing on the GPU. Compare the performance with your CPU-based implementation.

4. Rewrite the scatterplot program for use by the elderly. Issues include readability and ease of use. Test your results on someone over the age of 70. Incorporate their feedback into a revised version of the program.

History of Computer Graphics and Visualization

Some of the key events and developments that have advanced the computer graphics field are listed below. Students of data and information visualization would be well served by gaining a better understanding of the history of this field. Disclaimer: this history is by no means complete, and possibly has some inaccuracies in it. The authors welcome contributions and corrections, and we will maintain a "live" version of this document on the book's web site.

The 1960s:

- The term *computer graphics* was coined by William Fetter, Boeing (1960).

- First computer-animated film (*Two-Gyro Gravity-Gradient Attitude Control System*, by Edward Zajak, Bell Labs) (1961).

- First video game (Spacewar) developed by Steve Russell at MIT (1961).

- Sketchpad, by Ivan Sutherland, MIT—first extensive interactive drawing program (1963).

- First computer model of a human figure, by William Fetter, Boeing, for use in the study of cockpit design (1964).

- First computer animation language (BEFLIX), by Ken Knowlton, Bell Labs (1965).

- Jack Bresenham develops efficient algorithm to scan convert lines (1965).

- First computer-generated art show, Stuttgart (1965).

- Ivan Sutherland creates first head-mounted display (1966).

- Ralph Baer develops first home video game (Odyssey) that allowed users to move points around a screen (1966).

- Scan-line hidden surface removal algorithm developed by Wylie, Romney, Evans, and Erdahl (1967).

- Jacques Bertin's *Semiologie Graphique* is published (1967).

- Ray tracing invented by Appel (1968).

- First frame buffer built (three bits), at Bell Labs (1969).

- Area subdivision hidden surface removal algorithm developed by Warnock (1969).

The 1970s:

- Intensity interpolated shading developed by Gouraud (1971).

- Goldstein and Nagel perform first ray tracing using Boolean set operations (the basis of constructive solid geometry) (1971).

- First 8-bit frame buffer (with color map) built by Richard Shoup, Xerox PARC (1972). Evans and Sutherland started marketing frame buffers in 1973–74, with first ones sold to NYIT.

- Depth-sorting hidden surface removal algorithm developed by Newell, Newell, and Sancha (1972).

- *Westworld* debuts—first significant entertainment film that employed computer animation (1973).

- Herman Chernoff introduces the use of cartoon faces to convey multivariate data (1973).

- Ed Catmull pioneers texture mapping on curved surfaces (1974).

- Sutherland and Hodgman develop a polygon clipping algorithm (1974).

- PRIM-9, the first interactive visualization system for visual data analysis, is presented by Fishkiller, Friedman, and Tukey (1974).

- Phong Bui-Tuong develops the specular illumination model and normal interpolation shading (1975).

- Scatterplot Matrix introduced by John Hartigan (1975).

- Jim Blinn introduces environmental mapping (1976).

- Frank Crow develops solutions to the aliasing problem (1977).

- Jack Bresenham develops an efficient algorithm to scan convert circles (1977).

- Jim Blinn introduces bump mapping (1978).

- Cyrus and Beck develop a parametric line-clipping algorithm (1978).

- Linked brushing invented by Carol Newton (1978).

- First synthesis of rendering transparent surfaces, by Kay and Greenberg (1979).

- Herman and Liu demonstrate volume rendering on tomographic data (1979).

The 1980s:

- Turner Whitted creates a general ray-tracing paradigm that incorporates reflection, refraction, antialiasing, and shadows (1980).

- Fisheye lens developed by George Furnas (1981).

- *TRON* released by Disney films, containing 15 minutes and 235 scenes of computer-generated images. Companies involved were MAGI, Triple I, Digital Effects, and Robert Abel and Associates (1982).

- Octrees introduced as a mechanism for geometric modeling by Meager (1982).

- Silicon Graphics is founded by James Clark (1982).

- James Blinn wins first SIGGRAPH Computer Graphics Achievement Award (1983).

- Particle systems introduced by William Reeves (1983).

- Radiosity introduced by Goral, Torrance, Greenberg, and Battaile (1984).

- Liang and Barsky develop an efficient clipping algorithm for rectilinear clipping regions (1984).

- Grand Tour for exploring multivariate data invented by Daniel Asimov (1985).

- Parallel Coordinates introduced by Al Inselberg (1985).

- Pixar is bought from Lucasfilm by Steve Jobs (1986).

- Marching Cubes algorithm published by Lorensen and Cline (1987).

- *Tin Toy* wins Academy Award for best animated short film (1989).

The 1990s:

- First IEEE Visualization Conference (1990).

- Hanrahan and Lawson introduce Renderman (1990).

- Treemaps introduced by Ben Shneiderman (1991).

- IBM releases Visualization Data Explorer, later to become OpenDX (1991).

- Advanced Visual Systems releases AVS (1991).

- Silicon Graphics, Inc., release the OpenGL specifications (1992).

- First CAVE virtual reality environment presented at SIGGRAPH by the University of Illinois (1992).

- *Doom* and *Myst* released (1993).

- Table Lens introduced by Ramesh Rao and Stuart Card (1994).

- XmdvTool released to the public domain (1994).

- Keim introduces pixel-oriented techniques in VisDB (1994).

- First Information Visualization Conference (1995).

- Buena Vista Pictures releases *Toy Story*, the first full-length, computer-generated feature film (1995).

- First-generation GPUs released—ATI Rage, Nvidia TNT2, and 3Dfx Voodoo3 (1996).

- *Quake* released (1996).

- Founding of Spotfire, Inc. (1996); acquired by TIBCO in 2007.

- Second-generation GPUs released—NVidia GeForce 256, ATI Radeon 7500, and S3 Savage3D (1998).

- Alias Maya released (1998).

- Pixar's *Geri's Game* wins Academy Award for animated short film (1998).

- *Star Wars Episode I: The Phantom Menace* is released, containing 68 digital characters (including Jar Jar Binks) (1999).

The 2000s:

- Third-generation GPUs released—Nvidia GeForce 256, ATI Radeon 8500, and Microsoft Xbox (2001).

- Fourth-generation GPUs released—Nvidia GeForce FX and ATI Radeon 9700 (2003).

- Founding of Tableau Software, Inc. (2003).

- Thomas and Cook publish *Illuminating the Path: Research and Development Agenda Visual Analytics* (2005).

- First Visual Analytics Science and Technology Symposium (2006).

Example Data Sets

In this book, we use a variety of data sets to help explain techniques and illustrate design principles, all available from the book's web site (http://www.idvbook.com/). By using data from a wide range of disciplines, we hope to convey to the reader exactly how widespread the applications for visualization are; indeed, many innovations in the field have resulted from the exploration of ways to visualize data in new fields. It also is our experience that visualization specialists can find roles for themselves in virtually any domain, which enables us to expand our understanding of new disciplines while making a significant contribution to the advancement of both the visualization field and the application domain area.

One of the most common roadblocks to visualizing data is converting files from their original format (usually dependent on the tools used to acquire the data) to one that is acceptable to the visualization tool you wish to use. Thus, by providing a number of sample data sets, along with detailed descriptions of their formats, we hope to facilitate users in this process. All data sets used in this textbook can be found at the book's web site, along with links to other data repositories and sites containing very detailed descriptions and software for different popular data formats.

The Iris Data Set

The Iris data set, a small, well-understood and known data set, consists of the measurements of four attributes of 150 iris flowers from three types of irises. The typical task for the Iris data set is to classify the type of iris based on the measurements. It is one of the most analyzed data sets in statistics, data mining, and multivariate visualization. It was first published by R. A. Fisher in 1936 [127] and is widely available (our copy came from StatLib at CMU (http://lib.stat.cmu.edu)). The file is in CSV format, which can be imported to Excel and other programs. The data dimensions are as follows:

1. sepal length in cm;

2. sepal width in cm;

3. petal length in cm;

4. petal width in cm;

5. class:

   - Iris Setosa
   - Iris Versicolour
   - Iris Virginica

The Detroit Data Set

This is a small data set dealing with homicide rates in Detroit between the years 1961 and 1973. The goal should be to try to find the variables that best predict the homicide rate. The original data were collected by J.C. Fisher and used in his paper [128]. The copy we distribute is also from StatLib at CMU and is in ASCII format. There is one record per year.

The data dimensions are as follows:

- FTP—Full-time police per 100,000 population;

- UEMP—% unemployed in the population;

- MAN—number of manufacturing workers in thousands;

- LIC—Number of handgun licenses per 100,000 population;

- GR—Number of handgun registrations per 100,000 population;

- CLEAR—% homicides cleared by arrests;

- WM—Number of white males in the population;

- NMAN—Number of non-manufacturing workers in thousands;

- GOV—Number of government workers in thousands;

- HE—Average hourly earnings;

- WE—Average weekly earnings;

- HOM—Number of homicides per 100,000 of population;

- ACC—Death rate in accidents per 100,000 population;

- ASR—Number of assaults per 100,000 population.

The Breakfast Cereal Data Set

This data set contains nutritional information for 77 different breakfast cereals. It was used for the 1993 Statistical Graphics Exposition as a challenge data set. We retrieved this data from StatLib at CMU. The data is from the nutritional labels and is in CSV format. The variables are:

- cereal name;

- manufacturer (e.g., Kellogg's);

- type (cold/hot);

- calories (number);

- protein (g);

- fat (g);

- sodium (mg);

- dietary fiber (g);

- complex carbohydrates (g);

- sugars (g);

- display shelf (1, 2, or 3, counting from the floor);

- potassium (mg);

- vitamins and minerals (0, 25, or 100, respectively);

- weight (in ounces) of one serving (serving size);

- cups per serving.

Manufacturers are represented by their first initial: A = American Home Food Products, G = General Mills, K = Kelloggs, N = Nabisco, P = Post, Q = Quaker Oats, R = Ralston Purina.

The CT Head Data Set

This data set consists of a 113-slice MRI data set of a CT study of a cadaver head. Slices are stored in individual files as a 256×256 binary array (no header). Format is 16-bit integers (Mac ordering)—two consecutive bytes make up one binary integer. Data was acquired using a General Electric CT Scanner and provided courtesy of North Carolina Memorial Hospital. The data was acquired from http://graphics.stanford.edu/data/voldata/.

The UVW Data Set

This is a 3D vector data set generated via a computational fluid dynamics simulator. The data is in ASCII format and represents one time slice of unsteady velocity in a turbulent channel flow. After a 2-line header, the rows of the file consist of 6 dimensions—x, y, z, u, v, and w. The dimensions are 96 by 65 by 48. The data set was provided by Drs. Jiacai Lu and Gretar Tryggvason, ME Department, Worcester Polytechnic Institute. Note, there is roughly a 20:1:1 ratio between u, v, and w.

The Dow Jones Industrial Average Data Set

This is a time-series data set containing more than 100 years of daily averages for the Dow Jones. The source is http://www.analyzeindices.com/dow-jones-history.shtml, but it can also be found on StatLib. The format is ASCII text, with each line being of the form YYMMDD, closing value.

The Colorado Elevation Data Set

This is an array of elevations in Colorado. The data is included in the distribution of OpenDX (http://www.opendx.org/). The format is a binary file with a 268-byte header followed by a 400 by 400 array of 1-byte elevations.

The City-Temperature Data Set

This is an ASCII file containing the average January temperatures for a number of U.S. cities. It consists of the city name and state, the average temperature, and the longitude and latitude. It is in Excel format.

Sample Programs

Many different languages and programming environments can be used to design visualizations. Some, such as AVS and OpenDX, use a visual programming structure that allows users to construct programs via point-and-click. Other languages, such as Java and C++, have bindings to different graphics libraries (2D and 3D), that allow you to build significant applications, though the programmer needs a fair amount of programming experience to accomplish this. In between are languages such as Processing that try to hide some of the low-level details of the programming language, allowing you to rapidly construct nontrivial visualizations. In this appendix, we show some examples of such programs. Additional code is available on the book's web site.

A Processing Program for Terrain Visualization

```
/**
 * TopoSurface - by Matt Ward
 * This program reads in a file of elevation data and displays
 * a rubber sheet view.  Interactions supported include zooming,
 * panning, and rotation.  Panning is via mouse motions, while
 * zooming and rotation are keyboard clicks.
 */
int[][] distances = new int[400][400]; // buffer for elevation data
int shiftX, shiftY; // translation amounts
float angleX, angleY, angleZ; // rotation amounts
int camera_distance; // zooming amount

void setup() {
  size(400,400, P3D); // elevation data is 400 by 400
```

```
    shiftX = width/2; // center the initial translation
    shiftY = height/2;
    angleX = 0;
    angleY = 0;
    angleZ = 0;
    camera_distance = 500;

// open a file and read its binary data
byte b[] = loadBytes("colorado_elev.vit");

// skip 268 byte header and convert bytes to ints
  for(int i = 0; i < 400; i++)
   for(int j = 0;j < 400; j++)
      distances[i][j] = b[268 + i*400 + j] & 0xff;
}

void draw() {
  background(0);
  lights();
// set camera to look at middle of data
  camera(200, 200, camera_distance,
         200, 200, 0,
         0.0, 1.0, 0.0);
// interpret left mouse clicks as translates
  if(mousePressed && mouseButton == LEFT)  {
    shiftX = mouseX - width/2;
    shiftY = mouseY - height/2;
  }
  translate(shiftX, shiftY);
// now perform all rotations
  rotateY(angleY);
  rotateX(angleX);
  rotateZ(angleZ);
// don't draw edges, set fill to white, and draw the surface
  noStroke();
  fill(255, 255, 255);
  drawSurface(distances);
}

// handle all keystroke events for zoom and rotate (fixed amounts)
  void keyPressed()  {
    if(key == '-') camera_distance += 100;
    else  if (key == '+') camera_distance -= 100;
    else if(key == 'x') angleX += .25;
    else if(key == 'X') angleX -= .25;
    else if(key == 'y') angleY += .25;
```

```
      else if(key == 'Y') angleY -= .25;
      else if(key == 'z') angleZ += .25;
      else if(key == 'Z') angleZ -= .25;
  }

// to draw the surface, make a bunch of triangle strips
void drawSurface(int distances[][])  {

int x = 1; // x and y are the distances between adjacent data points
int y = 1;
float px = -width/2, py = -height/2; // we want things centered on
                                     // origin
float pts = 399; // the number of triangles in a strip

for(int j = 0;j < pts;j++)  {
// create a triangle strip for each row in the data
  beginShape(TRIANGLE_STRIP);
// first vertices are along edge
    vertex(px,py, (float)distances[j][0]);
    vertex(px,py+y, (float)distances[j+1][0]);
// for rest of vertices, alternate between 2 rows
    for (int i = 0; i < pts; i++) {
      px = px + x;
      vertex(px, py, (float)distances[j][i+1]);
      vertex(px, py+y, (float)distances[j+1][i+1]);
      }
  endShape();
// shift row and reset x to edge
  py = py + y;
  px = -width/2;
  }
}
```

A Processing Program to View Slices of Flow Data

```
/**
 * FlowSlicer - visualizing 3D flow data.  Written by Matt Ward
 *
 * Loads the file uvw.dat, which is an ascii file with about 400K
 * 3D vectors. The format is [x y z u v w] in floating point.
 * The output is an animation of the slices on a uniform grid
 * with 2 of the 3 vector components creating a line in the
 * direction of the vector.
 */
```

```
String[] lines; // lines of the input data
float[][][] u, v, w; // storage for the 3D vectors
int slice = 0;  // slice of the volume being visualized
void setup() {
  size(800, 800);
  background(0);
  stroke(255);
  frameRate(1); // put a little space between frams
  lines = loadStrings("uvw.dat");  // data set is hard coded
  u = new float[96][65][48];  // as are the dimensions!
  v = new float[96][65][48];
  w = new float[96][65][48];
  int index = 2;  // first 2 lines are metadata
  for(int i = 0; i < 48; i++)
    for(int j = 0;j < 65;j++)
      for(int k = 0;k < 96; k++)  {
        String[] pieces = split(lines[index], ' ');
                            // break line into tokens
        u[k][j][i] = float(pieces[3]) * 5.;
               // note dx/u is scaled different from others
        v[k][j][i] = float(pieces[4]) * 100.;
        w[k][j][i] = float(pieces[5]) * 100.;
        index++;  // get the next line of data
      }
}

// draw the current slice
void draw() {
  int sx, sy, ex, ey;
  background(0);  // clear the display first
  for(int j = 0;j < 65;j++)
    for(int k = 0; k < 96; k++)  {
      sx = j * 8;  // I space the points out so vectors don't overlap
      sy = k * 8;
      ex = sx + (int)u[k][j][slice];
                            // endpoint is based on 2 vector components
      ey = sy + (int)w[k][j][slice];
      line(sx, sy, ex, ey);
    }
  slice++;  // increment the slice - if the last one, start over
  if(slice >= 48) {
    slice = 0;
  }
}
```

A Java Program to View Slices of Flow Data

```
-------------FlowView.java-------------------------------------
/* Program to view uvw.dat, a 3D flow data set.  Written by Zhenyu Guo.
 * Uses 2 classes - FlowView and Voxel (programs similar
 * to VolumeSlicer).
 * Note - it takes a little while to read in data.
 */

import java.util.*;
import java.awt.*;
import java.awt.event.*;
import java.awt.image.MemoryImageSource;
import javax.swing.*;
import java.io.*;
import javax.swing.event.ChangeEvent;
import javax.swing.event.ChangeListener;

public class FlowView {

private JFrame frm;

private JPanel p1;

JLabel jlabel;
JSlider jslider;
JComboBox jcb;

SlicingFlowData svd;

//  set volume size - Note this is fixed
int l = 96;
int h = 65;
int w = 48;

// set up UI
public FlowView() {

frm = new JFrame("Flow Dataset Visualization");
Container c = frm.getContentPane();
c.setLayout(null);

p1 = new JPanel();
svd = new SlicingFlowData();
svd.setBackground(Color.WHITE);
svd.orientation = 0;
```

```
                svd.setBounds(0,0,1400,900);
                c.add(p1);
                c.add(svd);
                jslider = new JSlider(0, 100, 0);
                jslider.setMaximum(w-1);
                jslider.addChangeListener(listener);
                jlabel = new JLabel("0");
                jcb = new JComboBox();
                jcb.addItem("aligned with x");
                jcb.addItem("aligned with y");
                jcb.addItem("aligned with z");
                jcb.addActionListener(new action());
                p1.add(jcb);
                p1.add(jslider);
                p1.add(jlabel);
                p1.setBounds(100,900,200,100);

                frm.setSize(1450, 1050);
                frm.setLocation(0, 0);
                frm.setVisible(true);
                frm.setDefaultCloseOperation(JFrame.EXIT_ON_CLOSE);
                }


                // respond to slider changes
                ChangeListener listener = new ChangeListener() {
                        public void stateChanged(ChangeEvent e) {
                            if (e.getSource() == jslider) {
                                int i = jslider.getValue();
                                jlabel.setText(String.valueOf(i));
                                svd.pos = i;
                                Graphics g = svd.getGraphics();
                                svd.paintComponent(g);
                            }
                        }
                    };

                // respond to orientation selection
                    class action implements ActionListener {
                public void actionPerformed(ActionEvent e) {

                // decide which button is pressed and execute operation
                if (e.getSource() == jcb){
                int i = jcb.getSelectedIndex();
                svd.orientation = i;
                jlabel.setText("0");
```

```
jslider.setValue(0);
if(i==0){
jslider.setMaximum(w - 1);
}else if (i==1){
jslider.setMaximum(h - 1);
}else if(i==2){
jslider.setMaximum(l - 1);
}
Graphics g = svd.getGraphics();
                svd.paintComponent(g);
}
}
}

// Start it up
    public static void main(String[] args) {
     try {
     new MainFrame();
     } catch (Exception e) {
     e.printStackTrace();
     }
    }
}

class SlicingFlowData extends JPanel {

Voxel [][][] dataset;  // each voxel has a 3D vector in it

Color [] ColorMap;  // a discrete ramp that is then interpolated

//  set volume size
int l = 96;
int h = 65;
int w = 48;

//  three orientations for a cut slice
//  acceptable value: 0, 1 or 2
int orientation;

//  the cut slice position
int pos = 0;

double minMagnitude = 10000000;
double maxMagnitude = -10000;

SlicingFlowData() {
```

```
dataset = new Voxel [l][h][w];
Read();
initColorMap();
}

// A yellow-to-blue discrete ramp
void initColorMap(){
ColorMap = new Color[9];
ColorMap[0] = new Color(255, 255, 217);
ColorMap[1] = new Color(237, 248, 177);
ColorMap[2] = new Color(199, 233, 180);
ColorMap[3] = new Color(127, 205, 187);
ColorMap[4] = new Color(65, 182, 196);
ColorMap[5] = new Color(29, 145, 192);
ColorMap[6] = new Color(34, 94, 168);
ColorMap[7] = new Color(37, 52, 148);
ColorMap[8] = new Color(8, 29, 88);
}


// how to paint for visualization
public void paintComponent(Graphics g) {
clear(g);
Graphics2D g2d = (Graphics2D) g;

int pixDis = 14;  // set separation between base points of vectors
int maxArrowLength = 12;  // set maximum length of arrow

int startX = 10;  // set the position for the initial arrow
int startY = 10;

int r = 1;  // half the radius of the circle at the head of the arrow

BasicStroke bs0 = (BasicStroke) g2d.getStroke();
BasicStroke bs = new BasicStroke(2.5f);
g2d.setStroke(bs);

if (orientation == 0) {
// find min and max sizes in this projection
double min = 100000;
double max = -100000;
for (int i = 0; i < l; i++) {
for (int j = 0; j < h; j++) {
Voxel v = dataset[i][j][pos];
double m = v.orientation_x*v.orientation_x
                    + v.orientation_y*v.orientation_y;
```

```
if(m<min){
min = m;
}
if(m>max){
max = m;
}
}
}
min = Math.sqrt(min);
max = Math.sqrt(max);

// compute position, dimensions, and color for each vector
for (int i = 0; i < l; i++) {
for (int j = 0; j < h; j++) {
int x = startX + i*pixDis;
int y = startY + j*pixDis;
Voxel v = dataset[i][j][pos];
double m = Math.sqrt(v.orientation_x*v.orientation_x
                     + v.orientation_y*v.orientation_y);
int deltaX = (int)(v.orientation_x * (double)maxArrowLength
                     * ((m-min)/(max-min)));
int deltaY = (int)(v.orientation_y * (double)maxArrowLength
                     * ((m-min)/(max-min)));
g2d.setColor(getColor(v.magnitude));
// draw the vector with a filled circle at the head
g2d.drawLine(x, y, x + deltaX, y + deltaY);
g2d.drawOval(x + deltaX-r, y + deltaY-r, 2*r, 2*r);
}
}
// do the same for the other orientations
} else if (orientation == 1) {
double min = 100000;
double max = -100000;
for (int i = 0; i < l; i++) {
for (int j = 0; j < w; j++) {
Voxel v = dataset[i][pos][j];
double m = v.orientation_x*v.orientation_x + v.orientation_z
                     * v.orientation_z;
if(m<min){
min = m;
}
if(m>max){
max = m;
}
}
}
```

```
min = Math.sqrt(min);
max = Math.sqrt(max);
for (int i = 0; i < l; i++) {
for (int j = 0; j < w; j++) {
int x = startX + i*pixDis;
int y = startY + j*pixDis;
Voxel v = dataset[i][pos][j];
double m = Math.sqrt(v.orientation_x*v.orientation_x
                     + v.orientation_z*v.orientation_z);
int deltaX = (int)(v.orientation_x * (double)maxArrowLength
                     * ((m-min)/(max-min)));
int deltaY = (int)(v.orientation_z * (double)maxArrowLength
                     * ((m-min)/(max-min)));
g2d.setColor(getColor(v.magnitude));
g2d.drawLine(x, y, x + deltaX, y + deltaY);
g2d.drawOval(x + deltaX -r, y + deltaY-r, 2*r, 2*r);
}
}
}else if (orientation == 2) {
double min = 100000;
double max = -100000;
for (int i = 0; i < h; i++) {
for (int j = 0; j < w; j++) {
Voxel v = dataset[pos][i][j];
double m = v.orientation_y*v.orientation_y
                     + v.orientation_z*v.orientation_z;
if(m<min){
min = m;
}
if(m>max){
max = m;
}
}
}
min = Math.sqrt(min);
max = Math.sqrt(max);
for (int i = 0; i < h; i++) {
for (int j = 0; j < w; j++) {
int x = startX + i*pixDis;
int y = startY + j*pixDis;
Voxel v = dataset[pos][i][j];
double m = Math.sqrt(v.orientation_y*v.orientation_y
                     + v.orientation_z*v.orientation_z);
int deltaX = (int)(v.orientation_y * (double)maxArrowLength
                     * ((m-min)/(max-min)));
int deltaY = (int)(v.orientation_z * (double)maxArrowLength
```

```
                                    * ((m-min)/(max-min)));
g2d.setColor(getColor(v.magnitude));
g2d.drawLine(x, y, x + deltaX, y + deltaY);
g2d.drawOval(x + deltaX-r, y + deltaY-r, 2*r, 2*r);
}
}
}


g2d.setStroke(bs0);
}


// The color is a yellow-to-blue ramp, interpolated from a discrete
// set of 8 colors
Color getColor(double magnitude){
double colorRange = this.maxMagnitude - this.minMagnitude;
// compute the index into the discrete ramp
double v = 8.0 * (magnitude - this.minMagnitude) / colorRange;
int lowColorIdx = (int)v;
// if this is the maximum magnitude, just return highest color
if(lowColorIdx==8){
return this.ColorMap[lowColorIdx];
}
// need to interpolate between this color and next
int highColorIdx = lowColorIdx + 1;

// interpolation to get a color
double r = (v-(double)lowColorIdx)*
          ((double)this.ColorMap[highColorIdx].getRed()-
          (double)this.ColorMap[lowColorIdx].getRed()) +
          (double)this.ColorMap[lowColorIdx].getRed();
double g = (v-(double)lowColorIdx)*
          ((double)this.ColorMap[highColorIdx].getGreen()-
          (double)this.ColorMap[lowColorIdx].getGreen()) +
          (double)this.ColorMap[lowColorIdx].getGreen();
double b = (v-(double)lowColorIdx)*
          ((double)this.ColorMap[highColorIdx].getBlue()-
          (double)this.ColorMap[lowColorIdx].getBlue()) +
          (double)this.ColorMap[lowColorIdx].getBlue();

return new Color((int)r, (int)g, (int)b);
}

// input the data and compute min and max magnitudes
void Read() {
String s = "uvw.dat";  // the input filename
try {
```

```
File f = new File(s);
System.out.println("reading: " + s);
if (!f.exists()) {
System.out.println(s + "doesn't exist");
}
FileInputStream inputStream = new FileInputStream(f);
BufferedReader br = new BufferedReader(new InputStreamReader(inputStream));

String [] line;  // one line of input file

// pass the first two lines - these are header information
br.readLine();
br.readLine();

// read a single file - note we scale v and w, as otherwise u dominates
for(int k=0; k<w; k++){
for(int j=0; j<h; j++){
for(int i=0; i<l; i++){
line = br.readLine().split(" ");
Voxel curReadingVoxel = new Voxel(Double.parseDouble(line[0]),
Double.parseDouble(line[1]), Double.parseDouble(line[2]),
Double.parseDouble(line[3]), Double.parseDouble(line[4])* 20.,
Double.parseDouble(line[5]) * 20.);
dataset[i][j][k] = curReadingVoxel;
}
}
}

//get max and min magnitude
for(int k=0; k<w; k++){
for(int j=0; j<h; j++){
for(int i=0; i<l; i++){
double mag = dataset[i][j][k].getMagnitude();
if(mag<minMagnitude){
minMagnitude = mag;
}
if(mag>maxMagnitude){
maxMagnitude = mag;
}
}
}
}


} catch (Exception e) {
e.printStackTrace();
```

```
    }
    }

    void clear(Graphics g) {
    super.paintComponent(g);
    }
    }

    --------------Voxel.java-----------------------------
    // A class to hold a 3D vector from a flow field.
    // Written by Zhenyu Guo.

    public class Voxel {

    double pos_x, pos_y, pos_z;
    double magnitude;
    double orientation_x, orientation_y, orientation_z;

    Voxel(){
    }

    Voxel(double _pos_x, double _pos_y, double _pos_z, double u,
            double v, double w){
    this.pos_x = _pos_x;
    this.pos_y = _pos_y;
    this.pos_z = _pos_z;

    this.magnitude = Math.sqrt(u*u + v*v + w*w);

    this.orientation_x = u/this.magnitude;
    this.orientation_y = v/this.magnitude;
    this.orientation_z = w/this.magnitude;
    }


    double getMagnitude(){
    return this.magnitude;
    }
    }
```

Bibliography

[1] J. Abello, F. van Ham, and N. Krishnan. "ASK-GraphView: A Large Scale Graph Visualization System." *IEEE Trans. Visualization and Computer Graphics* 12:5 (2006), 669–676.

[2] Inc. ADVIZOR Solutions. "ADVIZOR Visual Discovery Software." http:// www.advizorsolutions.com/, accessed February 2003.

[3] Maneesh Agrawala, Wilmot Li, and Floraine Berthouzoz. "Design Principles for Visual Communication." *Communications of the ACM* 54:4 (2011), 60–69.

[4] Wolfgang Aigner, Silvia Miksch, Bettina Thurnher, and Stefan Biffl. "PlanningLines: Novel Glyphs for Representing Temporal Uncertainties and Their Evaluation." In *Proceedings of the International Conference Information Visualisation (IV)*, pp. 457–463. Los Alamitos, CA: IEEE Computer Society, 2005.

[5] Wolfgang Aigner, Silvia Miksch, Heidrun Schumann, and Christian Tominski. *Visualization of Time-Oriented Data.* London: Springer, 2011.

[6] D. J. Aks and J. T. Enns. "Visual Search for Size Is Influenced by a Background Texture Gradient." *Journal of Experimental Psychology: Human Perception & Performance* 22:6 (1996), 1467–1481.

[7] Réka Albert and Albert-László Barabási. "Statistical Mechanics of Complex Networks." *Reviews of Modern Physics* 74:1 (2002), 47.

[8] V. V. Alexandrov and N. D. Gorsky. *From Humans to Computers: Cognition through Visual Perception*, World Scientific Series in Computer Science, 22. Singapore: World Scientific, 1991.

[9] James P. Allen. *Middle Egyptian: An Introduction to the Language and Culture of Hieroglyphs*, tenth edition. Cambridge, UK: Cambridge University Press, 2000.

[10] Erik W. Anderson, Kristin C. Potter, Laura E. Matzen, Jason F. Shepherd, Gilbert A. Preston, and Cláudio T. Silva. "A User Study of Visualization

Effectiveness Using EEG and Cognitive Load." *Computer Graphics Forum* 30:3 (2011), 791–800.

[11] E. Anderson. "A Semigraphical Method for the Analysis of Complex Problems." *Proceedings of the National Academy of Science* 13 (1957), 923–927.

[12] K. Andrews and H. Heidegger. "Information Slices: Visualizing and Exploring Large Hierarchies Using Cascading, Semicircular Discs." Late Breaking Hot Topics paper presented at IEEE Symposium on Information Visualization (InfoVis'98), Research Triangle Park, North Carolina, 1998.

[13] D. F. Andrews. "Plots of High Dimensional Data." *Biometrics* 28 (1972), 125–136.

[14] Gennady L. Andrienko and Natalia V. Andrienko. "Interactive Maps for Visual Data Exploration." *International Journal of Geographical Information Science* 13:4 (1999), 355–374.

[15] Natalia V. Andrienko and Gennady L. Andrienko. "Informed Spatial Decisions through Coordinated Views." *Information Visualization* 2:4 (2003), 270–285.

[16] Natalia Andrienko and Gennady Andrienko. *Exploratory Analysis of Spatial and Temporal Data: A Systematic Approach.* Berlin: Springer, 2006.

[17] Gennady Andrienko, Natalia Andrienko, Peter Bak, Daniel Keim, and Stefan Wrobel. *Visual Analytics of Movement.* Berlin: Springer, 2013.

[18] M. Ankerst, D. Keim, and H. Kriegel. "Circle Segments: A Technique for Visually Exploring Large Multidimensional Data Sets." Hot Topics paper presented at presented at IEEE Visualization '96, San Francisco, CA, October 27–November 1, 1996.

[19] Mihael Ankerst, Stefan Berchtold, and Daniel A. Keim. "Similarity Clustering of Dimensions for an Enhanced Visualization of Multidimensional Data." In *INFOVIS '98 Proceedings of the 1998 IEEE Symposium on Information Visualization*, pp. 52–60. Washington, DC: IEEE Computer Society, 1998.

[20] Francis J. Anscombe. "Graphs in statistical analysis." *The American Statistician* 27:1 (1973), 17–21.

[21] Hassan Aref, Richard D. Charles, and T. Todd Elvins. "Scientific Visualization of Fluid Flow." In *Frontiers of Scientific Visualization*, edited by Clifford A. Pickover and Stuart K. Tewksbury, pp. 7–44. New York: John Wiley and Sons, Inc., 1994.

[22] David Asimov. "The Grand Tour: A Tool for Viewing Multidimensional Data." *SIAM Journal of Scientific and Statistical Computing* 6:1 (1985), 128–143.

[23] AVS. "Advanced Visual Systems Home Page." http://www.avs.com/, accessed July 1, 2008.

[24] M. P. Baker and C. Bushell. "After the Storm: Considerations for Information Visualization." *IEEE Computer Graphics and Applications* 15 (1995), 12–15.

[25] Lyn Bartram, Colin Ware, and Tom Calvert. "Filtering and Integrating Visual Information with Motion." *Information Visualization* 1:1 (2002), 66–79.

[26] Lyn Bartram, Colin Ware, and Tom Calvert. "Moticons: Direction, distraction, and task." *International Journal of Computer-Human Studies* 58:5 (2003), 515–545.

[27] G. Di Battista, P. Eades, R. Tamassia, and I. G. Tollis. *Graph Drawing: Algorithms for the Visualization of Graphs.* Upper Saddle River, NJ: Prentice Hall, 1998.

[28] Richard A. Becker, Stephen G. Eick, and Allan R. Wilks. "Visualizing Network Data." *IEEE Transactions on Visualization and Computer Graphics* 1:1 (1995), 16–28.

[29] Jeff Beddow. "Shape Coding of Multidimensional Data on a Microcomputer Display." In *VIS '90: Proceedings of the 1st IEEE Conference on Visualization '90*, pp. 238–246. Los Alamitos, CA: IEEE Computer Society Press, 1990.

[30] R. Daniel Bergeron and Georges G. Grinstein. "A Reference Model for Scientific Visualization." In *Proceedings Eurographics '89*, pp. 393–399. Aire-la-Ville, Switzerland: Eurographics Association, 1989.

[31] L. D. Bergman, B. E. Rogowitz, and L. A. Treinish. "A Rule-Based Tool for Assisting Colormap Selection." In *VIS '95: Proceedings of the 6th Conference on Visualization '95*, p. 118. Washington, DC: IEEE Computer Society, 1995.

[32] Berkeley Institute of Design. "Prefuse Home Page." http://prefuse.org, accessed July 1, 2008.

[33] Jacques Bertin and Myriam Daru. "Matrix Theory of Graphics: Jacques Bertin's Theories." *Information Design Journal* 10:1 (2000), 5–19.

[34] Jacques Bertin. *Semiology of Graphics: Diagrams, Networks, Maps.* Madison, WI: University of Wisconsin Press, 1983. Translated by Wiliam J. Berg. Originally published in 1967 in French.

[35] Clifford Beshers and Steven Feiner. "Automated Design of Virtual Worlds for Visualizing Multivariate Relations." In *VIS '92: Proceedings of the Third Conference on Visualization '92*, pp. 283–290. Los Alamitos, CA: IEEE Computer Society Press, 1992.

[36] Clifford Beshers and Steven Feiner. "Auto Visual: Rule-Based Design of Interactive Multivariate Visualizations." *IEEE Computer Graphics and Applications* 13:4 (1993), 41–49.

[37] C. G. Beshers and S. K. Feiner. "Automated Design of Data Visualizations." In *Scientific Visualization: Advances and Challenges*, edited by L. Rosemblum et al., pp. 88–102. New York: Academic Press, 1994.

[38] Claudio Bettini, Curtis Dyreson, William Evans, Richard Snodgrass, and X. Wang. *Time Granularities in Databases, Data Mining, and Temporal Reasoning.* Berlin: Springer, 2000.

[39] Faber Birren. *A Grammar of Color: A Basic Treatise on the Color System of Albert H. Munsell.* New York: Van Nostrand Reinhold Company, 1969.

[40] James F. Blinn. "A Generalization of Algebraic Surface Drawing." *ACM Trans. Graph.* 1:3 (1982), 235–256.

[41] Jules Bloomenthal and Brian Wyvill, editors. *Introduction to Implicit Surfaces.* San Francisco: Morgan Kaufmann Publishers Inc., 1997.

[42] Markus Bögl, Wolfgang Aigner, Peter Filzmoser, Tim Lammarsch, Silvia Miksch, and Alexander Rind. "Visual Analytics for Model Selection in Time Series Analysis." *IEEE Transactions on Visualization and Computer Graphics, Special Issue "VIS 2013"* 19:12 (2013), 2237–2246. Available online (http://publik.tuwien.ac.at/files/PubDat_220251.pdf).

[43] O. J. Braddick and I. E. Holliday. "Serial Search for Targets Defined by Divergence or Deformation of Optic Flow." *Perception* 20 (1991), 345–354. Available online (http://www.perceptionweb.com/abstract.cgi?id=p200345).

[44] Matthew Brehmer and Tamara Munzner. "A Multi-level Typology of Abstract Visualization tasks." *IEEE Transactions Visualization and Computer Graphics* 19:12 (2013), 2376–2385.

[45] C. A. Brewer. "Guidelines for Use of the Perceptual Dimensions of Color for Mapping and Visualization." In *Color Hard Copy and Graphic Arts III*, Society of Photo-Optical Instrumentation Engineers (SPIE) Conference Series, 2171, edited by J. Bares, pp. 54–63. Bellingham, WA: SPIE, 1994.

[46] Manfred Brill, Hans Hagen, Hans-Christian Rodrian, Wladimir Djatschin, and Stanislav V. Klimenko. "Streamball Techniques for Flow Visualization." In *VIS '94: Proceedings of the Conference on Visualization '94*, pp. 225–231. Los Alamitos, CA: IEEE Computer Society Press, 1994.

[47] D. Brodbeck and L. Girardin. "Design Study: Using Multiple Coordinated Views to Analyze Geo-referenced High-Dimensional Datasets." In *Proceedings of the International Conference on Coordinated and Multiple Views in Exploratory Visualization*, pp. 104–111. Los Alamitos, CA: IEEE Computer Society Press, 2003.

[48] Dominique Brodbeck, Matthew Chalmers, Aran Lunzer, and Pamela Cotture. "Domesticating Bead: Adapting an Information Visualization System to a Financial Institution." In *Proceedings of the IEEE Symposium on Information Visualization '97*, pp. 73–80. Los Alamitos, CA: IEEE Computer Society Press, 1997.

[49] C. Brown and B. Shepherd. *Graphics File Formats: Reference and Guide.* Greenwich, CT: Manning Publications, 1995.

[50] J. L. Brown. "Flicker and Intermittent Stimulation." In *Vision and Visual Perception*, edited by C. H. Graham, pp. 251–320. New York: John Wiley and Sons, 1965.

[51] M. Bruls, K. Huizing, and J. van Wijk. "Squarified Treemaps." In *Proceedings of Joint Eurographics and IEEE TCVG Symposium on Visualization*, pp. 33–42. Los Alamitos, CA: IEEE Computer Society Press, 2000. Available online (citeseer.ist.psu.edu/bruls99squarified.html).

[52] Steve Bryson and Creon Levit. "The Virtual Windtunnel: An Environment for the Exploration of Three-Dimensional Unsteady Flows." In *VIS '91: Proceedings of the Second Conference on Visualization*, pp. 17–24. Los Alamitos, CA: IEEE Computer Society Press, 1991.

[53] Christopher J. C. Burges. "Dimension Reduction: A Guided Tour." *Foundations and Trends in Machine Learning* 2:4 (2010), 275–365.

[54] Brian Cabral and Leith Casey Leedom. "Imaging Vector Fields Using Line Integral Convolution." In *SIGGRAPH '93: Proceedings of the 20th Annual Conference on Computer Graphics and Interactive Techniques*, pp. 263–270. New York: ACM Press, 1993.

[55] T. C. Callaghan. "Dimensional Interaction of Hue and Brightness in Preattentive Field Segregation." *Perception & Psychophysics* 36:1 (1984), 25–34.

[56] T. C. Callaghan. "Interference and Domination in Texture Segregation: Hue, Geometric Form, and Line Orientation." *Perception & Psychophysics* 46:4 (1989), 299–311.

[57] T. C. Callaghan. "Interference and Dominance in Texture Segregation." In *Visual Search*, edited by D. Brogan, pp. 81–87. New York: Taylor & Francis, 1990.

[58] Stuart K. Card and Jock Mackinlay. "The Structure of the Information Visualization Design Space." In *Proceedings of the IEEE Symposium on Information Visualization, 1997*, pp. 92–99. Los Alamitos, CA: IEEE Press, 1997.

[59] Stuart K. Card, Jock D. Mackinlay, and Ben Shneiderman, editors. *Readings in Information Visualization: Using Vision to Think*. San Francisco: Morgan Kaufmann Publishers Inc., 1999.

[60] M. Carpendale, D. Cowperthwaite, and F. Fracchia. "Three-Dimensional Pliable Surfaces: For the Effective Presentation of Visual Information." In *Proceedings of the 8th Annual ACM Symposium on User Interface and Software Technology*, pp. 217–226. New York: ACM Press, 1995.

[61] M. Carpendale, D. Cowperthwaite, and F. Fracchia. "Extending Distortion Viewing from 2D to 3D." *IEEE Computer Graphics and Applications* 17 (1997), 42–51.

[62] M. S. T. Carpendale, D. J. Cowperthwaite, M. Tigges, A. Fall, and F. D. Fracchia. "The Tardis: A Visual Exploration Environment for Landscape Dynamics." In *Visual Data Exploration and Analysis VI*, Proc. SPIE, 3643, pp. 110–119. Bellingham, WA: SPIE, 1999.

[63] Stephen M. Casner. "Task-analytic approach to the automated design of graphic presentations." *ACM Trans. Graph.* 10:2 (1991), 111–151.

[64] C. Cauvin, C. Schneider, and G. Cherrier. "Cartographic Transformations and the Piezopleth Method." *The Cartographic Journal* 26:2 (1989), 96–104.

[65] Center for Integrative Biomedical Computing. "SCIRun Home Page." http://software.sci.utah.edu/scirun.html, accessed July 1, 2008.

[66] K. Chang. *Introduction to Geographic Information System*, Fourth edition. New York: McGraw Hill, 2007.

[67] D. W. Chapman. "Relative Effects of Determinate and Indeterminate." *Amer. J. Psychology* 44 (1932), 163–174.

[68] Chaomei Chen and Mary P. Czerwinski. "Empirical Evaluation of Information Visualizations: An Introduction." *Int. J. Hum.-Comput. Stud.* 53:5 (2000), 631–635.

[69] Hong Chen. "Toward Design Patterns for Dynamic Analytical Data Visualization." In *Electronic Imaging 2004*, pp. 75–86. Bellingham, WA: International Society for Optics and Photonics, 2004.

[70] Chaomei Chen. "Top 10 Unsolved Information Visualization Problems." *IEEE Comput. Graph. Appl.* 25:4 (2005), 12–16.

[71] H. Chernoff. "The Use of Faces to Represent Points in k-Dimensional Space Graphically." *Journal of the American Statistical Association* 68 (1973), 361–368.

[72] Ed Chi. "A Framework for Information Visualization Spreadsheets." Ph.D. thesis, University of Minnesota, 1999.

[73] Ed H. Chi. "A Taxonomy of Visualization Techniques Using the Data State Reference Model." In *INFOVIS '00: Proceedings of the IEEE Symposium on Information Vizualization 2000*, p. 69. Washington, DC: IEEE Computer Society, 2000.

[74] E. Chi. *A Framework for Visualizing Information*. New York: Springer, 2002.

[75] Jon Christensen, Joe Marks, and Stuart Shieber. "An Empirical Study of Algorithms for Point-Feature Label Placement." *ACM Trans. Graph.* 14:3 (1995), 203–232.

[76] Mei C. Chuah and Stephen G. Eick. "Information Rich Glyphs for Software Management Data." *IEEE Comput. Graph. Appl.* 18:4 (1998), 24–29.

[77] CIE. "Official Recommendations on Uniform Color Spaces, Color-Difference Equations, and Metric Color Terms. Commission Internationale de L'Éclairge." CIE Publication No. 15, Supplement Number 2 (E-1.3.1), 1976.

[78] J.C. Claussen and T. Wilhelm. "Introduction to Network Complexity." In *International Workshop and Conference on Complex Networks and Their Applications*. Norwich, UK: PUBLISHER, 2008.

[79] W. Cleveland and R. McGill. "Graphical Perception: Theory, Experimentation and Application to the Development of Graphical Methods." *J. Am. Stat. Assoc.* 79:387 (1984), 531–554.

[80] William S. Cleveland. *The Elements of Graphing Data*. Belmont, CA: Wadsworth, Inc., 1985.

[81] William S. Cleveland. *Visualizing Data*. Summit, NJ: Hobart Press, 1993.

[82] Christopher Collins. "DocuBurst: Document Content Visualization Using Language Structure." Poster presented at the Symposium on Information Visualization (InfoVis '06), Baltimore, MD, October 29–November 3, 2006. Available online (http://faculty.uoit.ca/collins/publications/docs/ivposter2006.pdf).

[83] D. Cook and D. Swayne. *Interactive and Dynamic Graphics for Data Analysis: With R and GGobi.* New York: Springer, 2007.

[84] K. A. Cook and J. J. Thomas. *Illuminating the Path: The Research and Development Agenda for Visual Analytics.* Los Alamitos, CA: IEEE Computer Society Press, 2005.

[85] L. F. Costa, Francisco A. Rodrigues, Gonzalo Travieso, and Paulino Ribeiro Villas Boas. "Characterization of Complex Networks: A Survey of Measurements." *Advances in Physics* 56:1 (2007), 167–242.

[86] Nelson Cowan. "Evolving Conceptions of Memory Storage, Selective Attention, and Their Mutual Constraints within the Human Information-Processing System." *Psychological Bulletin* 104 (1988), 163–191.

[87] K. C. Cox, S. G. Eick, and T. He. "3D Geographic Network Displays." *SIGMOD Record* 25:4 (1996), 50–54.

[88] David Crystal. "Logograms." In *The Cambridge Encyclopedia of Language*, pp. 200–201. Cambridge, UK: Cambridge University Press, 1987.

[89] J. E. Cutting and R. T. Millard. "Three Gradients and the Perception of Flat and Curved Surfaces." *Journal of Experimental Psychology: General* 13:2 (1984), 198–216.

[90] Hervé Delingette, Stéphane Cotin, and Nicholas Ayache. "A Hybrid Elastic Model Allowing Real-Time Cutting, Deformations and Force-Feedback for Surgery Training and Simulation." In *CA '99: Proceedings of the Conference on Computer Animation*, pp. 70–81. Washington, DC: IEEE Computer Society, 1999.

[91] Borden Dent. "A Note on the Importance of Shape in Cartogram Communication." *The Journal of Geography* 71:7 (1972), 393–401.

[92] Borden Dent. "Communication Aspects of Value-By-Area Cartograms." *The American Cartogapher* 2:2 (1975), 154–168.

[93] Borden D. Dent. *Cartography: Thematic Map Design*, Fourth edition. Dubuque, IA: William C. Brown, 1996.

[94] Alan Dix, Janet E. Finlay, Gregory D. Abowd, and Russell Beale. *Human-Computer Interaction*, Third edition. Upper Saddle River, NJ: Prentice Hall, 2003.

[95] Srinivas Doddi, Madhav V. Marathe, Andy Mirzaian, Bernard M. E. Moret, and Binhai Zhu. "Map Labeling and Its Generalizations." In *SODA '97: Proceedings of the Eighth Annual ACM-SIAM Symposium on Discrete Algorithms*, pp. 148–157. Philadelphia: Society for Industrial and Applied Mathematics, 1997.

[96] Daniel Dorling. *Area Cartograms: Their Use and Creation.* Bristol, UK: Department of Geography, University of Bristol, 1996.

[97] James A. Dougenik, Nicholas Chrisman, and Duane R. Niemeyer. "An Algorithm to Construct Continuous Area Cartograms." *The Professional Geographer* 37:1 (1985), 75–81.

[98] Pierre Dragicevic and Stephane Huot. "SpiraClock: A Continuous and Non-Intrusive Display for Upcoming Events." In *Proceedings ACM SIGCHI Conference Human Factors in Computing Systems (CHI)*, pp. 604–605. New York: ACM Press, 2002. Extended Abstracts.

[99] J. Driver, P. McLeod, and Z. Dienes. "Motion Coherence and Conjunction Search: Implications for Guided Search Theory." *Perception & Psychophysics* 51:1 (1992), 79–85.

[100] S. du Toit, A. Steyn, and R. Stumpf. *Graphical Exploratory Data Analysis.* Berlin: Springer-Verlag, 1986.

[101] J. Duncan and G. W. Humphreys. "Visual Search and Stimulus Similarity." *Psychological Review* 96:3 (1989), 433–458. Available online (http://view.ncbi. nlm.nih.gov/pubmed/2756067).

[102] J. Duncan. "Boundary Conditions on Parallel Processing in Human Vision." *Perception* 18:4 (1989), 457–469. Available online (http://view.ncbi.nlm.nih. gov/pubmed/2813022).

[103] J. Dykes, A. M. MacEachren, and M.-J. Kraak. *Exploring Geovisualization.* Burlington, MA: Elsevier, 2005.

[104] Herbert Edelsbrunner and Roman Waupotitsch. "A Combinatorial Approach to Cartograms." *Computational Geometry* 7:5–6 (1997), 343–360.

[105] Martin Dodge (editor), Mary McDerby (co editor), and Martin Turner. *Geographic Visualization: Concepts, Tools and Applications.* New York: Wiley, 2008.

[106] H. E. Egeth and S. Yantis. "Visual Attention: Control, Representation, and Time Course." *Annu. Rev. Psychol.* 48 (1997), 269–297.

[107] Stephen G. Eick and Graham J. Wills. "Navigating Large Networks with Hierarchies." In *Proceedings of the 4th Conference on Visualization '93*, pp. 204–210. Washington, DC: IEEE Computer Society, 1993.

[108] S. G. Eick, J. L. Steffen, and E. E. Sumner. "Seesoft—A Tool for Visualizing Line Oriented Software Statistics." *IEEE Transactions on Software Engineering* 18:11 (1992), 957–968.

[109] Geoffrey Ellis and Alan Dix. "An Explorative Analysis of User Evaluation Studies in Information Visualisation." In *BELIV '06: Proceedings of the 2006 AVI Workshop on Beyond Time and Errors*, pp. 1–7. New York: ACM Press, 2006.

[110] Geoffrey Ellis, Enrico Bertini, and Alan Dix. "The Sampling Lens: Making Sense of Saturated Visualisations." In *CHI '05 Extended Abstracts on Human Factors in Computing Systems*, pp. 1351–1354. New York: ACM Press, 2005.

[111] John Ellson, Emden R. Gansner, Lefteris Koutsofios, Stephen North, and Gordon Woodhull. "Graphviz: Open Source Graph Drawing Tools." In *Graph Drawing: 9th International Symposium, GD 2001 Vienna, Austria, September 23–26, 2001, Revised Papers*, Lecture Notes in Computer Science, 2265, edited by Petra Mutzel, Michael Jünger, and Sebastian Leipert, pp. 483–484. Berlin: Springer, 2002.

[112] Niklas Elmqvist and Jean-Daniel Fekete. "Hierarchical Aggregation for Information Visualization: Overview, Techniques, and Design Guidelines." *Visualization and Computer Graphics, IEEE Transactions on* 16:3 (2010), 439–454.

[113] Linda S Elting, James M Walker, Charles G Martin, Scott B Cantor, and Edward B Rubenstein. "Influence of Data Display Formats on Decisions to Stop Clinical Trials." *British Medical Journal* 318 (1999), 1527–1531.

[114] ERDAS Inc. "ERDAS Home Page." http://gi.leica-geosystems.com/, accessed July 1, 2008.

[115] ESRI. "ArcView." http://www.esri.com/software/arcgis/arcview/index.html, 2003.

[116] ESRI. "List of Supported Map Projections." http://webhelp.esri.com/arcgisdesktop/9.2/index.cfm?TopicName=List_of_supported_map_projections, August 3, 2007.

[117] ESRI. "MapLex." http://www.esri.com/library/whitepapers/pdfs/maplexwp.pdf, August 1998.

[118] Jonathan Feinberg. "Wordle Home Page." http://www.wordle.net/, accessed August 31, 2009.

[119] S. K. Feiner and Clifford Beshers. "Worlds within Worlds: Metaphors for Exploring n-Dimensional Virtual Worlds." In *Proceedings of the 3rd Annual ACM SIGGRAPH Symposium on User Interface Software and Technology*, pp. 76–83. New York: ACM Press, 1990.

[120] Jean-Daniel Fekete. "The InfoVis Toolkit." http://ivtk.sourceforge.net, 2005.

[121] Jean-Daniel Fekete and Catherine Plaisant. "Excentric Labeling: Dynamic Neighborhood Labeling for Data Visualization." In *Proceedings of the SIGCHI Conference on Human Factors in Computing Systems*, pp. 512–519. New York: ACM Press, 1999.

[122] Ronen Feldman and James Sanger. *The Text Mining Handbook: Advanced Approaches in Analyzing Unstructured Data.* Cambridge, UK: Cambridge University Press, 2006.

[123] Stephen Few. *Show Me the Numbers: Designing Tables and Graphs to Enlighten.* Oakland, CA: Analytics Press, 2004.

[124] Stephen Few. *Information Dashboard Design: The Effective Visual Communication of Data.* Cambridge, MA: O'Reilly Media, Inc., 2006.

[125] Stephen Few. *Now You See It: Simple Visualization Techniques for Quantitative Analysis.* Oakland, CA: Analytics Press, 2009.

[126] Fabian Fischer, Florian Mansmann, Daniel A. Keim, Stephan Pietzko, and Marcel Waldvogel. "Large-Scale Network Monitoring for Visual Analysis of Attacks." In *Visualization for Computer Security: 5th International Workshop, VizSec 2008, Cambridge, MA, USA, September 15, 2008, Proceedings*, Lecture Notes in Computer Science, 5210, pp. 111–118. Berlin: Springer-Verlag, 2008.

[127] R. A. Fisher. "The Use of Multiple Measurements in Taxonomic Problems." *Annual Eugenics* 7:Part II (1936), 179–188.

[128] J. C. Fisher. "Homicide in Detroit: The Role of Firearms." *Criminology* 14 (1976), 387–400.

[129] J. J. Flannery. "The Relative Effectiveness of Some Common Graduated Point Symbols in the Presentation of Quantitative Data." *The Canadian Cartographer* 2 (2009), 96–109.

[130] James D. Foley, Andries Van Dam, Steven K. Feiner, John F. Hughes, and Richard L. Phillips. *Introduction to Computer Graphics*. Reading, MA: Addison-Wesley, 1994.

[131] Michael Formann and Frank Wagner. "A Packing Problem with Applications to Lettering of Maps." In *SCG '91: Proceedings of the Seventh Annual Symposium on Computational Geometry*, pp. 281–288. New York: ACM Press, 1991.

[132] Andrew U. Frank. "Different Types of 'Times' in GIS." In *Spatial and Temporal Reasoning in Geographic Information Systems*, Chapter 3, pp. 40–62. New York: Oxford University Press, 1998.

[133] Herbert Freeman. "Automated Cartographic Text Placement." *Pattern Recogn. Lett.* 26:3 (2005), 287–297.

[134] J. Friedman, E. Farrell, R. Goldwyn, M. Miller, and J. Sigel. "A Graphic Way of Describing Changing Multivariate Patterns." In *Proceeding of the Sixth Interface Symposium on Computer Science and Statistics*, pp. 56–59. North Hollywood, CA: Western Periodicals Co., 1972.

[135] M. Friendly. "A Brief History of Data Visualization." In *Handbook of Computational Statistics: Data Visualization*, III, edited by C. Chen, W. Härdle, and A. Unwin, pp. 15–56. Heidelberg: Springer-Verlag, 2006.

[136] Michael Friendly. "Michael Friendly's Home Page." http://www.math.yorku.ca/SCS/friendly.html, 2008.

[137] Ying-Huey Fua, Matthew O. Ward, and Elke A. Rundensteiner. "Hierarchical Parallel Coordinates for Exploration of Large Datasets." In *VIS '99: Proceedings of the Conference on Visualization '99*, pp. 43–50. Los Alamitos, CA: IEEE Computer Society Press, 1999.

[138] Ying-Huey Fua, Matthew O. Ward, and Elke A. Rundensteiner. "Structure-Based Brushes: A Mechanism for Navigating Hierarchically Organized Data and Information Spaces." *IEEE Trans. Visualization and Computer Graphics* 6:2 (2000), 150–159.

[139] Anton Fuhrmann and Eduard Gröller. "Real-Time Techniques for 3D Flow Visualization." In *Proceedings of the Conference on Visualization '98*, pp. 305–312. Los Alamitos, CA: IEEE Computer Society, 1998.

[140] G. Furnas. "Generalized Fisheye Views." In *Proceedings of the SIGCHI Conference on Human Factors in Computing Systems*, pp. 16–23. New York: ACM Press, 1986.

[141] Everette S. Gardner. "Exponential Smoothing: The State of the Art." *Journal of Forecasting* 4:1 (1985), 1–28.

[142] J. W. Gebb, G. H. Mowbray, and C. L. Byham. "Difference Lumens for Photic Intermittence." *Quarterly Journal of Experimental Psychology* 7 (1955), 49–55.

[143] J. Geier, L. Bernath, M. Hudak, and L. Sera. "Straightness as the Main Factor of the Hermann Grid Illusion." *Perception* 37 (2008), 651–665.

[144] Gary Geisler. "Making Information More Accessible: A Survey of Information, Visualization Applications and Techniques." http://www.ischool.utexas.edu/~geisler/info/infovis/paper.html, January 31, 1998.

[145] "GGobi Home Page." http://www.ggobi.org, accessed July 1, 2008.

[146] E. W. Gilbert. "Pioneer Maps of Health and Disease in England." *Geographical Journal* 124 (1958), 172–183.

[147] E. W. Gilbert. "The Map as Intent: Variations on the Theme of John Snow." *Cartographica* 30 (2004), 1–14.

[148] A. S. Glassner. *Principles of Digitial Image Synthesis,* Vol. 1. San Francisco: Morgan Kaufmann, 1995.

[149] R. Gnanadesikan. *Methods of Statistical Data Analysis of Multivariate Observations.* New York: John Wiley and Sons, 1977.

[150] Goddard Institute for Space Studies. "GISS Surface Temperature Analysis: Global Maps from GHCN Data." http://data.giss.nasa.gov/gistemp/maps/, accessed July 1, 2008.

[151] Joseph Goldberg and Jonathan Helfman. "Eye Tracking for Visualization Evaluation: Reading Values on Linear versus Radial Graphs." *Information Visualization* 10:3 (2011), 182–195.

[152] Gene Golovchinsky, Klaus Reichenberger, and Thomas Kamps. "Subverting Structure: Data-Driven Diagram Generation." In *Proceedings of the IEEE Conference on Visualization '95*, pp. 217–223. Los Alamitos, CA: IEEE Computer Society, 1995.

[153] R. Gonzalez and R. Woods. *Digital Image Processing.* Upper Saddle River, NJ: Prentice Hall, 2007.

[154] Iqbal A. Goralwalla, M. Tamer Özsu, and Duane Szafron. "An Object-Oriented Framework for Temporal Data Models." In *Temporal Databases: Research and Practice*, edited by Etzion et al., pp. 1–35. Berlin: Springer, 1998.

[155] C. Gorg, Z. Liu, N. Parekh, K. Singhal, and J. Stasko. "Jigsaw Meets Blue Iguanodon—The VAST 2007 Contest." In *Proceedings of the 2007 IEEE Symposium on Visual Analytics Science and Technology*, pp. 235–236. Washington, DC: IEEE Computer Society, 2007.

[156] "GraphViz—Graph Visualization Software." http://www.graphviz.org, accessed July 1, 2008.

[157] GRASS Development Team. "Grass GIS Home Page." http://grass.itc.it/, accessed July 1, 2008.

[158] M. Greenacre. *Correspondence Analysis in Practice*, Second edition. Boca Raton, FL: Chapman and Hall/CRC, 2007.

[159] D. L. Gresh, B. E. Rogowitz, R. L. Winslow, D. F. Scollan, and C. K. Yung. "WEAVE: A System for Visually Linking 3D and Statistical Visualizations, Applied to Cardiac Simulation and Measurement Data." In *VIS '00: Proceedings of the conference on Visualization '00*, pp. 489–492. Los Alamitos, CA: IEEE Computer Society Press, 2000. Available online (http://www.research.ibm.com/visualanalysis/papers/weave.pdf).

[160] G. Grinstein, D. Keim, and T. Munzner. "Grand Challenges in Information Visualization." Panel from VisWeek 2008, Columbus, OH, October 20, 2008. Report available at http://www.cs.uml.edu/~grinstei/GrandChallengesPanelVisWeek2008.pdf.

[161] Georges G. Grinstein, Ronald M. Pickett, and M. Williams. "EXVIS: An Exploratory Data Visualization Environment." In *Proceedings Graphics Interface '89*, pp. 254–261. Toronto: Canadian Information Processing Society, 1989.

[162] Georges G. Grinstein, Patrick E. Hoffman, and Ronald M. Pickett. "Benchmark Development for the Evaluation of Visualization for Data Mining." In *Information Visualization in Data Mining and Knowledge Discovery*, edited by U. Fayyad, G. Grinstein, and A. Wierse, pp. 129–176. San Francisco: Morgan Kaufmann Publishers, Inc., 2002.

[163] Theresia Gschwandtner, Wolfgang Aigner, Katharina Kaiser, Silvia Miksch, and Andreas Seyfang. "CareCruiser: Exploring and Visualizing Plans, Events, and Effects Interactively." In *Proceedings of the IEEE Pacific Visualization Symposium (PacificVis 2011)*, pp. 43–50. Los Alamitos, CA: IEEE Computer Society, 2011.

[164] Antal Guszlev. "Map Projections." http://lazarus.elte.hu/~guszlev/vet/, June 2003.

[165] Helmut Haase and Christoph Dohrmann. "Doing It Right: Psychological Tests to Ensure the Quality of Scientific Visualization." In *Proceedings of the Eurographics Workshop on Virtual Environments and Scientific Visualization*, pp. 243–256. London: Springer-Verlag, 1996.

[166] Elżbieta Hajnicz. *Time Structures: Formal Description and Algorithmic Representation*, Lecture Notes in Computer Science, 1047. Berlin: Springer, 1996.

[167] C. Hansen and C. Johnson, editors. *The Visualization Handbook.* Burlington, MA: Elsevier Butterworth-Heinemann, 2005.

[168] Robert M. Haralick, K. Shanmugam, and Its'hak Dinstein. "Textural Features for Image Classification." *Systems, Man and Cybernetics, IEEE Transactions on* 3:6 (1973), 610–621.

[169] John Brian Harley and David Woodward. *The History of Cartography: Cartography in Prehistoric, Ancient, and Medieval Europe and the Mediterranean.* Clifton, NJ: Humana Press, 1987.

[170] Robert L. Harris. *Information Graphics: A Comprehensive Illustrated Reference.* New York: Oxford University Press, 1999.

[171] J. Hartigan. "Printer Graphics for Clustering." *J. of Stat. Comp. and Sim* 4 (1975), 187–213.

[172] Susan Havre, Elizabeth Hetzler, and Lucy Nowell. "ThemeRiver: Visualizing Theme Changes Over Time." In *Proceedings of the IEEE Symposium on Information Visualization (InfoVis)*, pp. 115–124. Los Alamitos, CA: IEEE Computer Society, 2000.

[173] S. Havre, E. Hetzler, P. Whitney, and L. Nowell. "Themeriver: Visualizing Thematic Changes in Large Document Collections." *IEEE Transactions on Visualization and Computer Graphics* 8:1 (2002), 9–20.

[174] Christopher G. Healey. "Perception in Visualization." http://www.csc.ncsu.edu/faculty/healey/PP/index.html, 2009.

[175] Christopher G. Healey and James T. Enns. "Building Perceptual Textures to Visualize Multidimensional Datasets." In *Proceedings of the Conference on Visualization '98*, pp. 111–118. IEEE Computer Soceity Press: Los Alamitos, CA, 1998.

[176] Christopher G. Healey and James T. Enns. "Large Datasets at a Glance: Combining Textures and Colors in Scientific Visualization." *IEEE Transactions on Visualization and Computer Graphics* 5 (1999), 145–167.

[177] Christopher G. Healey. "Choosing Effective Colours for Data Visualization." In *Proceedings of the 7th Conference on Visualization '96*, pp. 263–270. Los Alamitos, CA: IEEE Computer Society Press, 1996.

[178] M. A. Hearst. "Tilebars: Visualization of Term Distribution Information in Full Text Information Access." In *Proceedings of the SIGCHI Conference on Human factors in Computing Systems*, pp. 59–66. New York: ACM Press/Addison-Wesley Publishing Co., 1995.

[179] Marti Hearst. *Search User Interfaces.* Cambridge, UK: Cambridge University Press, 2009.

[180] Jeffrey Heer and George G. Robertson. "Animated Transitions in Statistical Data Graphics." *Visualization and Computer Graphics, IEEE Transactions on* 13:6 (2007), 1240–1247.

[181] Jeffrey Heer and Ben Shneiderman. "Interactive Dynamics for Visual Analysis." *Queue* 10:2 (2012), 30.

[182] Jeffrey Heer, Stuart K. Card, and James A. Landay. "Prefuse: A Toolkit for Interactive Information Visualization." In *CHI '05: Proceedings of the SIGCHI Conference on Human Factors in Computing Systems*, pp. 421–430. New York: ACM Press, 2005.

[183] Jeffrey Heer, Maneesh Agrawala, and Wesley Willett. "Generalized Selection via Interactive Query Relaxation." In *Proceedings of the SIGCHI Conference on Human Factors in Computing Systems*, pp. 959–968. New York: ACM Press, 2008.

[184] Roland Heilmann, Daniel A. Keim, Christian Panse, and Mike Sips. "RecMap: Rectangular Map Approximations." In *INFOVIS '04: Proceedings of the IEEE Symposium on Information Visualization*, pp. 33–40. Washington, DC: IEEE Computer Society, 2004.

[185] Jeffrey J. Hemphill. "TIN Errors—Flat Triangles, Slivers and the 'Wedding Cake Effect'." *La Conchita.* http://www.geog.ucsb.edu/~jeff/projects/la_conchita/tinerror/1869_tinerror.html, accessed July 1, 2008.

[186] Ivan Herman, Guy Melançon, and M. Scott Marshall. "Graph Visualization and Navigation in Information Visualization: A Survey." *IEEE Transactions on Visualization and Computer Graphics* 6:1 (2000), 24–43. Available online (citeseer.ist.psu.edu/herman00graph.html).

[187] William L. Hibbard, Charles R. Dyer, and Brian E. Paul. "A Lattice Model for Data Display." In *VIS '94: Proceedings of the Conference on Visualization '94*, pp. 310–317. Los Alamitos, CA: IEEE Computer Society Press, 1994.

[188] Patrick Hoffman, Georges Grinstein, Kenneth Marx, Ivo Grosse, and Eugene Stanley. "DNA Visual and Analytic Data Mining." In *VIS '97: Proceedings of the 8th Conference on Visualization '97*, pp. 437–ff. Los Alamitos, CA: IEEE Computer Society Press, 1997.

[189] Patrick Edward Hoffman. "Table Visualizations: A Formal Model and Its Applications." Ph.D. thesis, University of Massachusetts Lowell, 2000.

[190] J. Hohnsbein and S. Mateeff. "The Time It Takes to Detect Changes in the Speed and Direction of Visual Motion." *Vision Research* 38:17 (1998), 2569–2573.

[191] Danny Holten. "Hierarchical Edge Bundles: Visualization of Adjacency Relations in Hierarchical Data." *IEEE Transactions on Visualization and Computer Graphics* 12:5 (2006), 741–748.

[192] A. Hotho, A. Nurnberger, and G. Paaß. "A Brief Survey of Text Mining." *LDV Forum-GLDV Journal for Computational Linguistics and Language Technology* 20:1 (2005), 19–62.

[193] Stephen D. Houston. *The First Writing: Script Invention as History and Process*, Illustrated edition. Cambridge, UK: Cambridge University Press, 2004.

[194] P. Huber. "Projection Pursuit." *Annals of Statistics* 13 (1985), 435–475.

[195] Jon Hutchins. "Dodgers Loop Sensor Data Set." *UCI Machine Learning Repository*, http://archive.ics.uci.edu/ml/datasets/Dodgers+Loop+Sensor, 2006.

[196] IBM. "Many Eyes Home Page." http://manyeyes.alphaworks.ibm.com/, accessed August 31, 2009.

[197] Peter Imrich, Klaus Mueller, Dan Imre, Alla Zelenyuk, and Wei Zhu. "Interactive Poster: 3D ThemeRiver." In *Poster Compendium of IEEE Symposium on Information Visualization (InfoVis)*. Los Alamitos, CA: IEEE Computer Society, 2003.

[198] Information Interfaces Group. "Jigsaw: Visualization for Investigative Analysis." http://www.cc.gatech.edu/gvu/ii/jigsaw/, accessed August 31, 2009.

[199] Alfred Inselberg. "The Plane with Parallel Coordinates." *The Visual Compter* 1:2 (1985), 69–91.

[200] Instituteo de Expanseo Commercial. "Brasil: Graphicos Economicos-Estatisticas." Technical report, Rio de Janeiro, Brazil, 1929.

[201] Victoria Interrante and Sunghee Kim. "Investigating the Effect of Texture Orientation on the Perception of 3D Shape." In *Human Vision and Electronic Imaging VI*, Proceedings of SPIE, 4299, edited by Bernice E. Rogowitz and Thrasyvoulos N. Pappas, pp. 330–339. Bellingham, WA: SPIE, 2001.

[202] Victoria Interrante, Sunghee Kim, and Haleh Hagh-Shenas. "Conveying 3D Shape with Texture: Recent Advances and Experimental Results." In *Human Vision and Electronic Imaging VII*, Proceedings of SPIE, 4662, edited by Bernice E. Rogowitz and Thrasyvoulos N. Pappas, pp. 197–206. Bellingham, WA: SPIE, 2002.

[203] T. K. Poiker J. Thurston and J. Patrick Moore. *Integrated Geospatial Technologies: A Guide to GPS, GIS, and Data Logging*, First edition. Hoboken, NJ: Wiley, 2003.

[204] Anil K. Jain and Richard C. Dubes. *Algorithms for Clustering Data*. Upper Saddle River, NJ: Prentice Hall, Inc., 1988.

[205] Dean Jenkins and Stephen Gerred. *ECGs by Example*, First edition. Edinburgh: Churchill Livingstone, 1997.

[206] Brian Johnson and Ben Shneiderman. "Tree-Maps: A Space-Filling Approach to the Visualization of Hierarchical Information Structures." In *VIS '91: Proceedings of the 2nd Conference on Visualization '91*, pp. 284–291. Los Alamitos, CA: IEEE Computer Society Press, 1991.

[207] C. R. Johnson, R. Moorhead, T. Munzner, H. Pfister, P. Rheingans, and T. S. Yoo, editors. *NIH-NSF Visualization Research Challenges Report*. Los Alamitos, CA: IEEE Computer Society Press, 2006.

[208] Chris R. Johnson. "Top Scientific Visualization Research Problems." *IEEE Comput. Graph. Appl.* 24:4 (2004), 13–17.

[209] Bela Julész, E. N. Gilbert, L. A. Shepp, and H. L. Frisch. "Inability of Humans to Discriminate between Visual Textures that Agree in Second-Order Statistics—Revisited." *Perception* 2 (1973), 391–405.

[210] Bela Julész, E. N. Gilbert, and J. D. Victor. "Visual Discrimination of Textures with Identical Third-Order Statistics." *Biological Cybernetics* 31:3 (1978), 137–140.

[211] Bela Julész. *Foundations of Cyclopean Perception.* Chicago: University of Chicago Press, 1971.

[212] Bela Julész. "Experiments in the Visual Perception of Texture." *Scientific American* 232:4 (1975), 34–43.

[213] Bela Julész. "Textons, the Elements of Texture Perception, and Their Interactions." *Nature* 290:5802 (1981), 91–97.

[214] Bela Julész. "A Theory of Preattentive Texture Discrimination Based on First-Order Statistics of Textons." *Biological Cybernetics* 41:2 (1981), 131–138.

[215] Bela Julész. "A Brief Outline of the Texton Theory of Human Vision." *Trends in Neuroscience* 7:2 (1984), 41–45.

[216] T. Kamps. *Diagram Design: A Constructive Theory.* New York: Springer, 1999.

[217] R. Kasturi and R. C. Jain, editors. *Computer Vision: Principles.* Los Alamitos, CA: IEEE Computer Society Press, 1991.

[218] T. Keahey. "Area-Normalized Thematic Views." Paper presented at the 19th International Cartographic Coference, Ottawa, Canada, August 14, 1999.

[219] T. Keahey and E. Robertson. "Techniques for Nonlinear Magnification Transformations." In *Proceedings of the IEEE Symposium on Information Visualization '96*, pp. 38–45. Los Alamitos, CA: IEEE Computer Society, 1996.

[220] T. Keahey and E. Robertson. "Nonlinear Magnification Fields." In *Proceedings of the IEEE Symposium on Information Visualization '97*, pp. 51–58. Los Alamitos, CA: IEEE Computer Society, 1997.

[221] Daniel A. Keim and Hans-Peter Kriegel. "VisDB: Database Exploration Using Multidimensional Visualization." *IEEE Comput. Graph. Appl.* 14:5 (1994), 40–49.

[222] D. A. Keim and D. Oelke. "Literature Fingerprinting: A New Method for Visual Literary Analysis." In *Proceedings of the IEEE Symposium on Visual Analytics Science and Technology (VAST 2007)*, pp. 115–122. Los Alamitos, CA: IEEE Computer Society Press, 2007.

[223] Daniel A. Keim, Mihael Ankerst, and Hans-Peter Kriegel. "Recursive Pattern: A Technique for Visualizing Very Large Amounts of Data." In *VIS '95: Proceedings of the 6th Conference on Visualization '95*, pp. 279–286. Los Alamitos, CA: IEEE Computer Society, 1995.

[224] Daniel A. Keim, E. Koutsofios, and S. C. North. "Visual Exploration of Large Telecommunication Data Sets." In *Proceedings of the Workshop on User Interfaces to Data Intensive Systems*, pp. 12–20. Los Alamitos, CA: IEEE Computer Society, 1999.

[225] Daniel A. Keim, Ming C. Hao, and Umeshwar Dayal. "Hierarchical Pixel Bar Charts." *IEEE Trans. Vis. Comput. Graph.* 8:3 (2002), 255–269.

[226] Daniel A. Keim, Ming C. Hao, Umeshwar Dayal, and Meichun Hsu. "Pixel Bar Charts: A Visualization Technique for Very Large Multi-attribute Data Sets?" *Information Visualization* 1:1 (2002), 20–34.

[227] Daniel A. Keim, Christian Panse, and Mike Sips. "Visual Data Mining of Large Spatial Data Sets." In *Databases in Networked Information Systems*, Lecture Notes in Computer Science, 2822, pp. 201–215. Berlin: Springer, 2003.

[228] Daniel A. Keim, Christian Panse, Mike Sips, and Stephen C. North. "PixelMaps: A New Visual Data Mining Approach for Analyzing Large Spatial Data Sets." In *Proceedings of the Third IEEE International Conference on Data Mining*, pp. 565–568. Los Alamitos, CA: IEEE Computer Society, 2003.

[229] Daniel A. Keim, Stephen C. North, and Christian Panse. "CartoDraw: A Fast Algorithm for Generating Contiguous Cartograms." *IEEE Transactions on Visualization and Computer Graphics* 10:1 (2004), 95–110.

[230] Daniel A. Keim, Christian Panse, Mike Sips, and Stephen C. North. "Pixel Based Visual Mining of Geo-Spatial Data." *Computers and Graphics* 28:3 (2004), 327–344. Available online (http://kops.ub.uni-konstanz.de/volltexte/ 2008/6967).

[231] Daniel A. Keim, Christian Panse, and Stephen C. North. "Medial-Axis-Based Cartograms." *IEEE Comput. Graph. Appl.* 25:3 (2005), 60–68.

[232] D. A. Keim. "Pixel-Oriented Database Visualizations." *ACM SIGMOD Record* 25:4 (1996), 35–39.

[233] Daniel A. Keim. "Designing Pixel-Oriented Visualization Techniques: Theory and Applications." *IEEE Transactions on Visualization and Computer Graphics* 6:1 (2000), 59–78.

[234] Daniel A. Keim. "Information Visualization and Visual Data Mining." *IEEE Transactions on Visualization and Computer Graphics* 8:1 (2002), 1–8.

[235] Christa Kelleher and Thorsten Wagener. "Ten Guidelines for Effective Data Visualization in Scientific Publications." *Environmental Modelling & Software* 26:6 (2011), 822–827.

[236] Peter R. Keller and Mary M. Keller. *Visual Cues: Practical Data Visualization.* Los Alamitos, CA: IEEE Computer Society Press, 1994.

[237] G. David Kerlick. "Moving Iconic Objects in Scientific Visualization." In *VIS '90: Proceedings of the 1st Conference on Visualization '90*, pp. 124–130. Los Alamitos, CA: IEEE Computer Society Press, 1990.

[238] Andreas Kerren, Helen C. Purchase, and Matthew O. Ward, editors. *Multivariate Network Visualization*, Lecture Notes in Computer Science, 8380. Berlin: Springer, 2014.

[239] Jongkwang Kim and Thomas Wilhelm. "What Is a Complex Graph?" *Physica A: Statistical Mechanics and its Applications* 387:11 (2008), 2637–2652.

[240] Sunghee Kim, Haleh Hagh-Shenas, and Victoria Interrante. "Conveying Shape with Texture: An Experimental Investigation of the Impact of Texture Type on Shape Categorization Judgments." In *Proceedings of the Ninth Annual IEEE Conference on Information Visualization*, pp. 163–170. Washington, DC: IEEE Computer Society, 2003.

[241] Sunghee Kim, Haleh Hagh-Shenas, and Victoria Interrante. "Showing Shape with Texture: Two Directions Seem Better than One." In *Human Vision and Electronic Imaging VIII*, Proceedings of SPIE, 5007, edited by Bernice E. Rogowitz and Thrasyvoulos N. Pappas, pp. 332–339. Bellingham, WA: SPIE, 2003.

[242] Gordon Kindlmann and James W. Durkin. "Semi-automatic Generation of Transfer Functions for Direct Volume Rendering." In *VVS '98: Proceedings of the 1998 IEEE Symposium on Volume Visualization*, pp. 79–86. New York: ACM Press, 1998.

[243] R. M. Kirby, H. Marmanis, and David H. Laidlaw. "Visualizing Multivalued Data from 2D Incompressible Flows Using Concepts from Painting." In *VIS '99: Proceedings of the Conference on Visualization '99*, 20, pp. 333–340. Los Alamitos, CA: IEEE Computer Society Press, 1999.

[244] Kitware, Inc. "VTK Home Page." http://www.vtk.org, accessed July 1, 2008.

[245] R. Victor Klassen and Steven J. Harrington. "Shadowed Hedgehogs: A Technique for Visualizing 2D Slices of 3D Vector Fields." In *VIS '91: Proceedings of the 2nd Conference on Visualization '91*, pp. 148–153. Los Alamitos, CA: IEEE Computer Society Press, 1991.

[246] B. Kleiner and J. Hartigan. "Representing Points in Many Dimensions by Trees and Castles." *Journal of the American Statistical Association* 76 (1981), 260–269.

[247] Christopher J. Kocmoud and Donald H. House. "Continuous Cartogram Construction." In *Proceedings of the Confrence on Visualization '98*, pp. 197–204. Los Alamitos, CA: IEEE Computer Society Press, 1998.

[248] T. Kohonen. *Self-Organizing Maps*, Springer Series in Information Sciences, 30, Third edition. Berlin: Springer, 2001.

[249] Polina Kondratieva, Jens Kruger, and Rudiger Westermann. "The Application of GPU Particle Tracing to Diffusion Tensor Field Visualization." In *Proceedings of the IEEE Visualization Conference*, pp. 73–78. Los Alamitos, CA: IEEE Computer Society, 2005.

[250] Robert Kosara, Gerald N. Sahling, and Helwig Hauser. "Linking Scientific and Information Visualization with Interactive 3D Scatterplots." *WSCG (Short Papers)* 12:1–3 (2004), 133–140.

[251] S. M. Kosslyn. *Elements of Graph Design*. New York: W. H. Freeman and Co., 1994.

[252] S. M. Kosslyn. *Graph Design for the Eye and Mind*. New York: Oxford University Press, 2006.

[253] E. Koutsofios, D. A. Keim, and S. C. North. "Visualizing Large Telecommunication Data Sets." *IEEE Computer Graphics and Applications Journal* 19:3 (1999), 16–19.

[254] Eleftherios E. Koutsofios, Stephen C. North, Russell Truscott, and Daniel A. Keim. "Visualizing Large-Scale Telecommunication Networks and Services (Case Study)." In *VIS '99: Proceedings of the Conference on Visualization '99*, pp. 457–461. Los Alamitos, CA: IEEE Computer Society Press, 1999.

[255] Menno-Jan Kraak and Ferjan Ormeling. *Cartography: Visualization of Geospatial Data*, Second edition. Upper Saddle River, NJ: Pearson Education, 2003.

[256] Menno-Jan Kraak and Ferjan Ormeling. *Cartography: Visualization of Geospatial Data*, Second edition. Harlow, UK: Pearson Education, 2003.

[257] Menno-Jan Kraak, Ferjan Ormeling, and Menno-Jan Kroak. *Cartography: Visualization of Spatial Data*. Reading, MA: Addison-Wesley Publishing Co., 1996.

[258] M. Kreuseler, N. Lopez, and H. Schumann. "A Scalable Framework for Information Visualization." In *Proceedings of IEEE Symposium on Information Visualization 2000*, pp. 27–36. Los Alamitos, CA: IEEE Computer Society, 2000.

[259] J. B. Kruskal and M. Wish. *Multidimensional Scaling*. Quantitative Applications in the Social Sciences Series, Newbury Park: Sage Publications, 1978.

[260] R. Kurzweil. *The Age of Spiritual Machines*. London: Penguin, 2000.

[261] P. Laarhoven and E. Aarts. *Simulated Annealing: Theory and Applications*. Mathematics and Its Applications, Dordrecht: Kluwer Academic Publishers, 1987.

[262] Tim Lammarsch, Wolfgang Aigner, Alessio Bertone, Johannes Gärtner, Eva Mayr, Silvia Miksch, and Michael Smuc. "Hierarchical Temporal Patterns and Interactive Aggregated Views for Pixel-based Visualizations." In *Proceedings of the International Conference Information Visualisation (IV)*, pp. 44–49. Los Alamitos, CA: IEEE Computer Society, 2009.

[263] David A. Lane. "UFAT: A Particle Tracer for Time-Dependent Flow Fields." In *VIS '94: Proceedings of the Conference on Visualization '94*, pp. 257–264. Los Alamitos, CA: IEEE Computer Society Press, 1994.

[264] John T. Langton, Astrid A. Prinz, and Timothy J. Hickey. "NeuroVis: Combining Dimensional Stacking and Pixelization to Visually Explore, Analyze, and Mine Multidimensional Multivariate Data." In *Visualization and Data Analysis (VDA 2007)*, Proceedings of SPIE, 6495, pp. 64950H–1–64950H–12. Bellingham, WA: SPIE, 2007.

[265] E. Lawler, J. Lenstra, A A. Rinnooy Kan, and D. Shmoys. *The Traveling Salesman Problem: A Guided Tour of Combinatorial Optimization*. New York: J. Wiley, 1985.

[266] J. LeBlanc, M. Ward, and N. Wittels. "Exploring N-Dimensional Databases." In *Proceedings of the 1st Conference on Visualization '90*, pp. 230–237. Los Alamitos, CA: IEEE Computer Society Press, 1990.

[267] Bongshin Lee, Catherine Plaisant, Cynthia Sims Parr, Jean-Daniel Fekete, and Nathalie Henry. "Task Taxonomy for Graph Visualization." In *Proceedings of the 2006 AVI Workshop on Beyond Time and Errors: Novel Evaluation Methods for Information Visualization*, pp. 1–5. New York: ACM Press, 2006.

[268] Y. K. Leung and M. D. Apperley. "A Review and Taxonomy of Distortion-Oriented Presentation Techniques." *ACM Transactions on Computer-Human Interaction* 1:2 (1994), 126–160.

[269] Martin D. Levine. *Vision in Man and Machine*. New York: McGraw-Hill, 1985.

[270] Haim Levkowitz. "Color Icons: Merging Color and Texture Perception for Integrated Visualization of Multiple Parameters." In *VIS '91: Proceedings of the 2nd Conference on Visualization '91*, pp. 164–170. Los Alamitos, CA: IEEE Computer Society Press, 1991.

[271] Haim Levkowitz. *Color Theory and Modeling for Computer Graphics, Visualization, and Multimedia Applications*. Norwell, MA: Kluwer Academic Publishers, 1997.

[272] B. Lichtenbelt, R. Crane, and S. Naqvi. *Introduction to Volume Rendering*. Upper Saddle River, NJ: Prentice Hall, 1998.

[273] Sharon Lin, Julie Fortuna, Chinmay Kulkarni, Maureen Stone, and Jeffrey Heer. "Selecting Semantically-Resonant Colors for Data Visualization." *Computer Graphics Forum* 32:3pt4 (2013), 401–410.

[274] Ling Liu and Tamer M. Özsu. *Encyclopedia of Database Systems*. Berlin: Springer, 2009.

[275] G. Liu, C. G. Healey, and J. T. Enns. "Target Detection and Localization in Visual Search: A Dual Systems Perspective." *Perception & Psychophysics* 65:5 (2003), 678–694.

[276] H. Lohninger. "INSPECT: A Program System to Visualize and Interpret Chemical Data." *Chemometrics and Intelligent Laboratory Systems* 22 (1994), 147–153.

[277] M. Looks, B. Goertzel, and C. Pennachin. "Novamente: An Integrative Architecture for Artificial General Intelligence." In *Proceedings of the AAAI Fall Symposium on Achieving Human-Level Intelligence through Integrated Systems and Research, AAAI Fall Symposium Series*, pp. 54–61. Menlo Park, CA: AAAI Press, 2004.

[278] William E. Lorensen and Harvey E. Cline. "Marching Cubes: A High Resolution 3D Surface Construction Algorithm." In *SIGGRAPH '87: Proceedings of the 14th Annual Conference on Computer Graphics and Interactive Techniques*, pp. 163–169. New York: ACM Press, 1987.

[279] A. M. MacEachren and M.-J. Kraak. "Research Challenges in Geovisualization." *Cartography and Geographic Information Science* 28:1 (2001), 3–12.

[280] A. M. MacEachren, B. P. Buttenfield, J. B. Campbell, D. W. DiBiase, and M. Monmonier. "Visualization." In *Geography's Inner Worlds*, edited by Ronald F. Abler, Melvin G. Marcus, and Judy M. Olson, pp. 99–137. Piscataway, NJ: Rutgers University Press, 1992.

[281] Alan M. MacEachren. *How Maps Work: Presentation, Visualization, and Design.* New York: The Guilford Press, 1995.

[282] A. Mack and I. Rock. *Inattentional Blindness.* Cambridge, MA: MIT Press, 1998.

[283] J. Mackinlay, G. Robertson, and S. Card. "The Perspective Wall: Detail and Context Smoothly Integrated." In *Proceedings of the SIGCHI Conference on Human Factors in Computing Systems: Reaching through Technology*, pp. 173–179. New York: ACM Press, 1991.

[284] Jock Mackinlay. "Automating the Design of Graphical Presentations of Relational Information." *ACM Trans. Graph.* 5:2 (1986), 110–141.

[285] Macrofocus GmbH. "Macrofocus Home Page." http://www.macrofocus.com, accessed July 1, 2008.

[286] Florian Mansmann, Fabian Fischer, Daniel A. Keim, and Stephen C. North. "Visualizing Large-Scale IP Traffic Flows." Paper presented at the 12th International Workshop on Vision, Modeling, and Visualization, Saarbrücken, Germany, 2007.

[287] Allen R. Martin and Matthew O. Ward. "High Dimensional Brushing for Interactive Exploration of Multivariate Data." In *Proceedings of the 6th Conference on Visualization '95*, pp. 271–278. Los Alamitos, CA: IEEE Computer Society Press, 1995.

[288] S. Mateeff, G. Dimitrov, and J. Hohnsbein. "Temporal Thresholds and Reaction Time to Changes in Velocity of Visual Motion." *Vision Research* 35:3 (1995), 355–363.

[289] Tony McLoughlin, Robert S. Laramee, Ronald Peikert, Frits H. Post, and Min Chen. "Over Two Decades of Integration-Based, Geometric Flow." *Computer Graphics Forum* 29 (2009), 1807–1829.

[290] J. Mezzich and D. Worthington. "A Comparison of Graphical Representations of Multidimensional Psychiatric Diagnostic Data." In *Graphical Representation of Multivariate Data*, edited by P. Wang, pp. 123–141. New York: Academic Press, 1978.

[291] Ted Mihalisin, John Timlin, and John Schwegler. "Visualizing Multivariate Functions, Data, and Distributions." *IEEE Comput. Graph. Appl.* 11:3 (1991), 28–35.

[292] Silvia Miksch and Wolfgang Aigner. "A Matter of Time: Applying a Data-Users-Tasks Design Triangle to Visual Analytics of Time-Oriented Data." *Computers & Graphics, Special Section on Visual Analytics* 38 (2014), 286–290. Available online (http://www.ifs.tuwien.ac.at/~silvia/pub/publications/miksch_cag_design-triangle-2014.pdf).

[293] John J. Miller and Edward J. Wegman. "Construction of Line Densities for Parallel Coordinate Plots." In *Computing and Graphics in Statistics*, edited by A. Buja and P. Tukey, pp. 107–123. New York: Springer-Verlag, 1991.

[294] A. H. Miller, E. N. Goldenberg, and L. Erbring. "Type-set Politics: Impact of Newspapers on Public Confidence." *American Political Science Review* 73 (1979), 67–84.

[295] George A. Miller. "The Magic Number Seven, Plus or Minus Two: Some Limits on Our Capacity for Processing Information." *Psychological Review* 63:2 (1956), 81–97.

[296] Sushmita Mitra and Tinku Acharya. "Gesture Recognition: A Survey." *Systems, Man, and Cybernetics, Part C: Applications and Reviews, IEEE Transactions on* 37:3 (2007), 311–324.

[297] E. Morse, M. Lewis, and K. A. Olsen. "Evaluating Visualizations: Using a Taxonomic Guide." *Int. J. Hum.-Comput. Stud.* 53:5 (2000), 637–662.

[298] G. H. Mowbray and J. W. Gebhard. "Differential Sensitivity of the Eye to White Light." *Science* 121 (1955), 137–175.

[299] H. J. Müller, G. W. Humphreys, P. T. Quinlan, and M. J. Riddoch. "Combined-Feature Coding in the Form Domain." In *Visual Search*, edited by D. Brogan, pp. 47–55. New York: Taylor & Francis, 1990.

[300] K. Mullet and D. Sano. *Designing Visual Interfaces*. Mountain View, CA: SunSoft Press, 1995.

[301] A. H. Munsell. *A Color Notation*. Boston: Geo. H. Ellis Co., 1905.

[302] Tamara Munzner. "H3: Laying Out Large Directed Graphs in 3D Hyperbolic Space." In *Proceedings of the 1997 IEEE Symposium on Information Visualization*, pp. 2–10. Washington, DC: IEEE Computer Society, 1997.

[303] Tamara Munzner. "Exploring Large Graphs in 3D Hyperbolic Space." *IEEE Computer Graphics & Applications* 18:4 (1998), 18–23.

[304] Ken Nakayama and Gerald H. Silverman. "Serial and Parallel Processing of Visual Feature Conjunctions." *Nature* 320:6059 (1986), 264–265.

[305] NCSA. "Visualization Study of the NSFNET." http://archive.ncsa.uiuc.edu/SCMS/DigLib/text/technology/Visualization-Study-NSFNET-Cox.html, 2003.

[306] NOAA. "Online Climate Data Repository." http://www.ncdc.noaa.gov/oa/climate/climatedata.html, accessed July 1, 2008.

[307] Matej Novotny and Helwig Hauser. "Outlier-Preserving Focus+Context Visualization in Parallel Coordinates." *IEEE Transactions on Visualization and Computer Graphics* 12:5 (2006), 893–900.

[308] OpenDX.org. "OpenDX Home Page." http://www.opendx.org/, accessed July 1, 2008.

[309] T. Ott and F. Swiaczny. *Time-Integrative Geographic Information Systems: Management and Analysis of Spatio-temporal Data*, First edition. Berlin: Springer, 2001.

[310] I. Overington. *Computer Vision: A Unified, Biologically-Inspired Approach.* Amsterdam: Elsevier Science, 1992.

[311] Giuliano Andrea Pagani and Marco Aiello. "Cost and Benefits of Denser Topologies for the Smart Grid." In *Computer and Information Sciences III*, edited by Erol Gelenbe and Ricardo Lent, pp. 73–81. London: Springer, 2013.

[312] W. B. Paley. "TextArc: Showing Word Frequency and Distribution in Text." Poster presented at IEEE Symposium on Information Visualization, Boston, MA, October 27–November 1, 2002.

[313] Rick Parent. *Computer Animation: Algorithms and Techniques*, Third edition. Burlington, MA: Morgan Kaufmann/Elsevier, 2012.

[314] Robert E. Patterson, Leslie M. Blaha, Georges G. Grinstein, Kristen K. Liggett, David E. Kaveney, Kathleen C. Sheldon, Paul R. Havig, and Jason A. Moore. "A Human Cognition Framework for Information Visualization." *Computers & Graphics* 42 (2014), 42–58.

[315] Theodosios Pavlidis. *Algorithms for Graphics and Image Processing.* Berlin: Springer-Verlag, 1982.

[316] Roger D. Peng and Leah J. Welty. "The NMMAPSdata Package." *R News* 4:2 (2004), 10–14.

[317] Wei Peng, Matthew O. Ward, and Elke A. Rundensteiner. "Clutter Reduction in Multi-Dimensional Data Visualization Using Dimension Reordering." In *INFOVIS '04: Proceedings of the IEEE Symposium on Information Visualization*, pp. 89–96. Washington, DC: IEEE Computer Society, 2004.

[318] Doantam Phan, Ling Xiao, Ron Yeh, Pat Hanrahan, and Terry Winograd. "Flow Map Layout." In *INFOVIS '05: Proceedings of the Proceedings of the 2005 IEEE Symposium on Information Visualization*, p. 29. Washington, DC: IEEE Computer Society, 2005.

[319] R. Pickett and G. Grinstein. "Iconographic Displays for Visualizing Multidimensional Data." In *Proceedings of the 1988 IEEE Conference on Systems, Man, and Cybernetics*, pp. 164–170. Los Alamitos, CA: IEEE Computer Society Press, 1988.

[320] Filip Piekniewski and Leszek Rybicki. "Visualizing and Analyzing Multidimensional Output from MLP Networks via Barycentric Projections." In *Artificial Intelligence and Soft Computing—ICAISC 2004: 7th International Conference, Zakopane, Poland, June 7–11, 2004, Proceedings*, Lecture Notes in Computer Science, 3070, pp. 247–252. Berlin/Heidelberg: Springer, 2004.

[321] Catherine Plaisant. "The Challenge of Information Visualization Evaluation." In *AVI '04: Proceedings of the Working Conference on Advanced Visual Interfaces*, pp. 109–116. New York: ACM Press, 2004.

[322] William Playfair. *The Commercial and Political Atlas and Statistical Breviary*, Reprint of Third edition. New York: Cambridge University Press, 2005.

[323] J. Pomerantz and E. A. Pristach. "Emergent Features, Attention, and Perceptual Glue in Visual Form Perception." *Journal of Experimental Psychology: Human Perception & Performance* 15:4 (1989), 635–649.

[324] Frits H. Post, Frank J. Post, Theo Van Walsum, and Deborah Silver. "Iconic Techniques for Feature Visualization." In *Proceedings of the IEEE Conference on Visualization*, pp. 288–295. Los Alamitos, CA: IEEE Computer Society, 1995.

[325] P. T. Quinlan and G. W. Humphreys. "Visual Search for Targets Defined by Combinations of Color, Shape, and Size: An Examination of Task Constraints on Feature and Conjuction Searches." *Perception & Psychophysics* 41:5 (1987), 455–472.

[326] "The R Project for Statistical Computing." http://www.r-project.org/, accessed July 1, 2009.

[327] Erwin Raisz. *Principles of Cartography.* New York: McGraw-Hill, 1962.

[328] R. Rao and S. Card. "The Table Lens: Merging Graphical and Symbolic Representations in an Interactive Focus + Context Visualization for Tabular Information." In *Proceedings of the SIGCHI Conference on Human Factors in Computing Systems: Celebrating Interdependence*, pp. 318–322. New York: ACM Press, 1994.

[329] A. Ravishankar Rao and Gerald L. Lohse. "Identifying High Level Features of Texture Perception." *CVGIP: Graph. Models Image Process.* 55:3 (1993), 218–233.

[330] A. Ravishankar Rao and Gerald L. Lohse. "Towards a Texture Naming System: Identifying Relevant Dimensions of Texture." In *Proceedings of the IEEE Conference on Visualization '93*, pp. 220–227. Los Alamitos, CA: IEEE Computer Society, 1993.

[331] Hannes Reijner. "The Development of the Horizon Graph." In *Electronic Proceedings of the Vis08 Workshop: From Theory to Practice: Design, Vision and Visualization*, edited by Lyn Bartram, Maureen Stone, and Diane Gromala, http://www.stonesc.com/Vis08_Workshop/DVD/, 2008.

[332] Benjamin Renoust. "Analysis and Visualisation of Edge Entanglement in Multiplex Networks." Ph.D. thesis, University of Massachusetts Lowell, 2014.

[333] Roland Rensink. "The Need for Attention to See Change." http://www.psych.ubc.ca/~rensink/flicker, March 2, 2003.

[334] R. A. Rensink. "Seeing, Sensing, and Scrutinizing." *Vision Research* 40:10-12 (2000), 1469–1487.

[335] R. J. Resnick, M. O. Ward, and E. A. Rundensteiner. "FED: A Framework for Iterative Data Selection in Exploratory Visualization." In *Proceedings of the 10th International Conference Scientific and Statistical Database Management*, pp. 180–189. Washington, DC: IEEE Computer Society, 1998.

[336] Penny Rheingans and Brice Tebbs. "A Tool for Dynamic Explorations of Color Mappings." In *Proceedings of the 1990 Symposium on Interactive 3D Graphics*, pp. 145–146. New York: ACM Press, 1990.

[337] William Ribarsky, Eric Ayers, John Eble, and Sougata Mukherjea. "Glyphmaker: Creating Customized Visualizations of Complex Data." *Computer* 27:7 (1994), 57–64.

[338] Alexander Rind, Silvia Miksch, Wolfgang Aigner, Thomas Turic, and Margit Pohl. "VisuExplore: Gaining New Medical Insights from Visual Exploration." In *Proceedings of the 1st International Workshop on Interactive Systems in Healthcare (WISH@CHI2010)*, edited by Gillian R. Hayes and Desney S. Tan, pp. 149–152. New York: ACM Press, 2010. Available online (http://ike.donau-uni.ac.at/publications/PDF/2010/CHI2010/final/rind_2010_wish_visuexplore.pdf).

[339] Alexander Rind, Tim Lammarsch, Wolfgang Aigner, Bilal Alsallakh, and Silvia Miksch. "TimeBench: A Data Model and Software Library for Visual Analytics of Time-Oriented Data." *IEEE Transactions on Visualization and Computer Graphics, Special Issue "VIS 2013"* 19 (2013), 2247–2256. Available online (http://publik.tuwien.ac.at/files/PubDat_219700.pdf).

[340] B. Roberts, M. G. Harris, and T. A. Yates. "The Roles of Inducer Size and Distance in the Ebbinghaus Illusion (Titchener Circles)." *Perception* 34:7 (2005), 847–56.

[341] George G. Robertson, Jock D. Mackinlay, and Stuart K. Card. "Cone Trees: Animated 3D Visualizations of Hierarchical Information." In *Proceedings of the SIGCHI Conference on Human Factors in Computing Systems*, pp. 189–194. New York: ACM Press, 1991.

[342] George Robertson, Mary Czerwinski, Kevin Larson, Daniel C. Robbins, David Thiel, and Maarten van Dantzich. "Data Mountain: Using Spatial Memory for Document Management." In *Proceedings of the 11th Annual ACM Symposium on User Interface Software and Technology*, pp. 153–162. New York: ACM Press, 1998.

[343] Philip K. Robertson. "A Methodology for Scientific Data Visualisation: Choosing Representations Based on a Natural Scene Paradigm." In *VIS '90: Proceedings of the First Conference on Visualization '90*, pp. 114–123. Los Alamitos, CA: IEEE Computer Society Press, 1990.

[344] Bernice E. Rogowitz and Lloyd A. Treinish. "An Architecture for Rule-Based Visualization." In *VIS '93: Proceedings of the 4th Conference on Visualization '93*, pp. 236–243. Washington, DC: IEEE Computer Society, 1993.

[345] Randall M. Rohrer, John L. Sibert, and David S. Ebert. "The Shape of Shakespeare: Visualizing Text Using Implicit Surfaces." In *INFOVIS '98: Proceedings of the 1998 IEEE Symposium on Information Visualization*, pp. 121–129. Washington, DC: IEEE Computer Society, 1998.

[346] Timo Ropinski, Steffen Oeltze, and Bernhard Preim. "Survey of Glyph-Based Visualization Techniques for Spatial Multivariate Medical Data." *Computers & Graphics* 35:2 (2011), 392–401.

[347] Geraldine E. Rosario, Elke A. Rundensteiner, David C. Brown, Matthew O. Ward, and Shiping Huang. "Mapping Nominal Values to Numbers for Effective Visualization." *Information Visualization* 3:2 (2004), 80–95.

[348] Steven F. Roth, John Kolojejchick, Joe Mattis, and Jade Goldstein. "Interactive Graphic Design Using Automatic Presentation Knowledge." In *CHI*

'94: Proceedings of the SIGCHI Conference on Human Factors in Computing Systems, pp. 112–117. New York: ACM Press, 1994.

[349] S. F. Roth, P. Lucas, J. A. Senn, C. C. Gomberg, M. B. Burks, P. J. Stroffolino, A. J. Kolojechick, and C. Dunmire. "Visage: A User Interface Environment for Exploring Information." In *INFOVIS '96: Proceedings of the 1996 IEEE Symposium on Information Visualization (INFOVIS '96)*, pp. 3–12. Washington, DC: IEEE Computer Society, 1996.

[350] Sam T. Roweis and Lawrence K. Saul. "Nonlinear Dimensionality Reduction by Locally Linear Embedding." *Science* 290:5500 (2000), 2323–2326. Available online (http://www.sciencemag.org/content/290/5500/2323.abstract).

[351] Elke A. Rundensteiner, Matthew O. Ward, Zaixian Xie, Qingguang Cui, Charudatta V. Wad, Di Yang, and Shiping Huang. "XmdvtoolQ: Quality-Aware Interactive Data Exploration." In *SIGMOD '07: Proceedings of the 2007 ACM SIGMOD International Conference on Management of Data*, pp. 1109–1112. New York: ACM Press, 2007.

[352] T. A. Runkler. *Data Analytics: Models and Algorithms for Intelligent Data Analysis*. Bücher: Springer Vieweg, 2012.

[353] S. J. Russell and P. Norvig. *Artificial Intelligence: A Modern Approach*, Second edition. Upper Saddle River, NJ: Prentice Hall, 2002.

[354] Takafumi Saito, Hiroko Nakamura Miyamura, Mitsuyoshi Yamamoto, Hiroki Saito, Yuka Hoshiya, and Takumi Kaseda. "Two-Tone Pseudo Coloring: Compact Visualization for One-Dimensional Data." In *Proceedings of the IEEE Symposium on Information Visualization (InfoVis)*, pp. 173–180. Los Alamitos, CA: IEEE Computer Society, 2005.

[355] Gerard Salton and Christopher Buckley. "Term-Weighting Approaches in Automatic Text Retrieval." *Information Processing and Management* 24:5 (1988), 513–523.

[356] G. Salton, A. Wong, and C. S. Yang. "A Vector Space Model for Automatic Indexing." *Commun. ACM* 18:11 (1975), 613–620.

[357] Hanan Samet. *The Design and Analysis of Spatial Data Structures*. Reading, MA: Addison-Wesley, 1990.

[358] Beatriz Sousa Santos and Paulo Dias. "Evaluation in Visualization: Some Issues and Best Practices." In *Visualization and Data Analysis 2014*, SPIE Proceedings, 9017, p. 90170O. Bellingham, WA: SPIE, 2013.

[359] Purvi Saraiya, Chris North, and Karen Duca. "An Insight-Based Methodology for Evaluating Bioinformatics Visualizations." *IEEE Transactions on Visualization and Computer Graphics* 11:4 (2005), 443–456.

[360] M. Sarkar, S. Snibbe, O. Tversky, and S. Reiss. "Stretching the Rubber Sheet: A Metaphor for Viewing Large Layouts on Small Screens." In *Proceedings of the 6th Annual ACM Symposium on User Interface Software and Technology*, pp. 81–91. New York: ACM Press, 1993.

[361] SAS Institute. "SAS Home Page." http://www.sas.com, accessed July 1, 2008.

[362] J. L. Schafer. *Analysis of Incomplete Multivariate Data.* Boca Raton, FL: CRC Press, 1997.

[363] Sebastian Schmidt, Miguel A. Nacenta, Raimund Dachselt, and Sheelagh Carpendale. "A Set of Multi-touch Graph Interaction Techniques." In *ACM International Conference on Interactive Tabletops and Surfaces*, pp. 113–116. New York: ACM Press, 2010.

[364] M. Schrauf, B. Lingelbach, E. Lingelbach, and E. R. Wist. "The Hermann Grid and the Scintillation Effect." *Perception* 24, Supplement A (1995), 88–89.

[365] W. J. Schroeder, C. R. Volpe, and W. E. Lorensen. "The Stream Polygon: A Technique for 3D Vector Field Visualization." In *VIS '91: Proceedings of the 2nd Conference on Visualization '91*, pp. 126–132. Los Alamitos, CA: IEEE Computer Society Press, 1991.

[366] Will Schroeder, Ken Martin, and Bill Lorensen. *The Visualization Toolkit: An Object-Oriented Approach to 3D Graphics*, Fourth edition. Clifton Park, NY: Kitware, Inc., 2006.

[367] Hans-Jörg Schulz, Thomas Nocke, Magnus Heitzler, and Heidrun Schumann. "A Design Space of Visualization Tasks." *IEEE Transactions Visualization and Computer Graphics* 19:12 (2013), 2366–2375.

[368] Michael Sedlmair, Petra Isenberg, Dominikus Baur, and Andreas Butz. "Information Visualization Evaluation in Large Companies: Challenges, Experiences and Recommendations." *Information Visualization* 10:3 (2011), 248–266.

[369] S. Selvin, D. Merrill, J. Schulman, S. Sacks, L. Bedell, and L. Wong. "Transformations of Maps to Investigate Clusters of Disease." *Social Science and Medicine* 26:2 (1988), 215–221.

[370] Hikmet Senay and Eve Ignatius. "A Knowledge-Based System for Visualization Design." *IEEE Comput. Graph. Appl.* 14:6 (1994), 36–47.

[371] L. Shapiro and G. Stockman. *Computer Vision.* Upper Saddle River, NJ: Prentice Hall, 2001.

[372] John Sharko, Georges Grinstein, and Kenneth A. Marx. "Vectorized Radviz and Its Application to Multiple Cluster Datasets." *IEEE Transactions on Visualization and Computer Graphics* 14:6 (2008), 1427–1444.

[373] Helen Sharp, Yvonne Rogers, and Jenny Preece. *Interaction Design: Beyond Human-Computer Interaction*, Second edition. New York: J. Wiley, 2007.

[374] Ben Shneiderman and Catherine Plaisant. *Designing the User Interface: Strategies for Effective Human-Computer Interaction*, Fourth edition. Boston: Addison Wesley, 2004.

[375] Ben Shneiderman. "Dynamic Queries for Visual Information Seeking." *IEEE Software* 11 (1994), 70–77.

[376] Ben Shneiderman. "The Eyes Have It: A Task by Data Type Taxonomy for Information Visualizations." In *Proceedings of the 1996 IEEE Symposium on*

Visual Languages, pp. 336–343. Los Alamitos, CA: IEEE Computer Society, 1996.

[377] Ben Shneiderman. "Extreme Visualization: Squeezing a Billion Records into a Million Pixels." In *SIGMOD '08: Proceedings of the 2008 ACM SIGMOD International Conference on Management of Data*, pp. 3–12. New York: ACM Press, 2008.

[378] J. Siegel, E. Farrell, R. Goldwyn, and H. Friedman. "The Surgical Implication of Physiologic Patterns in Myocardial Infarction Shock." *Surgery* 72 (1972), 126–141.

[379] Simeon Simoff, Michael H. Böhlen, and Arturas Mazeika, editors. *Visual Data Mining: Theory, Techniques and Tools for Visual Analytics.* Berlin: Springer, 2008.

[380] D. J. Simons and D. T. Levin. "Change Blindness." *Trends in Cognitive Sciences* 1 (1997), 261–267.

[381] D. J. Simons. "In Sight, Out of Mind: When Object Representations Fail." *Psychological Science* 7:5 (1996), 301–305.

[382] D. J. Simons. "Current Approaches to Change Blindness." *Visual Cognition* 7:1/2/3.

[383] Terry A. Slocum, Robert B. McMaster, Fritz C. Kessler, and Hugh H. Howard. *Thematic Cartography and Geovisualization*, Third edition. Upper Saddle River, NJ: Prentice Hall, 2009.

[384] Terry A. Slocum. *Thematic Cartography and Visualization.* Upper Saddle River, NJ: Prentice Hall, 1999.

[385] Lindsay I. Smith. "A Tutorial on Principal Component Analysis." http://www.cs.otago.ac.nz/cosc453/student_tutorials/principal_components.pdf, February 26, 2002.

[386] Douglas Smith. "Beyond the Cave: Lascaux and the Prehistoric in Post-War French Culture." *French Studies* 58 (2004), 219–232.

[387] R. J. Snowden. "Texture Segregation and Visual Search: A Comparison of the Effects of Random Variations along Irrelevant Dimensions." *Journal of Experimental Psychology: Human Perception & Performance* 24:5 (1998), 1354–1367.

[388] John P. Snyder. *Map Projections: A Working Manual.* Washington, DC: US Government Printing Office, 1987.

[389] Pierre Soille. *Morphological Image Analysis: Principles and Applications.* Berlin: Springer-Verlag Telos, 1999.

[390] Robert Spence. *Information Visualization: Design for Interaction*, Second edition. Upper Saddle River, NJ: Prentice Hall, 2007.

[391] L. Spillmann. "The Hermann Grid Illusion: A Tool for Studying Human Perceptive Field Organization." *Perception* 23 (1994), 691–708.

[392] SPSS Inc. "SPSS Home Page." http://www.spss.com, accessed July 1, 2008.

[393] John Stasko and Eugene Zhang. "Focus+Context Display and Navigation Techniques for Enhancing Radial, Space-Filling Hierarchy Visualizations." In *Proceedings of the IEEE Symposium on Information Visualization*, pp. 57–65. Los Alamitos, CA: IEEE Computer Society, 2000.

[394] StatLib. "StatLib—Datasets Archive." http://lib.stat.cmu.edu/datasets/, accessed July 1, 2008.

[395] Peter Stearns. *The Encyclopedia of World History.* New York: Houghton-Mifflin, 2001.

[396] Daniel Steinbock. "TagCrowd Home Page." http://www.tagcrowd.com/, accessed August 31, 2009.

[397] Andreas Steiner. "A Generalisation Approach to Temporal Data Models and Their Implementations." Ph.D. thesis, Swiss Federal Institute of Technology, 1998.

[398] Debbie Stone, Caroline Jarrett, Mark Woodroffe, and Shailey Minocha. *User Interface Design and Evaluation.* The Morgan Kaufmann Series in Interactive Technologies, San Francisco: Morgan Kaufmann Publishers, Inc., 2005.

[399] Magnus Strengert, Marcelo Magallón, Daniel Weiskopf, Stefan Guthe, and Thomas Ertl. "Hierarchical Visualization and Compression of Large Volume Datasets Using GPU Clusters." In *Proceedings of the Eurographics Symposium on Parallel Graphics and Visualization*, pp. 41–48. Aire-la-Ville, Switzerland: Eurographics Association, 2004.

[400] H. Strobelt, D. Oelke, C. Rohrdantz, A. Stoffel, D. Keim, and O. Deussen. "Document Cards: A Top Trumps Visualization for Documents." *IEEE Info-Vis 2009: IEEE Transactions on Visualization and Computer Graphics* 15:6 (2009), 1145–1152.

[401] Steven H. Strogatz. "Exploring Complex Networks." *Nature* 410:6825 (2001), 268–276.

[402] Steve Summit. "Data File Formats." http://www.eskimo.com/~scs/datafiles.html, accessed July 1, 2008.

[403] Tableau Software. "Tableau Home Page." http://www.tableausoftware.com, accessed July 1, 2008.

[404] H. Tamura, S. Mori, and T. Yamawaki. "Textural Features Corresponding to Visual Perception." *IEEE Transactions on Systems, Man, and Cybernetics* 8:6 (1978), 460–473.

[405] Alexandru Telea. *Data Visualization: Principles and Practice.* Wellesley, MA: A K Peters, 2008.

[406] T. Tenev and R. Rao. "Managing Multiple Focal Levels in Table Lens." In *Proceedings of the 1997 IEEE Symposium on Information Visualization*, pp. 59–63. Washington, DC: IEEE Computer Society, 1997.

[407] J. Thomas, P. Cowley, O. Kuchar, L. Nowell, J. Thomson, and P. Chung Wong. "Discovering Knowledge Through Visual Analysis." *Journal of Universal Computer Science* 7:6 (2001), 517–529. Available online (http://www.jucs.org/jucs_7_6/discovering_knowledge_through_visual).

[408] David Thompson, Jeff Braun, and Ray Ford. *OpenDX: Paths to Visualization.* Missoula, MT: VIS, Inc., 2004.

[409] TIBCO Software, Inc. "Spotfire Home Page." http://spotfire.tibco.com, accessed July 1, 2008.

[410] Vladimir Tikunov and Sabir Gusein-Zade. "A New Technique for Constructing Continuous Cartograms." *Cartography and Geographic Information Systems* 20:3 (1993), 66–85.

[411] Vladimir Tikunov and Sabir Gusein-Zade. "Map Transformations." *Geography Review* 9:1 (1995), 19–23.

[412] W. R. Tobler. "Cartograms and Cartosplines." In *Proceedings of the 1976 Workshop on Automated Cartography and Epidemiology*, pp. 53–58. Washington, DC: Department of Health Education and Welfare, 1976.

[413] W. R. Tobler. "Pseudo-Cartograms." *The American Cartographer* 13:1 (1986), 43–40.

[414] Tom Sawyer Software. "Tom Sawyer Home Page." http://www.tomsawyer. com, accessed July 1, 2008.

[415] Christian Tominski and Hans-Jörg Schulz. "The Great Wall of Space-Time." In *Proceedings of the Workshop on Vision, Modeling & Visualization (VMV)*, pp. 199–206. Eurographics Association, 2012. Available online (http://dx.doi. org/10.2312/PE/VMV/VMV12/199-206).

[416] Christian Tominski and Heidrun Schumann. "Enhanced Interactive Spiral Display." In *Proceedings of the Annual SIGRAD Conference, Special Theme: Interactivity*, pp. 53–56. Linköping, Sweden: Linköping University Electronic Press, 2008.

[417] Christian Tominski, James Abello, and Heidrun Schumann. "Axes-Based Visualizations with Radial Layouts." In *Proceedings of the ACM Symposium on Applied Computing (SAC)*, pp. 1242–1247. New York: ACM Press, 2004.

[418] Melanie Tory and Torsten Müller. "Evaluating Visualizations: Do Expert Reviews Work?" *IEEE Computer Graphics and Applications* 25:5 (2005), 8–11.

[419] Anne M. Treisman and Garry Gelade. "A Feature-Integration Theory of Attention." *Cognitive Psychology* 12:1 (1980), 97–136. Available online (http: //dx.doi.org/10.1016/0010-0285(80)90005-5).

[420] Anne Treisman and S. Gormican. "Feature Analysis in Early Vision: Evidence from Search Asymmetries." *Psychological Review* 95:1 (1988), 15–48.

[421] Anne Treisman and J. Souther. "The Roles of Attention and Top-Down Constraints in Conjoining Letters to Form Words." *Journal of Experimental Psychology: Human Perception & Performance* 12 (1986), 107–141.

[422] Anne M. Treisman. "Preattentive Processing in Vision." *Computer Vision, Graphics, and Image Processing* 31:2 (1985), 156–177.

[423] Anne M. Treisman. "Search, Similarity, and Integration of Features between and within Dimensions." *Journal of Experimental Psychology: Human Perception & Performance* 17:3 (1991), 652–676.

[424] E. R. Tufte. *The Visual Display of Quantitative Information.* Cheshire, CT: Graphics Press, 1983.

[425] E. R. Tufte. *Envisioning Information.* Cheshire, CT: Graphics Press, 1990.

[426] E. R. Tufte. *Visual Explanations.* Cheshire, CT: Graphics Press, 1997.

[427] E. R. Tufte. *Beautiful Evidence.* Cheshire, CT: Graphics Press, 2006.

[428] P. D. Tynan and R. Sekuler. "Motion Processing in Peripheral Vision: Reaction Time and Perceived Velocity." *Vision Research* 22:1 (1982), 61–68.

[429] Fan-Yin Tzeng and Kwan-Liu Ma. "Intelligent Feature Extraction and Tracking for Visualizing Large-Scale 4D Flow Simulations." In *SC '05: Proceedings of the 2005 ACM/IEEE Conference on Supercomputing*, p. 6. Washington, DC: IEEE Computer Society Press, 2005.

[430] University of California, Irvine Department of Information and Computer Science. "UCI KDD Data Archive." http://kdd.ics.uci.edu/, accessed July 1, 2008.

[431] University of Maryland HCI Lab Data Repository. "SEMVAST: Scientific Evaluation Methods for Visual Analytics Science and Technology." http://www.cs.umd.edu/hcil/semvast/, accessed August 27, 2009.

[432] Eliane R. A. Valiati, Marcelo S. Pimenta, and Carla M. D. S. Freitas. "A Taxonomy of Tasks for Guiding the Evaluation of Multidimensional Visualizations." In *BELIV '06: Proceedings of the 2006 AVI Workshop on Beyond Time and Errors*, pp. 1–6. New York: ACM Press, 2006.

[433] A. van Doorn and J. Koenderink. "Spatial Properties of the Visual Detectability of Moving Spatial White Noise." *Experimental Brain Research* 45:1–2 (1982), 189–195. Available online (http://dx.doi.org/10.1007/BF00235778).

[434] A. van Doorn and J. Koenderink. "Temporal Properties of the Visual Detectability of Moving Spatial White Noise." *Experimental Brain Research* 45:1–2 (1982), 179–188.

[435] J. J. van Wijk and W. Nuij. "Smooth and Efficient Zooming and Panning." In *Proceedings of the IEEE Symposium on Information Visualization 2003*, pp. 15–23. Los Alamitos, CA: IEEE Computer Society Press, 2003.

[436] Andrew Vande Moere. "Time-Varying Data Visualization Using Information Flocking Boids." In *Proceedings of the IEEE Symposium on Information Visualization (InfoVis)*, pp. 97–104. Los Alamitos, CA: IEEE Computer Society, 2004.

[437] Vero Insight. "MineSet Home Page." http://www.vero-insight.com/, 2009.

[438] Fernanda B. Viégas, Danah Boyd, David H. Nguyen, Jeffrey Potter, and Judith Donath. "Digital Artifacts for Remembering and Storytelling: PostHistory and Social Network Fragments." In *Proceedings of the Annual Hawaii International Conference on System Sciences (HICSS)*, pp. 109–118. Los Alamitos, CA: IEEE Computer Society, 2004.

[439] VRVis. "High Quality Volume Rendering with 2D and 3D Textures." http://old.vrvis.at/via/resources/PR-CBerger-2/index.html, accessed August 1, 2008.

[440] F. Wanner, C. Rohrdantz, F. Mansmann, D. Oelke, and D. A. Keim. "Visual Sentiment Analysis of RSS News Feeds Featuring the US Presidential Election in 2008." Paper presented at the Workshop on Visual Interfaces to the Social and the Semantic Web, Sanibel Island, FL, February 8, 2009.

[441] M. O. Ward and B. N. Lipchak. "A Visualization Tool for Exploratory Analysis of Cyclic Multivariate Data." *Metrika* 51:1 (2000), 27–38.

[442] Matthew O. Ward and Kevin J. Theroux. "Perceptual Benchmarking for Multivariate Data Visualization." In *DAGSTUHL '97: Proceedings of the Conference on Scientific Visualization*, pp. 314–321. Washington, DC: IEEE Computer Society, 1997.

[443] Matthew O. Ward and Jing Yang. "Interaction Spaces in Data and Information Visualization." In *Eurographics Symposium on Visualization (VisSym)*, edited by Oliver Deussen, Charles D. Hansen, Daniel A. Keim, and Dietmar Saupe, pp. 137–145. Aire-la-Ville, Switzerland: Eurographics Association, 2004.

[444] Matthew O. Ward. "XmdvTool: Integrating Multiple Methods for Visualizing Multivariate Data." In *VIS '94: Proceedings of the Conference on Visualization '94*, pp. 326–333. Los Alamitos, CA: IEEE Computer Society Press, 1994.

[445] Matthew O. Ward. "A Taxonomy of Glyph Placement Strategies for Multidimensional Data Visualization." *Information Visualization* 1:3–4 (2002), 194–210.

[446] Colin Ware and William Knight. "Using Visual Texture for Information Display." *ACM Trans. Graph.* 14:1 (1995), 3–20.

[447] Colin Ware. "Color Sequences for Univariate Maps: Theory, Experiments and Principles." *IEEE Comput. Graph. Appl.* 8:5 (1988), 41–49.

[448] Colin Ware. *Information Visualization: Perception for Design.* San Francisco: Morgan Kaufmann Publishers Inc., 2000.

[449] A. Watt and M. Watt. *Advanced Rendering and Animation Techniques: Theory and Practice.* Reading, MA: Addison-Wesley, 1991.

[450] M. Wattenberg and F. B. Viégas. "The Word Tree, an Interactive Visual Concordance." *IEEE Transactions on Visualization and Computer Graphics* 14:6 (2008), 1221–1228.

[451] Martin Wattenberg. "Arc Diagrams: Visualizing Structure in Strings." In *Proceedings of the IEEE Symposium on Information Visualization (INFOVIS 2002)*, pp. 110–116. Washington, DC: IEEE Computer Society Press, 2002.

[452] Duncan J. Watts and Steven H. Strogatz. "Collective Dynamics of 'Small-World' Networks." *Nature* 393:6684 (1998), 440–442.

[453] Marc Weber, Marc Alexa, and Wolfgang Müller. "Visualizing Time-Series on Spirals." In *Proceedings of the IEEE Symposium on Information Visualization (InfoVis)*, pp. 7–14. Los Alamitos, CA: IEEE Computer Society, 2001.

[454] WEBSOM research group. "WEBSOM Map—Million Documents." http://websom.hut.fi/websom/milliondemo/html/root.html, accessed August 31, 2009.

[455] Edward J. Wegman and Jeffrey L. Solka. "On Some Mathematics for Visualizing High Dimensional Data." *Sankhya—The Indian Journal of Statistics, Series A* 64:2 (2002), 429–452.

[456] Stephen Wehrend and Clayton Lewis. "A Problem-Oriented Classification of Visualization Techniques." In *VIS '90: Proceedings of the First Conference on Visualization '90*, pp. 139–143. Los Alamitos, CA: IEEE Computer Society Press, 1990.

[457] C. Weigle, W. Emigh, G. Liu, R. Taylor, J. Enns, and C. Healey. "Oriented Sliver Textures: A Technique for Local Value Estimation of Multiple Scalar Fields." In *Proceedings Graphics Interface 2000*, pp. 163–170. Toronto: Canadian Information Processing Society, 2000.

[458] Scott D. Westrem. "Making a Mappamundi: The Hereford Map." http://www.sochistdisc.org/2002_articles/westrem.htm, 2008.

[459] Leland Wilkinson. *SYSTAT for DOS: Advanced Applications, Version 6.* Evanston, IL: SYSTAT, Inc., 1994.

[460] Leland Wilkinson. *The Grammar of Graphics.* Statistics and Computing, New York: Springer-Verlag, 2005.

[461] G. Wills. "Selection: 524,288 Ways to Say 'This Is Interesting'." In *Proceedings of the IEEE Symposium on Information Visualization '96*, pp. 54–60. Los Alamitos, CA: IEEE Computer Society Press, 1996.

[462] Craig M. Wittenbrink, Alex T. Pang, and Suresh K. Lodha. "Glyphs for Visualizing Uncertainty in Vector Fields." *IEEE Transactions on Visualization and Computer Graphics* 2:3 (1996), 266–279.

[463] J. M. Wolfe and K. R. Cave. "Deploying Visual Attention: The Guided Search Model." In *AI and the Eye*, edited by T. Troscianko and A. Blake, pp. 79–103. Chichester, UK: John Wiley & Sons, Inc., 1989.

[464] J. M. Wolfe and S. L. Franzel. "Binocularity and Visual Search." *Perception & Psychophysics* 44 (1988), 81–93.

[465] J. M. Wolfe, K. R. Cave, and S. L. Franzel. "Guided Search: An Alternative to the Feature Integration Model for Visual Search." *Journal of Experimental Psychology: Human Perception & Performance* 15:3 (1989), 419–433. Available online (http://view.ncbi.nlm.nih.gov/pubmed/2527952).

[466] J. M. Wolfe, K. P. Yu, M. I. Stewart, A. D. Shorter, S. R. Friedman-Hill, and K. R. Cave. "Limitations on the Parallel Guidance of Visual Search: Color × Color and Orientation × Orientation Conjunctions." *Journal of Experimental Psychology: Human Perception & Performance* 16:4 (1990), 879–892.

[467] J. M. Wolfe, S. R. Friedman-Hill, M. I. Stewart, and K. M. O'Connell. "The Role of Categorization in Visual Search for Orientation." *Journal of Experimental Psychology: Human Perception & Performance* 18:1 (1992), 34–49.

[468] J. M. Wolfe, N. Klempen, and K. Dahlen. "Postattentive Vision." *Journal of Experimental Psychology: Human Perception & Performance* 26:2 (2000), 693–716.

[469] J. M. Wolfe. "Guided Search 2.0: A Revised Model of Visual Search." *Psychonomic Bulletin & Review* 1:2 (1994), 202–238.

[470] P. Wong and R. Bergeron. "Multiresolution Multidimensional Wavelet Brushing." In *Proceedings of the 7th Conference on Visualization '96*, pp. 141–148. Los Alamitos, CA: IEEE Computer Society Press, 1996.

[471] Pak Chung Wong, Harlan Foote, Dan Adams, Wendy Cowley, and Jim Thomas. "Dynamic Visualization of Transient Data Streams." In *Proceedings of the IEEE Symposium on Information Visualization*, pp. 97–104. Los Alamitos, CA: IEEE Computer Society Press, 2003.

[472] Pak Chung Wong, Han-Wei Shen, and Chaomei Chen. "Top Ten Interaction Challenges in Extreme-Scale Visual Analytics." In *Expanding the Frontiers of Visual Analytics and Visualization*, edited by J. Dill, R. Earnshaw, D. Kasik, J. Vince, and P.C. Wong, pp. 197–207. New York: Springer, 2012.

[473] H. Wright. *Introduction to Scientific Visualization.* New York: Springer, 2007.

[474] Michael Wybrow, Niklas Elmqvist, Jean-Daniel Fekete, Tatiana von Landesberger, Jarke J van Wijk, and Björn Zimmer. "Interaction in the Visualization of Multivariate Networks." In *Multivariate Network Visualization*, Lecture Notes in Computer Science, 8380, edited by Andreas Kerren, Helen C. Purchase, and Matthew O. Ward, pp. 97–125. New York: Springer, 2014.

[475] G. Wyvill, C. McPheeters, and B. Wyvill. "Data Structure for Soft Objects." *The Visual Computer* 2 (1986), 227–234.

[476] Zaixian Xie, Shiping Huang, Matthew O. Ward, and Elke A. Rundensteiner. "Exploratory Visualization of Multivariate Data with Variable Quality." In *Proceedings of the IEEE Symposium on Visual Analysis Science and Technology*, pp. 183–190. Los Alamitos, CA: IEEE Computer Society Press, 2006.

[477] XmdvTool Project. "XmdvTool Home Page." http://davis.wpi.edu/~xmdv, accessed July 1, 2008.

[478] Jing Yang, Matthew O. Ward, and Elke A. Rundensteiner. "InterRing: An Interactive Tool for Visually Navigating and Manipulating Hierarchical Structures." In *Proceedings of the IEEE Symposium on Information Visualization '02*, pp. 77–84. Washington, DC: IEEE Computer Society, 2002.

[479] J. Yang, W. Peng, M. O. Ward, and E. A. Rundensteiner. "Interactive Hierarchical Dimension Ordering, Spacing and Filtering for Exploration of High Dimensional Datasets." In *Proceedings of the IEEE Symposium on Information Visualization*, pp. 105–112. Washington, DC: IEEE Computer Society, 2003.

[480] Jing Yang, Matthew O. Ward, Elke A. Rundensteiner, and S. Huang. "Visual Hierarchical Dimension Reduction for Exploration of High Dimensional Datasets." In *VISSYM '03: Proceedings of the Symposium on Data Visualisation 2003*, pp. 19–28. Aire-la-Ville, Switzerland: Eurographics Association, 2003.

[481] Jing Yang, Matthew O. Ward, Elke A. Rundensteiner, and Anilkumar Patro. "InterRing: A Visual Interface for Navigating and Manipulating Hierarchies." *Information Visualization* 2:1 (2003), 16–30.

[482] J. Yang, A. Patro, S. Huang, N. Mehta, M. O. Ward, and E. A. Rundensteiner. "Value and Relation Display for Interactive Exploration of High Dimensional Datasets." In *Proceedings of the IEEE Symposium on Information Visualization*, pp. 73–80. Washington, DC: IEEE Computer Society, 2004.

[483] Fanhai Yang, Howard Goodell, Ronald Pickett, Robert Bobrow, Alexander Baumann, Alexander Gee, and Georges Grinstein. "Data Exploration Combining Kinetic and Static Visualization Displays." In *Proceedings of the Fourth International Conference on Coordinated and Multiple Views in Exploratory Visualization*, pp. 21–30. Washington, DC: IEEE Computer Society, 2006.

[484] D. Yang, Elke A. Rundensteiner, and Matthew O. Ward. "Analysis Guided Visual Exploration of Multivariate Data." In *Proceedings of the IEEE Symposium on Visual Analytics Science and Technology*, pp. 83–90. Washington, DC: IEEE Computer Society, 2007.

[485] Jing Yang, Daniel Hubball, Matthew Ward, Elke Rundensteiner, and William Ribarsky. "Value and Relation Display: Interactive Visual Exploration of Large Data Sets with Hundreds of Dimensions." *IEEE Trans. Visualization and Computer Graphics* 13:3 (2007), 494–507.

[486] Li Yang. "Pruning and Visualizing Generalized Association Rules in Parallel Coordinates." *IEEE Transactions on Knowledge and Data Engineering* 17:1 (2005), 60–70.

[487] Ji Soo Yi, Youn ah Kang, John T. Stasko, and Julie A. Jacko. "Toward a Deeper Understanding of the Role of Interaction in Information Visualization." *IEEE Trans. Visualization and Computer Graphics* 13 (2007), 1224–1231.

[488] Jian Zhao, Fanny Chevalier, and Ravin Balakrishnan. "KronoMiner: Using Multi-Foci Navigation for the Visual Exploration of Time-Series Data." In *Proceedings of the 2011 Annual Conference on Human Factors in Computing Systems*, pp. 1737–1746. New York: ACM Press, 2011.

[489] J. Zhou, G. Grinstein, and K. Marx. "A New Gene Selection Method for Visual Analysis." Scientific Report No. 015, University of Massachusetts Lowell, 2007.

[490] G. K. Zipf. *Human Behavior and the Principle of Least Effort: An Introduction to Human Ecology.* Reading, MA: Addison-Wesley Press, 1949.

[491] Christian Zuchner. "Grotte Chauvet Archaeologically Dated." http://www.rupestre.net/tracce/12/chauv.html, 2000.

[492] Torre Zuk, Lothar Schlesier, Petra Neumann, Mark S. Hancock, and Shee-lagh Carpendale. "Heuristics for Information Visualization Evaluation." In *BELIV '06: Proceedings of the 2006 AVI Workshop on Beyond Time and Errors*, pp. 1–6. New York: ACM Press, 2006.

[493] Zuse Institute Berlin. "LicFactory Home Page." http://www.zib.de/visual/software/LicFactory/, accessed August 1, 2008.

Index